F 1563 P323 1989

Panama, a country study

Panama
a country study

Federal Research Division
Library of Congress
Edited by
Sandra W. Meditz
and
Dennis M. Hanratty
Research Completed
December 1987

On the cover: Cuna Indian *mola* design of a man gathering coconuts

Fourth Edition, 1989; First Printing, 1989.

Library of Congress Cataloging-in-Publication Data

Panama: a country study.

(Area handbook series) (DA Pam 550-46)
Supt. of Docs. no.: D 101.22:550-46/987
"Research completed December 1987"
Bibliography: pp. 295-311.
Includes index.
1. Panama. I. Meditz, Sandra W., 1950-   . II. Hanratty, Dennis M., 1950-   . III. Library of Congress. Federal Research Division. IV. Series. V. Series: DA Pam 550-46.
F1563.P323   1989   972.87   88-600486

Headquarters, Department of the Army
DA Pam 550-46

For sale by the Superintendent of Documents, U.S. Government Printing Office
Washington, D.C. 20402

Foreword

This volume is one in a continuing series of books now being prepared by the Federal Research Division of the Library of Congress under the Country Studies—Area Handbook Program. The last page of this book lists the other published studies.

Most books in the series deal with a particular foreign country, describing and analyzing its political, economic, social, and national security systems and institutions, and examining the interrelationships of those systems and the ways they are shaped by cultural factors. Each study is written by a multidisciplinary team of social scientists. The authors seek to provide a basic understanding of the observed society, striving for a dynamic rather than a static portrayal. Particular attention is devoted to the people who make up the society, their origins, dominant beliefs and values, their common interests and the issues on which they are divided, the nature and extent of their involvement with national institutions, and their attitudes toward each other and toward their social system and political order.

The books represent the analysis of the authors and should not be construed as an expression of an official United States government position, policy, or decision. The authors have sought to adhere to accepted standards of scholarly objectivity. Corrections, additions, and suggestions for changes from readers will be welcomed for use in future editions.

Louis R. Mortimer
Acting Chief
Federal Research Division
Library of Congress
Washington, D.C. 20540

Acknowledgments

The authors wish to acknowledge the contributions of the following individuals who, under the chairmanship of Richard F. Nyrop, wrote the 1980 edition of *Panama: A Country Study*. The authors of the 1980 edition were as follows: Jan Knippers Black, "Historical Setting"; Richard F. Nyrop, "The Society and Its Environment"; Darrel R. Eglin, "The Economy"; James D. Rudolph, "Government and Politics"; and Eugene K. Keefe, "National Security." Their work provided the organization and structure of much of the present volume, as well as substantial portions of the text.

The authors are grateful to individuals in various agencies of the United States government and in international and private institutions who gave of their time, research materials, and special knowledge to provide information and perspective. Officials at the World Bank were especially helpful in providing economic data. Similarly, officials of the United States Department of Defense, both in Washington and Panama, supplied up-to-date information on Panama's defense forces.

The authors also wish to thank those who contributed directly to the preparation of the manuscript. These include Richard F. Nyrop, who reviewed all drafts and served as liaison with the sponsoring agency; Barbara Auerbach, Ruth Nieland, Michael Pleasants, and Gage Ricard, who edited the chapters; Martha E. Hopkins, who managed editing and book production; and Barbara Edgerton, Janie L. Gilchrist, Monica Shimmin, and Izella Watson, who did the word processing. Catherine Schwartzstein performed the final prepublication editorial review, and Amy Bodnar, of Communicators Connections, compiled the index. Diann Johnson of the Library of Congress Printing and Processing Section performed phototypesetting, under the supervision of Peggy Pixley.

David P. Cabitto, who was assisted by Sandra K. Cotugno and Kimberly A. Lord, provided invaluable graphics support. Susan M. Lender reviewed the map drafts, which were prepared by Harriett R. Blood, Kimberly A. Lord, and Greenhorne and O'Mara, Inc. Paulette Marshall of the Library of Congress deserves special thanks for designing the illustrations for the book's cover and the title page of each chapter.

The authors also would like to thank several individuals who provided research support. Sisto Flores supplied information on ranks and insignia, Joan C. Barch wrote the section on geography in Chapter 2, and Richard A. Haggerty supplied a variety of information for inclusion in both the text and the bibliography.

Finally, the authors acknowledge the generosity of the individuals and public and private agencies who allowed their photographs to be used in this study. We are indebted especially to those who contributed original work not previously published.

Contents

List of Figures

Preface

Like its predecessor, this study is an attempt to treat in a compact and objective manner the dominant social, political, economic, and military aspects of contemporary Panama. Sources of information included scholarly books, journals, and monographs, official reports of governments and international organizations, numerous periodicals, and interviews with individuals having special competence in Panamanian and Latin American affairs. Chapter bibliographies appear at the end of the book; brief comments on sources recommended for further reading appear at the end of each chapter. Measurements are given in the metric system; a conversion table is provided to assist readers unfamiliar with metric measurements (see table 1, Appendix A). A glossary is also included.

Although there are numerous variations, Spanish surnames generally consist of two parts: the patrilineal name followed by the matrilineal. In the instance of Omar Torrijos Herrera, for example, Torrijos is his father's name, Herrera, his mother's maiden name. In non-formal use, the matrilineal name is often dropped. Thus, after the first mention, we have usually referred simply to Torrijos. A minority of individuals use only the patrilineal name.

Country Profile

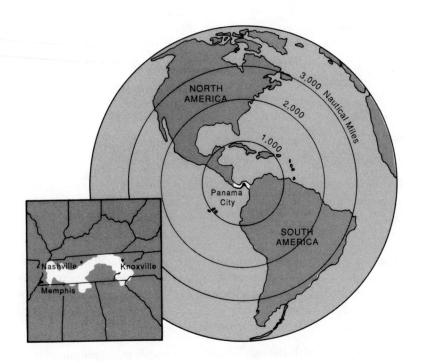

Country

Formal Name: Republic of Panama (República de Panamá).

Short Form: Panama.

Term for Citizens: Panamanian(s).

Capital: Panama City (Panamá).

Geography

Size: Approximately 77,082 square kilometers.

Topography: Dominant feature of landform is central spine of highlands forming continental divide. Highest elevations near borders with Costa Rica and Colombia. Lowest elevations at waist of country where it is crossed by Panama Canal. Most of population concentrated on Pacific side of divide southwestward from Panama City.

Climate: Tropical climate with high temperatures and humidity year round; pleasanter conditions prevailing in highlands and on Pacific side of continental divide. Seasons determined by rainfall rather than by changes in temperature. Prolonged rainy season between May and December; short dry season between December and April in parts of Pacific slope and for shorter periods on Atlantic slope of divide.

Society

Population: In mid-1987 population estimated at 2.3 million; rate of annual growth calculated at about 2.2 percent in the 1980s.

Education and Literacy: Compulsory attendance to age fifteen or completion of six-year primary level. Education free at public primary, secondary, and high schools; nominal tuition at University of Panama. About 87 percent of population over age 10 literate.

Health: Although high proportion of medical facilities and personnel located in major urban areas, most people had ready access to medical care of some kind, and extension of modern medical facilities to rural areas continued in late 1980s. Life expectancy at birth in 1985 seventy-one years.

Language: Spanish the official language and mother tongue of over 87 percent of the people. Antilleans—about 8 percent of the population—primarily spoke English, and Indians—about 5 percent—spoke their own tongues, but with a growing number adopting Spanish as second language.

Ethnic Groups: Society composed of three principal groups: Spanish-speaking mestizos, representing the vast majority of inhabitants; English-speaking Antillean blacks, constituting approximately 8 percent of the population; and tribal Indians, making up about 5 percent of the population. Mestizos originally identified as people of mixed Indian-Spanish heritage, but term now refers to any racial mixture where the individual conforms to the norms of Hispanic culture. Also some unmixed Caucasians.

Religion: Overwhelmingly Roman Catholic. Ratio of priests to population quite low, and relatively few Panamanians enter priesthood. Antilleans predominantly Protestant.

Economy

Gross Domestic Product (GDP): US$4.9 billion in 1985, more than US$2,000 per capita. Growth of GDP estimated at 2.8 percent for 1986, demonstrating some economic recovery following very low or negative growth as a result of recession after 1982.

Agriculture: About 9 percent of GDP in 1985. Crops represented just over 63 percent of value added in agriculture. Main crops—bananas, sugarcane, rice, corn, coffee, beans, tobacco, melons, and flowers. Livestock (producing primarily red meat) accounted for nearly 30 percent of value added in agriculture; fishing (primarily shrimp), just over 4 percent; and forestry, nearly 3 percent. Largely self-sufficient in foods except wheat.

Industry: Nearly 18 percent of GDP in 1985, including primarily manufacturing and mining (over 9 percent of GDP), construction (nearly 5 percent of GDP), and energy (over 3 percent of GDP). Manufacturing consisted mainly of import substitution, consumer goods. A few larger plants, including oil refining, electric power, cement, and sugar. Manufacturing concentrated near major cities.

Services: Over 73 percent of GDP in 1985. Sector included transportation, banking and other financial services, government services, wholesale and retail trade, and other services.

Currency: Balboa equal to United States dollar. Balboas available only in coins. Dollars circulated as the only paper currency.

Imports: US$1.34 billion in 1985, including primarily manufactured goods, crude oil, machinery and transportation equipment, chemicals, and food products.

Exports: US$414.5 million in 1985, mainly refined petroleum, bananas, sugar, manufactured goods, shrimp, and clothing.

Balance of Payments: Traditionally, no short-run constraints because of monetary system. Large exports of services, including those to former Canal Zone, nearly compensated for deficits in merchandise trade balance. Substantial inflow of capital. Beginning in June 1987, however, extensive capital flight, bank closures, and cutoffs of United States aid as a result of the volatile political situation posed serious short- and long-term financial problems for Panama.

Fiscal Year (FY): Calendar year.

Fiscal Policy: Public-sector expenditures considerably above revenues, resulting in large external public debt—one of the world's largest on a per capita basis. Austerity and structural adjustment programs imposed in 1983–84 successful in reducing deficit, but debt service remained a major burden in the late 1980s.

Transportation and Communications

Ports: Fourteen ports, the most important Balboa (Pacific) and Cristóbal (Atlantic) at entrances to Panama Canal.

Railroads: There were 3 separate, unconnected systems totalling 238 kilometers. Main line between Panama City and Colón (seventy-six kilometers). Other two in west, originating in David and Almirante, respectively, and continuing across the Costa Rican border.

Roads: In 1984 about 9,535 kilometers, 32 percent asphalted. Principal axes are Pan-American Highway, running across Panama from Costa Rica toward Colombia, and Trans-isthmian Highway from Panama City to Colón.

Airports: Eight main fields, including one international airport: General Omar Torrijos International Airport, more commonly known as Tocumen International Airport, near Panama City.

Oil Pipeline: Trans-isthmian pipeline completed in 1982. Approximately eighty-one kilometers long, running from Puerto Armuelles to Chiriquí Grande.

Telecommunications: Well-developed internal and external systems.

Government and Politics

Government: Executive—under provisions of 1972 Constitution, as amended in 1978 and 1983, chief executive is president of the republic, assisted by two vice presidents, all elected by popular vote for five-year terms. In late 1980s, de facto executive authority remained, however, in hands of commander of Panama Defense Forces (Fuerzas de Defensa de Panamá—FDP). Legislature—sixty-seven-member unicameral Legislative Assembly created in 1983; members popularly elected for five-year terms that run concurrently with presidential term. Judiciary—Highest court is Supreme Court made up of nine members and nine alternates who serve ten-year terms after nomination by the executive branch and ratification by Legislative Assembly. Supreme Court divided into three chambers for civil, penal, and administrative cases. Lower courts include superior tribunals, circuit courts, municipal courts, and night courts. Public Ministry, headed by attorney general, acts as state representative within judiciary.

Politics: Political culture traditionally characterized by personalism (*personalismo*), the tendency to give one's political loyalties to an individual rather than to a party or ideology. Politics from 1968 coup until his death in 1981 dominated by General Omar Torrijos Herrera, formally head of government from 1968 to 1978 and thereafter de facto head of government while commander of the National Guard. Torrijos's influence continued after his death, as both military and civilian leaders sought to lay claim to his political and social heritage. Proliferation of parties after 1980, when political system opened up again. Most activity divided into two main coalitions: pro-government and opposition. Pro-government coalition headed by party created by Torrijos: Democratic Revolutionary Party (Partido Revolucionario Democrático—PRD). Nation's principal opposition party was Authentic Panameñista Party (Partido Panameñista Auténtico—PPA) led by veteran politician Arnulfo Arias Madrid. Political crisis over lack of democratization and scandals associated with the FDP commander, General Manuel Antonio Noriega Morena, began in June 1987 and escalated throughout the year and into 1988. Opposition forces remained fragmented, but popular protests were orchestrated by the National Civic Crusade (Cruzada Civilista Nacional—CCN), a coalition of civic, business, and professional forces.

International Relations: Traditionally dominated by bilateral relations with United States; special relationship created by 1977 Panama Canal treaties continued to be most important aspect of foreign relations in late 1980s. Relations very strained and troubled, however, in late 1987 because of United States concerns over the lack of democratization and serious allegations of involvement of the FDP commander in drug trafficking and money laundering. Following negotiation of Panama Canal treaties, Panama has given more attention to other commercial and trade relations and especially to the Central American peace process.

International Agreements and Membership: The country is party to Inter-American Treaty of Reciprocal Assistance (Rio Treaty) and Treaty for the Prohibition of Nuclear Weapons in Latin America (Tlatelolco Treaty) and is bound by provisions of Panama Canal treaties. Also a member of Organization of American States, United Nations and its specialized agencies, World Bank, International Monetary Fund, and Inter-American Development Bank, as well as an active member of the Nonaligned Movement.

National Security

Armed Forces: Panama Defense Forces (Fuerzas de Defensa de Panamá—FDP) include military forces, police forces, and National Guard, with total strength of about 15,000.

Military Units: Principally ground forces with four combat battalions, four support battalions, eight infantry companies, and one cavalry squadron. Also a small air force and navy, as well as paramilitary National Guard.

Equipment: Limited equipment inventory. Most infantry weapons, military vehicles, naval craft, and aircraft from United States. Two largest (thirty-meter) patrol craft from Britain.

Foreign Military Treaties: Bilateral treaties with United States for canal defense.

Police: Police forces subordinate to FDP and include a variety of uniformed, undercover, and civilian forces. Most significant are National Department of Investigations (Departamento Nacional de Investigaciones—DENI), undercover security police, and First Public Order Company (Doberman), which handles riot control.

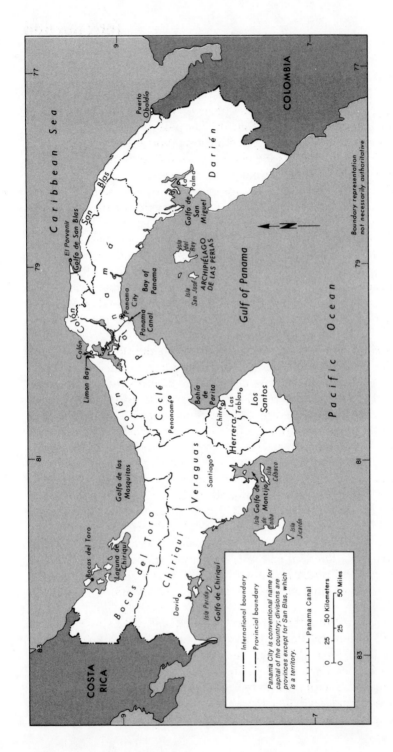

Figure 1. Administrative Divisions of Panama, 1987

Introduction

PANAMA'S HISTORY, as well as its present-day social, economic, and political life, has been dominated by the country's significant geographic position. Encompassing the lowest and narrowest portion of the isthmus connecting North America and South America, Panama has for centuries served as a land bridge and transit zone between continents and oceans.

The narrowness of the isthmus inspired various attempts to facilitate passage between the Atlantic and Pacific oceans. Following their arrival in Panama in 1501, the Spanish turned Panama into a principal crossroads and marketplace of the great Spanish Empire (see The Conquest; The Spanish Colony, ch. 1). They built the Camino Real, or royal road, to link settlements on the Pacific and Atlantic coasts and used the road to transport treasures from the west coast of South America—especially Peruvian gold and silver— to Spanish galleons waiting on the Atlantic coast for the trip to Spain.

As early as 1520, however, frustrated by the slowness and hazards of the Camino Real, the Spanish undertook surveys to determine the feasibility of constructing a canal across the isthmus. The United States, seeking a quicker passage to its west coast because of the discovery of gold in California in 1848, promoted the construction of a trans-isthmian railroad, which was completed in the 1850s. But it was the French who first undertook what the Spanish ultimately had abandoned as impractical—and undesirable because it would be an attractive target for other world powers. Under the direction of Ferdinand de Lesseps, the builder of the Suez Canal, the French in 1879 attempted to construct a canal across the isthmus. The project was abandoned in 1889 because of the combined effects of disease, faulty design, and, finally, bankruptcy. The United States soon took on the project, building on what the French had done, and the first ship passed through the Panama Canal on August 15, 1914 (see Building the Canal, ch. 1).

Since that time, the Panama Canal has been the single greatest factor influencing Panama's society, economy, political life, and foreign relations. Panamanian society in the 1980s continued to reflect Panama's unusual position as a transit zone and the home of the canal, factors that subjected Panama to a variety of outside influences and gave the country an ethnic diversity not commonly associated with Latin America (see Ethnic Groups, ch. 2). Like other former Spanish colonies, Panama's population was over-whelmingly Spanish-speaking and Roman Catholic; most inhab-itants were regarded as mestizos—a term that originally referred to those of mixed Spanish and Indian heritage, but increasingly had come to mean any racial mixture in individuals conforming to the norms of Hispanic culture. In addition to mestizos and tribal Indians, Panama contained a significant minority of Antillean blacks (8 percent of the population)—Protestant, English-speaking descen-dants of Caribbean laborers who built the canal. There also were significant numbers of Chinese, Jews, Arabs, Greeks, East Asians, South Asians, Lebanese, Europeans, and North Americans—both immigrants and expatriate residents—who came to Panama to take advantage of commercial opportunities associated with the canal.

The Panama Canal has also shaped Panama's economic develop-ment. First, the canal has been a major source of wealth for Panama because of revenue generated by canal traffic, the influx of work-ers who built and later maintained the canal, and the large United States civilian and military presence associated with the canal. Until the Latin American economic slump in the mid-1980s, Panama was generally regarded as wealthy in the regional context, although the distribution of income remained skewed. Reflecting this rela-tive wealth, Panama registered one of the highest levels of per capita income in the developing world (US$2,100) in 1985. Second, because of the canal and other transport and service activities deriv-ing from the country's location, Panama's economy always has been service-oriented rather than productive. Services accounted for 73 percent of the gross domestic product (GDP—see Glossary) in 1985, the highest level in the world. The Panama Canal was the primary activity in the nation's services sector, but that sector was expanded through increased government services and initiatives such as the Colón Free Zone (CFZ—see Glossary), a trans-isthmian pipeline, and the International Financial Center, which promoted offshore banking and foreign investment in Panama (see Panama Canal; Services, ch. 3).

A third characteristic of Panama's economy was the country's use of the United States dollar as its paper currency. The local cur-rency, the balboa (see Glossary), was available only in coins. Reli-ance on the United States dollar meant that the country could neither print nor devalue currency as a means of establishing and implementing monetary policies. Finally, Panama's development in terms of both location of economic activity and concentration of population followed an axis across the isthmus between Colón at the Atlantic terminus of the Panama Canal and Panama City on the Pacific coast. Over half of the population and most nonagricultural economic activity were located there.

In addition to its major influence on social and economic life in Panama, the canal also bound Panama inexorably to the United States—and therein lies the canal's dominance of Panamanian politics and foreign policy. In essence, the canal itself spurred the creation of the modern-day nation of Panama. In order to obtain the rights to construct a canal, the United States fostered separatist sentiment in Panama, then a department of Colombia, and engineered Panama's independence from Colombia in 1903. Panama became a virtual protectorate of the United States, and the pattern of United States intervention set at independence was to be repeated numerous times throughout the first half of the twentieth century (see The United States Protectorate, ch. 1).

This close relationship was from the start, however, colored by resentment and bitterness. The Hay-Bunau-Varilla Treaty of 1903, by which the United States acquired the right to construct a canal, was the primary source of this discontent—at least initially—for several reasons. First, Panama was not even a party to the treaty, which was signed by the United States and a French-born entrepreneur. Second, and more important, the treaty gave the United States "in perpetuity" a sixteen-kilometer-wide strip of territory known as the Canal Zone that split the nation into two unconnected pieces. (In return, Panama was to receive an annuity.) Sovereignty or jurisdiction over the Canal Zone, profits from canal operations, frustration over the continued highly visible presence and domination of the United States in Panama, and other related issues became and remained the primary focus of both internal politics and foreign relations for Panama. Nationalism, consistently a powerful force in Panama in the twentieth century, was directed primarily against the United States presence. National leaders of all political persuasions both cultivated and capitalized on public discontent with the United States. Indeed, these leaders kept popular resentment narrowly focused on the United States lest it turn on the Panamanian elite, commonly known as the oligarchy, which traditionally controlled Panama's political, economic, and social life (see Urban Society, ch. 2).

The quest for a more equitable treaty governing the Panama Canal has dominated Panamanian-United States relations throughout the twentieth century. The Hay-Bunau-Varilla Treaty was modified several times. But Panama's hopes for a completely new treaty were not realized until 1977, when the two countries brought to fruition negotiations that had been initiated as early as 1971 (see The Treaty Negotiations, ch. 1). Panama and the United States actually signed two treaties on September 7, 1977. The first, the Panama Canal Treaty, abrogated all previous treaties with respect to the canal and transferred legal jurisdiction over the Canal Zone to Panama. The treaty created a United States agency, the Panama Canal Commission, to operate, manage, and maintain the canal until noon, December 31, 1999, at which time Panama will secure unfettered ownership and management of the canal. The commission consists of five United States citizens and four Panamanians working under an American administrator and a Panamanian deputy until 1990; thereafter the commission will work under a Panamanian administrator appointed by the winner of the 1989 presidential elections in Panama, but approved by the United States president with the advice and consent of the United States Senate. In other words, the canal will remain under the effective control of the United States government throughout the treaty period (see The 1977 Treaties and Associated Agreements, ch. 1; for texts of the treaties, see Appendix B).

The second treaty, the Treaty Concerning the Permanent Neutrality and Operation of the Panama Canal, popularly known as the Neutrality Treaty, was vigorously resisted by the Panamanian negotiators and remains particularly galling to the government and the public. It provides for joint Panamanian and United States responsibility for the protection of the canal, but because it has no termination date, it smacks of the detested "in perpetuity" phrase of the original 1903 treaty. Panamanian concern over possible United States intervention in Panamanian affairs based on this treaty was sharpened by various unilateral interpretations and conditions that were attached to the treaties by the United States Senate during its ratification proceedings. One condition attached to the Neutrality Treaty in effect stipulated that even after December 31, 1999, the United States could use military forces in Panama "to reopen the Canal or restore the operations of the Canal." Although the Panamanian government and public were incensed over this attachment, Panama continued with the ratification. It did, however, append the following statement to the two documents: "The Republic of Panama will reject, in unity and with decisiveness and firmness, any attempt by any country to intervene in its internal or external affairs."

Thus, despite the high hopes of all concerned, the negotiation of new treaties failed to resolve Panamanian discontent. Issues related to the canal continued to muddy the waters of United States-Panamanian relations in 1988 (see Relations with the United States: The Panama Canal; Other Aspects of Panamanian-United States Relations, ch. 4). United States-Panamanian relations also were strained by growing United States dissatisfaction with Panama's military-dominated political system. Panama's failure to establish a democratic form of government was an especially sore point for the United States government because "democratization" in Panama was an American condition for support of the Panama Canal treaties.

Panama's political system dates back to the year 1968—a watershed in Panamanian history. In that year the National Guard staged a coup—not for the first time—and established an enduring pattern of direct and then indirect military control of the government. Despite the subsequent construction of a democratic facade in the late 1970s, de facto control of the nation's politics in 1988 remained firmly in the hands of the commander of the National Guard's successor organization, the Panama Defense Forces (Fuerzas de Defensa de Panamá—FDP).

The 1968 coup also represents a major turning point in Panamanian history because it brought to power Brigadier General Omar Torrijos Herrera, a charismatic leader whose populist legacy—known as Torrijismo—radically altered Panamanian politics. Prior to the advent of Torrijos, Panamanian politics were dominated almost exclusively by a small number of aristocratic families. This oligarchy, largely urban, tended to be white or light-skinned and valued its purported racial purity; aristocrats intermarried and held tightly to their elite status. But Torrijos built a popular base from the ranks of the National Guard, which was composed mostly of provincial black and lower- or middle-class mestizos like Torrijos himself, as well as an assortment of campesinos and urban workers (see The Government of Torrijos and the National Guard, ch. 1; Nationalism, Populism, and Militarism: The Legacy of Omar Torrijos, ch. 4). Torrijos fostered public works and agrarian reform and put the National Guard to work on programs to improve conditions in rural areas and to bring the poorer classes to power.

Initially at least, Panama enjoyed an economic boom under Torrijos. After the passage of strict secrecy laws, Panama became an international banking center, and the CFZ became the world's second largest free-trade zone (after Hong Kong). But Panama's foreign debt also soared because of the extensive borrowing from abroad used to finance the expansion in public services, and Panama eventually registered one of the highest per capita debt levels in the world (see Growth and Structure of the Economy; External Debt, ch. 3). Panama's high growth rate through 1982 fell off sharply as the world economy went into a recession. Unemployment, rural poverty, and a low rate of private investment also plagued the country.

In the late 1970s, Torrijos's populist alliance already showed signs of eroding, primarily because of the severe economic downturn that had forced Torrijos to retract many of the progressive measures previously enacted to benefit labor and land reform. But the unpopularity of the canal treaties and the "democratization" process that Torrijos had initiated to win United States support for the treaties also were prime factors. Torrijos, for example, had permitted political parties, previously banned, to resume activity. In 1978 elections were held for a new legislature, and Torrijos formally stepped down as head of the government in favor of Aristides Royo, a government technocrat who was chosen by the legislature to serve a six-year term as president. Torrijos nevertheless remained commander of the National Guard and, as such, the holder of real power in Panama.

Torrijos's sudden death in a July 1981 airplane crash gave rise to a power struggle in Panama that was filled by a succession of figurehead presidents controlled by a series of National Guard and FDP commanders, who engaged in fierce internal maneuvering. The newly erected democratic facade remained in place and on paper was strengthened by the promulgation of constitutional amendments in 1983, which, among other things, permitted the direct election of a president (see The Constitutional Framework, ch. 4). Elections were duly held in 1984, but widespread allegations of fraud, increasingly supported by credible evidence, undercut the importance of the event as a demonstration of Panama's return to democracy. The FDP's handpicked candidate was elected, and the FDP commander remained the true source of political power in Panama.

General Manuel Antonio Noriega Moreno, the ambitious former head of military intelligence in Panama, assumed control of the National Guard in 1983 and launched a successful effort to consolidate his power. He oversaw the transformation of the National Guard from a small paramilitary organization into the much larger and more capable FDP, ostensibly capable of defending the expanded national territory (now including the former Canal Zone) and of joining the United States in defending the Panama Canal (see Missions and Organization of the Defense Forces, ch. 5). Because of the strong United States vested interest in the security of the canal, this transformation was accomplished with extensive United States training, equipment, and financial assistance. Ironically, however, the growing size and strength of the FDP, which were fostered in accordance with perceived United States strategic interests, led to a situation that the United States increasingly regarded as inimical to its own interests as well as those of the

Panamanian people. The FDP, which traditionally has exhibited strong institutional cohesiveness and loyalty to its commander, increasingly has become a formidable power base for enhancing and institutionalizing political control by the FDP commander.

Despite Noriega's firm hold on power in Panama, a series of events in the mid-1980s tarnished his already unsavory international reputation and threatened his regime. The first occurrence was the violent death in September 1985 of Dr. Hugo Spadafora, a vociferous Noriega critic. Spadafora, who purported to have hard evidence of Noriega's involvement in drug trafficking, was brutally murdered, and there were credible reports of FDP involvement in the death (see Political Developments in the Post-Torrijos Era, ch. 4). Panamanians were shocked, but the threat to Noriega came not from popular discontent, but rather from the decision of then-president Nicolás Ardito Barletta Vallarino to investigate the murder. To prevent such an action, Noriega forced Ardito Barletta to resign in favor of his vice president, Eric Arturo Delvalle Henríquez. Noriega successfully weathered this initial storm, but at the cost of an overt demonstration of the extent of military control over an ostensibly civilian regime.

The second and more serious threat to Noriega and, by extension, to the FDP, came in June 1987, when Colonel Roberto Díaz Herrera, chief of staff of the FDP, was forced to retire and then publicly denounced Noriega and other FDP officers for a variety of corrupt practices, including engineering the 1984 election fraud, ordering the murder of Spadafora, and causing the death of Torrijos. Díaz Herrera later also spoke of Noriega's involvement in drug trafficking. Díaz Herrera's revelations were shocking, not so much because of what they said about Noriega and the FDP—Panamanians had long suspected these things—but because Díaz Herrera was the first high-ranking FDP officer to break the FDP code of silence. He had spoken apparently out of pique at Noriega's failure to live up to an earlier agreement among FDP leaders to rotate the position of commander. Revenge for this forced retirement also motivated Díaz Herrera's denunciation of Noriega.

One result of the revelations was an internal political crisis in Panama that as of a year later remained unresolved. In June 1987, a coalition of civic, business, and professional groups formed the National Civic Crusade (Cruzada Civilista Nacional—CCN), and thousands of Panamanians participated in marches and street demonstrations to demand Noriega's resignation. Noriega and the FDP responded harshly, and there were credible reports of widespread police brutality. Noriega also attempted—mostly unsuccessfully—to portray the conflict as a class and racial struggle (i.e., white elite opposition to the black and mestizo masses and FDP) as well as a Yankee (see Glossary) conspiracy to retain United States control of the canal.

The chain of events in June 1987 also led to the direct involvement of the United States in the crisis. On June 26, 1987, the United States Senate passed a resolution calling for a transition to genuine democracy in Panama. The Panamanian government responded by organizing a demonstration against the United States embassy and arresting United States diplomatic and military personnel. As a consequence, on July 1, 1987, the United States suspended all military and economic assistance to Panama. It also halted repairs to Panamanian military equipment and supplies of tear gas and spare parts. For the rest of the year and into the new year, the United States government continued to consider ways of escalating the economic pressures on Panama and periodically took additional steps in that direction. In December, for example, the United States Congress suspended Panama's sugar quota for exports to the United States, cut off all nonhumanitarian aid, prohibited joint military exercises, and mandated United States opposition to any international development bank loan for Panama until Noriega handed over power to a democratically elected civilian government.

By the end of 1987, the United States government apparently had decided that Noriega was expendable and that serious efforts should be made to force him from power. United States assistant secretary of defense Richard Armitage headed an end-of-the-year effort to draw up a plan for Noriega's departure from Panama. But Noriega, who had been aware of the negotiations, denounced the plan in January 1988.

The already volatile situation flared up further in February 1988, when grand juries in Miami and Tampa, Florida, indicted Noriega on numerous counts of racketeering, drug trafficking, and money laundering. The indictments accused him of using his country as a vast clearinghouse for drugs and money tied to the Colombian cocaine trade. Suspicions and growing evidence of such activities by Noriega (as well as arms trafficking and intelligence activities) had long abounded, but the United States government previously had not acted on the evidence, purportedly because Noriega was considered by successive administrations as an important ally. Some United States government elements apparently had regarded him as vital for the protection of United States strategic interests in Panama; others, as an important source of intelligence information on Cuba. Moreover, Noriega had reportedly assisted United States efforts to oppose the Sandinista regime in Nicaragua. But support for Noriega died out after the events of June 1987 and the indictments.

The evolving crisis took another unexpected turn later in February 1988, when Panamanian president Delvalle attempted to fire Noriega, who then, with the solid backing of FDP officers, convened the legislature, which voted to oust Delvalle and replace him with education minister Manuel Solís Palma. Delvalle went into hiding in Panama, and, ironically, this aristocrat, formerly branded as "Noriega's man," became the unlikely leader of the opposition to Noriega. Washington refused to recognize Solís Palma and initiated an additional economic squeeze designed to bring Noriega down. In March 1988, the United States government froze Panamanian assets (about US$50 million) in United States banks, withheld its monthly payment for the use of the canal, and suspended trade preferences on imports from Panama. (All payments due to the Panamanian government were placed in escrow, payable only to the "legitimate" government of Delvalle.) The United States also decertified Panama as an ally in the drug-fighting war, which, according to a 1986 law, would mandate an aid cut-off and justify other discretionary sanctions, which were not imposed at that time. This measure was largely symbolic, however, because aid had already been terminated in December 1987.

Because Panama was dependent on the United States dollar, these economic measures meant that Panama had no cash with which to pay its employees—or to meet its interest payments on loans from international lending institutions or private banks. Panama's banks closed in early March 1988, and by mid-March half of the estimated US$23 billion in foreign deposits had left the country. Indeed, capital flight had proceeded steadily ever since the June 1987 crisis. Even before the capital flight, the economy was stagnating and suffering from high unemployment and low or negative growth in GDP. In short, the Panamanian economy was near collapse. Although the economic measures adopted by the United States were intended to dry up the Noriega regime's cash and thereby force him out without permanently damaging the economy, analysts began to fear that the long-term effects of the crisis on the Panamanian economy would be devastating and that the once-prosperous banking sector would be irrevocably damaged.

The CCN reacted to the economic crisis in Panama by calling a general strike that brought Panama's economy to a virtual standstill for the month of March. Widely regarded as largely upper-class, white, and elite, the CCN had not engendered widespread popular or labor support up to that point, but in March 1988 its followers appeared to be growing. The populace engaged in a series of protests and strikes over the government's failure to pay public-sector employees and pensioners. Several parties and the hierarchy of the Roman Catholic Church (traditionally conservative and previously impartial) voiced support for the crusade. Noriega did not appear to have much support outside the FDP and the official government party that had been created by Torrijos—the Democratic Revolutionary Party (Partido Revolucionario Democrático—PRD).

After the exertion of economic pressure by the United States—combined with growing internal opposition to the Noriega regime—many observers expected Noriega to be forced to step aside in the near future. But such was not the case. Noriega showed remarkable durability and ingenuity in adopting countermeasures that permitted his regime to survive. In an important move aimed at cutting off the flow of information among opposition forces, Noriega periodically closed down independent and opposition radio and television stations and newspapers. Faced with CCN strikes and demonstrations and spontaneous acts of protest by various groups (e.g., teachers, telephone workers, mill workers, and hospital workers), Noriega responded with violence. Troops teargassed demonstrating teachers, stormed Panama's largest hospital when hospital workers staged a protest, occupied flour mills, forcefully reopened the port of Balboa after dock workers went on strike, stormed a luxury hotel to arrest opposition figures, intimidated shops and supermarkets into reopening, forced banks to reopen for limited operations, and purged (forcibly retired or imprisoned) FDP officers implicated in a mid-March 1988 coup attempt or suspected of disloyalty. Acting under a declared state of urgency, Noriega increasingly moved to take over all key economic sectors and public services so that he could survive a prolonged economic battle.

In addition to instituting measures designed to quell popular protests, Noriega showed great resourcefulness in his quest for cash dollars. By the end of March, he had amassed enough cash to meet some of the government's payrolls. His sources of cash included cash salary payments to Panamanians working for United States military forces in Panama, the Panama Canal Commission, and various foreign banks; the conversion of Panamanian assets of the Latin American Export Bank into hard currency in Europe; and taxes paid by United States companies with branches in Panama. The United States government later tried to close off the latter flow of dollars, but regulations prohibiting payments to the government of Panama were so general that they were difficult to enforce. Another factor in Noriega's ability to weather the cash crisis was the introduction of an alternative currency system that used government checks, issued in small denominations. These "Panadollars" could not be cashed at banks, but were widely exchanged in lieu of cash.

Noriega's successful containment of the violence in Panama, defeat of the attempted coup, and acquisition of cash apparently reinforced his determination to stay in power. In March 1988, Noriega began to toy with both opposition and United States government attempts to negotiate his departure. But he ultimately rejected all proposed deals, even though between March and May the United States increasingly backed down on its initial requirements and met virtually all demands put forth by Noriega, including his insistence that the indictments be dropped.

Thus, by June 1988, the situation had reached an impasse. The opposition in Panama remained committed to ousting Noriega and restoring democracy to the country, but its protest activities were sporadic and its leaders disheartened. In fact, most CCN leaders had left the country. There was some discussion of opposition negotiations with Noriega, but few observers expected any such attempts to prove fruitful. The United States government maintained all economic sanctions previously imposed against Panama, and on June 6 announced its intention of more rigidly enforcing regulations prohibiting payments to the government of Panama. United States government officials also made vague threats about other future actions against Panama, but they publicly ruled out any military intervention in the absence of a direct threat to the Panama Canal, and most observers noted the lack of other viable United States options. The prospect of Latin American mediation to achieve a negotiated settlement offered some hope of an end to the crisis, but there was no apparent progress in this direction as of August 1988. Meanwhile, the Panamanian economy, although outwardly functioning more normally, continued its steady deterioration, as evidenced by continued layoffs, bankruptcies, a sharp decline in the GDP, and defaults on payments of the foreign debt.

The acknowledged failure of the combined efforts of the United States government and the Panamanian opposition to force out Noriega resulted from several factors that observers discussed at great length in the media and on which they generally agreed. First, the Panamanian opposition did not develop into a "people's power" movement such as those that had successfully toppled dictators in the Philippines and Haiti earlier in the 1980s. The Panamanian opposition was widespread, but it remained fragmented, lacked a charismatic leader, failed to foster allies within the FDP (a tactic used successfully elsewhere), and never engendered widespread support among labor or the masses. In its attempt to develop support, the opposition was hindered somewhat by a perceived class distinction between the elite upper- and middle-class, business-dominated CCN and the masses, who had traditionally supported and benefited from FDP rule. Noriega played on this mass susceptibility to class animosity. There was growing evidence that the populace regarded the FDP under Noriega as corrupt and self-serving and found his personal corruption distasteful, but fear and perceived class interests continued to override any desire for social change. Moreover, observers noted that the Panamanian opposition, as well as the general populace, remained steadfastly cautious and nonviolent and was easily intimidated by the FDP.

The second major reason for Noriega's retention of power was the strength and cohesiveness of the FDP—attributes that had been largely underestimated by the United States government and others. The FDP, out of both fear and entrenched self-interest, remained loyal to Noriega. Although his position was undermined somewhat by the defection of close associates, Noriega still was able to put down the March 1988 coup attempt quite easily. Subsequently, he managed to purge suspected dissidents and surrounded himself with loyal supporters and cronies. In May 1988, Noriega created a twenty-member Strategic Military Council headed by a colonel and composed of three lieutenant colonels, ten majors, and six captains. Observers believed that this lower-ranking group increasingly bypassed the more senior general staff. Noriega also tripled the size of his personal security force, staffing it largely with Cubans and other non-Panamanians, and he reportedly also brought in Cuban military advisers and weapons. In short, Noriega moved both to consolidate his hold over the FDP and to tighten the FDP's grip on the country.

Finally, and perhaps most basically, Noriega survived the crisis because the economic sanctions imposed by the United States government did not have the quick and catastrophic effect envisioned by policy makers. Despite the dependence of Panama on dollars, the Panamanian economy proved to be surprisingly resilient. In addition, the sanctions were ineffective because they did not directly affect Noriega, who managed to weather his liquidity crisis because of a continuous influx of both legal and illegal cash. The sanctions hit hardest on the middle class and private sector and created hardships for the masses. In the long run, however, the economy was seriously damaged, perhaps irreparably. Moreover, some observers noted that the economic sanctions may unintentionally have destroyed the private sector, which is the base for moderate, democratic forces in Panama. In related events, observers noted the ruling PRD's apparent move to the left with the appointment of new cabinet members in late April 1988 and the increasingly pro-Cuban and pro-leftist leanings of the FDP.

The focus of United States and international attention on Noriega—first attempting to remove him from power and then analyzing where such attempts went wrong—tended to obscure more enduring problems affecting Panama's future. In mid-1988 analysts uniformly agreed that, even without Noriega, who was not likely to leave soon, restoring order, rebuilding the damaged economy, and revamping the political system were formidable tasks. Noriega's departure would ease but not solve Panama's political problems. The opposition remained divided and political parties factionalized. Indeed, in February 1988, two parties reportedly formed their own opposition movement—the Popular Civic Movement (Movimiento Civilista Popular—MCP)—separate from the CCN. Moreover, the lack of a clear national leader as an alternative to Noriega or another FDP officer was a serious impediment to opposition success. Delvalle was tainted by his former association with Noriega; veteran politician Arnulfo Arias Madrid died in August 1988; and other party leaders reportedly lacked charisma.

Finally, and most important, the extensive, institutionalized control of national life by the FDP and the endemic corruption within the FDP (including widespread involvement in drug trafficking and money laundering) stood in the way of any rapid or easy transition to democracy in Panama. In the summer of 1988, some observers reported that certain FDP elements were discontent with Noriega. They predicted that Panamanian military officers would eventually remove Noriega from power. Prospects for an end to corruption and a return to democratic civilian rule in Panama, however, would not necessarily be improved by a military coup that ousted Noriega alone.

The FDP's reputation for corruption also fueled United States fears about the future of the Panama Canal. The prospects for an efficient, professional, and nonpartisan administration of the canal and related activities under Panamanian leadership were not good based on the evidence of Panama's corrupt, politicized management of the trans-isthmian railroad, ports, and other former Canal Zone property turned over to it in 1979. Indeed, some analysts believed that even before the crisis ignited in June 1987, maladministration, political patronage, and corruption had become so pronounced and extensive that they jeopardized the future of Panama's economy.

Panama's future thus remained clouded in mid-1988. Although life had in some senses returned to normal following the turmoil that had flared up in June 1987, the political system remained un~~presentative~~ and potentially unstable, the economy chaotic, and relations with the United States severely strained.

August 15, 1988

* * *

As of late March 1989, there had been no major changes in the situation in Panama since research and writing of this book were completed. But observers agreed that the United States attempt to oust Noriega had failed. Despite his increasing international isolation and lack of popular support, Noriega had survived, and, against all odds, the battered economy had not collapsed.

In the spring of 1989, political activity in Panama focused on preparations for the presidential election set for May 7, 1989. Progovernment parties—the PRD, Labor and Agrarian Party (Partido Laborista Agrario—PALA), Republican Party (Partido Republicano—PR), National Liberal Party (Partido Liberal Nacional—PLN), and several other small parties—had formed a new electoral coalition, the National Liberation Coalition (Coalición de Liberación Nacional—COLINA). COLINA's slate of candidates, announced in early February 1989, included Carlos Alberto Duque Jaén of the PRD for president, Ramón Sieiro Murgas of PALA for first vice president, and Aquilino Boyd, the government's ambassador to the Organization of American States, for second vice president. All three were widely regarded as staunch Noriega supporters: Duque, a business partner of Noriega; Sieiro, Noriega's brother-in law; and Boyd, a Noriega regime loyalist.

Opposing the government coalition were three major opposition parties—the Christian Democratic Party (Partido Demócrato Cristiano—PDC), National Liberal Republican Movement (Movimiento Liberal Republicano Nacional—MOLIRENA), and Authentic Liberal Party (Partido Liberal Auténtico—PLA), which had banded together in a coalition known as the Civic Democratic Opposition Alliance (Alianza Democrática de Oposición Cívica—Civic ADO or ADOC). Civic ADO also had the support of the Crusade (CCN), the small Popular Action Party (Partido de Acción Popular—PAPO), and a dissident faction of the Authentic Panameñista Party (Partido Panameñista Auténtico—PPA), which had split after the death of Arias Madrid in August 1988. When the Electoral Tribunal gave official recognition and control of the party to a small faction headed by Hildebrando Nicosia Pérez, who had broken with Arias Madrid in the mid-1980s, the majority faction, led by Guillermo

Endara, left the PPA and formed the Arnulfist Party. The Arnulfist Party threw its considerable weight behind Civic ADO, and its leader, Guillermo Endara, was put forward as Civic ADO's presidential candidate. In addition to Endara, Civic ADO's electoral slate included Ricardo Arias Calderón of the PDC for first vice president and Guillermo Ford of MOLIRENA for second vice president. The official PPA refused to join either coalition, preferring to run its own slate of candidates headed by Nicosia for president.

Observers predicted that the government-sponsored candidates would prevail. The Noriega regime was widely expected to ensure the victory of its candidates through a combination of electoral fraud and pre-electoral tactics designed to intimidate and divide the opposition. Indeed, the opposition claimed that thousands of names of opposition party supporters had already disappeared from the lists of eligible voters. Moreover, in the period leading up to the election, the Noriega regime was reportedly using its control of the three-member Electoral Tribunal to capitalize on internal divisions in legitimate opposition parties. In disputes over party leadership, the tribunal had consistently ruled in favor of minority factions presumed more loyal to Noriega, most notably in the case of the PPA. Analysts regarded such rulings as attempts to "steal" these opposition parties and undercut their electoral strength. Some observers even postulated that Nicosia had purposely split the PPA in order to create a rift in the opposition, reduce support for Civic ADO, and enhance the electoral prospects of COLINA.

The pre-electoral period in Panama was a tense one with respect not only to internal Panamanian politics but also to relations between Panama and the United States. In addition to its political machinations, the Noriega regime's continued harassment of Americans in Panama, incursions onto United States military facilities, hostile propaganda, and charges of violations of the Panama Canal treaties exacerbated the already poor relations between the two countries. Observers believed that the future tone and direction of the relationship would be determined to a large extent by the outcome of the May 1989 election. The United States would face difficult policy decisions over how to react to the expected electoral fraud; what to do about the economic sanctions, which were unpopular and ineffective but still officially in place; and how to handle the turn-over of directorship of the Panama Canal Commission to a Panamanian in 1990, given the high probability of an undemocratic and hostile regime in Panama.

Panama itself faced an uncertain future. Although victory for pro-Noriega forces seemed assured in the short term, in the longer term they were expected to confront increasing regional and international isolation, continued United States opposition, and, most seriously, bleak economic prospects because of the dramatic drop in GDP and government income and the equally drastic rise in capital flight and unemployment. The once vital Panamanian economy was a shambles, and its future looked grim, indeed.

March 27, 1989

* * *

Late on the night of May 10, 1989, the Electoral Tribunal announced that the May 7 elections—presidential, legislative, and local—had been annulled because of violence and "foreign interference." The announcement followed three days of uncertainty, controversy, and incipient violence during which both sides claimed victory although official results had not been forthcoming. Duque declared himself the winner on election night, and partial results slowly released by the government over the next three days showed him leading by a two-to-one margin. But the Roman Catholic Church in Panama, independent exit polls, and international election observers supported the opposition's contention that it had won by a margin of about three to one.

The opposition stated unequivocally that the elections were fraudulent and that the official results were based on fake tally sheets. Most observers agreed with them. They cited numerous instances of military and paramilitary raids on vote-counting centers during which original tally sheets were seized or destroyed. It appeared that the Noriega regime, unable to steal the election unobtrusively because of the wide margin of the opposition's victory, had resorted to crude and overt fraud to ensure the victory of its hand-picked candidates.

In addition, the regime responded to opposition demonstrations with violence, forcibly dispersing protesters. On May 10, members of Noriega's civilian paramilitary squads, known as Dignity Battalions, which were believed to be composed primarily of members of the FDP, attacked and savagely beat opposition candidates Endara, Arias Calderón, and Ford during a motorcade and popular demonstration to protest the electoral fraud. The Noriega regime responded to international condemnation of its actions by expelling foreign journalists and harassing United States diplomatic and military personnel stationed in Panama.

Despite its use of fraud and violence, however, the Noriega regime ultimately gave up on any attempt to claim victory in the elections and instead nullified them. Opposition and church leaders rejected the annulment and demanded official recognition of the opposition's electoral victory and a turnover of power to the newly elected government on September 1, 1989, as scheduled. In addition, the opposition called for a twenty-four-hour general strike to be held on May 17.

Most Latin American nations, except for Cuba and Nicaragua, also condemned the annulment but warned against United States military intervention. A special meeting of the Organization of American States to discuss the situation was scheduled for May 17, and the Group of Eight (a coalition of eight Latin American democracies from which Panama had been suspended in February 1988) expressed "profound concern" over events in Panama. West European nations also denounced the Noriega regime's actions.

For its part, the United States stood by its earlier condemnation of the elections as fraudulent, deplored the use of violence, refused to recognize the Noriega regime, and called on Panamanians to overthrow Noriega. The United States took steps to protect its personnel and property in Panama and to prepare for a possible evacuation of United States personnel and their dependents from Panama. It also ordered the deployment to Panama of an additional brigade of combat troops, recalled its ambassador, and engaged in diplomatic initiatives to isolate Noriega and encourage a regional solution to the crisis.

Thus, the political crisis that had begun in Panama in June 1987 remained unresolved and had, in fact, escalated to a new and more dangerous level. The situation remained very tense as observers awaited Noriega's further efforts to exert control and the domestic and international responses to his actions.

May 15, 1989   Sandra W. Meditz

Chapter 1. Historical Setting

Cuna Indian mola *design of a Panamanian coin featuring Spanish explorer* Vasco Núñez de Balboa

THE HISTORY OF the Panamanian isthmus, since Spaniards first landed on its shores in 1501, is a tale of treasure, treasure seekers, and peoples exploited; of clashes among empires, nations, and cultures; of adventurers and builders; of magnificent dreams fulfilled and simple needs unmet. In the wake of Vasco Núñez de Balboa's torturous trek from the Atlantic to the Pacific in 1513, conquistadors seeking gold in Peru and beyond crossed the seas and recrossed with their treasures bound for Spain. The indigenous peoples who survived the diseases, massacres, and enslavement of the conquest ultimately fled into the forest or across to the San Blas Islands. Indian slaves were soon replaced by Africans.

A century before the English settled Massachusetts Bay, Panama was the crossroads and marketplace of the great Spanish Empire, the third richest colony of the New World. In the seventeenth century, however, the thriving colony fell prey to buccaneers of the growing English Empire, and Panama entered a period of decline and neglect that lasted until gold was discovered in California.

The geopolitical significance of Panama has been recognized since the early 1500s, when the Spanish monarchs considered digging a canal across the isthmus. United States interest, intensified in the 1850s by the California gold rush, resulted in the construction of a trans-isthmian railroad. In 1879 a French company under the direction of Ferdinand de Lesseps, builder of the Suez Canal, began constructing a canal in Panama. The project fell victim to disease, faulty design, and ultimately bankruptcy and was abandoned in 1889.

By the turn of the twentieth century, the United States had become convinced that a canal should be built to link the two oceans. In addition to the geographic advantages of the isthmus, President Theodore Roosevelt was attracted by the separatist tendencies of Panama, then a department of Colombia. When Panama rebelled against Colombia in 1903, Roosevelt deployed United States naval vessels to discourage the Colombian forces and proudly claimed the role of midwife at the birth of the Republic of Panama.

Since its completion in 1914, the Panama Canal has been Panama's economic base, and the United States presence has been the republic's major source of frustration. The provisions of the treaty concluded in 1903 between John Hay and Philippe Bunau-Varilla (the Hay-Bunau-Varilla Treaty) granted the Canal Zone "in perpetuity" to the United States and made Panama a virtual

3

protectorate of the United States. Relations with the United States in general, and the status of the Canal Zone in particular, long remained the overriding concerns of the formulators of Panama's foreign policy and strongly influenced domestic politics and international relations.

Despite the negotiation of treaty amendments in 1936 and 1955, limiting the freedom of the United States to intervene in Panama's internal affairs, various problems between the two countries continued to generate resentment among Panamanians. Aside from the larger issue of jurisdiction over the zone—which split the country into two parts—Panamanians complained that they did not receive their fair share of the receipts from the canal, that commissaries in the zone had damaged their commercial interests, that Panamanian workers in the zone were discriminated against in economic and social matters, and that the large-scale presence of the United States military in the zone and in bases outside the zone cast a long shadow over national sovereignty.

After serious rioting in 1964 that indicated the intensity of nationalistic aspirations concerning the status of the canal, the United States agreed to enter into negotiations for a new treaty. Meanwhile, studies relating to the construction of a new canal were undertaken. In 1971 after a four-year interlude, negotiations were renewed. In 1977 two new treaties were signed, one providing for Panamanian assumption of control over the canal in the year 2000 and the other providing for a permanent joint guarantee of the canal's neutrality.

The focal point of consensus in Panamanian political life, cutting across both social and partisan divides, has been nationalism. Nationalistic sentiments, directed primarily against the highly visible and dominant presence of the United States, have been catered to in varying degrees by all who have held positions of leadership or have sought popular support. Public demonstrations and riots, as occurred in 1927, 1947, 1959, and 1964, have been effective in influencing policy, especially in relation to the country's stance vis-à-vis the United States. National leaders have alternately responded to and contributed to an explosive climate of public opinion. They have carefully kept popular resentment narrowly focused on the United States presence lest discontent turn on the Panamanian elite, generally referred to as the oligarchy.

Until the National Guard seized control in 1968, power had been wielded almost exclusively by a small number of aristocratic families. The middle class was constrained from challenging the system because most of its members depended on government jobs. Also, the slow pace of industrialization had limited the political role of urban labor. The lower classes lacked organization and leadership. They had been distracted from recognizing common problems by the ethnic antagonisms between those of Spanish or mestizo background and the more recent immigrants, Antillean blacks from Jamaica and other parts of the West Indies.

Brigadier General Omar Torrijos Herrera, who in 1969 as commander of the National Guard assumed the role of head of government, had some initial success in building a popular base for his government among small farmers and urban workers. His domestic program emphasized public works—especially the construction of roads, bridges, schools, and low-cost public housing—and an agrarian reform program. In addition, he encouraged the entry of foreign banks and firms as part of his effort to create jobs and increase incomes.

In negotiating new Panama Canal treaties, Torrijos, like other leaders before him, walked the tightrope of taking a strong stand on the issue to maintain popular support, while keeping popular frustrations within controllable limits and without appearing so militant as to alarm the United States. Successful in this endeavor, by the time the new treaties were signed in 1977, Torrijos had held power longer than any other leader in Panama's history.

Nevertheless, by the late 1970s, clear signs appeared to show that Torrijos's populist alliance was eroding. Observers attributed the decline in support to a variety of factors, including severe economic problems that led to backtracking on social programs, opposition among Panamanians to the 1977 Panama Canal treaties, and the very ''democratization'' process that Torrijos initiated to gain United States support for the canal treaties.

In October 1978, the 1972 Constitution had been reformed to allow the legalization of political parties, and exiled political leaders were permitted to return to Panama. Torrijos formally stepped down as head of government, and a civilian president was elected. Torrijos, however, clearly remained the dominant force in the political system. Torrijos's shocking, sudden death in an airplane crash in July 1981 created a power vacuum in Panama. The newly erected democratic facade persisted, however, with a succession of civilian presidents controlled by the National Guard and its emergent leader, General Manuel Antonio Noriega Moreno, who (as of late 1987) had been in command since August 1983. Noriega successfully transformed the National Guard into the far larger Panama Defense Forces (Fuerzas de Defensa de Panamá—FDP), a formidable power base for his increasing political control.

The Conquest

Estimates vary greatly of the number of Indians who inhabited the isthmus when the Spanish explorers arrived. By some accounts, the population was considerably greater than that of contemporary Panama. Some Panamanian historians have suggested that there might have been a population of 500,000 Indians from some 60 "tribes," but other researchers have concluded that the Cuna alone numbered some 750,000.

Besides the Cuna, who constituted by far the largest group in the area, two other major groups, the Guaymí and the Chocó, have been identified by ethnologists (see Indians, ch. 2). The Guaymí, of the highlands near the Costa Rican border, are believed to be related to Indians of the Nahuatlan and Mayan nations of Mexico and Central America. The Chocó on the Pacific side of Darién Province appear to be related to the Chibcha of Colombia (see fig. 1).

Although the Cuna, now found mostly in the Comarca de San Blas, an indigenous territory or reserve considered part of Colón Province for some official purposes, have been categorized as belonging to the Caribbean culture, their origin continues to be a subject of speculation. Various ethnologists have indicated the possibility of a linguistic connection between the name *Cuna* and certain Arawak and Carib tribal names. The possibility of cultural links with the Andean Indians has been postulated, and some scholars have noted linguistic and other affinities with the Chibcha. The implication in terms of settlement patterns is that the great valleys of Colombia, which trend toward the isthmus, determined migration in that direction.

Lines of affiliation have also been traced to the Cueva and Coiba tribes, although some anthropologists suggest that the Cuna might belong to a largely extinct linguistic group. Some Cuna believe themselves to be of Carib stock, while others trace their origin to creation by the god Olokkuppilele at Mount Tacarcuna, west of the mouth of the Río Atrato in Colombia.

Among all three Indian groups—the Cuna, Guaymí, and Chocó—land was communally owned and farmed. In addition to hunting and fishing, the Indians raised corn, cotton, cacao, various root crops and other vegetables, and fruits. They lived then—as many still do—in circular thatched huts and slept in hammocks. Villages specialized in producing certain goods, and traders moved among them along the rivers and coastal waters in dugout canoes. The Indians were skillful potters, stonecutters, goldsmiths, and silversmiths. The ornaments they wore, including breastplates and earrings of beaten gold, reinforced the Spanish myth of El Dorado, the city of gold.

Rodrigo de Bastidas, a wealthy notary public from Seville, was the first of many Spanish explorers to reach the isthmus. Sailing westward from Venezuela in 1501 in search of gold, he explored some 150 kilometers of the coastal area before heading for the West Indies. A year later, Christopher Columbus, on his fourth voyage to the New World, touched several points on the isthmus. One was a horseshoe-shaped harbor that he named Puerto Bello (beautiful port), later renamed Portobelo.

Vasco Núñez de Balboa, a member of Bastidas's crew, had settled in Hispaniola (the island encompassing present-day Dominican Republic and Haiti) but stowed away on a voyage to Panama in 1510 to escape his creditors. At that time, about 800 Spaniards lived on the isthmus, but soon the many jungle perils, doubtless including malaria and yellow fever, had killed all but 60 of them. Finally, the settlers at Antigua del Darién (Antigua), the first city to be duly constituted by the Spanish crown, deposed the crown's representative and elected Balboa and Martin Zamudio co-mayors (see fig. 2).

Balboa proved to be a good administrator. He insisted that the settlers plant crops rather than depend solely on supply ships, and Antigua became a prosperous community. Like other conquistadors, Balboa led raids on Indian settlements, but unlike most, he proceeded to befriend the conquered tribes. He took the daughter of a chief as his lifelong mistress.

On September 1, 1513, Balboa set out with 190 Spaniards—among them Francisco Pizarro, who later conquered the Inca Empire in Peru—a pack of dogs, and 1,000 Indian slaves. After twenty-five days of hacking their way through the jungle, the party gazed on the vast expanse of the Pacific Ocean. Balboa, clad in full armor, waded into the water and claimed the sea and all the shores on which it washed for his God and his king.

Balboa returned to Antigua in January 1514 with all 190 soldiers and with cotton cloth, pearls, and 40,000 pesos in gold. Meanwhile, Balboa's enemies had denounced him in the Spanish court, and King Ferdinand appointed a new governor for the colony, then known as Castilla del Oro. The new governor, Pedro Arias de Avila, who became known as "Pedrarias the Cruel," charged Balboa with treason. In 1517 Balboa was arrested, brought to the court of Pedrarias, and executed.

In 1519 Pedrarias moved his capital away from the debilitating climate and unfriendly Indians of the Darién to a fishing village on the Pacific coast (about four kilometers east of the present-day

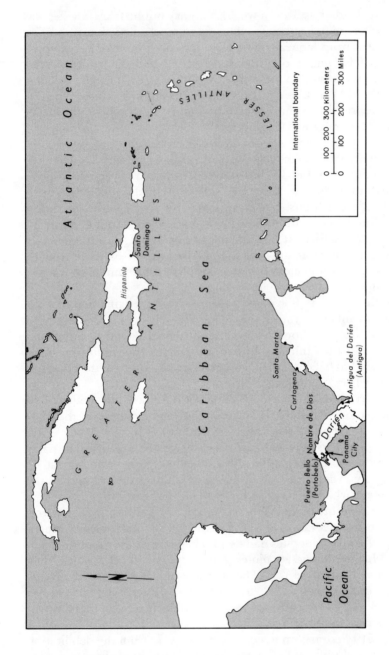

Figure 2. The Isthmus and Surrounding Areas in the Fifteenth and Sixteenth Centuries

capital). The Indians called the village Panama, meaning "plenty of fish." In the same year, Nombre de Dios, a deserted early settlement, was resettled and until the end of the sixteenth century served as the Caribbean port for trans-isthmian traffic. A trail known as the Camino Real, or royal road, linked Panama and Nombre de Dios. Along this trail, traces of which can still be followed, gold from Peru was carried by muleback to Spanish galleons waiting on the Atlantic coast.

The increasing importance of the isthmus for transporting treasure and the delay and difficulties posed by the Camino Real inspired surveys ordered by the Spanish crown in the 1520s and 1530s to ascertain the feasibility of constructing a canal. The idea was finally abandoned in mid-century by King Philip II (1556–98), who concluded that if God had wanted a canal there, He would have built one.

Pedrarias's governorship proved to be disastrous. Hundreds of Spaniards died of disease and starvation in their brocaded silk clothing; thousands of Indians were robbed, enslaved, and massacred. Thousands more of the Indians succumbed to European diseases to which they had no natural immunity. After the atrocities of Pedrarias, most of the Indians fled to remote areas to avoid the Spaniards.

The regulations for colonial administration set forth by the Spanish king's Council of the Indies decreed that the Indians were to be protected and converted to Christianity. The colonies, however, were far from the seat of ultimate responsibility, and few administrators were guided by the humane spirit of those regulations. The Roman Catholic Church, and particularly the Franciscan order, showed some concern for the welfare of the Indians, but on the whole, church efforts were inadequate to the situation.

The Indians, nevertheless, found one effective benefactor among their Spanish oppressors. Bartolomé de las Casas, the first priest ordained in the West Indies, was outraged by the persecution of the Indians. He freed his own slaves, returned to Spain, and persuaded the council to adopt stronger measures against enslaving the Indians. He made one suggestion that he later regretted—that Africans, whom the Spaniards considered less than human, be imported to replace the Indians as slaves.

In 1517 King Charles V (1516–56) granted a concession for exporting 4,000 African slaves to the Antilles. Thus the slave trade began and flourished for more than 200 years. Panama was a major distribution point for slaves headed elsewhere on the mainland. The supply of Indian labor had been depleted by the mid-sixteenth century, however, and Panama began to absorb many of the slaves.

A large number of slaves on the isthmus escaped into the jungle. They became known as *cimarrones* (sing., *cimarrón*), meaning wild or unruly, because they attacked travelers along the Camino Real. An official census of Panama City in 1610 listed 548 citizens, 303 women, 156 children, 146 mulattoes, 148 Antillean blacks, and 3,500 African slaves.

The Spanish Colony

The period of free, though licensed, exploration gave way to a period in which the king exercised royal control by appointing governors and their staffs. All were to be paid from crown revenues expected from the royal profits on the colony. The king's representative was responsible for ensuring such returns; he tracked all gold, pearls, and income from trade and conquest; he weighed out and safeguarded the king's share.

Governors had some summary powers of justice, but *audiencias* (courts) were also established. The first such *audiencia,* in Santo Domingo, Hispaniola, had jurisdiction over the whole area of conquest. As settlement spread, other *audiencias* were set up. By a decree of 1538, all Spanish territory from Nicaragua to Cape Horn was to be administered from an *audiencia* in Panama. This *audiencia* lasted only until 1543 because of the impossibility of exercising jurisdiction over so vast an area. A new Panamanian *audiencia,* with jurisdiction over an area more nearly coinciding with the territory of present-day Panama, was established in 1563. The viceroy's position was revived for the rich empires of Mexico and Peru. After 1567 Panama was attached to the Viceroyalty of Peru but retained its own *audiencia.*

Beginning early in the sixteenth century, Nombre de Dios in Panama, Vera Cruz in Mexico, and Cartagena in Colombia were the only three ports in Spanish America authorized by the crown to trade with the homeland. By the mid-1560s, the system became regularized, and two fleets sailed annually from Spain, one to Mexico, and the other to southern ports. These fleets would then rendezvous at Havana and return together to Cádiz, Spain. In principle, this rigid system remained in effect until the eighteenth century. From the middle of the seventeenth century, however, as the strength and prosperity of Spain declined, annual visits became the exception.

Shipments of bullion and goods were to be delivered to Panama on the Pacific side for transport over the isthmus and return to Spain. Panama's own contribution to the loading of the fleet was relatively small. Gold production was never great, and little exportable surplus of agricultural and forest products was available.

Nothing was manufactured; in fact, Spain discouraged the production of finished goods. The colony's prosperity, therefore, fluctuated with the volume of trade, made up largely of Peruvian shipments. When the Inca gold was exhausted, great quantities of silver mined in Peru replaced gold in trade for 150 years, supplemented eventually by sugar, cotton, wine, indigo, cinchona, vanilla, and cacao.

Except for traffic in African slaves, foreign trade was forbidden unless the goods passed through Spain. Africans were brought to the colonies on contract (*asiento*) by Portuguese, English, Dutch, and French slavers, who were forbidden to trade in any other commodities. Spanish efforts to retain their monopoly on the rich profits from trade with their colonies provided a challenge to the rising maritime nations of Europe. Intermittent maritime warfare resulted in the Caribbean and later in the Pacific. The first serious interference with trade came from the English.

From 1572 to 1597, Francis Drake was associated with most of the assaults on Panama. Drake's activities demonstrated the indefensibility of the open roadstead of Nombre de Dios. In 1597 the Atlantic terminus of the trans-isthmian route was moved to Portobelo, one of the best natural harbors anywhere on the Spanish Main (the mainland of Spanish America).

Despite raids on shipments and ports, the registered legal import of precious metals increased threefold between 1550 and 1600. Panama's prosperity was at its peak during the first part of the seventeenth century. This was the time of the famous *ferias* (fairs, or exchange markets) of Portobelo, where European merchandise could be purchased to supply the commerce of the whole west coast south of Nicaragua. When a *feria* ended, Portobelo would revert to its quiet existence as a small seaport and garrison town.

Panama City also flourished on the profits of trade. Following reconstruction after a serious fire in 1644, contemporary accounts credit Panama City with 1,400 residences "of all types" (probably including slave huts); most business places, religious houses, and substantial residences were rebuilt of stone. Panama City was considered, after Mexico City and Lima, the most beautiful and opulent settlement in the West Indies.

Interest in a canal project was revived early in the seventeenth century by Philip III of Spain (1598–1621). The Council of the Indies dissuaded the king, arguing that a canal would draw attack from other European nations—an indication of the decline of Spanish sea power.

During the first quarter of the seventeenth century, trade between Spain and the isthmus remained undisturbed. At the same time,

England, France, and the Netherlands, one or all almost constantly at war with Spain, began seizing colonies in the Caribbean. Such footholds in the West Indies encouraged the development of the buccaneers—English, French, Dutch, and Portuguese adventurers who preyed on Spanish shipping and ports with the tacit or open support of their governments. Because of their numbers and the closeness of their bases, the buccaneers were more effective against Spanish trade than the English had been during the previous century.

The volume of registered precious metal arriving in Spain fell from its peak in 1600; by 1660 volume was less than the amount registered a century before. Depletion of Peruvian mines, an increase in smuggling, and the buccaneers were causes of the decline.

Henry Morgan, a buccaneer who had held Portobelo for ransom in 1668, returned to Panama with a stronger force at the end of 1670. On January 29, 1671, Morgan appeared at Panama City. With 1,400 men he defeated the garrison of 2,600 in pitched battle outside the city, which he then looted. The officials and citizens fled, some to the country and others to Peru, having loaded their ships with the most important church and government funds and treasure. Panama City was destroyed by fire, probably from blown up powder stores, although the looters were blamed. After 4 weeks, Morgan left with 175 mule loads of loot and 600 prisoners. Two years later, a new city was founded at the location of the present-day capital and was heavily fortified.

The buccaneer scourge rapidly declined after 1688 mainly because of changing European alliances. By this time Spain was chronically bankrupt; its population had fallen; and it suffered internal government mismanagement and corruption.

Influenced by buccaneer reports about the ease with which the isthmus could be crossed—which suggested the possibility of digging a canal—William Paterson, founder and ex-governor of the Bank of England, organized a Scottish company to establish a colony in the San Blas area. Paterson landed on the Caribbean coast of the Darién late in 1698 with about 1,200 persons. Although well received by the Indians (as was anyone not Spanish), the colonists were poorly prepared for life in the tropics with its attendant diseases. Their notion of trade goods—European clothing, wigs, and English Bibles—was of little interest to the Indians. These colonists gave up after 6 months, unknowingly passing at sea reinforcements totaling another 1,600 people. The Spanish reacted to these new arrivals by establishing a blockade from the sea. The English capitulated and left in April 1700, having lost many lives, mostly from malnutrition and disease.

In Spain Bourbon kings replaced the Hapsburgs in 1700, and some liberalization of trade was introduced. These measures were too late for Panama, however. Spain's desperate efforts to maintain its colonial trade monopoly had been self-defeating. Cheaper goods supplied by England, France, and the Netherlands were welcomed by colonial officials and private traders alike. Dealing in contraband increased to the detriment of official trade. Fewer merchants came to the Portobelo *feria* to pay Spain's inflated prices because the foreign suppliers furnished cheaper goods at any port at which they could slip by or bribe the coastal guards. The situation worsened; only five of the previously annual fleets were dispatched to Latin America between 1715 and 1736, a circumstance that increased contraband operations.

Panama's temporary loss of its independent *audiencia,* from 1718 to 1722, and the country's attachment to the Viceroyalty of Peru were probably engineered by powerful Peruvian merchants. They resented the venality of Panamanian officials and their ineffectiveness in suppressing the pirates (outlaws of no flag, as distinct from the buccaneers of the seventeenth century). Panama's weakness was further shown by its inability to protect itself against an invasion by the Miskito Indians of Nicaragua, who attacked from Laguna de Chiriquí. Another Indian uprising in the valley of the Río Tuira caused the whites to abandon the Darién.

The final blow to Panama's shrinking control of the transit trade between Latin America and Spain came before the mid-eighteenth century. As a provision of the Treaty of Utrecht at the end of the War of the Spanish Succession in 1713, Britain secured the right to supply African slaves to the Spanish colonies (4,800 a year for 30 years) and also to send 1 ship a year to Portobelo. The slave trade provision evidently satisfied both countries, but the trade in goods did not. Smuggling by British ships continued, and a highly organized contraband trade based in Jamaica—with the collusion of Panamanian merchants—nearly wiped out the legal trade. By 1739 the importance of the isthmus to Spain had seriously declined; Spain again suppressed Panama's autonomy by making the region part of the Viceroyalty of New Granada (encompassing present-day Colombia, Venezuela, Ecuador, and Panama).

In the same year, war broke out between Britain and Spain. A British military force took Portobelo and destroyed it. Panamanian historians maintain that this attack diverted Spanish trade from the trans-isthmian route. The Seville-Cádiz monopoly of colonial trade had been breached by royal decrees earlier in the century, and precedent was thus furnished for the merchants of the Latin American colonies to agitate for direct trade with Spain and for intercolonial trade. After 1740 the Pacific coast ports were permitted to trade directly via ships rounding Cape Horn, and the Portobelo *feria* was never held again.

Relaxing the trading laws benefited both Spanish America and Spain, but Panama's economic decline was serious. Transit trade had for so long furnished the profits on which Panama had flourished that there had been no incentive to develop any other economic base. After the suppression of its *audiencia* in 1751, Panama became a quiet backwater, a geographically isolated appendage of New Granada, scarcely self-supporting even in food and producing little for export.

In 1793, near the close of the colonial period, the first recorded attempt at a comprehensive census of the area that had comprised the Panamanian *audiencia* was made. Incomplete and doubtless omitting most of the Indian and *cimarrón* population, specifically excluding soldiers and priests, the census recorded 71,888 inhabitants, 7,857 of whom lived in Panama City. Other principal towns had populations ranging from 2,000 to a little over 5,000.

Social hierarchy in the colony was rigid. The most prestigious and rewarding positions were reserved for the *peninsulares*, those actually born in Spain. Criollos, those of Spanish ancestry but born in the colonies, occupied secondary posts in government and trade. Mestizos, usually offspring of Hispanic fathers and Indian mothers, engaged in farming, retail trade, and the provision of services. African and Indian slaves constituted an underclass. To the extent possible, Indians who escaped enslavement avoided Hispanic society altogether.

The church held a special place in society. Priests accompanied every expedition and were always counselors to the temporal leaders. The first bishop on the mainland came with Pedrarias. The bishop's authority, received from the king, made him in effect a vice governor. The bishopric was moved from Darién to Panama City in 1521. The relationship between church and government in the colony was closer than in Spain. Both the Roman Catholic Church and the monastic orders gained great wealth through tithes and land acquisition.

The Colombia Department

Independence from Spain

Lacking communication except by sea, which the Spanish generally controlled, Panama remained aloof from the early efforts of the Spanish colonies to separate from Spain. Revolutionaries of other colonies, however, did not hesitate to use Panama's strategic

Church of Natá, built in 1522; believed to be the oldest church still in use on the mainland of the Americas

potential as a pawn in revolutionary maneuvers. General Francisco Miranda of Venezuela, who had been attracting support for revolutionary activities as early as 1797, offered a canal concession to Britain in return for aid. Thomas Jefferson, while minister to France, also showed interest in a canal, but the isolationist policies of the new United States and the absorption of energies and capital in continental expansion prevented serious consideration.

Patriots from Cartagena attempted to take Portobelo in 1814 and again in 1819, and a naval effort from liberated Chile succeeded in capturing the island of Taboga in the Bay of Panama. Panama's first act of separation from Spain came without violence. When Simón Bolívar's victory at Boyacá on August 7, 1819, clinched the liberation of New Granada, the Spanish viceroy fled Colombia for Panama, where he ruled harshly until his death in 1821. His replacement in Panama, a liberal constitutionalist, permitted a free press and the formation of patriotic associations. Raising troops locally, he soon sailed for Ecuador, leaving a native Panamanian, Colonel Edwin Fábrega, as acting governor.

Panama City immediately initiated plans to declare independence, but the city of Los Santos preempted the move by proclaiming freedom from Spain on November 10, 1821. This act precipitated a meeting in Panama City on November 28, which is celebrated as the official date of independence. Considerable discussion followed as to whether Panama should remain part of Colombia (then comprising both the present-day country and Venezuela) or unite with Peru. The bishop of Panama, a native Peruvian who realized the commercial ties that could be developed with his country, argued for the latter solution but was voted down. A third possible course of action, a union with Mexico proposed by emissaries of that country, was rejected.

Panama thus became part of Colombia, then governed under the 1821 Constitution of Cúcuta, and was designated a department with two provinces, Panamá and Veraguas. With the addition of Ecuador to the liberated area, the whole country became known as Gran Colombia. Panama sent a force of 700 men to join Bolívar in Peru, where the war of liberation continued.

The termination of hostilities against the royalists in 1824 failed to bring tranquillity to Gran Colombia. The constitution that Bolívar had drafted for Bolivia was put forward by him to be adopted in Gran Colombia. The country was divided principally over the proposal that a president would serve for life. The president would not be responsible to the legislature and would have power to select his vice president. Other provisions, generally centralist in their tendencies, were repugnant to some, while a few desired a monarchy. Panama escaped armed violence over the constitutional question but joined other regions in petitioning Bolívar to assume dictatorial powers until a convention could meet. Panama announced its union with Gran Colombia as a "Hanseatic State," i.e., as an autonomous area with special trading privileges, until the convention was held.

In 1826 Bolívar honored Panama when he chose it as the site for a congress of the recently liberated Spanish colonies. Many leaders of the revolutions in Latin America considered the establishment of a single government for the former Spanish colonies the natural follow-up to driving out the *peninsulares*. Both José de San Martin and Miranda proposed creating a single vast monarchy ruled by an emperor descended from the Incas. Bolívar, however, was the one who made the most serious attempt to unite the Spanish American republics.

Although the league or confederation envisioned by Bolívar was to foster the blessings of liberty and justice, a primary purpose was to secure the independence of the former colonies from renewed attacks by Spain and its allies. In this endeavor Bolívar sought Britain's protection. He was reluctant to invite representatives of the United States, even as observers, to the congress of plenipotentiaries lest their collaboration compromise the league's position with the British. Furthermore, Bolívar felt that the neutrality of the

United States in the war between Spain and its former colonies would make its representation inappropriate. In addition, slavery in the United States would be an obstacle in discussing the abolition of the African slave trade. Bolívar nevertheless acquiesced when the governments of Colombia, Mexico, and Central America (see Glossary) invited the United States to send observers.

Despite the sweeping implications of the Monroe Doctrine, President John Quincy Adams—in deciding to send delegates to the Panama conference—was not disposed to obligate the United States to defend its southern neighbors. Adams instructed his delegates to refrain from participating in deliberations concerning regional security and to emphasize discussions of maritime neutrality and commerce. Nevertheless, many members of the United States Congress opposed participation under any conditions. By the time participation was approved, the delegation had no time to reach the conference. The British and Dutch sent unofficial representatives.

The Congress of Panama, which convened in June and adjourned in July of 1826, was attended by four American states—Mexico, Central America, Colombia, and Peru. The "Treaty of Union, League, and Perpetual Confederation" drawn up at that congress would have bound all parties to mutual defense and to the peaceful settlement of disputes. Furthermore, because some feared that monarchical elements sympathetic to Spain and its allies might regain control of one of the new republics, the treaty included a provision that if a member state substantially changed its form of government, it would be excluded from the confederation and could be readmitted only with the unanimous consent of all other members.

The treaty was ratified only by Colombia and never became effective. Bolívar, having made several futile attempts to establish lesser federations, declared shortly before his death in 1830 that "America is ungovernable; those who served the revolution have plowed the sea." Despite his disillusion, however, he did not see United States protection as a substitute for collective security arrangements among the Spanish-speaking states. In fact, he is credited with having said, "The United States seems destined by Providence to plague America with misery in the name of Liberty."

Three abortive attempts to separate the isthmus from Colombia occurred between 1830 and 1840. The first was undertaken by an acting governor of Panama who opposed the policies of the president, but the Panamanian leader reincorporated the department of Panama at the urging of Bolívar, then on his deathbed. The second attempted separation was the scheme of an unpopular dictator, who was soon deposed and executed. The third secession, a response to civil war in Colombia, was declared by a popular assembly, but reintegration took place a year later.

The California Gold Rush and the Railroad

Even before the United States acquired California after the Mexican War (1846–48), many heading for California used the isthmus crossing in preference to the long and dangerous wagon route across the vast plains and rugged mountain ranges. Discovery of gold in 1848 increased traffic greatly. In 1847 a group of New York financiers organized the Panama Railroad Company. This company secured an exclusive concession from Colombia allowing construction of a crossing, which might be by road, rail, river, or a combination. After surveys, a railroad was chosen, and a new contract so specifying was obtained in 1850. The railroad track followed generally the line of the present canal. The first through train from the Atlantic to the Pacific side ran on the completed track on January 28, 1855.

The gold rush traffic, even before the completion of the railroad, restored Panama's prosperity. Between 1848 and 1869, about 375,000 persons crossed the isthmus from the Atlantic to the Pacific, and 225,000 crossed in the opposite direction. Prices for food and services were greatly inflated, producing enormous profits from meals and lodging.

The railroad also created a new city and port at the Atlantic terminus of the line. The town that immediately sprang up to accommodate the railroad offices, warehouses, docks, and shops and to lodge both railroad workers and passengers soon became, and remains, the second largest in the country. United States citizens named it Aspinwall, after one of the founders of the Panama Railroad Company, but the Panamanians christened it Colón, in honor of Columbus. Both names were used for many years, but because the Panamanians insisted that no such place as Aspinwall existed and refused to deliver mail so addressed, the name Colón prevailed.

The gold rush and the railroad also brought the United States "Wild West" to the isthmus. The forty-niners tended to be an unruly lot, usually bored as they waited for a ship to California, frequently drunk, and often armed. Many also displayed prejudice verging on contempt for other races and cultures. The so-called Watermelon War of 1856, in which at least sixteen persons were killed, was the most serious clash of races and cultures of the period.

In 1869 the first transcontinental railroad was completed in the United States. This development reduced passenger and freight traffic across the isthmus and diminished the amount of gold and silver shipped east. During the height of the gold rush, however, from 1855 to 1858, only one-tenth of the ordinary commercial freight was destined for or originated in California. The balance concerned trade of the North Americans with Europe and Asia. The railroad company, because of its exceptionally high return on a capitalization that never exceeded US$7 million, paid a total of nearly US$38 million in dividends between 1853 and 1905. Panama received US$25,000 from Colombia's annuity and benefited from transient trade and some inflow of capital.

The Uncompleted French Canal

Throughout the nineteenth century, governments and private investors in the United States, Britain, and France intermittently displayed interest in building a canal across the Western Hemisphere. Several sites were considered, but from the start the ones in Nicaragua and Panama received the most serious attention. President Andrew Jackson sent Charles A. Biddle as his emissary in the 1830s to investigate both routes, but the project was aborted when Biddle abandoned his government mission and negotiated instead with Colombian capitalists for a private concession.

Nevertheless, Colombia continued to express interest in negotiating with the United States on building a canal. The two countries signed a treaty in 1846. The treaty removed the existing restrictive tariffs and gave the United States and its citizens the right of free transit of persons and goods over any road or canal that might be constructed in the isthmus. In addition, the United States guaranteed the neutrality of the isthmus and Colombia's sovereignty over it, with a view to ensuring uninterrupted transit for the duration of the treaty, which was to be twenty years or as long thereafter as the parties gave no notice to revise it. Called the Bidlack-Mallarino Treaty of 1846, it was actually ratified and became effective in 1848.

Because the canal interests of Britain and the United States had continued to clash, particularly in Nicaragua, Britain and the United States sought to ease tensions by entering into the Clayton-Bulwer Treaty of 1850. The governments agreed specifically that neither would acquire rights to or construct a Nicaraguan canal without the participation of the other. This general principle was extended to any canal or railroad across Central America, to include the Isthmus of Tehuantepec in Mexico and Panama. In effect, since neither government was then willing or able to begin a canal, the treaty was for the time an instrument of neutrality.

Colombia's attempt to attract canal interest finally brought French attention to bear on Panama. After several surveys, a concession of exclusive rights was obtained from Colombia, and a

19

company was formed in 1879 to construct a sea-level canal generally along the railroad route. Ferdinand de Lesseps, of Suez Canal fame, headed the company. The terms of the concession required completion in twelve years, with the possibility of a six-year extension at Colombia's discretion. The lease was for ninety years and was transferable, but not to any foreign government. The company also purchased most of the stock of the Panama Railroad Company, which, however, continued to be managed by Americans.

A ceremonious commencement of work was staged by de Lesseps on January 1, 1880, but serious earth moving did not start until the next year. As work progressed, engineers judged that a sea-level canal was impracticable. De Lesseps, a promoter but not an engineer, could not be convinced until work had gone on for six years. Actual labor on a lock canal did not start until late in 1888, by which time the company was in serious financial difficulty. At the peak of its operations the company employed about 10,000 workers.

De Lesseps had to contend not only with enemies who hampered financing by spreading rumors of failure and dumping stocks and bonds on the market but also with venal French politicians and bureaucrats who demanded large bribes for approving the issue of securities. His efforts to get the French government to guarantee his bonds were blocked by the United States, on the grounds that such action would lead to government control in violation of the Monroe Doctrine. The end result in January 1889 was the appointment of a receiver to liquidate the company, whereupon all work stopped.

Despite the French company's disastrous financial experience, an estimated two-fifths of the excavation necessary for the eventual canal had been completed. Many headquarters and hospital buildings were finished. Some of the machinery left on the site was usable later, and the railroad had been maintained. Another legacy of the French company's bankruptcy was a large labor force, now unemployed, mostly Antillean blacks. More than half were repatriated, but thousands remained, many of whom eventually worked on the United States canal.

The Spillover from Colombia's Civil Strife

During the last half of the nineteenth century, violent clashes between the supporters of the Liberal and Conservative parties in Colombia left the isthmus's affairs in constant turmoil. Local self-government for the department of Panama was extended when the Liberals were in power and withdrawn when the Conservatives prevailed. The Catholic Church was disestablished under the

Liberals and reestablished under the Conservatives. The fortunes of local partisans rose and fell abruptly and often violently.

According to one estimate, the period witnessed forty administrations of the Panamanian department, fifty riots and rebellions, five attempted secessions, and thirteen interventions by the United States, acting under the provisions of the Bidlack-Mallarino Treaty. Partisan clashes and foreign intervention exacerbated racial antagonisms and economic problems and intensified grievances against the central government of Colombia.

Between 1863 and 1886, the isthmus had twenty-six presidents. Coups d'état, rebellions, and violence were almost continuous, staged by troops of the central government, by local citizens against centrally imposed edicts, and by factions out of power. The chaotic conditions that had prevailed under the federalist constitution of 1863 culminated in the 1884 election of Rafael Núñez as president of Colombia, supported by a coalition of moderate Liberals and Conservatives. Núñez called all factions to participate in a new constituent assembly, but his request was met by an armed revolt of the radical Liberals.

Early in 1885, a revolt headed by a radical Liberal general and centered in Panama City developed into a three-way fight. Colón was virtually destroyed. United States forces landed at the request of the Colombian government but were too late to save the city. Millions of dollars in claims were submitted by companies and citizens of the United States, France, and Britain, but Colombia successfully pleaded its lack of responsibility.

Additional United States naval forces occupied both Colón and Panama City and guarded the railroad to ensure uninterrupted transit until Colombian forces landed to protect the railroad. The new constitution of 1886 established the Republic of Colombia as a unitary state; departments were distinctly subordinate to the central government, and Panama was singled out as subject to the direct authority of the government. The United States consul general reported that three-quarters of the Panamanians wanted independence from Colombia and would revolt if they could get arms and be sure of freedom from United States intervention.

Panama was drawn into Colombia's War of a Thousand Days (1899–1902) by rebellious radical Liberals who had taken refuge in Nicaragua. As in the rest of Colombia, opinion in Panama was divided, and revolts in the southwest had hardly been suppressed when Liberals from Nicaragua invaded the Pacific coastal region and nearly succeeded in taking Panama City in mid-1900. The fortunes of war varied, and although a local armistice gave supporters of the Colombian government temporary security in the

Panama City-Colón region, the rebels were in control throughout the isthmus. Meanwhile, by early 1902 the rebels had been defeated in most of Colombia proper. At that point, the Colombian government asked the United States to intercede and bring about an armistice in Panama, which was arranged aboard the U.S.S. *Wisconsin* in the Bay of Panama in 1902.

Throughout the period of turmoil, the United States had retained its interest in building a canal through either Nicaragua or Panama. An obstacle to this goal was overcome in December 1901 when the United States and Britain signed the Hay-Pauncefote Treaty. This treaty nullified the provisions of the Clayton-Bulwer Treaty of 1850 and signified British acceptance of a canal constructed solely by or under the auspices of the United States with guarantees of neutrality.

The United States Protectorate

The 1903 Treaty and Qualified Independence

Naval operations during the Spanish-American War (1898–99) served to convince President Theodore Roosevelt that the United States needed to control a canal somewhere in the Western Hemisphere. This interest culminated in the Spooner Bill of June 29, 1902, providing for a canal through the isthmus of Panama, and the Hay-Herrán Treaty of January 22, 1903, under which Colombia gave consent to such a project in the form of a 100-year lease on an area 10 kilometers wide. This treaty, however, was not ratified in Bogotá, and the United States, determined to construct a canal across the isthmus, intensively encouraged the Panamanian separatist movement.

By July 1903, when the course of internal Colombian opposition to the Hay-Herrán Treaty became obvious, a revolutionary junta had been created in Panama. José Augustin Arango, an attorney for the Panama Railroad Company, headed the junta. Manuel Amador Guerrero and Carlos C. Arosemena served on the junta from the start, and five other members, all from prominent Panamanian families, were added. Arango was considered the brains of the revolution, and Amador was the junta's active leader.

With financial assistance arranged by Philippe Bunau-Varilla, a French national representing the interests of de Lesseps's company, the native Panamanian leaders conspired to take advantage of United States interest in a new regime on the isthmus. In October and November 1903, the revolutionary junta, with the protection of United States naval forces, carried out a successful uprising against the Colombian government. Acting, paradoxically, under the Bidlack-Mallarino Treaty of 1846 between the United States and Colombia—which provided that United States forces could intervene in the event of disorder on the isthmus to guarantee Colombian sovereignty and open transit across the isthmus—the United States prevented a Colombian force from moving across the isthmus to Panama City to suppress the insurrection.

President Roosevelt recognized the new Panamanian junta as the de facto government on November 6, 1903; de jure recognition came on November 13. Five days later Bunau-Varilla, as the diplomatic representative of Panama (a role he had purchased through financial assistance to the rebels), concluded the Isthmian Canal Convention with Secretary of State John Hay in Washington. Bunau-Varilla had not lived in Panama for seventeen years before the incident, and he never returned. Nevertheless, while residing in the Waldorf-Astoria Hotel in New York City, he wrote the Panamanian declaration of independence and constitution and designed the Panamanian flag. Isthmian patriots particularly resented the haste with which Bunau-Varilla concluded the treaty, an effort partially designed to preclude any objections an arriving Panamanian delegation might raise. Nonetheless, the Panamanians, having no apparent alternative, ratified the treaty on December 2, and approval by the United States Senate came on February 23, 1904.

The rights granted to the United States in the so-called Hay-Bunau-Varilla Treaty were extensive. They included a grant "in perpetuity of the use, occupation, and control" of a sixteen-kilometer-wide strip of territory and extensions of three nautical miles into the sea from each terminal "for the construction, maintenance, operation, sanitation, and protection" of an isthmian canal.

Furthermore, the United States was entitled to acquire additional areas of land or water necessary for canal operations and held the option of exercising eminent domain in Panama City. Within this territory Washington gained "all the rights, power, and authority . . . which the United States would possess and exercise if it were the sovereign . . . to the entire exclusion" of Panama.

The Republic of Panama became a de facto protectorate of the larger country through two provisions whereby the United States guaranteed the independence of Panama and received in return the right to intervene in Panama's domestic affairs. For the rights it obtained, the United States was to pay the sum of US$10 million and an annuity, beginning 9 years after ratification, of US$250,000 in gold coin. The United States also purchased the rights and properties of the French canal company for US$40 million.

Colombia was the harshest critic of United States policy at the time. A reconciliatory treaty with the United States providing an indemnity of US$25 million was finally concluded between these two countries in 1921. Ironically, however, friction resulting from the events of 1903 was greatest between the United States and Panama. Major disagreements arose concerning the rights granted to the United States by the treaty of 1903 and the Panamanian constitution of 1904. The United States government subsequently interpreted these rights to mean that the United States could exercise complete sovereignty over all matters in the Canal Zone. Panama, although admitting that the clauses were vague and obscure, later held that the original concession of authority related only to the construction, operation, and defense of the canal and that rights and privileges not necessary to these functions had never been relinquished.

Organizing the New Republic

The provisional governing junta selected when independence was declared governed the new state until a constitution was adopted in 1904. Under its terms, Amador became Panama's first president.

The constitution was modeled, for the most part, after that of the United States, calling for separation of powers and direct elections for the presidency and the legislature, the National Assembly. The assembly, however, elected three persons to stand in the line of succession to the presidency. This provision remained in effect until 1946, when a new constitution provided for direct election of the vice president. The new republic was unitary; municipalities were to elect their own officials, but provincial authorities were to be appointed by the central government. The most controversial provision of the constitution was that which gave the United States the right to intervene to guarantee Panamanian sovereignty and to preserve order.

A two-party system of Liberals and Conservatives was inherited from Colombia, but the party labels had even less precise or ideological meaning in Panama than they had in the larger country. By the early 1920s, most of the Conservative leaders of the independence generation had died without leaving political heirs. Thus, cleavages in the Liberal Party led to a new system of personalistic parties in shifting coalitions, none of which enjoyed a mass base. Politics remained the exclusive preserve of the oligarchy, which tended to be composed of a few wealthy, white families.

Having successfully severed their ties with Colombia, the seces-
sionists of Panama's central government were soon faced with a
secessionist problem of their own. The Cuna of the San Blas Islands
were unwilling to accept the authority of Panama, just as they had
been unwilling to accept the authority of Colombia or Spain. The
Panamanian government exercised no administrative control over
the islands until 1915, when a departmental government was established; its main office was in El Porvenir. At that time, forces of
the Colonial Police, composed of blacks, were stationed on several
islands. Their presence, along with a number of other factors, led
to a revolt in 1925.

In 1903 on the island of Narganá, Charlie Robinson was elected
chief. Having spent many years on a West Indian ship, he began
a "civilizing" program. His cause was later taken up by a number of young men who had been educated in the cities on the mainland. These Young Turks advocated forcibly removing nose rings,
substituting dresses for *molas* (see Glossary), and establishing dance
halls like those in the cities. They were actively supported by the
police, who arrested men who did not send their daughters to the
dance hall; the police also allegedly raped some of the Indian
women. By 1925 hatred for these modernizers and for the police
was intense throughout the San Blas Islands.

The situation was further complicated by the factionalism that
resulted when Panama separated from Colombia. The leader of
one of these factions, Simral Coleman, with the help of a sympathetic American explorer, Richard Marsh, drew up a "declaration of independence" for the Cuna, and on February 25, 1925,
the rebellion was underway. During the course of the rebellion,
about twenty members of the police were killed. A few days later
a United States cruiser appeared; with United States diplomatic
and naval officials serving as intermediaries, a peace treaty was
concluded. The most important outcome of this rebellion against
Panama was a treaty that in effect recognized San Blas as a semiautonomous territory.

Building the Canal

When the United States canal builders arrived in 1904 to begin
their momentous task, Panama City and Colón were both small,
squalid towns. A single railroad stretched between the towns, running alongside the muddy scars of the abortive French effort. The
new builders were haunted by the ghosts of de Lesseps's failure and
of the workers, some 25,000 of whom had died on the project. These
new builders were able, however, to learn from de Lesseps's mis-
takes and to build on the foundations of the previous engineering.

The most formidable task that the North Americans faced was that of ridding the area of deadly mosquitoes.

After a couple of false starts under a civilian commission, President Roosevelt turned the project over to the United States Army Corps of Engineers, guided by Colonel George Washington Goethals. Colonel William Crawford Gorgas was placed in charge of sanitation. In addition to the major killers—malaria and yellow fever—smallpox, typhoid, dysentery, and intestinal parasites threatened the newcomers.

Because the mosquito carrying yellow fever was found in urban areas, Gorgas concentrated his main efforts on the terminal cities. "Gorgas gangs" dug ditches to drain standing water and sprayed puddles with a film of oil. They screened and fumigated buildings, even invading churches to clean out the fonts of holy water. They installed a pure water supply and a modern system of sewage disposal. Goethals reportedly told Gorgas that every mosquito killed was costing the United States US$10. "I know, Colonel," Gorgas reportedly replied, "but what if one of those ten-dollar mosquitoes were to bite you?" Gorgas's work is credited with saving at least 71,000 lives and some 40 million days of sickness. The cleaner, safer conditions enabled the canal diggers to attract a labor force. By 1913 approximately 65,000 men were on the payroll. Most were West Indians, although some 12,000 workers were recruited from southern Europe. Five thousand United States citizens filled the administrative, professional, and supervisory jobs. To provide these men with the comforts and amenities to which they were accustomed, a paternalistic community was organized in the Canal Zone.

The most challenging tasks involved in the actual digging of the canal were cutting through the mountain ridge at Culebra; building a huge dam at Gatún to trap the Río Chagres and form an artificial lake; and building three double sets of locks—Gatun Locks, Pedro Miguel Locks, and Miraflores Locks—to raise the ships to the lake, almost twenty-six meters above sea level, and then lower them. On August 15, 1914, the first ship made a complete passage through the canal.

By the time the canal project was completed, its economic impact had created a new middle class. In addition, new forms of discrimination occurred. Panamanian society had become segregated not only by class but by race and national origin as well (see Ethnic Groups and Social Organization, ch. 2). Furthermore, United States commercial competition and political intervention had already begun to generate resentment among Panamanians.

Excavation for the Panama Canal
at the Culebra Cut, December 1904
Courtesy National Archives

United States Intervention and Strained Relations

In the very first year of the Hay-Bunau-Varilla Treaty, dissension had already arisen over the sovereignty issue. Acting on an understanding of its rights, the United States had applied special regulations to maritime traffic at the ports of entry to the canal and had established its own customs, tariffs, and postal services in the zone. These measures were opposed by the Panamanian government.

Mounting friction finally led Roosevelt to dispatch Secretary of War William Howard Taft to Panama in November 1904. His visit resulted in a compromise agreement, whereby the United States retained control of the ports of Ancón and Cristóbal, but their facilities might be used by any ships entering Panama City and Colón. The agreement also involved a reciprocal reduction of tariffs and the free passage of persons and goods from the Canal Zone into the republic. Compromises were reached in other areas, and both sides emerged with most of their grievances blunted if not wholly resolved.

Before the first year of independence had passed, the intervention issue also complicated relations. Threats to constitutional government in the republic by a Panamanian military leader,

27

General Estéban Huertas, had resulted, at the suggestion of the United States diplomatic mission, in disbanding the Panamanian army in 1904. The army was replaced by the National Police, whose mission was to carry out ordinary police work. By 1920 the United States had intervened four times in the civil life of the republic. These interventions involved little military conflict and were, with one exception, at the request of one Panamanian faction or another.

The internal dynamics of Panamanian politics encouraged appeals to the United States by any currently disgruntled faction for intervention to secure its allegedly infringed rights. United States diplomatic personnel in Panama also served as advisers to Panamanian officials, a policy resented by nationalists. In 1921 the issue of intervention was formally raised by the republic's government. When asked for a definitive, written interpretation of the pertinent treaty clauses, Secretary of State Charles Evans Hughes pointed to inherent difficulties and explained that the main objectives of the United States were to act against any threat to the Canal Zone or the lives and holdings of non-Panamanians in the two major cities.

Actual intervention took several forms. United States officials supervised elections at the request of incumbent governments. To protect lives of United States citizens and property in Chiriquí Province, an occupation force was stationed there for two years over the protests of Panamanians who contended that the right of occupation could apply only to the two major cities. United States involvement in the 1925 rent riots in Panama City was also widely resented. After violent disturbances during October, and at the request of the Panamanian government, 600 troops with fixed bayonets dispersed mobs threatening to seize the city.

At the end of the 1920s, traditional United States policy toward intervention was revised. In 1928 Secretary of State Frank B. Kellogg reiterated his government's refusal to countenance illegal changes of government. In the same year, however, Washington declined to intervene during the national elections that placed Florencio H. Arosemena in office. The Arosemena government was noted for its corruption. But when a coup d'état was undertaken to unseat Arosemena, the United States once again declined to intervene. Though no official pronouncement of a shift in policy had been made, the 1931 coup d'état—the first successful one in the republic's history—marked a watershed in the history of United States intervention.

Meanwhile, popular sentiment on both sides calling for revisions to the treaty had resulted in the Kellogg-Alfaro Treaty of 1925. The United States in this instrument agreed to restrictions on private commercial operations in the Canal Zone and also agreed to a tightening of the regulations pertaining to the official commissaries. At the same time, however, the United States gained several concessions involving security. Panama agreed to automatic participation in any war involving the United States and to United States supervision and control of military operations within the republic. These and other clauses aroused strong opposition and, amid considerable tumult, the National Assembly on January 26, 1927, refused to consider the draft treaty.

The abortive Kellogg-Alfaro Treaty involved the two countries in a critical incident with the League of Nations. During the fall of 1927, the League Assembly insisted that Panama could not legally participate in the proposed arrangement with the United States. The assembly argued that an automatic declaration of war would violate Panama's obligations under the League Covenant to wait three months for an arbitral decision on any dispute before resorting to war. The discussion was largely academic inasmuch as the treaty had already been effectively rejected, but Panama proposed that the dispute over sovereignty in the Canal Zone be submitted to international arbitration. The United States denied that any issue needed arbitration.

A New Accommodation

In the late 1920s, United States policymakers noted that nationalist aspirations in Latin America were not producing desired results. United States occupation of the Dominican Republic, Haiti, and Nicaragua had not spawned exemplary political systems, nor had widespread intervention resulted in a receptive attitude toward United States trade and investments. As the subversive activities of Latin American Nazi and Fascist sympathizers gained momentum in the 1930s, the United States became concerned about the need for hemispheric solidarity.

The gradual reversal of United States policy was heralded in 1928 when the Clark Memorandum was issued, formally disavowing the Roosevelt Corollary (see Glossary) to the Monroe Doctrine. In his inaugural address in 1933, President Franklin D. Roosevelt enunciated the Good Neighbor Policy. That same year, at the Seventh Inter-American Conference in Montevideo, the United States expressed a qualified acceptance of the principle of nonintervention; in 1936 the United States approved this principle without reservation.

In the 1930s, Panama, like most countries of the Western world, was suffering economic depression. Until that time, Panamanian politics had remained a competition among individuals and families within a gentleman's club—specifically, the Union Club of Panama City. The first exception to this succession was Harmodio Arias Madrid (unrelated to the aristocratic family of the same name) who was elected to the presidency in 1932. A mestizo from a poor family in the provinces, he had attended the London School of Economics and had gained prominence through writing a book that attacked the Monroe Doctrine.

Harmodio and his brother Arnulfo, a Harvard Medical School graduate, entered the political arena through a movement known as Community Action (Acción Communal). Its following was primarily mestizo middle class, and its mood was antioligarchy and anti-Yankee (see Glossary). Harmodio Arias was the first Panamanian president to institute relief efforts for the isolated and impoverished countryside. He later established the University of Panama, which became the focal point for the political articulation of middle-class interests and nationalistic zeal.

Thus, a certain asymmetry developed in the trends underway in the 1930s that worked in Panama's favor. While the United States was assuming a more conciliatory stance, Panamanians were losing patience, and a political base for virulent nationalism was emerging.

A dispute arose in 1932 over Panamanian opposition to the sale of 3.2-percent beer in the Canal Zone competing with Panamanian beers. Tension rose when the governor of the zone insisted on formally replying to the protests, despite the Panamanian government's well-known view that proper diplomatic relations should involve only the United States ambassador. In 1933 when unemployment in Panama reached a dangerous level and friction over the zone commissaries rekindled, President Harmodio Arias went to Washington.

The result was agreement on a number of issues. The United States pledged sympathetic consideration of future arbitration requests involving economic issues that did not affect the vital aspects of canal operation. Special efforts were to be made to protect Panamanian business interests from the smuggling of cheaply purchased commissary goods out of the zone. Washington also promised to seek appropriations from Congress to sponsor the repatriation of the numerous immigrant canal workers, who were aggravating the unemployment situation. Most important, however, was President Roosevelt's acceptance, in a joint statement with Harmodio Arias, that United States rights in the zone applied only for the purposes of "maintenance, operation, sanitation, and protection" of the canal. The resolution of this long-standing issue, along with a clear recognition of Panama as a sovereign nation, was a significant move in the direction of the Panamanian interpretation of the proper United States position in the isthmus.

This accord, though welcomed in Panama, came too early to deal with a major problem concerning the US$250,000 annuity. The devaluation of the United States dollar in 1934 reduced its gold content to 59.6 percent of its former value. This meant that the US$250,000 payment was nearly cut in half in the new devalued dollars. As a result, the Panamanian government refused to accept the annuity paid in the new dollars.

Roosevelt's visit to the republic in the summer of 1934 prepared the way for opening negotiations on this and other matters. A Panamanian mission arrived in Washington in November, and discussions on a replacement for the Hay-Bunau-Varilla Treaty continued through 1935. On March 2, 1936, Secretary of State Cordell Hull and Assistant Secretary of State Sumner Welles joined the Panamanian negotiators in signing a new treaty—the Hull-Alfaro Treaty—and three related conventions. The conventions regulated radio communications and provided for the United States to construct a new trans-isthmian highway connecting Panama City and Colón.

The treaty provided a new context for relations between the two countries. It ended the protectorate by abrogating the 1903 treaty guarantee of the republic's independence and the concomitant right of intervention. Thereafter, the United States would substitute negotiation and purchase of land outside the zone for its former rights of expropriation. The dispute over the annuity was resolved by agreeing to fix it at 430,000 balboas (the balboa being equivalent to the devalued dollar), which increased the gold value of the original annuity by US$7,500. This was to be paid retroactively to 1934 when the republic had begun refusing the payments.

Various business and commercial provisions dealt with long-standing Panamanian complaints. Private commercial operations unconnected with canal operations were forbidden in the zone. This policy and the closing of the zone to foreign commerce were to provide Panamanian merchants with relief from competition. Free entry into the zone was provided for Panamanian goods, and the republic's customhouses were to be established at entrances to the zone to regulate the entry of goods finally destined for Panama.

The Hull-Alfaro revisions, though hailed by both governments, radically altered the special rights of the United States in the isthmus, and the United States Senate was reluctant to accept the alterations. Article X of the new treaty provided that in the event of any threat to the security of either nation, joint measures could be taken after consultation between the two. Only after an exchange of interpretative diplomatic notes had permitted Senator Key Pittman, chairman of the Foreign Relations Committee, to advise his colleagues that Panama was willing under this provision to permit the United States to act unilaterally, did the Senate give its consent on July 25, 1939.

The Bisected Republic

The War Years

After ratifying the Hull-Alfaro Treaty in 1939, Panama and the United States began preparation for and collaboration in the coming war effort. Cooperation in this area proceeded smoothly for more than a year, with the republic participating in the series of conferences, declarations, and protocols that solidified the support of the hemisphere behind Washington's efforts to meet the threat of Axis aggression. This cooperation halted with the inauguration of Arnulfo Arias.

Arnulfo Arias was elected to the presidency at least three times after 1940 (perhaps four or five if, as many believe, the vote counts of 1964 and 1984 were fraudulent), but he was never allowed to serve a full term. He was first elected when he headed a mass movement known as Panameñismo. Its essence was nationalism, which in Panama's situation meant opposition to United States hegemony. Arias aspired to rid the country of non-Hispanics, which meant not only North Americans, but also West Indians, Chinese, Hindus, and Jews. He also seemed susceptible to the influence of Nazi and Fascist agents on the eve of the United States declaration of war against the Axis.

North Americans were by no means the only ones in Panama who were anxious to be rid of Arias. Even his brother, Harmodio, urged the United States embassy to move against the leader. United States officials made no attempt to conceal their relief when the National Police, in October 1941, took advantage of Arias's temporary absence from the country to depose him.

Arnulfo Arias had promulgated a new constitution in 1941, which was designed to extend his term of office. In 1945 a clash between Arias's successor, Ricardo Adolfo de la Guardia, and the National Assembly led to the calling of a constituent assembly that elected a new president, Enrique A. Jiménez, and drew up a new constitution. The constitution of 1946 erased the innovations introduced by Arias and restored traditional concepts and structures of government.

In preparation for war, the United States had requested 999-year leases on more than 100 bases and sites. Arias balked, but ultimately

*Ship passes through the Panama Canal
at the Gaillard Cut, Cucaracha Slide, June 1921
Courtesy National Archives*

approved a lease on one site after the United States threatened to occupy the land it wanted. De la Guardia proved more accommodating; he agreed to lease the United States 134 sites in the republic but not for 999 years. He would extend the leases only for the duration of the war plus one year beyond the signing of the peace treaty.

The United States transferred Panama City's water and sewer systems to the city administration and granted new economic assistance, but it refused to deport the West Indians and other non-Hispanics or to pay high rents for the sites. Among the major facilities granted to the United States under the agreement of 1942 were the airfield at Río Hato, the naval base on Isla Taboga, and several radar stations.

The end of the war brought another misunderstanding between the two countries. Although the peace treaty had not entered into effect, Panama demanded that the bases be relinquished, resting its claim on a subsidiary provision of the agreement permitting renegotiation after the cessation of hostilities. Overriding the desire of the United States War Department to hold most of the bases for an indefinite period, the Department of State took cognizance of growing nationalist dissatisfaction and in December 1946 sent Ambassador Frank T. Hines to propose a twenty-year extension of the leases on thirteen facilities. President Jiménez authorized a draft treaty over the opposition of the foreign minister and exacerbated latent resentment. When the National Assembly met in 1947 to consider ratification, a mob of 10,000 Panamanians armed with stones, machetes, and guns expressed opposition. Under these circumstances the deputies voted unanimously to reject the treaty. By 1948 the United States had evacuated all occupied bases and sites outside the Canal Zone.

The upheaval of 1947 was instigated in large measure by university students. Their clash with the National Police on that occasion, in which both students and policemen were killed, marked the beginning of a period of intense animosity between the two groups. The incident was also the first in which United States intentions were thwarted by a massive expression of Panamanian rage.

The National Guard in Ascendance

A temporary shift in power from the civilian aristocracy to the National Police occurred immediately after World War II. Between 1948 and 1952, National Police Commander José Antonio Remón installed and removed presidents with unencumbered ease. Among his behind-the-scenes manipulations were the denial to Arnulfo Arias of the presidency he apparently had won in 1948, the installation of Arias in the presidency in 1949, and the engineering of Arias's removal from office in 1951. Meanwhile, Remón increased salaries and fringe benefits for his forces and modernized training methods and equipment; in effect, he transformed the National Police from a police into a paramilitary force. In the spheres of security and public order, he achieved his long-sought goal by transforming the National Police into the National Guard in 1953 and introduced greater militarization into the country's only armed force. The missions and functions were little changed by the new title, but for Remón, this change was a step toward a national army (see Historical Background, ch. 5).

From several preexisting parties and factions, Remón also organized the National Patriotic Coalition (Coalición Patriótica Nacional—CPN). He ran successfully as its candidate for the presidency in 1952. Remón followed national tradition by enriching himself through political office. He broke with tradition, however, by promoting social reform and economic development. His agricultural and industrial programs temporarily reduced the country's overwhelming economic dependence on the canal and the zone.

Remón's reformist regime was short-lived, however. In 1955 he was machine-gunned to death at the racetrack outside Panama City.

The first vice president, José Ramón Guizado, was impeached for the crime and jailed, but he was never tried, and the motivation for his alleged act remained unclear. Some investigators believed that the impeachment of Guizado was a smokescreen to distract attention from others implicated in the assassination, including United States organized crime figure ''Lucky'' Luciano, dissident police officers, and both Arias families. The second vice president, Ricardo Arias (of the aristocratic Arias family), served out the remainder of the presidential term and dismantled many of Remón's reforms.

Remón did not live to see the culmination of the major treaty revision he initiated. In 1953 Remón had visited Washington to discuss basic revisions of the 1936 treaty. Among other things, Panamanian officials wanted a larger share of the canal tolls, and merchants continued to be unhappy with the competition from the nonprofit commissaries in the Canal Zone. Remón also demanded that the discriminatory wage differential in the zone, which favored United States citizens over Panamanians, be abolished.

After lengthy negotiations a Treaty of Mutual Understanding and Cooperation was signed on January 23, 1955. Under its provisions commercial activities not essential to the operation of the canal were to be cut back. The annuity was enlarged to US$1,930,000. The principle of ''one basic wage scale for all . . . employees . . . in the Canal Zone'' was accepted and implemented. Panama's request for the replacement of the ''perpetuity'' clause by a ninety-nine-year renewable lease was rejected, however, as was the proposal that its citizens accused of violations in the zone be tried by joint United States-Panamanian tribunals.

Panama's contribution to the 1955 treaty was its consent to the United States occupation of the bases outside of the Canal Zone that it had withheld a few years earlier. Approximately 8,000 hectares of the republic's territory were leased rent-free for 15 years for United States military maneuvers. The Río Hato base, a particularly important installation in defense planning, was thus regained for the United States Air Force. Because the revisions had the strong support of President Ricardo Arias, the National Assembly approved them with little hesitation.

The Politics of Frustrated Nationalism

The CPN placed another candidate, Ernesto de la Guardia, in the presidency in 1956. The Remón government had required parties to enroll 45,000 members to receive official recognition. This membership requirement, subsequently relaxed to 5,000, had excluded all opposition parties from the 1956 elections except the

National Liberal Party (Partido Liberal Nacional—PLN), which traced its lineage to the original Liberal Party.

De la Guardia was a conservative businessman and a member of the oligarchy. By Panamanian standards, he was by no means anti-Yankee (see Glossary), but his administration presided over a new low in United States-Panamanian relations. The Egyptian nationalization of the Suez Canal in 1956 raised new hopes in the republic, because the two canals were frequently compared in the world press. Despite Panama's large maritime fleet (the sixth greatest in the world), Britain and the United States did not invite Panama to a special conference of the major world maritime powers in London to discuss Suez. Expressing resentment, Panama joined the communist and neutral nations in a rival Suez proposal. United States secretary of state John Foster Dulles's unqualified statement on the Suez issue on September 28, 1956—that the United States did not fear similar nationalization of the Panama Canal because the United States possessed "rights of sovereignty" there—worsened matters.

Panamanian public opinion was further inflamed by a United States Department of the Army statement in the summer of 1956 that implied that the 1955 treaty had not in fact envisaged a total equalization of wage rates. The United States attempted to clarify the issue by explaining that the only exception to the "equal pay for equal labor" principle would be a 25-percent differential that would apply to all citizens brought from the continental United States.

Tension mounted in the ensuing years. In May 1958 students demonstrating against the United States clashed with the National Guard. The violence of these riots, in which nine died, was a forecast of the far more serious difficulties that followed a year later. In November 1959 anti-United States demonstrations occurred during the two Panamanian independence holidays. Aroused by the media, particularly by articles in newspapers owned by Harmodio Arias, Panamanians began to threaten a "peaceful invasion" of the Canal Zone, to raise the flag of the republic there as tangible evidence of Panama's sovereignty. Fearful that Panamanian mobs might actually force entry into the Canal Zone, the United States called out its troops. Several hundred Panamanians crossed barbed-wire restraints and clashed with Canal Zone police and troops. A second wave of Panamanian citizens was repulsed by the National Guard, supported by United States troops.

Extensive and violent disorder followed. A mob smashed the windows of the United States Information Agency library. The United States flag was torn from the ambassador's residence and trampled.

Aware that public hostility was getting out of hand, political leaders attempted to regain control over their followers but were unsuccessful. Relations between the two governments were severely strained. United States authorities erected a fence on the border of the Canal Zone, and United States citizens residing in the Canal Zone observed a voluntary boycott of Panamanian merchants, who traditionally depended heavily on these patrons.

On March 1, 1960—Constitution Day—student and labor groups threatened another march into the Canal Zone. The widespread disorders of the previous fall had had a sobering effect on the political elite, who seriously feared that new rioting might be transformed into a revolutionary movement against the social system itself. Both major coalitions contesting the coming elections sought to avoid further difficulties, and influential merchants, who had been hard hit by the November 1959 riots, were apprehensive. Reports that the United States was willing to recommend flying the republic's flag in a special site in the Canal Zone served to ease tensions. Thus, serious disorders were averted.

De la Guardia's administration had been overwhelmed by the rioting and other problems, and the CPN, lacking effective opposition in the National Assembly, began to disintegrate. Most dissenting factions joined the PLN in the National Opposition Union, which in 1960 succeeded in electing its candidate, Roberto Chiari, to the presidency. De la Guardia became the first postwar president to finish a full four-year term in office, and Chiari had the distinction of being the first opposition candidate ever elected to the presidency.

Chiari attempted to convince his fellow oligarchs that change was inevitable. He cautioned that if they refused to accept moderate reform, they would be vulnerable to sweeping change imposed by uncontrollable radical forces. The tradition-oriented deputies who constituted a majority in the National Assembly did not heed his warning. His proposed reform program was simply ignored. In foreign affairs, Chiari's message to the Assembly on October 1, 1961, called for a new revision of the Canal Zone arrangement. When Chiari visited Washington from June 12–13, 1962, he and President John F. Kennedy agreed to appoint high-level representatives to discuss controversies between their countries regarding the Canal Zone. The results of the discussions were disclosed in a joint communiqué issued on July 23, 1963.

Agreement had been reached on the creation of the Bi-National Labor Advisory Committee to consider disputes arising between Panamanian employees and zone authorities. The United States had agreed to withhold taxes from its Panamanian employees to be remitted to the Panamanian government. Pending congressional approval, the United States agreed to extend to Panamanian employees the health and life insurance benefits available to United States citizens in the zone.

Several other controversial matters, however, remained unresolved. The United States agreed to increase the wages of Panamanian employees in the zone, but not as much as the Panamanian government requested. No agreement was reached in response to Panamanian requests for jurisdiction over a corridor through the zone linking the two halves of the country.

Meanwhile, the United States had initiated a new aid program for all of Latin America—the Alliance for Progress. Under this approach to hemisphere relations, President Kennedy envisioned a long-range program to raise living standards and advance social and economic development. No regular United States government development loans or grants had been available to Panama through the late 1950s. The Alliance for Progress, therefore, was the first major effort of the United States to improve basic living conditions. Panama was to share in the initial, large-scale loans to support self-help housing. Nevertheless, pressure for major revisions of the treaties and resentment of United States recalcitrance continued to mount.

The Negotiation of New Treaties

The 1964 Riots

Public demonstrations and riots arising from popular resentment over United States policies and the overwhelming presence of United States citizens and institutions had not been uncommon, but the rioting that occurred in January 1964 was uncommonly serious. The incident began with a symbolic dispute over the flying of the Panamanian flag in the Canal Zone.

For some time the dispute had been seriously complicated by differences of opinion on that issue between the Department of Defense and the Department of State. On the one hand, the military opposed accepting a Panamanian flag, emphasizing the strategic importance of unimpaired United States control in the Canal Zone and the dangerous precedent that appeasement of the rioters' demands would set for future United States-Panamanian relations. The Department of State, on the other hand, supported the flag proposal as a reasonable concession to Panamanian demands and a method of avoiding major international embarrassment. Diplomatic officials also feared that the stability of Panamanian political institutions themselves might be threatened by extensive violence and mob action over the flag issue.

The United States finally agreed to raise the Panamanian and United States flags side by side at one location. The special ceremony on September 21, 1960, at the Shaler Triangle was attended by the new governor of the zone, Major General William A. Carter, along with all high United States military and diplomatic officers and the entire Panamanian cabinet. Even this incident, however, which marked official recognition of Panama's "titular" sovereignty, was marred when the United States rejected de la Guardia's request to allow him to raise the flag personally. De la Guardia, as a retaliatory measure, refused to attend the ceremony and extended invitations to the presidential reception after the ceremony only to the United States ambassador and his senior diplomatic aides; United States Canal Zone and military officials were excluded.

Panamanians remained dissatisfied as their flag appeared at only one location in the Canal Zone, while the United States flag flew alone at numerous other sites. An agreement was finally reached that at several points in the Canal Zone the United States and Panamanian flags would be flown side by side. United States citizens residing in the Canal Zone were reluctant to abide by this agreement, however, and the students of an American high school, with adult encouragement, on two consecutive days hoisted the American flag alone in front of their school.

Word of the gesture soon spread across the border, and on the evening of the second day, January 9, 1964, nearly 200 Panamanian students marched into the Canal Zone with their flag. A struggle ensued, and the Panamanian flag was torn. After that provocation, thousands of Panamanians stormed the border fence. The rioting lasted 3 days, and resulted in more than 20 deaths, serious injuries to several hundred persons, and more than US$2 million of property damage.

At the outbreak of the fighting, Panama charged the United States with aggression. Panama severed relations with the United States and appealed to the Organization of American States (OAS) and the United Nations (UN). On January 10 the OAS referred the case to the Inter-American Peace Committee. When the UN Security Council met, United States ambassador Adlai E. Stevenson noted that the Inter-American Peace Committee had already scheduled an on-the-spot investigation and urged that the problem be considered in the regional forum. A proposal by the Brazilian delegate that the president of the Security Council address an appeal to the two parties to exercise restraint was agreed on, and the UN took no further action.

The United States had hoped to confine the controversy to the Inter-American Peace Committee. But when negotiations broke down, Panama insisted that the Organ of Consultation under the 1947 Inter-American Treaty of Reciprocal Assistance (the so-called Rio Treaty) be convoked. The OAS Council, acting provisionally as the Organ of Consultation, appointed an investigating committee consisting of all the members of the Council except the two disputants. A joint declaration recommended by the Committee was signed by the two countries in April, and diplomatic relations were restored. The controversy smoldered for almost a year, however, until President Lyndon B. Johnson announced that plans for a new canal would be drawn up and that an entirely new treaty would be negotiated.

Negotiations were carried on throughout the first half of the presidency of Chiari's successor, Marcos Aurelio Robles. When the terms of three draft treaties—concerning the existing lock canal, a possible sea-level canal, and defense matters—were revealed in 1967, Panamanian public reaction was adverse. The new treaties would have abolished the resented "in perpetuity" clause in favor of an expiration date of December 13, 1999, or the date of the completion of a new sea-level canal if that were earlier. Furthermore, they would have compensated the Panamanian government on the basis of tonnage shipped through the canal, an arrangement that could have increased the annuity to more than US$20 million.

The intensity of Panamanian nationalism, however, was such that many contended that the United States should abandon involvement in Panama altogether. Proposals for the continued United States military bases in the Canal Zone, for the right of the United States to deploy troops and armaments anywhere in the republic, and for a joint board of nine governors for the zone, five of which were to be appointed by the United States, were particularly unpopular. Robles initially attempted to defend the terms of the drafts. When he failed to obtain treaty ratification and he learned that his own coalition would be at a disadvantage in the upcoming elections, he declared that further negotiations would be necessary.

The Oligarchy under Fire

In the mid-1960s, the oligarchy was still tenuously in charge of Panama's political system. Members of the middle class, consisting largely of teachers and government workers, occasionally gained political prominence. Aspiring to upper-class stations, they failed to unite with the lower classes to displace the oligarchy. Students were the most vocal element of the middle class and the group most disposed to speak for the inarticulate poor; as graduates, however, they were generally co-opted by the system.

A great chasm separated the rural section from the urban population of the two major cities. Only the rural wageworkers, concentrated in the provinces of Bocas del Toro and Chiriquí, appeared to follow events in the capital and to express themselves on issues of national policy. Among the urban lower classes, antagonism between the Spanish speakers and the English- and French-speaking blacks inhibited organization in pursuit of common interests.

Literacy was high—about 77 percent—despite the scarcity of secondary schools in the rural areas. Voter turnout also tended to be high, despite the unreliability of vote counts. (A popular saying is "He who counts the votes elects.") Concentration on the sins of the United States had served as a safety valve, diverting attention from the injustices of the domestic system.

The multi-party system that existed until the coup d'état of 1968 served to regulate competition for political power among the leading families. Individual parties characteristically served as the personal machines of leaders, whose clients (supporters or dependents) anticipated jobs or other advantages if their candidate were successful. Of the major parties competing in the 1960s, only the highly factionalized PLN had a history of more than two decades. The only parties that had developed clearly identifiable programs were the small Socialist Party and the Christian Democratic Party (Partido Demócrato Cristiano—PDC). The only party with a mass base was the Panameñista Party (Partido Panameñista—PP), the electoral vehicle of the erratic former president, Arnulfo Arias. The Panameñista Party appealed to the frustrated, but lacked a clearly recognizable ideology or program.

Seven candidates competed in the 1964 presidential elections, although only three were serious contenders. Robles, who had served as minister of the presidency in Chiari's cabinet, was the candidate of the National Opposition Union, comprising the PLN and seven smaller parties. After lengthy backstage maneuvers, Robles was endorsed by the outgoing president. Juan de Arco Galindo, a former member of the National Assembly and public works minister and brother-in-law of former President de la Guardia, was the candidate of the National Opposition Alliance (Alianza Nacional de Oposición) coalition, comprising seven parties headed by the CPN. Arnulfo Arias was supported by the PP, already the largest single party in the country.

As usual, the status of the canal was a principal issue in the campaign. Both the liberal and the CPN coalitions cultivated nationalist sentiment by denouncing the United States. Arias, abandoning his earlier nationalistic theme, assumed a cooperative and conciliatory stance toward the United States. Arias attracted lower-class

41

support by denouncing the oligarchy. The Electoral Tribunal announced that Robles had defeated Arias by a margin of more than 10,000 votes of the 317,312 votes cast. The CPN coalition trailed far behind the top two contenders. Arias supporters, who had won a majority of the National Assembly seats, attributed Robles's victory to the "miracle of Los Santos"; they claimed that enough corpses voted for Robles in that province to enable him to carry the election.

The problems confronting Robles were not unlike those of his predecessors but were aggravated by the consequences of the 1964 riots. In addition to the hardships and resentments resulting from the losses of life and property, the riots had the effect of dramatically increasing the already serious unemployment in the metropolitan areas. Despite his nationalistic rhetoric during the campaign, the new president was dependent on United States economic and technical assistance to develop projects that Chiari's government, also with United States assistance, had initiated. Chiari emphasized building schools and low-cost housing. He endorsed a limited agrarian-reform program. Like his predecessor, Robles sought to increase the efficiency of tax collection rather than raise taxes.

By 1967 the coalitions were being reshuffled in preparation for the 1968 elections. By the time Arias announced his candidacy, he had split both the coalitions that had participated in the 1964 elections and had secured the support of several factions in a coalition headed by the Panameñista Party. Robles's endorsement went to David Samudio of the PLN. A civil engineer and architect of middle-class background, Samudio had served as an assemblyman and had held several cabinet posts, including that of finance minister under Robles. In addition to the PLN, he was supported by the Labor and Agrarian Party (Partido Laborista Agrario—PALA) and other splinter groups. (Party labels are deceptive; the PALA, for example, had neither an agrarian base nor organized labor support.) A PDC candidate, Antonio González Revilla, also entered the race.

Because many of Arias's supporters believed that the 1964 election had been rigged, the principal issue in the 1968 campaign became the prospective validity of the election itself. The credibility crisis became acute in February 1968 when the president of the Electoral Tribunal, a Samudio supporter, closed the central registration office in a dispute with the other two members of the tribunal, Arias supporters, over electoral procedures. The government brought suit before the Supreme Court for their dismissal, on the grounds that each man had a son who was a candidate for elective office. Thereupon González Revilla, with the backing of

Arias, petitioned the National Assembly to begin impeachment proceedings against Robles for illegal interferences in electoral matters. Among other issues, Robles was accused of diverting public funds to Samudio's campaign.

The National Assembly met in special session and appointed a commission to gather evidence. Robles, in turn, obtained a judgment from a municipal court that the assembly was acting unconstitutionally. The National Assembly chose to ignore a stay order issued by the municipal court pending the reconvening of the Supreme Court on April 1, and on March 14 it voted for impeachment. On March 24, the National Assembly found Robles guilty and declared him deposed. Robles and the National Guard ignored the proceedings, maintaining that they would abide by the decision of the Supreme Court when it reconvened.

The Supreme Court, with only one dissenting vote, ruled the impeachment proceedings unconstitutional. The Electoral Tribunal subsequently ruled that thirty of the parliamentary deputies involved in the impeachment proceedings were ineligible for reelection. Robles, with the support of the National Guard, retained the presidency.

The election took place on May 12, 1968, as scheduled, and tension mounted over the succeeding eighteen days as the Election Board and the Electoral Tribunal delayed announcing the results. Finally the Election Board declared that Arias had carried the election by 175,432 votes to 133,887 for Samudio and 11,371 for González Revilla. The Electoral Tribunal, senior to the Board and still loyal to Robles, protested, but the commander of the National Guard, Brigadier General Bolívar Vallarino, despite past animosity toward Arias, supported the conclusion of the Board.

Arias took office on October 1, demanding the immediate return of the Canal Zone to Panamanian jurisdiction and announcing a change in the leadership of the National Guard. He attempted to remove the two most senior officers, Vallarino and Colonel José María Pinilla, and appoint Colonel Bolívar Urrutia to command the force. On October 11 the National Guard, for the third time, removed Arias from the presidency. With seven of his eight ministers and twenty-four members of the National Assembly, Arias took refuge in the Canal Zone.

The Government of Torrijos and the National Guard

The overthrow of Arias provoked student demonstrations and rioting in some of the slum areas of Panama City. The peasants in Chiriquí Province battled guardsmen sporadically for several months, but the National Guard retained control. Urrutia was initially arrested but was later persuaded to join in the two-man provisional junta headed by Pinilla. Vallarino remained in retirement. The original cabinet appointed by the junta was rather broad based and included several Samudio supporters and one Arias supporter. After the first three months, however, five civilian cabinet members resigned, accusing the new government of dictatorial practices.

The provisional junta moved swiftly to consolidate government control. Several hundred actual or potential political leaders were arrested on charges of corruption or subversion. Others went into voluntary or imposed exile, and property owners were threatened with expropriation. The National Assembly and all political parties were disbanded, and the University of Panama was closed for several months while its faculty and student body were purged. The communications media were brought under control through censorship, intervention in management, or expropriation.

Pinilla, who assumed the title of president, had declared that his government was provisional and that free elections were to be scheduled. In January 1969, however, power actually rested in the hands of Omar Torrijos and Boris Martínez, commander and chief of staff, respectively, of the National Guard. In early March, a speech by Martínez promising agrarian reform and other measures radical enough to alarm landowners and entrepreneurs provoked a coup within the coup. Torrijos assumed full control, and Martínez and three of his supporters in the military government were exiled.

Torrijos stated that "there would be less impulsiveness" in government without Martínez. Torrijos did not denounce the proposed reforms, but he assured Panamanian and United States investors that their interests were not threatened.

Torrijos, now a brigadier general, became even more firmly entrenched in power after thwarting a coup attempted by Colonels Amado Sanjur, Luis Q. Nentzen Franco, and Ramiro Silvera in December 1969. While Torrijos was in Mexico, the three colonels declared him deposed. Torrijos rushed back to Panama, gathered supporters at the garrison in David, and marched triumphantly into the capital. The colonels followed earlier competitors of Torrijos into exile. Because the governing junta (Colonel Pinilla and his deputy, Colonel Urrutia) had not opposed the abortive coup, Torrijos replaced them with two civilians, Demetrio B. Lakas, an engineer well liked among businessmen, and Arturo Sucre, a lawyer and former director of the national lottery. Lakas was designated "provisional president," and Sucre was appointed his deputy.

In late 1969 a close associate of Torrijos announced the formation of the New Panama Movement. This movement was originally

Torrijos in the countryside

intended to organize peasants, workers, and other social groups and was patterned after that of Mexico's Institutional Revolutionary Party. No organizational structure was established, however, and by 1971 the idea had been abandoned. The government party was revived under a different name, the Democratic Revolutionary Party (Partido Revolucionario Democrático—PRD) in the late 1970s.

A sweeping cabinet reorganization and comments of high-ranking officials in 1971 portended a shift in domestic policy. Torrijos expressed admiration for the socialist trends in the military governments of Peru and Bolivia. He also established a mutually supportive relationship with Cuba's Fidel Castro Ruz. Torrijos carefully distanced himself from the Panamanian Marxist left. The political label he appeared to wear most comfortably was "populist." In 1970 he declared, "Having finished with the oligarchy, the Panamanian has his own worth with no importance to his origin, his cradle, or where he was born."

Torrijos worked on building a popular base for his government, forming an alliance among the National Guard and the various sectors of society that had been the objects of social injustice at the hands of the oligarchy, particularly the long-neglected campesinos. He regularly traveled by helicopter to villages throughout the interior to hear their problems and to explain his new programs.

In addition to the National Guard and the campesinos, the populist alliance that Torrijos formed as a power base included

45

students, the People's Party (Partido del Pueblo—PdP), and portions of the working classes. Support for Torrijos varied among interest groups and over time. The alliance contained groups, most notably the National Guard and students, that were traditionally antagonistic toward one another and groups that traditionally had little concern with national politics, e.g., the rural sector. Nationalism, in the form of support of the efforts of the Torrijos regime to obtain control over the canal through a new treaty with the United States, provided the glue for maintaining political consensus.

In the early 1970s, the strength of the alliance was impressive. Disloyal or potentially disloyal elements within the National Guard and student groups were purged; increased salaries, perquisites, and positions of political power were offered to the loyal majority. The adherence of the middle classes was procured partly through more jobs. In return for its support, the PdP was allowed to operate openly when all other political parties were outlawed.

The Torrijos effort to secure political support in the rural sector was an innovation in Panamanian politics. With the exception of militant banana workers in the western provinces of Chiriquí and Bocas del Toro, the campesinos traditionally have had little concern with national political issues. Unlike much of Latin America, in Panama the elite is almost totally urban based, rather than being a landed aristocracy (see Urban Society, ch. 2).

No elections were held under the military government until April 1970, when the town of San Miguelito, incorporated as the country's sixty-fourth municipal district, was allowed to elect a mayor, treasurer, and municipal council. Candidates nominated by trade groups and other nonpartisan bodies were elected indirectly by a council that had been elected by neighborhood councils. Subsequently, the new system was extended throughout the country, and in 1972 the 505-member National Assembly of Municipal Representatives met in Panama City to confirm Torrijos's role as head of government and to approve a new constitution. The new document greatly expanded governmental powers at the expense of civil liberties. The state also was empowered to ''oversee the rational distribution of land'' and, in general, to regulate or initiate economic activities. In an obvious reference to the Canal Zone, the Constitution also declared the ceding of national territory to any foreign country to be illegal.

The governmental initiatives in the economy, legitimated by the new Constitution, were already underway. The government had announced in early 1969 its intention to implement 1962 legislation by distributing 700,000 hectares of land within 3 years to 61,300 families. Acquisition and distribution progressed much more slowly than anticipated, however (see Land Tenure and Agrarian Reform, ch. 3).

Nevertheless, major programs were undertaken. Primary attention and government assistance went to farmers grouped in organizations that were initially described as cooperatives but were in fact commercial farming operations by state-owned firms. The government also established companies to operate banana plantations—partly because a substantial amount of the land obtained under the land-reform laws was most suited to banana cultivation and had belonged to international fruit companies.

Educational reforms instituted by Torrijos emphasized vocational and technical training at the expense of law, liberal arts, and the humanities. The programs introduced on an experimental basis in some elementary and secondary schools resembled the Cuban system of "basic schools in the countryside." New schools were established in rural areas in which half the student's time was devoted to instruction in farming. Agricultural methods and other practical skills were taught to urban students as well, and ultimately the new curriculum was to become obligatory even in private schools. Although the changes were being instituted gradually, they met strong resistance from the upper-middle classes and particularly from teachers.

Far-reaching reforms were also undertaken in health care. A program of integrated medical care became available to the extended family of anyone who had been employed for the minimal period required to qualify for social security. A wide range of services was available not only to the worker's spouse and children, but to parents, aunts, uncles, cousins—to any dependent relative. Whereas in the past medical facilities had been limited almost entirely to Panama City, under Torrijos hospitals were built in several provincial cities. Clinics were established throughout the countryside. Medical-school graduates were required to spend at least two years in a rural internship servicing the scattered clinics.

Torrijos also undertook an ambitious program of public works. The construction of new roads and bridges contributed particularly to greater prosperity in the rural areas. Although Torrijos showed greater interest in rural development than in urban problems, he also promoted urban housing and office construction in Panama City. These projects were funded, in part, by both increased personal and corporate taxes and increased efficiency in tax collection. The 1972 enactment of a new labor code attempted to fuse the urban working class into the populist alliance. Among other things the code provided obligatory collective agreements, obligatory payroll deduction of union fees, the establishment of a superior labor tribunal, and the incorporation of some 15,000 additional workers, including street vendors and peddlers, into labor unions. At the same time, the government attempted unsuccessfully to unite the nation's three major labor confederations into a single, government-sponsored organization.

Meanwhile, Torrijos lured foreign investment by offering tax incentives and provisions for the unlimited repatriation of capital. In particular, international banking was encouraged to locate in Panama, to make the country a regional financial center. A law adopted in 1970 facilitated offshore banking (see Glossary). Numerous banks, largely foreign owned, were licensed to operate in Panama; some were authorized solely for external transactions. Funds borrowed abroad could be loaned to foreign borrowers without being taxed by Panama (see Finance, ch. 3).

Most of the reforms benefiting workers and peasants were undertaken between 1971 and 1973. Economic problems beginning in 1973 led to some backtracking on social programs. A new labor law passed in 1976, for example, withdrew much of the protection provided by the 1972 labor code, including compulsory collective bargaining. The causes of these economic difficulties included such external factors as the decline in world trade, and thus canal traffic. Domestic problems included a decline in agricultural production that many analysts attributed to the failure of the economic measures of the Torrijos government. The combination of a steady decline in per capita gross national product (GNP—see Glossary), inflation, unemployment, and massive foreign debts adversely affected all sectors of society and contributed heavily to the gradual erosion of the populist alliance that had firmly supported Torrijos in the early 1970s.

Increasingly, corruption in governing circles and within the National Guard also had become an issue in both national and international arenas. Torrijos's opponents were quick to note that his relatives appeared in large numbers on the public payroll.

The Treaty Negotiations

During the first two years after the overthrow of Arias, while the National Guard consolidated its control of the government and Torrijos rooted out his competitors within the National Guard, the canal issue was downplayed and generally held in abeyance. By 1971, however, the negotiation of new treaties had reemerged as the primary goal of the Torrijos regime.

In the 1970s, about 5 percent of world trade, by volume, some 20 to 30 ships daily, were passing through the canal. Tolls had been kept artificially low, averaging a little more than US$10,000 for the 8- to 10-hour passage, and thus entailing a United States government subsidy. Nevertheless, canal use was declining in the 1970s because of alternate routes, vessels being too large to transit the canal, and the decline in world trade.

The canal, nevertheless, was clearly vital to Panama's economy. Some 30 percent of Panama's foreign trade passed through the canal. About 25 percent of the country's foreign exchange earnings and 13 percent of its GNP were associated with canal activities. The level of traffic and the revenue thereby generated were key factors in the country's economic life (see Role of the Canal From 1903 to 1977, ch. 3).

Under the 1903 treaty, the governor of the Canal Zone was appointed by the president of the United States and reported to the secretary of war. The governor also served as president of the Canal Zone Company and reported to a board of directors appointed by the secretary of war. United States jurisdiction in the zone was complete, and residence was restricted to United States government employees and their families. On the eve of the adoption of new treaties in 1977, residents of the Canal Zone included some 40,000 United States citizens, two-thirds of whom were military personnel and their dependents, and about 7,500 Panamanians. The Canal Zone was, in effect, a United States military outpost with its attendant prosperous economy, which stood in stark contrast to the poverty on the other side of its fences.

By the 1960s military activities in the zone were under the direction of the United States Southern Command (SOUTHCOM). The primary mission of SOUTHCOM was defending the canal. In addition, SOUTHCOM served as the nerve center for a wide range of military activities in Latin America, including communications, training Latin American military personnel, overseeing United States military assistance advisory groups, and conducting joint military exercises with Latin American armed forces (see United States Forces in Panama, ch. 5).

Negotiations for a new set of treaties were resumed in June 1971, but little was accomplished until March 1973 when, at the urging of Panama, the UN Security Council called a special meeting in Panama City. A resolution calling on the United States to negotiate a "just and equitable" treaty was vetoed by the United States on the grounds that the disposition of the canal was a bilateral matter. Panama had succeeded, however, in dramatizing the issue and gaining international support.

The United States signaled renewed interest in the negotiations in late 1973, when Ambassador Ellsworth Bunker was dispatched to Panama as a special envoy. In early 1974, Secretary of State

Henry Kissinger and Panamanian foreign minister Juan Antonio Tack announced their agreement on eight principles to serve as a guide in negotiating a "just and equitable treaty eliminating once and for all the causes of conflict between the two countries." The principles included recognition of Panamanian sovereignty in the Canal Zone; immediate enhancement of economic benefits to Panama; a fixed expiration date for United States control of the canal; increased Panamanian participation in the operation and defense of the canal; and continuation of United States participation in defending the canal.

American attention was distracted later in 1974 by the Watergate scandal, impeachment proceedings, and ultimately the resignation of President Richard M. Nixon. Negotiations with Panama were accelerated by President Gerald R. Ford in mid-1975 but became deadlocked on four central issues: the duration of the treaty; the amount of canal revenues to go to Panama; the amount of territory United States military bases would occupy during the life of the treaty; and the United States demand for a renewable forty- or fifty-year lease of bases to defend the canal. Panama was particularly concerned with the open-ended presence of United States military bases and held that the emerging United States position retained the bitterly opposed "perpetuity" provision of the 1903 treaty and thus violated the spirit of the 1974 Kissinger-Tack principles. The sensitivity of the issue during negotiations was illustrated in September 1975 when Kissinger's public declaration that "the United States must maintain the right, unilaterally, to defend the Panama Canal for an indefinite future" provoked a furor in Panama. A group of some 600 angry students stoned the United States embassy.

Negotiations remained stalled during the United States election campaign of 1976 when the canal issue, particularly the question of how the United States could continue to guarantee its security under new treaty arrangements, became a major topic of debate. Torrijos replaced Foreign Minister Tack with Aquilino Boyd in April 1976, and early the next year Boyd was replaced by Nicolás González Revilla. Rómulo Escobar Bethancourt, meanwhile, became Panama's chief negotiator. Panama's growing economic difficulties made the conclusion of a new treaty, accompanied by increased economic benefits, increasingly vital.

The new Panamanian negotiating team was thus encouraged by the high priority that President Jimmy Carter placed on rapidly concluding a new treaty. Carter added Sol Linowitz, former ambassador to the OAS, to the United States negotiating team shortly after taking office in January 1977. Carter held that United States

Panama Canal treaties signing ceremony,
September 7, 1977
Courtesy The White House

interests would be protected by possessing "an assured capacity or capability" to guarantee that the canal would remain open and neutral after Panama assumed control. This view contrasted with previous United States demands for an ongoing physical military presence and led to the negotiation of two separate treaties. This changed point of view, together with United States willingness to provide a considerable amount of bilateral development aid in addition to the revenues associated with Panama's participation in the operation of the canal, were central to the August 10, 1977, announcement that agreement had been reached on two new treaties.

The 1977 Treaties and Associated Agreements

On September 7, 1977, Carter and Torrijos met in Washington to sign the treaties in a ceremony that also was attended by representatives of twenty-six other nations of the Western Hemisphere. The Panama Canal Treaty, the major document signed on September 7, abrogated the 1903 treaty and all other previous bilateral agreements concerning the canal. The treaty was to enter into force six months after the exchange of instruments of ratification and to expire at noon on December 31, 1999 (see Appendix B). The Panama Canal Company and the Canal Zone government

51

would cease to operate and Panama would assume complete legal jurisdiction over the former Canal Zone immediately, although the United States would retain jurisdiction over its citizens during a thirty-month transition period. Panama would grant the United States rights to operate, maintain, and manage the canal through a new United States government agency, the Panama Canal Commission. The commission would be supervised by a board of five members from the United States and four from Panama; the ratio was fixed for the duration of the treaty. The commission would have a United States administrator and Panamanian deputy administrator until January 1, 1990, when the nationalities of these two positions would be reversed. Panamanian nationals would constitute a growing number of commission employees in preparation for their assumption of full responsibility in 2000. Another binational body, the Panama Canal Consultative Committee, was created to advise the respective governments on policy matters affecting the canal's operation.

Article IV of the treaty related to the protection and defense of the canal and mandated both nations to participate in that effort, though the United States was to hold the primary responsibility during the life of the treaty. The Combined Board, composed of an equal number of senior military representatives from each country, was established and its members charged with consulting their respective governments on matters relating to protection and defense of the canal (see Canal Defense, ch. 5). Guidelines for employment within the Panama Canal Commission were set forth in Article X, which stipulated that the United States would establish a training program to ensure that an increasing number of Panamanian nationals acquired the skills needed to operate and maintain the canal. By 1982 the number of United States employees of the commission was to be at least 20 percent lower than the number working for the Panama Canal Company in 1977. Both nations pledged to assist their own nationals who lost jobs because of the new arrangements in finding employment. The right to collective bargaining and affiliation with international labor organizations by commission employees was guaranteed.

Under the provisions of Article XII, the United States and Panama agreed to study jointly the feasibility of a sea-level canal and, if deemed necessary, to negotiate terms for its construction. Payments to Panama from the commission ("a just and equitable return on the national resources which it has dedicated to the . . . canal") were set forth in Article XIII. These included a fixed annuity of US$10 million, an annual contingency payment of up to US$10 million to be paid out of any commission profits, and

US$0.30 per Panama Canal net ton (see Glossary) of cargo that passed through the canal, paid out of canal tolls. The latter figure was to be periodically adjusted for inflation and was expected to net Panama between US$40 and US$70 million annually during the life of the treaty. In addition, Article III stipulated that Panama would receive a further US$10 million annually for services (police, fire protection, street cleaning, traffic management, and garbage collection) it would provide in the canal operating areas.

The second treaty, the Treaty Concerning the Permanent Neutrality and Operation of the Panama Canal, or simply the Neutrality Treaty, was a much shorter document. Because it had no fixed termination date, this treaty was the major source of controversy (see Appendix B). Under its provisions, the United States and Panama agreed to guarantee the canal's neutrality "in order that both in time of peace and in time of war it shall remain secure and open to peaceful transit by the vessels of all nations on terms of entire equality." In times of war, however, United States and Panamanian warships were entitled to "expeditious" transit of the canal under the provisions of Article VI. A protocol was attached to the Neutrality Treaty, and all nations of the world were invited to subscribe to its provisions.

At the same ceremony in Washington, representatives of the United States and Panama signed a series of fourteen executive agreements associated with the treaties. These included two Agreements in Implementation of Articles III and IV of the Panama Canal Treaty that detailed provisions concerning operation, management, protection, and defense, outlined in the main treaty. Most importantly, these two agreements defined the areas to be held by the United States until 2000 to operate and defend the canal. These areas were distinguished from military areas to be used jointly by the United States and Panama until that time, military areas to be held initially by the United States but turned over to Panama before 2000, and areas that were turned over to Panama on October 1, 1979 (see fig. 3).

One foreign observer calculated that 64 percent of the former Canal Zone, or 106,700 hectares, came under Panamanian control in 1979; another 18 percent, or 29,460 hectares, would constitute the "canal operating area" and remain under control of the Panama Canal Commission until 2000; and the remaining 18 percent would constitute the various military installations controlled by the United States until 2000. The agreements also established the Coordinating Committee, consisting of one representative of each country, to coordinate the implementation of the agreement with respect to Article III of the Panama Canal Treaty, and an analogous Joint

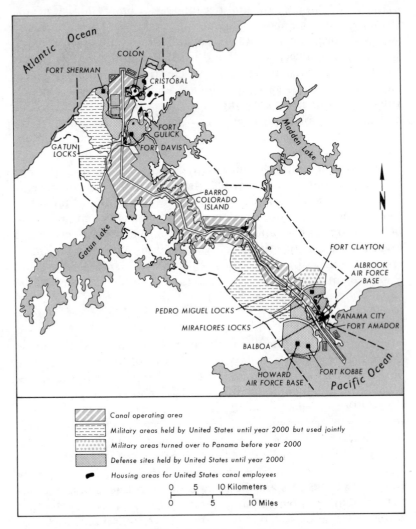

Figure 3. Dispensation of Land Within the Former Canal Zone

Committee to perform the defense-related functions called for in the agreement with respect to Article IV of the treaty.

Ancillary agreements signed on September 7 allowed the United States to conduct certain activities in Panama until 2000, including the training of Latin American military personnel at four schools located within the former Canal Zone; provided for cooperation to protect wildlife within the area; and outlined future United States economic and military assistance. This latter agreement, subject to the availability of congressionally approved funds, provided for United States loan guarantees, up to US$75 million over a 5-year period, for housing; a US$20-million loan guarantee by the United States Overseas Private Investment Corporation for financing projects in the Panamanian private sector; loans, loan guarantees, and insurance, up to a limit of US$200 million between 1977 and 1982, provided by the Export-Import Bank of the United States for financing Panamanian purchases of United States exports; and up to US$50 million in foreign military sales credits over a 10-year period.

The speeches of Carter and Torrijos at the signing ceremony revealed the differing attitudes toward the new accords by the two leaders. Carter declared his unqualified support of the new treaties. The statement by Torrijos was more ambiguous, however. While he stated that the signing of the new treaties "attests to the end of many struggles by several generations of Panamanian patriots," he noted Panamanian criticism of several aspects of the new accords, particularly of the Neutrality Treaty:

> Mr. President, I want you to know that this treaty, which I shall sign and which repeals a treaty not signed by any Panamanian, does not enjoy the approval of all our people, because the 23 years agreed upon as a transition period are 8,395 days, because during this time there will still be military bases which make my country a strategic reprisal target, and because we are agreeing to a treaty of neutrality which places us under the protective umbrella of the Pentagon. This pact could, if it is not administered judiciously by future generations, become an instrument of permanent intervention.

Torrijos was so concerned with the ambiguity of the Neutrality Treaty, because of Panamanian sensitivity to the question of United States military intervention, that, at his urging, he and President Carter signed the Statement of Understanding on October 14, 1977, to clarify the meaning of the permanent United States rights. This statement, most of which was subsequently included as an amendment to the Neutrality Treaty and incorporated into its instrument of ratification, included a declaration that the United States "right to act against any aggression or threat directed against the Canal . . . does not mean, nor shall it be interpreted as the right of intervention of the United States in the internal affairs of Panama." Despite this clarification, the plebiscite that took place the next week and served as the legal means of ratification in Panama, saw only two-thirds of Panamanians registering their approval of the new treaties, a number considerably smaller than that hoped for by the government.

Ratification in the United States necessitated the approval of two-thirds of the Senate. The debates, the longest in Senate history, began on February 7, 1978. The Neutrality Treaty was approved on March 16, and the main treaty on April 18, when the debate finally ended. To win the necessary sixty-seven Senate votes, Carter agreed to the inclusion of a number of amendments, conditions, reservations, and understandings that were passed during the Senate debates and subsequently included in the instruments of ratification signed by Carter and Torrijos in June.

Notable among the Senate modifications of the Neutrality Treaty were two amendments incorporating the October 1977 Statement of Understanding, and interpreting the "expeditious" transit of United States and Panamanian warships in times of war as being preferential. Another modification, commonly known as the DeConcini Condition, stated that "if the Canal is closed, or its operations are interfered with [the United States and Panama shall each] have the right to take such steps as each deems necessary, . . . including the use of military force in the Republic of Panama, to reopen the Canal or restore the operations of the Canal." Modifications of the Panama Canal Treaty included a reservation requiring statutory authorization for payments to Panama set forth in Article XIII and another stating that any action taken by the United States to secure accessibility to the Canal "shall not have as its purpose or be interpreted as a right of intervention in the internal affairs of the Republic of Panama or interference with its political independence or sovereign integrity." Reservations attached to both treaties made the United States provision of economic and military assistance, as detailed in the ancillary agreements attached to the treaties, nonobligatory.

The inclusion of these modifications, which were never ratified in Panama, was received there by a storm of protest. Torrijos expressed his concern in 2 letters, the first to Carter and another sent to 115 heads of state through their representatives at the UN. A series of student protests took place in front of the United States embassy. The DeConcini Condition was the major object of protest. Although the reservation to the Panama Canal Treaty was designed to mollify Panamanian fears that the DeConcini Condition marked a return to the United States gunboat diplomacy of the early twentieth century, this provision would expire in 2000, whereas the DeConcini Condition, because it was attached to the Neutrality Treaty, would remain in force permanently.

Despite his continuing concern with the ambiguity of the treaties with respect to the United States role in defense of the canal after 2000, the close Senate vote made Torrijos aware that he could not secure any further modification at that time. On June 16, 1978, he and Carter signed the instruments of ratification of each treaty in a ceremony in Panama City. Nevertheless, Torrijos added the following statement to both Panamanian instruments: "The Republic of Panama will reject, in unity and with decisiveness and firmness, any attempt by any country to intervene in its internal or external affairs." The instruments of ratification became effective on June 1, 1979, and the treaties entered into force on October 1, 1979.

Torrijos Government Undertakes "Democratization"

Ironically, the successful conclusion of negotiations with the United States and the signing of the Panama Canal treaties in August 1977 added to the growing political difficulties in Panama. Virtually all observers of Panamanian politics in the late 1970s agreed that the situation in the late 1970s could only be understood in terms of the central role traditionally played by nationalism in forming Panamanian political consensus. Before August 1977, opponents of Torrijos were reluctant to challenge his leadership because of his progress in gaining control over the Canal Zone. The signing of the treaties eliminated that restraint; in short, after August 1977, Panamanian resentment could no longer be focused exclusively on the United States.

The widespread feeling among Panamanians that the 1977 treaties were unacceptable, despite their being approved by a two-thirds majority in the October 1977 plebiscite, contributed to growing opposition to the government. Critics pointed especially to the amendments imposed by the United States Senate after the October 1977 plebiscite, which they felt substantially altered the spirit of the treaties. Furthermore, political opponents of Torrijos argued that the government purposely limited the information available on the treaties and then asked the people to vote "yes" or "no," in a plebiscite that the opposition maintained was conducted fraudulently.

Another factor contributing to the erosion of the populist alliance built by Torrijos during the early 1970s was the graduated and controlled process of "democratization" undertaken by the Torrijos government after signing the new canal treaties. In October 1978, a decade after the government declared political parties illegal in the aftermath of the 1968 military coup d'état, the 1972 Constitution was reformed to implement a new electoral law and legalize political parties. In the spirit of opening the political system that accompanied the ratification of the Panama Canal treaties, exiled political leaders, including former President Arnulfo Arias, were allowed to return to the country, and a flurry of political activity was evident during the subsequent eighteen months. Foremost among the activities were efforts to obtain the 30,000 signatures legally required to register a party for the October 1980 elections.

The 1978 amendments to the 1972 Constitution markedly decreased the powers of the executive branch of government and increased those of the legislature, but the executive remained the dominant branch. From October 1972 until October 1978, Torrijos had acted as the chief executive under the titles of head of government and "Maximum Leader of the Panamanian Revolution." After the 1978 amendments took effect, Torrijos gave up his position as head of government but retained control of the National Guard and continued to play an important role in the government's decision-making process. Before stepping down, Torrijos had agreed to democratize Panama's political system, in order to gain United States support for the canal treaties. In October 1978, the National Assembly elected a thirty-eight-year-old lawyer and former education minister, Aristides Royo, to the presidency and Ricardo de la Espriella to the vice presidency, each for a six-year term.

The PRD—a potpourri of middle-class elements, peasant and labor groups, and marginal segments of Panamanian society—was the first party to be officially recognized under the registration process that began in 1979. Wide speculation held that the PRD would nominate Torrijos as its candidate for the presidential race planned for 1984. Moreover, many assumed that with government backing, the PRD would have a substantial advantage in the electoral process.

In March 1979, a coalition of eight parties called the National Opposition Front (Frente Nacional de Oposición—FRENO) was formed to battle the PRD in the 1980 legislative elections, the first free elections to be held in a decade. FRENO was composed of parties on both the right and the left of center in the political spectrum, including the strongly nationalistic, anti-Yankee Authentic Panameñista Party (Partido Panameñista Auténtico—PPA), which was led by the aged but still popular former president, Arnulfo Arias; the PLN; the reform-oriented PDC; and the Social Democratic Party (Partido Social Democrático—PSD), which was left of center and reform-oriented. Three right-of-center parties—the Republican Party (Partido Republicano—PR), the Third Nationalist Party, and PALA—had also joined the FRENO coalition. The Independent Democratic Movement, a small, moderately left-of-center party, completed the coalition. Such diverse ideologies in the opposition party suggested a marriage of convenience. FRENO opposed the Panama Canal treaties and called for their revision on terms more favorable to Panama.

All qualified parties competed in the 1980 legislative elections, but these elections posed no threat to Torrijos's power base because political parties vied for only nineteen of the fifty-seven seats in the legislature. The other two-thirds of the representatives were appointed, in essence by Torrijos's supporters. The PRD won twelve of the available nineteen seats; the PLN won five seats, and the PDC, one. The remaining seat was won by an independent candidate running with the support of a communist party, the Panamanian People's Party (Partido Panameño del Pueblo—PPP). The PPP had failed to acquire the signatures required for a place on the ballot. Despite the lopsided victory of the pro-government party and the weakness of the National Legislative Council (budgeting and appropriations were controlled by President Royo, who had been handpicked by Torrijos), this election represented a small step toward restoring democratic political processes. The election also demonstrated that Panama's political party system was too fragmented to form a viable united front against the government.

The Post-Torrijos Era

Torrijos's Sudden Death

Omar Torrijos was killed in an airplane crash in western Panama on July 31, 1981. His death deprived Central America of a potential moderating influence when that region was facing increased destabilization, including revolutions in Nicaragua and El Salvador. His death also created a power vacuum in his own country and ended a twelve-year "dictatorship with a heart," as Torrijos liked to call his rule. He was succeeded immediately as National Guard commander by the chief of staff, Colonel Florencio Florez Aguilar, a Torrijos loyalist. Although Florez adopted a low profile and allowed President Royo to exercise more of his constitutional authority, Royo soon alienated the Torrijos clique, the private sector, and the National Guard's general staff, all of whom rejected his leadership style and his strongly nationalistic, anti-United States rhetoric. Royo had become the leader of leftist elements within the government, and he used his position to accuse the United States of hundreds of technical violations in the implementation of the canal treaties. The general staff considered the National Guard to be the country's principal guarantor of national stability and began to challenge the president's political authority. Royo attempted to use the PRD as his power base, but the fighting between leftists and conservatives within the party became too intense to control. Meanwhile, the country's many and diverse political parties, although discontented with the regime, were unable to form a viable and solid opposition.

Torrijos had been the unifying influence in Panama's political system. He had kept Royo in the presidency, the PRD functioning, and the National Guard united. The groups were loyal to him but distrustful of each other.

Florez completed twenty-six years of military service in March 1982 and was forced to retire. He was replaced by his own chief of staff, General Rubén Darío Paredes, who considered himself to be Torrijos's rightful successor and the embodiment of change and unity (Torrijos had been grooming Paredes for political office since 1975). In a press interview, Paredes stated that he had become ''what some people sometimes call a strong man.'' Without delay the new National Guard commander asserted himself in Panamanian politics and formulated plans to run for the presidency in 1984. Many suspected that Paredes had struck a deal with Colonel Manuel Antonio Noriega Moreno, who had been the assistant chief of staff for intelligence since 1970, whereby Noriega would assume command of the National Guard and Paredes would become president in 1984. Paredes publicly blamed Royo for the rapidly deteriorating economy and the pocketing of millions of dollars from the nation's social security system by government officials.

In July 1982, growing labor unrest led to an outbreak of strikes and public demonstrations against the Royo administration. Paredes, claiming that ''the people wanted change,'' intervened to remove Royo from the presidency. With National Guard backing, Paredes forced Royo and most of his cabinet to resign on July 30, 1982, almost one year to the day after the death of Torrijos. Royo was succeeded by Vice President Ricardo de la Espriella, a United States-educated former banking official. De la Espriella wasted no time in referring to the National Guard as a ''partner in power.''

In August 1982, President de la Espriella formed a new cabinet that included independents and members of the Liberal Party and the PRD; Jorge Illueca Sibauste, Royo's foreign minister, became the new vice president. Meanwhile, Colonel Armando Contreras became chief of staff of the National Guard. Colonel Noriega continued to hold the powerful position of assistant chief of staff for intelligence—the Panamanian government's only intelligence arm. In December 1982, Noriega became chief of staff of the National Guard.

Noriega Takes Control

In November 1982, a commission was established to draft a series of proposed amendments to the 1972 Constitution. The PRD supported the amendments and claimed that they would limit the power of the National Guard and help the country return to a fully democratic system of government. These amendments reduced the term of the president from six to five years, created a second vice presidency, banned participation in elections by active members of the National Guard, and provided for the direct election of all members of the legislature (renamed the Legislative Assembly) after nomination by legitimate political parties. These amendments were approved in a national referendum held on April 24, 1983, when they were considered to be a positive step toward lessening the power of the National Guard. In reality, however, the National Guard leadership would surrender only the power it was willing to surrender.

General Paredes, in keeping with the new constitutional provision that no active National Guard member could participate in an election, reluctantly retired in August 1983. He was succeeded immediately by Noriega, who was promoted to brigadier general. During the same month, Paredes was nominated as the PRD candidate for president. National elections were only five months away, and Paredes appeared to be the leading presidential contender. Nevertheless, in early September, President de la Espriella purged his cabinet of Paredes loyalists, and Noriega declared that he would not publicly support any candidate for president. These events convinced Paredes that he had no official government or military backing for his candidacy. He withdrew from the presidential race on September 6, 1983, less than a month after retiring from the National Guard. Although Paredes subsequently gained the support of the Popular Nationalist Party (Partido Nacionalista Popular—PNP) and was able to appear on the 1984 ballot, he was no longer a major presidential contender. Constitutional reforms notwithstanding, the reality of Panamanian politics dictated that no candidate could become president without the backing of the National Guard and, especially, its commander.

With Paredes out of the way, Noriega was free to consolidate power. One of his first acts was to have the Legislative Assembly approve a bill to restructure the National Guard, which thereafter would operate under the name of Panama Defense Forces (Fuerzas de Defensa de Panamá—FDP). Nominally, the president of the republic would head the FDP, but real power would be in the hands of Noriega, who assumed the new title of commander in chief of the FDP (see Missions and Organization of the Defense Forces, ch. 5).

Meanwhile, the PRD—the military-supported party—was left without a candidate. To strengthen its base for the upcoming election, the PRD created a coalition of six political parties called the National Democratic Union (Unión Nacional Democrática— UNADE), which included the PALA, PLN, and PR, as well as the smaller PP and the left-of-center Broad Popular Front (Frente Amplio Popular—FRAMPO). With the approval of the military, UNADE selected Nicolás Ardito Barletta Vallarino to be its presidential candidate. Ardito Barletta, a University of Chicago-trained economist and former minister of planning, had been a vice president of the World Bank (see Glossary) for six years before his nomination in February 1984. Ardito Barletta was considered well qualified for the presidency, but he lacked his own power base.

Opposing Ardito Barletta and the UNADE coalition was the Democratic Opposition Alliance (Alianza Democrática de Oposición—ADO) and its candidate, the veteran politician, Arnulfo Arias. ADO, formed by the PPA, the PDC, the center-right National Liberal Republican Movement (Movimiento Liberal Republicano Nacional—MOLIRENA), and an assortment of leftist parties, was a diverse coalition made up of rural peasants (especially from Arias's home province of Chiriquí) and lower- and middle-class elements that opposed military rule and government corruption. During the campaign, Arias emphasized the need to reduce military influence in Panamanian politics. He called for the removal of the defense bill passed in September 1983, which had given the FDP control over all security forces and services.

The campaign proved to be bitterly contested, with both sides predicting victory by a large margin. Arias and his backers claimed that Ardito Barletta was conducting the campaign unfairly. Indeed, UNADE took advantage of being the pro-government coalition and used government vehicles and funds to help conduct its campaign. In addition, most of the media—television, radio stations, and newspapers—favored the government coalition. For example, only one of the country's five daily newspapers supported the ADO.

Voting day, May 6, 1984, was peaceful. Violence broke out the next day between supporters of the two main candidates in front of the Legislative Palace, where votes were being counted. One person was killed, and forty others were injured. Irregularities and errors in the voter registration and in the vote count led to credible charges of electoral misconduct and fraud. Thousands of people, who believed that they had registered properly, showed up at the polling places only to discover that their names had been inexplicably left off the voting list. Large-scale vote-buying, especially in rural areas, was reported.

More serious problems developed during the next several days. Very few official vote tallies were being delivered from the precinct and district levels to the National Board of Vote Examiners, with no apparent reason for the delay. The vote count proceeded slowly amid a climate of suspicion and rumor. On May 9, the vote tabulation was suspended. On May 11, the members of the National Board of Vote Examiners declared that they could not fulfill their function because of 2,124 allegations of fraud, and they turned the process over to the Electoral Tribunal. The opposition coalition publicized evidence showing that many votes had been destroyed before they had been counted. These charges and all subsequent challenges by the opposition were rejected by the tribunal, even though the head of the three-member tribunal demanded a further investigation into the allegations. The election results were made public on May 16. Ardito Barletta won the election with 300,748 votes; Arias came in second with 299,035; retired General Paredes received 15,976. The military-supported candidate had won the election, and the threat to the political power of the FDP had been circumvented.

The United States government acknowledged that the election results were questionable but declared that Ardito Barletta's victory must be seen as an important forward step in Panama's transition to democracy. Relations between the United States and Panama worsened later in the year because of Panama's displeasure at the alleged slowness with which the United States-controlled Panama Canal Commission was replacing American workers with Panamanians.

The resignation of President Ricardo de la Espriella and his cabinet on February 13, 1984, was barely noticed during the intense election campaign. De la Espriella was forced out by Noriega. De la Espriella had opposed the military's manipulation of the election and strongly advocated free elections for 1984. During his brief tenure, de la Espriella had failed to institute any significant policy changes, and his presidency was lackluster. De la Espriella was succeeded immediately by Vice President Jorge Illueca, who formed a new cabinet.

Ardito Barletta, a straitlaced and soft-spoken technocrat, took office on October 11, 1984. He quickly launched an attack on the country's economic problems and sought help from the International Monetary Fund (IMF—see Glossary) to refinance part of the country's US$3.7-billion debt—the world's highest on a per-capita basis. He promised to modernize the government's bureaucracy and implement an economic program that would create a 5-percent annual growth rate. On November 13—to meet IMF requirements for a US$603-million loan renegotiation—he announced economic austerity measures, including a 7-percent tax on all services and reduced budgets for cabinet ministries and autonomous government agencies. He revoked some of the measures ten days later in response to massive protests and strikes by labor, student, and professional organizations.

Negative popular reaction to Ardito Barletta's efforts to revive the country's stagnant economy troubled opposition politicians, the military, and many of his own UNADE supporters. Ardito Barletta's headstrong administrative style also offended Panamanian politicians who had a customary backslapping and back-room style of politicking. Moreover, Arditto Barletta's economic program conflicted with the military's traditional use of high government spending to keep the poor and the political left placated.

On August 12, 1985, Noriega stated that the situation in the country was "totally anarchic and out of control"; he also criticized Ardito Barletta for running an incompetent government. Observers speculated that another reason—and probably the real one—for the ouster of Ardito Barletta was FDP opposition to the president's plan to investigate the murder of Dr. Hugo Spadafora, a prominent critic of the Panamanian military. Shortly before his death, Spadafora had announced that he had evidence linking Noriega to drug trafficking and illegal arms dealing. Relatives of Spadafora claimed that witnesses had seen him in the custody of Panamanian security forces in the Costa Rican border area immediately before his decapitated body was found on September 14, just a few miles north of the Panamanian border.

Because of uneasiness within the FDP over the Spadafora affair, Noriega, using Ardito Barletta's ineffectiveness as an excuse, pressured Ardito Barletta to resign, which he did on September 27, 1985, after only eleven months in office. Ardito Barletta was succeeded the next day by his first vice president, Eric Arturo Delvalle Henríquez, who announced a new cabinet on October 3, 1985.

* * *

A number of good books are available in English dealing with various periods of Panamanian history and with the construction of the canal and the diplomatic controversies that have arisen. David Howarth's *Panama* provides particularly good coverage of the period of conquest and colonization. The most comprehensive account of Panama's unhappy association with Colombia is found in Alex Pérez-Venero's *Before the Five Frontiers.*

The importance of the canal in Panamanian development is explored in the eminently readable and informative *The Path Between the Seas* by David McCullough. A painstakingly thorough study of bilateral relations that focuses on the Panama Canal dispute from its origin until ratification of the Panama Canal treaties is found in *U.S.-Panama Relations, 1903–1978* coauthored by David N. Farnsworth and James W. McKenney. Detailed information on the negotiations and related events leading to the 1977 treaties is found in *A Chronology of Events Relating to the Panama Canal,* prepared for the United States Senate Foreign Relations Committee.

Steve C. Ropp's *Panamanian Politics: From Guarded Nation to National Guard* focuses on Panamanian political history until 1980. No detailed studies can be found on Panamanian political developments since 1980, but articles authored by Robert F. Drinan, Roberto Eisenmann, Jr., and Robert F. Lamberg are useful. (For further information and complete citations, see Bibliography.)

Chapter 2. The Society and Its Environment

Cuna Indian mola *design of festival musician*

PANAMANIAN SOCIETY OF the 1980s reflected the country's unusual geographical position as a transit zone. Panama's role as a crossing point had long subjected the isthmus to a variety of outside influences not typically associated with Latin America. The population included East Asian, South Asian, European, North American, and Middle Eastern immigrants and their offspring, who came to Panama to take advantage of the commercial opportunities connected with the Panama Canal. Black Antilleans, descendants of Caribbean laborers who worked on the construction of the canal, formed the largest single minority group; as English-speaking Protestants, they were set apart from the majority by both language and religion. Tribal Indians, often isolated from the larger society, constituted roughly 5 percent of the population in the 1980s. They were distinguished by language, their indigenous belief systems, and a variety of other cultural practices.

Spanish-speaking Roman Catholics formed a large majority. They were often termed mestizos—a term originally denoting mixed Indian and Spanish parentage that was used in an unrestrictive fashion to refer to almost anyone having mixed racial inheritance who conformed to the norms of Hispanic culture.

Ethnicity was broadly associated with class and status, to the extent that white elements were more apparent at the top of the social pyramid and recognizably black and Indian features at the bottom. Members of the elite placed a high value on purported racial purity; extensive ties of intermarriage within the group tended to reinforce this self-image.

Class structure was marked by divisions based on wealth, occupation, education, family background, and culture, in addition to race. The roots of the traditional elite's control lay in the colonial era. The fundamental social distinction was that between wealthier, whiter settlers who managed to purchase political positions from the Spanish crown and poorer mestizos who could not. Landholding formed the basis for the elite's wealth, political office for their power. When the isthmus became more pivotal as a transit zone after completion of the canal, elite control became less focused on landholding and more concerned with food processing and transportation facilities. Occasionally a successful immigrant family acquired wealth as the decades passed. Nevertheless, the older families' control of the country's politics remained virtually intact until the 1968 military coup.

The relationship between landowners and tenants or squatters, between cattle ranchers and subsistence farmers, was the dynamic that underlay social relations in rural Panama in the twentieth century. Cattle ranching had expanded to meet the growing demand for meat in cities. Small farmers cleared the tropical forest for cattle ranchers, planted it for one to two seasons, and then moved on to repeat the process elsewhere. As the population and the demand for meat increased, so too did the rate of movement onto previously unsettled lands, creating a "moving agricultural frontier."

Migration, both to cities and to less settled regions in the country, was a critical component in contemporary social relations. City and countryside were linked because the urban-based elite owned ranches or plantations, farmers and ranchers provisioned cities, and migration was an experience common to tens of thousands of Panamanians. Land and an expanding urban economy were essential to absorb surplus labor from heavily populated regions of the countryside. It remained to be seen how the social system would function in the face of high urban unemployment in the more straitened economic circumstances of the late 1980s.

Geography

Panama is located on the narrowest and lowest part of the Isthmus of Panama that links North America and South America. This S-shaped part of the isthmus is situated between 7° and 10° north latitude and 77° and 83° west longitude. Slightly smaller than South Carolina, Panama encompasses approximately 77,082 square kilometers, is 772 kilometers in length, and is between 60 and 177 kilometers in width (see fig. 1).

Panama's two coastlines are referred to as the Caribbean (or Atlantic) and Pacific, rather than the north and south coasts. To the east is Colombia and to the west Costa Rica. Because of the location and contour of the country, directions expressed in terms of the compass are often surprising. For example, a transit of the Panama Canal from the Pacific to the Caribbean involves travel not to the east but to the northwest, and in Panama City the sunrise is to the east over the Pacific.

The country is divided into nine provinces, plus the Comarca de San Blas, which for statistical purposes is treated as part of Colón Province in most official documents. The provincial borders have not changed since they were determined at independence in 1903. The provinces are divided into districts, which in turn are subdivided into sections called *corregimientos*. Configurations of the *corregimientos* are changed periodically to accommodate population changes as revealed in the census reports.

The country's two international boundaries, with Colombia and Costa Rica, have been clearly demarcated, and in the late 1980s there were no outstanding disputes. The country claims the seabed of the continental shelf, which has been defined by Panama to extend to the 500-meter submarine contour. In addition, a 1958 law asserts jurisdiction over 12 nautical miles from the coastlines, and in 1968 the government announced a claim to a 200-nautical-mile Exclusive Economic Zone.

The Caribbean coastline is marked by several good natural harbors. However, Cristóbal, at the Caribbean terminus of the canal, had the only important port facilities in the late 1980s. The numerous islands of the Archipiélago de Bocas del Toro, near the Costa Rican border, provide an extensive natural roadstead and shield the banana port of Almirante. The over 350 San Blas Islands, near Colombia, are strung out for more than 160 kilometers along the sheltered Caribbean coastline.

The major port on the Pacific coastline is Balboa. The principal islands are those of the Archipiélago de las Perlas in the middle of the Gulf of Panama, the penal colony on the Isla de Coiba in the Golfo de Chiriquí, and the decorative island of Taboga, a tourist attraction that can be seen from Panama City. In all, there are some 1,000 islands off the Pacific coast.

The Pacific coastal waters are extraordinarily shallow. Depths of 180 meters are reached only outside the perimeters of both the Gulf of Panama and the Golfo de Chiriquí, and wide mud flats extend up to 70 kilometers seaward from the coastlines. As a consequence, the tidal range is extreme. A variation of about 70 centimeters between high and low water on the Caribbean coast contrasts sharply with over 700 centimeters on the Pacific coast, and some 130 kilometers up the Río Tuira the range is still over 500 centimeters.

The dominant feature of the country's landform is the central spine of mountains and hills that forms the continental divide (see fig. 4). The divide does not form part of the great mountain chains of North America, and only near the Colombian border are there highlands related to the Andean system of South America. The spine that forms the divide is the highly eroded arch of an uplift from the sea bottom, in which peaks were formed by volcanic intrusions.

The mountain range of the divide is called the Cordillera de Talamanca near the Costa Rican border. Farther east it becomes the Serranía de Tabasará, and the portion of it closer to the lower saddle of the isthmus, where the canal is located, is often called the Sierra de Veraguas. As a whole, the range between Costa Rica

71

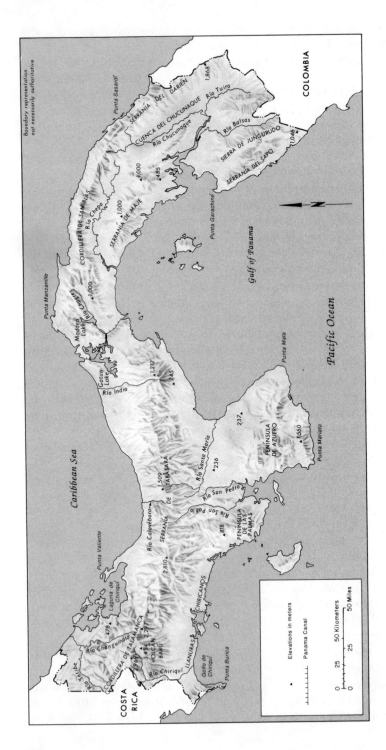

Figure 4. Topography and Drainage

and the canal is generally referred to by Panamanian geographers as the Cordillera Central.

The highest point in the country is the Volcán Barú (formerly known as the Volcán de Chiriquí), which rises to almost 3,500 meters. The apex of a highland that includes the nation's richest soil, the Volcán Barú is still referred to as a volcano, although it has been inactive for millennia.

Nearly 500 rivers lace Panama's rugged landscape. Mostly unnavigable, many originate as swift highland streams, meander in valleys, and form coastal deltas. However, the Río Chepo and the Río Chagres are sources of hydroelectric power.

The Río Chagres is one of the longest and most vital of the approximately 150 rivers that flow into the Caribbean. Part of this river was dammed to create Gatun Lake, which forms a major part of the transit route between the locks near each end of the canal. Both Gatun Lake and Madden Lake (also filled with water from the Río Chagres) provide hydroelectricity for the area of the former Canal Zone.

The Río Chepo, another major source of hydroelectric power, is one of the more than 300 rivers emptying into the Pacific. These Pacific-oriented rivers are longer and slower running than those of the Caribbean side. Their basins are also more extensive. One of the longest is the Río Tuira, which flows into the Golfo de San Miguel and is the nation's only river navigable by larger vessels.

Panama has a tropical climate. Temperatures are uniformly high—as is the relative humidity—and there is little seasonal variation. Diurnal ranges are low; on a typical dry-season day in the capital city, the early morning minimum may be 24°C and the afternoon maximum 29°C. The temperature seldom exceeds 32°C for more than a short time.

Temperatures on the Pacific side of the isthmus are somewhat lower than on the Caribbean, and breezes tend to rise after dusk in most parts of the country. Temperatures are markedly cooler in the higher parts of the mountain ranges, and frosts occur in the Cordillera de Talamanca in western Panama.

Climatic regions are determined less on the basis of temperature than on rainfall, which varies regionally from less than 1.3 to more than 3 meters per year. Almost all of the rain falls during the rainy season, which is usually from April to December, but varies in length from seven to nine months. The cycle of rainfall is determined primarily by two factors: moisture from the Caribbean, which is transported by north and northeast winds prevailing during most of the year, and the continental divide, which acts as a rainshield for the Pacific lowlands. A third influence that is present during the late autumn is the southwest wind off the Pacific. This wind brings some precipitation to the Pacific lowlands, modified by the highlands of the Península de Azuero, which form a partial rainshield for much of central Panama. In general, rainfall is much heavier on the Caribbean than on the Pacific side of the continental divide. The annual average in Panama City is little more than half of that in Colón. Although rainy-season thunderstorms are common, the country is outside the hurricane track.

Panama's tropical environment supports an abundance of plants. Forests dominate, interrupted in places by grasslands, scrub, and crops. Although nearly 40 percent of Panama is still wooded, deforestation is a continuing threat to the rain-drenched woodlands. Tree cover has been reduced by more than 50 percent since the 1940s. Subsistence farming, widely practiced from the northeastern jungles to the southwestern grasslands, consists largely of corn, bean, and tuber plots. Mangrove swamps occur along parts of both coasts, with banana plantations occupying deltas near Costa Rica. In many places, a multi-canopied rain forest abuts the swamp on one side of the country and extends to the lower reaches of slopes in the other.

Population

Regions of Settlement

Panama has no generally recognized group of geographic regions, and no single set of names is in common use. One system often used by Panamanian geographers, however, portrays the country as divided into five regions that reflect population concentration and economic development as well as geography.

Darién, the largest and most sparsely populated of the regions, extends from the hinterlands of Panama City and Colón to the Colombian border, comprising more than one-third of the national territory (see fig. 5). In addition to the province of Darién, it includes the Comarca de San Blas and the eastern part of Panamá Province. Darién—a name that was once applied to the entire isthmus—is a land of rain forest and swamp.

The Central Isthmus does not have precisely definable boundaries. Geographically, it is the low saddle of land that bisects the isthmus at the canal. It extends on the Pacific side from the Darién as far west as the town of La Chorrera. On the Atlantic, it includes small villages and clustered farms around Gatun Lake. East of the canal it terminates gradually as the population grows sparse, and the jungles and swamps of the Darién region begin. More a concept than a region, the Central Isthmus, with a width of about

100 kilometers, is the densely populated historical transportation route between the Atlantic and the Pacific and includes most of Colón Province.

Central Panama lies to the southwest of the canal and is made up of all or most of the provinces of Veraguas, Coclé, Herrera, and Los Santos. Located between the continental divide and the Pacific, the area is sometimes referred to as the Central Provinces. The sparsely populated Santa Fe District of Veraguas Province is located across the continental divide on the Atlantic side, however, and a frontier part of Coclé is also on the Atlantic side of the divide.

The hills and lowlands of Central Panama, dotted with farms and ranches, include most of the country's rural population. Its heartland is a heavily populated rural arc that frames the Bahía de Parita and includes most of the country's largest market towns, including the provincial capitals of Penonomé, Santiago, Chitré, and Las Tablas. This agriculturally productive area has a relatively long dry season and is known as the dry zone of Panama.

The remaining part of the Pacific side of the divide is taken up by Chiriquí Province. Some geographers regard it and Central Panama as a single region. But the lowlands of the two areas are separated by the hills of the Península de Las Palmas, and the big province of Chiriquí has sufficient individuality to warrant consideration as a separate region. The second largest and second most populous of the nine provinces, Chiriquí is to some extent a territory of pioneers as well as one of considerable economic importance. It is only in Chiriquí that the frontiers of settlement have pushed up well into the interior highlands, and the population has a particular sense of regional identity. A native of Chiriquí can be expected to identify himself, above all, as a Chiricano.

Atlantic Panama includes all of Bocas del Toro Province, the Caribbean coastal portions of Veraguas and Coclé, and the western districts of Colón. It is home to a scant 5 percent of the population, and its only important population concentrations are near the Costa Rican border where banana plantations are located.

Size and Growth

In mid-1987, Panama's population was estimated at 2.3 million, when 40 percent of the population was under 15 years of age (see fig. 6). This high proportion suggested continued pressure on the educational system to provide instruction and on the economy to create jobs in the next two decades. Population had increased more than 600 percent since the country's first census in 1911 (see table 2, Appendix A). The annual rate of increase ranged from less than 0.5 percent in the economically depressed 1920s to more than

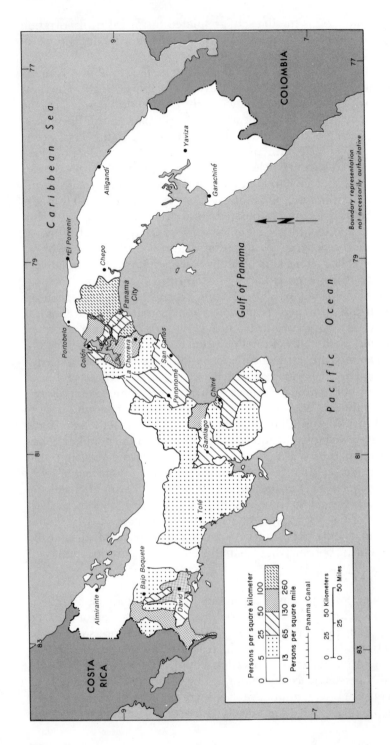

Figure 5. Population Density, 1980 Census

3 percent in the decade from 1910 to 1920 and in the 1960s. Demographers projected an annual growth rate of 2.2 percent in the 1980s, declining to 1.9 percent by 1990–95.

Provincial growth rates in the 1970s ranged from a low of 0.5 percent in Los Santos to a high of 3.5 percent in Panamá (see table 3, Appendix A). The population in Bocas del Toro, both in remote and rural areas, grew at an average annual rate of approximately 3.1 percent. This high growth rate was due to a significant influx of migrants in response to the development of the Cerro Colorado copper project in the eastern part of that province (see Mining, ch. 3). Population density was seventy-five persons per square kilometer. The highest densities and the region of the most concentrated urbanization were located in the corridor along the former Canal Zone from Colón to Panama City.

The crude death rate was 5 persons per 1,000 in the mid-1980s, a decline of nearly 50 percent from the mid-1960s. The crude birth rate was 27 per 1,000, a drop of one-third during the same period. Organized family planning began in 1966 with the establishment of the Panamanian Family Planning Organization, a private group. By 1969 the Ministry of Health was actively involved in family planning; clinics, information, and instruction were becoming more available to the population as a whole. By the late 1970s and early 1980s, more than 60 percent of women of childbearing age were using some form of contraception.

Ethnic Groups

Because the isthmus holds a central position as a transit zone, Panama has long enjoyed a measure of ethnic diversity. This diversity, combined with a variety of regions and environments, has given rise to a number of distinct subcultures. But in the late 1980s, these subcultures were often diffuse in the sense that individuals were frequently difficult to classify as members of one group or the other, and statistics about the groups' respective sizes were rarely precise. Panamanians nonetheless recognized racial and ethnic distinctions and considered them social realities of considerable importance.

Broadly speaking, Panamanians viewed their society as composed of three principal groups: the Spanish-speaking, Roman Catholic mestizo majority; the English-speaking, Protestant Antillean blacks; and tribal Indians. Small numbers of those of foreign extraction— Chinese, Jews, Arabs, Greeks, South Asians, Lebanese, West Europeans, and North Americans—were also present. They generally lived in the largest cities, and most were involved in the retail trade and commerce. There were a few retired United States citizens—

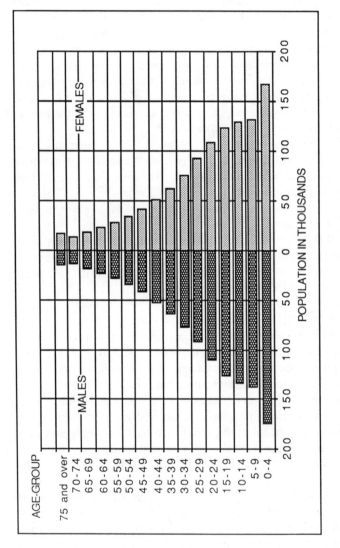

Source: Based on information from Panama, Directorate of Statistics and Census, *Estadística Panameña*, Vol. 970, Panama City, March 1985, 15.

Figure 6. Estimated Population by Age and Sex, 1987

mostly former Canal Zone officials—residing in Chiriquí. The Chinese were a major source of labor on the trans-isthmian railroad, completed in the mid-nineteenth century. Most went on to California in the gold rush beginning in 1848; of those who remained, most owned retail shops. They suffered considerable discrimination in the early 1940s under the nationalistic government of President Arnulfo Arias Madrid, who sought to rid Panama of non-Hispanics (see The War Years, ch. 1).

There were also small groups of Hispanic blacks, blacks (*playeros*), and Hispanic Indians (*cholos*) along the Atlantic coast lowlands and in the Darién. Their settlements, dating from the end of the colonial era, were concentrated along coasts and rivers. They had long relied on mixed farming and livestock raising, adapted to the particular exigencies of the tropical forest environment. In the mid-twentieth century, they began marketing small quantities of livestock, tropical fruits, rice, and coffee. In the 1980s, they were under pressure from the mestizo population, as farmers from the central provinces expanded into these previously isolated regions (see Rural Society, this ch.).

Antillean Blacks

Black laborers from the British West Indies came to Panama by the tens of thousands in the first half of the twentieth century. Most were involved in the effort to improve the isthmus transportation system, but many came to work on the country's banana plantations as well. By 1910 the Panama Canal Company had employed more than 50,000 workers, three-quarters of whom were Antillean blacks. They formed the nucleus of a community separated from the larger society by race, language, religion, and culture.

Since World War II, immigration from the Caribbean islands has been negligible. Roughly 7 to 8 percent of the population were Antillean blacks in the 1980s. Their share in the total population was decreasing, as younger generations descended from the original immigrants became increasingly assimilated into the Hispanic national society.

The Antillean community continued to be marked by its immigrant, West Indian origins in the 1980s. Some observers noted that Antillean families and gender ideals reflected West Indian patterns and that Antillean women were less submissive than their mestizo counterparts. The Antilleans were originally united by their persistent loyalty to the British crown, to which they had owed allegiance in the home islands. Many migrated to Panama with the intention of returning home as soon as they had earned enough money to permit them to retire. This apparently transient status, coupled with cultural differences, further separated them from the local populace. Another alienating factor was the hostility of Hispanic Panamanians, which increased as the Antilleans prolonged their stay and became entrenched in the canal labor force. They faced racial discrimination from North Americans as well. Their precarious status was underscored by the fact that the 1941 constitution deprived them of their Panamanian citizenship (it was restored by the 1946 constitution). The hostility they faced welded them into a minority united by the cultural antagonisms they confronted.

The cleavage between older and younger generations was particularly marked. Younger Antilleans who opted for inclusion in the Hispanic society at large generally rejected their parents' religion and language in so doing. Newer generations educated in Panamanian schools and speaking Spanish well identified with the national society, enjoying a measure of acceptance there. Nevertheless, there remained substantial numbers of older Antilleans who were trained in schools in the former Canal Zone and spoke English as a first language. They were adrift without strong ties to either the West Indian or the Panamanian Hispanic culture. Isolated from mainstream Panamanian society and increasingly removed from their Antillean origins, they existed, in a sense, on the margins of three societies.

In common with most middle- and many lower-class Panamanians, Antillean blacks valued education as a means of advancement. Parents ardently hoped to give their children as good an education as possible because education and occupation underlay the social hierarchy of the Antillean community. At the top of that hierarchy were ministers of the mainline Protestant religions, professionals such as doctors and lawyers, and white-collar workers. Nonetheless, even a menial worker could hope for respect and some social standing if he or she adhered to middle-class West Indian forms of marriage and family life, membership in an established church, and sobriety. The National Guard, formerly known as the National Police and subsequently called the Panama Defense Forces (Fuerzas de Defensa de Panamá—FDP), served as a means of integration into the national society and upward mobility for poorer blacks (Antilleans and Hispanics), who were recruited in the 1930s and 1940s when few other avenues of advancement were open to them (see Manpower, ch. 5).

Indians

According to the 1980 census, Panama's indigenous population numbered slightly over 93,000, or 5 percent of the total population (see table 4, Appendix A). Censuses showed Indians to be a declining proportion of the total population; they had accounted for nearly 6 percent of all Panamanians in 1960. The figures were only a rough estimate of the numbers of Indians in Panama, however. Precise numbers and even the exact status of several smaller tribes were uncertain, in part because many Indians were in the process of assimilation. Language, although the most certain means of identifying a person as an Indian, was by itself an unreliable guide. There were small groups of people who spoke only Spanish and yet preserved other indigenous practices and were considered Indians by their neighbors. The Guaymí, for example, showed little concern about linguistic purity and had adopted a wide variety of words of Spanish origin; nonetheless, they assiduously preserved indigenous religious belief and practice. By contrast, the far more acculturated Térraba would not use foreign words, even for non-indigenous items.

The Indian population was concentrated in the more remote regions of the country, and for most tribes, isolation was a critical element in their cultural survival. The Guaymí, numbering roughly 50,000 to 55,000, or slightly more than half of the Indian population, inhabited the remote regions of northwest Panama. The Cuna (also referred to as the Kuna) were concentrated mainly along the Caribbean coast east of Colón; their population was approximately 30,000, about one-third of all Indians.

In addition, there were a number of smaller groups scattered in the remote mountains of western Panama and the interior of Darién. The Chocó (or Embera) occupied the southeastern portion of Darién along the border with Colombia. Most were bilingual in Spanish and Chocó, and they reportedly had intermarried extensively with Colombian blacks. They appeared to be in a state of advanced acculturation.

The Bribri were a small section of the Talamanca tribe of Costa Rica. They had substantial contact with outsiders. Many were employed on banana plantations in Costa Rica, and Protestant missionaries were active among them, having made significant numbers of converts.

The Bókatá lived in eastern Bocas del Toro along the Río Calové-bora. Linguistically, Bókatá speech was similar to Guaymí, but the two languages were not mutually intelligible. The tribe had not been as exposed to outsiders as had the Guaymí. In the late 1970s, there were virtually no roads through Bókatá territory; by the mid-1980s, there was a small dirt road passable only in dry weather.

The Térraba were another small tribe, living in the environs of the Río Teribe. In the twentieth century, the tribe suffered major population swings. It was decimated by recurrent tuberculosis epidemics between 1910 and 1930, but population expanded rapidly with the availability of better medical care after the 1950s. Contact with outsiders also increased. A Seventh Day Adventist mission was active in the tribe for years, and there was substantial acculturation with the dominant mestizo culture. By the late 1980s, the Térraba had abandoned most of their native crafts production, and their knowledge of the region's natural history was declining. They even looted their ancestral burial mounds for gold to sell. They refused employment on nearby banana plantations until the early 1970s, when a flood swept away most of the alluvial soil they had farmed. The Guaymí attempted to include the Térraba in Guaymí territory, but the Térraba stoutly resisted these efforts.

All of the tribes were under the jurisdiction of both the provincial and national governments. The Indigenous Policy Section of the Ministry of Government and Justice bore primary responsibility for coordinating programs that affected Indians, serving as a liaison between the tribes and the national government. There were a number of special administrative arrangements made for those districts in which Indians constituted the majority of the population. The 1972 Constitution required the government to establish reserves (*comarcas*) for indigenous tribes, but the extent to which this mandate had been implemented varied. By the mid-1980s, the Cuna were established in the Comarca de San Blas and the Chocó had government approval for official recognition of their own *comarca* in Darién. The Guaymí and the government continued negotiations about the extent of Guaymí territory. The Guaymí contended that government proposals would leave about half the tribe outside the boundaries of the reserve.

Indian education has frequently been under the de facto control of missionaries. The national government made a late entry into the field, but by the late 1970s there were nearly 200 Indian schools with nearly 15,000 students. Nevertheless, illiteracy among Indians over 10 years of age was almost 80 percent, in comparison with less than 20 percent in the population at large.

Cuna

The vast majority of Cuna Indians inhabited the San Blas Islands, with an estimated 3,000 additional Cuna living in small scattered settlements in Darién and in Colombia. The San Blas Islands are clusters of small coral islands, each only a few feet above sea level, along Panama's northeast coast. They contain some fifty densely settled Cuna villages. The density of settlement was one indication of a dramatic increase in population. Official census figures

San Blas Cuna Indian villages
Courtesy Organization of American States

showed a population increase of nearly 60 percent between 1950 and 1980. The 1980 census revealed that village size ranged from 37 to nearly 1,500 inhabitants; half the total population was accounted for in 19 villages ranging in population from 300 to 1,000, with one-third in settlements of more than 1,000. The census seriously undercounted the total Cuna population, however, because it excluded absent workers, whose numbers were significant, given the prevalence of out-migration for wage labor.

Before settling on the San Blas Islands, the Cuna lived in inland settlements concentrated on rivers and streams throughout the Darién. Their contacts with outsiders were confined to trade with pirates and limited interaction with two abortive European colonies attempted in the region in the late seventeenth and early eighteenth centuries. Then, a 1787 treaty with Spain began roughly a century of profitable trade, and the Cuna specialized in coconut farming, which continues to produce their main cash crop. Pressure from mestizo and Chocó Indians migrating into the Darién from Colombia toward the end of the nineteenth century gradually pushed the Cuna toward the coast and the villages they still occupied in the late 1980s.

The Cuna's contact with outsiders remained limited and circumscribed until around 1910. Panamanian settlement was focused along the isthmus, and the Colombian government was, in every significant sense, very distant. Although the Cuna themselves traded with passing ships, they did not permit the crews to debark. An individual Cuna might, however, serve a stint as a sailor, and groups would take a large canoe full of trading goods to Colón.

The Cuna were extensively dependent on outside sources for goods—indigenously produced items played little role in farming and fishing. In contrast to many rural mestizos and Indians elsewhere in Panama, the terms on which they bought outside manufactures were relatively favorable. The Cuna dealt only in cash; they bought from many suppliers; and Cuna themselves owned retail stores in San Blas.

By the early years of the twentieth century, the modern settlement pattern of the San Blas Cuna was well defined. Settlements varied in scale from temporary working camps of one to two families to permanent communities numbering in the hundreds. Social life then, as now, was organized around the twin foci of household and village. Descent was reckoned bilaterally, individuals tracing their ancestors and their progeny through both males and females. The household was the most significant grouping of kin. A 1976 survey found that households numbered on average 9.9 persons, with multiple family households the rule. Larger groupings of kin had no formal role in social relations. Adult siblings were rarely close, and contacts between more distant relatives, such as cousins, were even more diffuse.

Cuna households, in their ideal form, were composed of a senior couple, their unmarried children, and their married daughters and sons-in-law and their offspring. The head of the household directed the work of those residing there; a son-in-law's position was extremely subordinate, particularly during the early years of his marriage. After several years of marriage, husbands usually tried to establish their own households, but the shortage of suitable land made this difficult.

Women were a major force in household decisions. Their sewing and household activities were respected work. Men dominated the public-political sphere of Cuna life, however, and women were overwhelmingly subordinate to men outside their homes. Only a few women had been elected to public office, but daughters of leaders sometimes held government appointments.

Politics and kinship were separate aspects of Cuna life. Kin, even close relatives, did not necessarily support one another on specific issues. Although the children of past leaders enjoyed some advantage in pursuing a career in politics, kinship did not define succession to political office.

Villages had formal, ranked elective political offices, including the chiefs and the chiefs' spokespersons (also known as interpreters). Most communities also had a set of committees charged with specific tasks. Chiefs (except in the most acculturated communities where the chiefs did not sing) derived their authority from their knowledge of the sacred chants, and the spokespersons derived theirs from their ability to interpret the chants for the people. Elected officials conducted elaborate meetings dealing with both religious and secular affairs. The number of officials, the presence or absence of a specifically designated meeting place, and the number and complexity of the meetings themselves were all measures of a village's stature.

Meetings or gatherings fell into two categories: chanting or singing gatherings attended by all members of a village and talking gatherings attended by adult men only. Singing gatherings were highly formalized, combining both indigenous and Spanish elements. The ritualized dialogue that chiefs chanted to their followers was common Indian practice throughout much of Latin America. Much of the actual vocabulary reflected Spanish influence. For example, the Cuna word for chief's spokesperson, *arkar,* is probably a corruption of the Spanish, *alcalde.*

Talking gatherings focused on exchanging information and taking care of matters that demanded action—relating travel experiences, requesting permission to leave, or resolving disputes, for example. Resolution was reached through consensus in a gradual process directed by the chief or chiefs. Votes were rarely taken, and then only in the more acculturated communities. Agreement was evident when no further contrary opinions were stated. Historically, if an agreement could not be reached, the community would split up.

Cuna also held general congresses as frequently as several times per year. Each village sent a delegation; the size varied but typically at least one chief and a chief's spokesperson were included. The rules of procedure were highly formalized. As with local gatherings, the emphasis was on reaching a consensus of the group rather than acquiring the votes necessary for a majority. And, again, agreement was evident when no further contrary opinions were stated or when they were shouted down by the rest of the delegates.

Villages had considerable discretionary powers, and they regulated who could settle there. Most refused to accept Colombian Cuna displaced by cattle ranchers. Others expressed disapproval of landless San Blasinos (residents of San Blas) from other villages marrying into their village. The power of villages to grant or withhold travel permits was used as a sanction against misconduct and a weapon in political disputes. Women were rarely permitted to travel outside San Blas, and until the mid-1960s, many villages required an absentee worker to come home for harvest and planting or pay for a substitute.

Villages varied in their willingness to accept innovations. In general, the Cuna of eastern San Blas were more conservative, while those of the western and central parts more readily accepted outside influences. Modernist villages sent more workers to the larger society; conservative communities tended to rely more extensively on agricultural income for their livelihood. Village politics were concerned with questions of inheritance, boundary disputes, land sales, and property theft.

Land was privately held. As population increased, landholding and inheritance were more critical. In theory, all children had an equal right to inherit their parents' fields. In practice, though, most land passed from father to son. Sons, after fulfilling the labor obligations to their in-laws, farmed with their fathers.

Some coconut groves were held in common by the descendants of the original owner; common ownership gave these groups of descendants a strategic importance in controlling resources. Cooperative societies played a significant role in various economic ventures and had a major impact on coconut production, transporting, and selling.

Slash-and-burn farming on uninhabited islands and the mainland was the major economic activity, providing most subsistence. Bananas were the primary subsistence crop; coconuts, the main cash crop. Sources of nonagricultural income included migrant wage labor, the sale of hand-sewn items by Cuna women, and tourism. Most of the tourists were day visitors, but there were several resorts in the San Blas Islands owned by Cuna, United States citizens, and Panamanians. The Cuna also owned retail stores on the San Blas Islands.

Migrant wage labor was the most common source of nonfarm income. The Cuna have a long history as migrant laborers, beginning with their service as sailors on passing ships in the nineteenth century. In the early decades of the twentieth century, Cuna did short stints in Panama City, Colón, and on banana plantations. Later they worked in the Canal Zone. The United Fruit Company banana plantations in Changuinola and Almirante were frequent destinations for Cuna. The company viewed the Cuna as exemplary employees, and a few were promoted to managerial or semimanagerial positions as of the late 1980s. Migrant labor was a part of the experience of almost every young male Cuna in his late teens or early twenties. In contrast with most of rural Panama, however, women left San Blas very infrequently. A mid-1970s survey found that less than 4 percent of San Blas women of all ages were living away.

Missionary activity among the Cuna began with the Roman Catholics in 1907 and Protestant denominations in 1913. Non-Panamanian Protestants were banned in 1925. A small Baptist mission returned with legal guarantees of freedom of confession in the 1950s. The presence of missionaries was a bone of contention between modernist and traditional Cuna for decades. Christianity spread unevenly through the archipelago, and the San Blasinos often resisted it tenaciously. Converts were often lax in their adherence to the new creeds; indigenous belief and practice remained prominent. The Baptist mission, noted one anthropologist, was "thoroughly Kuna-ized."

Ritual was a major focus of Cuna concern and a significant part of the relations between non-kin. It formed the basis for community solidarity and esprit. A man gained prestige through his mastery of rituals and chants. Virtually the entire village took part in female puberty rites, which were held several times each year; much social interaction followed ritualized patterns closely.

Lavish sharing was an esteemed virtue; stinginess was disparaged. Thus, the Cuna continued to celebrate community solidarity through feasting, gift giving, and ritual. The community offered food to visitors and entertained at public expense. The plethora of celebrations in the Cuna calendar offered ample occasions to display their generosity.

Many Cuna recognized the value of literacy, and schools had a long history in the archipelago. In the nineteenth century, some Cuna learned to read and write during periods of migrant labor. By the early 1900s, there were a few primary schools in San Blas. There was some resistance among the more conservative elements in Cuna society, but in general education encountered far less opposition than did missionaries' proselytizing. In the 1980s, most settlements of any size had a primary school; there were also several secondary schools. It was not uncommon for Cuna to migrate to further their education—there was a contingent of Cuna at the University of Panama, and a few had studied abroad. On islands with the longest history of schooling, illiteracy rates among those 10 years of age and older were in the range of 15 percent in the late 1970s. The 4 villages that had refused schools until the late 1960s and early 1970s averaged nearly 95 percent illiterate. Overall, more than half the Cuna population over ten years of age was literate, and a comparable proportion of those aged seven to fifteen were in school.

Cuna relations with outsiders, especially the Panamanian government, have frequently been stormy. In general, however, the Cuna have managed to hold their own more effectively than most indigenous peoples. Early in the twentieth century, there were several Cuna confederacies, each under the aegis of the main village's chief. The chiefs negotiated with outsiders on behalf of the villages within their alliance.

In 1930 the national government recognized the semiautonomous status of the San Blas Cuna; eight years later the government formed the official Cuna reserve, the Comarca de San Blas. The Carta Orgánica, legislated by Law 16 of 1953, established the administrative structure of the reservation.

Tensions between the state and the Cuna increased under the rule of Omar Torrijos Herrera (1968–81) as the government attempted to alter Cuna political institutions. Cuna were unhappy over the appointment of Hispanics rather than Cuna to sensitive posts. Relations reached a low point during the controversy surrounding government plans to promote tourism in the region, threatening San Blas's status as a reserve. The conflict ended, however, with the reaffirmation of the reserve's status. The extent of Cuna disagreements with the national government was reflected in their vote in the 1977 referendum on the Panama Canal treaties: San Blas was the only electoral district to reject the treaties. For

*Cuna girls
in traditional dress
Courtesy Agency for
International Development*

the Cuna, this action was less a statement about the fate of the former Canal Zone or Panamanian sovereignty than their rather strongly held views about their autonomy. Although many government-sponsored reforms were incorporated into Cuna political institutions, the San Blasinos continued to exercise a significant measure of autonomy.

Guaymí

The Guaymí Indians were concentrated in the more remote regions of Bocas del Toro, Chiriquí, and Veraguas. Because their territory was divided by the Cordillera Central, the Guaymí resided in two sections that were climatically and ecologically distinct. On the Pacific side, small hamlets were scattered throughout the more remote regions of Chiriquí and Veraguas; on the Atlantic side, the people remained in riverine and coastal environments.

Contact was recorded between outsiders and Guaymí in the seventeenth and eighteenth centuries. Spanish colonial policy tried to group the Indians into settlements (*reducciones*) controlled by missionaries. This policy enjoyed only limited success in the area of modern Panama. Although some Indians converted to Christianity and gradually merged with the surrounding rural mestizo populace, most simply retreated to more remote territories.

Roman Catholic missionaries had sporadic contact with the Guaymí after the colonial era. Protestant missionaries—mostly

Methodists and Seventh-Day Adventists—were active on the fringes of Guaymí territory on the Atlantic side, beginning in the early twentieth century. The Guaymí were impressed by missionaries because most missionaries, unlike mestizos, did not try to take advantage of them in economic dealings.

Present-day contact was most intense in Veraguas, where the mestizo farmers were expanding into previously remote lands at a rapid rate. Guaymí in Bocas del Toro and Chiriquí were less affected. The entry of these outsiders effectively partitioned Guaymí lands. There was a rise in the proportion of tribal members bilingual in Spanish and Guaymí, substantial numbers of whom eventually abandoned Guaymí and disclaimed their Indian identity.

Government schools, especially along the Atlantic portion of Guaymí territory, attracted Indian settlements. Many parents were anxious for their children to attend at least primary school. They arranged for their children to board as servants with Antillean black families living in town, so that the children could attend classes. The outcome was a substantial number of Guaymí young adults who were trilingual in Guaymí, Spanish, and English.

Guaymí subsistence relied on crop raising, small-scale livestock production, hunting, and fishing. In contrast to the slash-and-burn agriculture practiced by the majority mestizo population, Guaymí agriculture was more similar to the type of exploitation practiced in the pre-Columbian era. It placed less reliance on machete and match, and more emphasis on the gradual selective clearing and weeding of plots at the seedling stage of crop growth. The Guaymí burned some trees (that did not have to be felled), but generally left more vegetation to decay. This strategy did not subject the fragile tropical soils to the intense leaching that often follows clear cutting and burning of the tropical forest. The Guaymí agricultural system relied upon an intimate and detailed knowledge of the forest flora. The Guaymí marked seasons not as much by changes in temperature and precipitation as by differences in plants. They noted the times of the year by observing when various plants matured. As an agricultural system it was highly diversified, and the wide range of crop varieties planted conferred resistance to the diverse pests that afflict more specialized farming systems. As an example, Guaymí banana trees produced fruit for sale during all the years that blight had essentially shut down the commercial banana plantations in the region.

Like much of rural Panama, Guaymí territories were subjected to considerable pressure. The length of time land was left fallow decreased. In addition, there were few stands of even well-established secondary forest, let alone untouched tropical forest.

In the more intensively used regions, cultivators noted the proliferation of the short, coarse grasses that are the bane of traditional slash-and-burn agricultural systems (see Rural Society, this ch.).

The decline in stands of virgin and secondary forest led to a decrease in wildlife, which affected the Guaymí diet. Domestic livestock grew in importance as a source of protein because larger animals, such as tapir, deer, and peccary, once plentiful, were available only occasionally. Smaller livestock, such as poultry, was extremely vulnerable to disease and predation. Pigs and cattle were raised, but they were among the most consistently saleable products available; as a result, the Guaymí had to choose between protein and cash income. Overall, the diet was quite starchy, with bananas, manioc, and yams the main food items.

Wildlife was adversely affected by modern hunting techniques, also. Traditional hunting and fishing techniques had a minimal impact on the species involved. However, the small-caliber rifles, flashlights, and underwater gear used by Guaymí in the modern era were far more destructive.

The link of most Guaymí to the market economy was similar to that of many poorer rural mestizos. The Indians bought such items as clothing, cooking utensils, axes, blankets, alcohol, sewing machines, wristwatches, and radios. They earned the money for these purchases through period wage labor and the sale of livestock, crops, and crafts (the most unpredictable source of income).

Most Guaymí young men had some experience as wage laborers, although their opportunities were usually limited and uncertain. Some acquired permanent or semipermanent jobs. A few managed to get skilled employment as mechanics or overseers. Fewer still became teachers. The principal employers for Guaymí were the surrounding banana plantations and cattle ranches. Because government policy after the 1950s limited the hiring of foreign laborers on the plantations, Guaymí formed a major part of the banana plantation work force. A number of Indian families settled in towns to work on the plantations. Nonetheless, the wages Guaymí earned proved illusory since most, if not all, of their earnings were spent on living expenses while away from home.

The Guaymí link to the national economy not only provided cash for the purchase of a variety of consumer goods but also acted as a safety valve, relieving the pressure on land. Their dependence on this link was evident during the 1960s, when the Guaymí endured a real hardship because of a decline in demand for labor on banana plantations.

Settlement patterns among the Guaymí were intimately linked to kinship and social organization. Hamlets, each typically representing a single extended family, were scattered throughout the territory. There were no larger settlements of any permanence serving as trading or ceremonial centers. A few mestizo towns on the fringes of Guaymí territory served as trading posts.

Each hamlet was ideally composed of a group of consanguineally related males, their wives, and their unmarried children. Nevertheless, this general rule glossed over residence patterns of considerable fluidity and complexity. At least at some points in an individual's life, he or she resided in a three-generation household. Households, however, took many forms, including nuclear families; polygynous households; groups of brothers, their wives, and unmarried children; a couple, their unmarried children, and married sons and their wives and children; or a mother, her married sons, and their wives and children.

A hamlet defined an individual's social identity, and access to land and livelihood was gained through residence in a specific hamlet. Typically, a person's closest kin resided there. The wide variety of family forms represented in hamlets reflected the diverse ways individual Guaymí used the ties of kinship to gain access to land. Depending on the availability of plots, an individual couple might live with the husband's family (the ideal), the wife's kin, the husband's mother (if his parents did not live together), the husband's mother's kin, or his father's mother's kin.

Guaymí had pronounced notions about which tasks were appropriately male or female; but men would build fires, cook, and care for children if necessary and women would, as the occasion demanded, weed and chop firewood. Women were never supposed to clear forest, herd cattle, or hunt. Nonetheless, a measure of expediency dictated who actually performed the required duties. Because most men migrated to look for employment, a significant segment of the agricultural work force was absent for lengthy periods of time. Consequently, women assumed a larger share of the farmwork during those absences. Their own male kinsmen helped with the heavier tasks. Children began assisting their parents at approximately eight years of age. By the time a girl was fourteen to fifteen years old and a boy seventeen to eighteen, they were expected to do the work of an adult.

Sharing of food and labor was an important form of exchange among kin. If a hamlet needed food, a woman or child would be sent to solicit food from relatives. Kin also formed a common labor pool for virtually all agricultural work. Guaymí did not hire each other as wage laborers. Non-kin assisted each other only for specific festive or communal works. Within the hamlet, all able-bodied family members were expected to contribute labor. Kin from different hamlets exchanged labor on a day-by-day basis. Individuals were careful not to incur too many obligations so as not to compromise their own household's agricultural production. Those who received assistance were obliged to provide food, meat, and *chicha* (a kind of beer) for all the workers. Moreover, there was supposed to be enough food to send a bit home with each worker.

Marriage was the primary means by which Guaymí created social ties to other (non-kin) Guaymí. The ramifications of marriage exchanges extended far beyond the couple concerned. The selection of a spouse was the choice of an allied group and reflected broader concerns such as access to land and wealth, resolution of longstanding disputes, or acquisition of an ally in a previously nonaligned party.

Fathers usually arranged marriages for children. An agreement was marked by a visit of the groom and his parents to the home of the prospective bride and her family. The marriage itself was fixed through a series of visits between the two households involved. No formal ceremony marked the event. Ideally, marriage arrangements were to be balanced exchanges between two kin groups.

Initially the young couple resided with the bride's parents because a son-in-law owed his parents-in-law labor. Thus, a bride usually did not leave her natal hamlet for at least a year. For the husband, persuading his wife to leave her family and join his was a major, and often insurmountable, hurdle. If the marriage conformed to the ideal of a balanced exchange, however, a husband's task was considerably easier in that his wife had to join him or her brother would not receive a wife.

Young men in groups without daughters to exchange in marriage were at a disadvantage. Although they could (and did) ask for wives without giving a sister in return, the fathers of the brides gained significantly. A son-in-law whose family did not provide a bride to his wife's family faced longer labor obligations to his in-laws and uncertainty about when, or if, his wife would join him and his family.

A minority of all marriages were polygynous. Traditionally, a man's ability to support more than one wife was testimony to his wealth and prestige. Co-wives were often sisters. A man could marry his wife's younger sister after he had established a household and acquired sufficient resources to support two families. Wives lived together until their sons matured and married. At that time, an extended household would reconstitute itself around a woman and her married sons and their wives and children. Younger wives in polygynous marriages had a tendency to leave their husbands as they aged. A reasonably successful Guaymí man might expect to begin his married life in a monogamous union, have several wives as he grew more wealthy, and finish his life again in a monogamous marriage.

In general, there were few external indications of differences in wealth, and there was no formal ranking of status in Guaymí society. Prestige accrued to the individual Guaymí male who was able to demonstrate largesse in meeting his obligations to kin and in-laws. A young man began to gain the respect of his in-laws by providing them well with food and labor. He further demonstrated his abilities by farming his own plots well enough to provide for his family and those of his kin who visited.

An individual might also gain prestige through his ability to settle differences. Historically, disputes between Guaymí were settled at public meetings chaired by a person skilled in arbitration. An individual's prestige was in proportion to his ability to reach a consensus among the parties involved in the dispute. In present-day Guaymí society, a government-appointed representative decided the case. Guaymí gained prestige by proposing settlements more acceptable to the disputants than those of the government representative. As an individual's reputation spread, other disputants sought him out to arbitrate. The entire process emphasized the extent to which indigenous political structures were acephalous and loosely organized. There were no durable, well-organized, non-kin groups that functioned in the political sphere; decision making was largely informal and consensual.

In the 1980s, government plans to develop the Cerro Colorado copper mine, along the Cordillera Central in eastern Chiriquí Province, gave impetus to the efforts of some Guaymí to organize politically. Most of the mining project as well as a planned slurry pipeline, a highway, and the Changuinola I Hydroelectric Project were in territory occupied by the Guaymí. Guaymí attended a number of congresses to protect their claims to land and publicize their misgivings about the projects. The Guaymí were concerned about the government's apparent lack of interest in their plight, about the impact on their lands and their productivity, and about the effect of dam construction on fishing and water supplies. Guaymí were also worried that proposed cash indemnification payments for lands or damages would be of little benefit to them in the long run. As of late 1987, however, the matter had not been fully resolved.

Social Organization

Family and Kin

In the late 1980s, family and kin continued to play a central role in the social lives of most Panamanians. An individual without kin to turn to for protection and aid was in a precarious position. Loyalty to one's kin was an ingrained value, and family ties were considered one's surest defense against a hostile and uncertain world. This loyalty often outweighed that given to a spouse; indeed, a man frequently gave priority to his responsibility to his parents or siblings over that extended to his wife.

Co-resident parents, children, and others living with them constituted the basic unit of kinship. Family members relied upon each other for assistance in major undertakings throughout life. Extended kin were important as well. Grandparents, uncles, aunts, and cousins faithfully gathered to mark birthdays and holidays together. Married children visited their parents frequently—even daily. In some small remote villages and in some classes (such as the elite), generations of intermarriage created a high measure of interrelatedness, and almost everyone could trace a kinship link with everyone else. Co-residence, nonetheless, remained the basis for the most enduring ties an individual formed.

A significant portion of all marriage unions were consensual rather than contractual. A formal marriage ceremony often represented the culmination of a life together for many mestizo and Antillean couples. It served as a mark of economic success. Grown children sometimes promoted their parents' formal marriage. Alternatively, a priest might encourage it for an elderly sick person, as a prerequisite for receiving the rite of the anointing of the sick.

The stability of consensual marriages varied considerably. In rural areas where campesinos' livelihood was reasonably secure and population relatively stable, social controls bolstered informal unions. Mestizos themselves made no distinction between the obligations and duties of couples in a consensual or a legal marriage. Children suffered little social stigma if their parents were not legally married. If the union was unstable and there were children, the paternal grandparents sometimes took in both mother and children. Or, a woman might return to her mother's or her parents' household, leaving behind her children so that she could work. Nevertheless, there were a significant number of female-headed families, particularly in cities and among the poorest segment of the population.

Formally constituted legal marriage was the rule among the more prosperous campesinos, cattle ranchers, the urban middle class, and the elite. Marriage played a significant role for the elite in defining and maintaining the family's status. A concern for genealogy, imputed racial purity, and wealth were major considerations. Repeated intermarriage made the older elite families into a broadly interrelated web of kin. As one upper-class wife noted, ". . . no member of my family marries anyone whose greatgrandparents were unknown to us."

Men were expected to be sexually active outside of marriage. Keeping a mistress was acceptable in virtually every class. Among the wealthier classes, a man's relationship with his mistress could take on a quasi-formal, permanent quality. An elite male could entertain his mistress on all but the most formal social occasions, and he could expect to receive friends at the apartment he had provided for her. Furthermore, he would recognize and support the children she bore him.

The ideal focus for a woman, by contrast, was home, family, and children. Children were a woman's main goal and consolation in life. The tie between mother and child was virtually sacrosanct, and filial love and respect deeply held duties. Whatever her husband's extramarital activities, a woman's fidelity had to be above reproach. An elite or middle-class woman derived considerable solace from her status as a man's legal wife. Nevertheless, middle-class and more educated women often found their traditional role and the division of labor irksome and were particularly offended by the diversion of family funds into their husbands' pursuit of pleasure.

Campesinos, too, divided social life into its properly male and female spheres: "The man is in the fields, the woman is in the home." As a corollary, men were "of the street" and able to visit at will. Women who circulated too freely were likened to prostitutes; men who performed female tasks were thought to be dominated by their wives.

Childrearing practices reinforced the traditional male and female roles and values to a greater or lesser degree among all classes. Boys were permitted considerably more latitude and freedom than girls. Girls were typically tightly supervised, their companions screened, and their activities monitored.

Because children were deeply desired, their birth was celebrated, and a baptism was a major family event. The selection of godparents (*padrinos*) was an important step that could have a pronounced influence on the child's welfare and future. It resulted in a quasi-kinship relationship that carried with it moral, ceremonial, and religious significance, and broadened family ties of trust, loyalty, and support.

Parents tried to choose for their children godparents whom they respected, and trusted, and who were as high on the social scale as possible. A certain degree of formality and ceremony was expected of godparents in social interaction, but the bonds primarily involved protective responsibility and a willingness to render assistance in adversity.

Campesinos followed two distinct patterns in choosing godparents. The parents might choose a person of wealth, power, or prestige, thereby gaining an influential protector. Such a contact could give a parent the confidence to launch a child into an alien outside world, in which he or she might have little personal status or experience. By contrast, among some campesinos there was strong informal pressure in the opposite direction. They believed it was inappropriate to ask someone of higher economic status to act as a godparent, so they sought out instead a relative or friend, especially one who lived in the same area. The choice here tended to reinforce existing social ties and loyalties.

Rural Society

The opening of the trans-isthmian railroad in the mid-nineteenth century and the Panama Canal early in the twentieth century reinforced the distinctions basic to Panamanian society: the dichotomies between rural and urban inhabitants; small-scale, mixed agriculturalists and larger cattle ranchers; the landless and landowners; and mestizos and whites. By the late 1980s, urban-based control over rural lands was considerable. The metropolitan elite not only had substantial rural landholdings, but monopolized pivotal political posts as well. Wealthy city dwellers also controlled food-processing and transportation facilities. For the bulk of the mestizo peasants, though, limited population and ample reserves of land made elite control of resources less onerous than it might have been, as did the fact that urban elites tended to view their holdings less as agricultural enterprises than as estates in the countryside.

Traditional slash-and-burn agriculture was the basis of rural livelihood for most human settlement on the isthmus (see Agriculture, ch. 3). All able-bodied household members were expected to contribute to the family's support. The peasant family was a single production and consumption unit. There was a marked division of labor by sex, and most of the work associated with crops and planting was done by men. Mestizos recognized the significant contribution children made to the agricultural output of a household. Boys and girls gradually assumed responsibilities for assisting with the duties deemed appropriate to their gender. As children, especially boys, grew older, they received part of the income from the sale of crops or part of a field that was ''in their name.''

Agricultural production was geared to the household's consumption. A family typically kept some livestock and planted a variety of foodstuffs, of which maize was the principal crop. Peasants gained temporary access to land by entering an agreement to clear and maintain cattle pastures for absentee landowners. A family would agree to clear a stand of forest (ideally secondary growth) and plant it in crops for one to two years. At the end of the cycle, they would often seed the plot with grasses before moving on to a new site. Peasants also owed landowners a minimal number of days in labor each year. They faced further demands on their labor to build and maintain communal buildings, such as churches and schools, and to assist with certain public works required by the government.

Since the 1950s, however, traditional slash-and-burn farming and the system of social relations it supports have been in the throes of change. Increasing population pressure, the rapid expansion of cattle ranching, and production of a variety of other cash crops in the interior provinces have put pressure on the land base necessary to maintain slash-and-burn agriculture while preserving the tropical forest. Improved transportation has been accompanied by a rapid expansion in cattle ranching in regions hitherto inaccessible. The process as a whole has meant an increasing consolidation of landholdings and displacement of traditional small-scale farmers engaged in mixed crop and livestock production. The number of farms classified as family owned and operated has declined, in favor of larger units worked by agricultural laborers. This pattern has been accompanied by an increase in and intensification of land disputes.

The consolidation process has been particularly intense in the lowlands of the Pacific coast and in Colón Province southwest of the city of Colón. In these regions, the expansion of the road network and the increasing number of all-weather roads have given potential cattle ranchers access to the large urban beef markets in Colón and Panama City. Cattle ranches grew five-fold in size in the hinterlands of Colón Province in the 1960s. Similar forces had a comparable impact on the Pacific coast, where cattle ranching increased by more than 400 percent from the 1950s through the 1970s, and land values tripled.

The increased demands on the land base affected peasant farmers on many levels. Growing population pressure and the felling of most untouched stands of tropical forest meant a decrease of hunting and, therefore, of animal protein in the family diet. Peccary, deer, and iguana, once relatively common supplements to the mestizo diet, were less available. The same process limited the forest products available for home construction and firewood. Ironically, the expansion in cattle ranching limited the ability of small-scale farmers to keep larger livestock. The purchase price of cattle rose;

Mountainous countryside in Chiriquí Province
Courtesy Organization of American States

and, because increased planting meant that animals could not forage as freely as before, they had to be penned or fenced. Finally, where drought-resistant pasture grasses were seeded, the forest itself regenerated much more slowly—limiting still further the land's ability to support an expanding population of both cattle ranchers and small farmers.

The decline in the land available for slash-and-burn agriculture and the increase in cash cropping also drew peasants more deeply into commercialized agriculture in the 1980s. At the same time that small farmers faced declining harvests and increased pressure on the family's subsistence base, they were forced to compete in markets for cash crops where the price was largely determined by larger-scale producers. Most of their production of cash crops was sporadic and in response to unpredictable situations. Difficulties in marketing placed small producers at a further disadvantage.

Sugarcane provides an instructive example. Farmers often planted sugarcane as a second-year crop in the fields they had cleared. The crop was pressed on the draft-animal presses some families owned and used for home consumption. As transportation improved, more small farmers gained access to large-scale, commercial sugarcane mills and had the option of growing sugarcane on contract for the mills. Although this opportunity offered the cultivator a possible source of more reliable income, small farmers were disadvantaged in a number of ways. Planting cane precludes using a plot for foodstuffs during the second year of cultivation. In addition, it requires hired labor, and small-scale producers were hard pressed to offer wages competitive with those that larger farmers or the mills themselves could pay. Finally, small farmers were unable to control the timing of their harvesting, which is essential for gaining optimal yields, because producers had to cut and transport their harvest whenever they were able to contract laborers and truckers for hauling the crop to the mill.

By the late 1980s, peasant families had become vastly more dependent on the money economy. In many regions, consumer goods replaced the traditional craft items produced at home, and hired labor was used in preference to labor exchange among households. Neighbors previously linked through myriad ties of exchange and interdependence were now bound by their common link with external markets. The amount of cash purchases families had to make rose dramatically: corrugated roofing replaced thatch, metal cookware replaced gourds and wooden utensils, nails served instead of vines as fasteners, and, in rare instances, gas stoves were used instead of wood-burning ranges.

Peasant families had a variety of subsidiary sources of income at their disposal. Men and women alike had opportunities to earn a little cash income. Women husked and cleaned rice for neighbors who could afford to pay, sewed, made hats, cooked, and washed clothes, while men made furniture. Those fortunate enough to own draft animals or trucks hauled goods for other farmers. Depending on location, season, and a variety of other factors, there was occasional demand for casual laborers. Such options represented a "safety net" that farmers took advantage of when crops failed or harvests were short. Nevertheless, nonfarming sources of income did not represent a viable alternative to agriculture for most families.

The general increase in cash in circulation affected various segments of the rural population differently. Younger or more highly educated and trained workers were able to compete for better-paying jobs and thus outearn their parents. Despite this, the impact on family life was cushioned because parents never counted on controlling their grown children. In one sense, families were better off because well-employed children were better able to assist their elderly parents. Where the increased cash purchases included milled rice, women were spared the arduous task of husking and milling rice themselves. Educational opportunities benefited all able to take advantage of them. Women gained in particular from the increase in employment opportunities for primary-school teachers.

In addition to peasant farmers and ranchers, Panama had the core of a rural educated middle class by the mid-twentieth century. Frequently educated at the teachers' college in Santiago, in the province of Veraguas, these educated sons and daughters of more prosperous agriculturalists and small merchants were of marginal influence in comparison with the urban elite. Long excluded from any effective role in the nation's politics, they proved a bulwark of support for the Torrijos regime (see The Government of Torrijos and the National Guard, ch. 1).

Land reform legislation drafted under the influence of the Alliance for Progress in the early 1960s recognized the peasants' right to land (see The National Guard in Ascendance, ch. 1). Nevertheless, the law's consequences in the countryside were often unforeseen. The plots allocated under the law were usually too small to support slash-and-burn agriculture; they did not allow sufficient land for fallowing. And, for a substantial portion of peasant families, the cash outlay required to purchase land was prohibitive. Although the relatively poor were unable to assume such debts, the more prosperous were. Some of the more successful emigrants to the city managed to acquire land through land reform and rented it to farmers under terms equivalent to those previously available through larger absentee owners.

In the late 1960s and early 1970s, the government attempted to model its land reform efforts on a collective farming system borrowed from Chile (see Land Tenure and Agrarian Reform, ch. 3). The government acquired tax-delinquent properties and set up a variety of collectively operated agro-enterprises. The collectives enjoyed mixed success, however. They tended to be heavily mechanized and dependent on outside infusions of technical assistance and capital, while they generated only minimal employment. The most dramatic successes were achieved in regions like Veraguas Province where small farmers competed with cattle ranchers for land. Collectives were less successful in areas where smallholdings predominated.

Where small farmers held title to their lands—an infrequent pattern in traditional rural Panama—they often sold their lands to the larger, more heavily capitalized cattle ranches. The numbers of landless, or nearly landless, cultivators in search of plots to "borrow" for a season's planting rose. Substantial numbers of these displaced small farmers chose migration as an alternative.

Mestizo migrants from regions where cattle ranching was expanding entered the lowlands of the Atlantic coast and the Darién Peninsula in increasing numbers. Migrants arrived and cleared forest land (generally away from the rivers favored by the region's earlier black, Indian, Hispanic Indian, and Hispanic black settlers). The process then repeated itself: the new settlers remained for a few years until improved roads brought more cattle ranchers; the *colonos* (internal migrants) who originally cleared the forest then sold their lands and moved yet deeper into the tropical forest.

Migration

Migration has played an increasingly significant role in the lives of Panamanians and has followed a distinct pattern throughout the twentieth century. Population movement has been into those districts and provinces enjoying a period of economic prosperity, typically associated with the canal. As the economic boom peters out, the migrant population moves back to the primarily agricultural districts, to be reabsorbed into subsistence farming or small-scale businesses and services in the country's predominantly rural interior. The pattern has been repeated several times with the ebb and flow of economic activity. In the late 1980s, it remained to be seen what adaptations migrants would make given the shrinking rural land base.

The 1911 census provides a baseline for population movements throughout the century. At that time, the provinces of Chiriquí and Panamá accounted for nearly 40 percent of the total population. Chiriquí's growth was the result of migrants from Colombia in the nineteenth century; Panamá's came as a result of the canal construction begun just after the turn of the century. The central provinces—Veraguas, Coclé, Los Santos, and Herrera (in order of population)—accounted for slightly more than 40 percent of the total. The entire region had been populated along the coasts since the colonial era and had grown in response to increased demand for foodstuffs in Panama City and Colón in the second half of the nineteenth century. The decade following the census saw dramatic population growth in response to the United States presence and the building of the Panama Canal. The need to feed the massive numbers of Antillean black laborers who came to work on the construction project generated a boom in agriculture.

Subsequent censuses revealed a specific pattern of rural-rural and rural-urban migration. Some rural districts of a province lost population, while others even relatively close grew rapidly. The pattern reversed itself during periods of economic stagnation. Then, migrants retreated into subsistence agriculture in regions that had enjoyed limited participation in the previous boom. Between 1910 and 1920, for example, the Chepigana District in Darién was in the midst of a boom and enjoyed a significant influx of population, while the neighboring Pinogana District lost population. Their roles were reversed in the following decade.

The 1920s represented such a period of stagnation. The regions of highest growth in the previous decade grew much more slowly—if they grew at all. Colón and Bocas del Toro were the most heavily affected. Panamá Province continued to grow at rates slightly in excess of the national average; nonetheless, a large number of foreign workers left, as did a significant portion of the small business owners who had provisioned them and who were ruined by the decline in clientele.

Rural regions absorbed these surplus laborers and served as centers of population growth throughout the 1920s. Some such as Veraguas and Darién grew in excess of 5 percent annually during the intercensal period. District capitals in predominantly rural provinces tended to enjoy significant growth as well, probably as a result of their administrative functions, and the rise of banana plantations in Chiriquí attracted workers from throughout Central America.

The pattern reversed again in the late 1930s and mid-1940s. The immediate pre-World War II period as well as the war itself were times of significant economic expansion for the country as a whole. The province of Panamá headed the country in population growth, and the entire western portion of the province was a region of economic expansion. Colón, by contrast, lost in importance. Its annual rate of increase, 1.44 percent, was barely half the national average. The decline in Colón's fortunes reflected the centralization of economic and administrative activity in Panama City. Furthermore, Colón's importance as a port on the Atlantic diminished with the construction of the Trans-isthmian Highway (also known as the Boyd-Roosevelt Highway).

The economic expansion accompanying World War II eliminated problems associated with the increase in large-scale agro-enterprises in the interior. Although substantial numbers of small farmers were displaced, they were readily absorbed by the demand for labor in cities and the countryside. Even in the period of economic contraction following the war, cities in predominantly rural provinces enjoyed significant growth. The war fueled the development of small-scale industrial and processing activities throughout the country. The dimensions of this growth were such that large numbers of rural youngsters—sons and daughters of small farmers—remained in the provinces in which they were born rather than migrating to Panama City or the Canal Zone.

World War II also saw Panama's last major influx of foreign workers. Most of these workers left with the economic slowdown at the war's end. As in previous periods of economic contraction, increasing numbers of displaced migrants took refuge in subsistence farming. The late 1940s was a time of growth for the rural regions of the country.

Overall, population grew at an annual rate of 2.9 percent in the 1950s; Panama was in the midst of a demographic transition as birth rates remained high while death rates dropped. The press of the population on the land base reached critical proportions. Peasants, displaced by the spread of large-scale agro-enterprises in the country, found it more and more difficult to find unoccupied land to put into production. At the same time, rural-urban migrants found it increasingly difficult simply to return home and resume farming during periods of economic contraction.

The pressure on the land base was acute enough to precipitate significant conflict over holdings in the 1950s and 1960s. In the province of Panamá, peasants invaded and seized the land around Gatun Lake as well as some regions of the districts of La Chorrera, Capira, and Chaime. Although many of these squatters were successful in maintaining their claim on the holdings, most peasants in other parts of the country were not so fortunate. The expansion of large cattle ranches in much of Los Santos and Veraguas continued the migratory process begun earlier, and peasants were pushed farther and farther along the agricultural frontier.

Substantial numbers of these displaced peasants migrated to less settled regions in Chiriquí, Los Santos, and Veraguas. Likewise, banana plantations in Chiriquí and Bocas del Toro drew significant numbers of migrants. The principal destination for much of the rural populace, however, was Greater Panama City.

Nearly two-thirds of all migrants had as their destination the heavily urban province of Panamá—a proportion that has remained roughly constant since the 1950s. In terms of absolute numbers, Los Santos and Veraguas were the major contributors to the migration stream: together they accounted for one-third of all migrants. The relatively depressed districts around Colón contributed large numbers of migrants, as did a number of districts in Chiriquí and Bocas del Toro. Based on rates of out-migration rather than absolute numbers, Los Santos, Darién, and Coclé were the main places of origin.

Within the province of Panamá, the greater metropolitan area of Panama City attracted most migrants. The districts surrounding the city averaged a growth rate of more than 10 percent per year in the 1960s and 1970s. Panama City played a significant role in the migration patterns of virtually every other province in the country. Over 90 percent of the migrants from Darién went there,

as did roughly 80 percent of those from Coclé, Colón, Los Santos, and Veraguas. In the relatively prosperous mid-1960s to mid-1970s, most migrants managed to find employment. Many joined the ranks of peddlers and other small-scale self-employed individuals.

The manufacturing sector expanded significantly during the 1960s, resulting in a doubling of the industrial labor force. The service sector—traditionally the country's most dynamic—was fueled by the expansion of manufacturing as well as Panama's pivotal position as a transit zone. The service sector absorbed more than half the increase in the economically active population and grew at a rate of more than 6 percent annually. For the city-bound migrant, that meant jobs in public and domestic service and construction. Nevertheless, some observers expected the rate of migration to the metropolitan region to decline with economic reverses in the 1980s and the increase in opportunities in other regions, such as the Cerro Colorado copper project in Chiriquí.

Overall, the migration stream in the 1970s was composed of three components: rural-urban migrants (accounting for more than half of all migrants), urban-urban migrants (roughly one-quarter of all migrants), and urban-rural migrants (nearly 20 percent of those questioned about their place of residence 5 years earlier had been living in a city). The exact proportion and significance of urban-rural migration were difficult to judge. Approximately half the

105

migrants were former residents of the smaller cities of the interior and presumably had left their farms for seasonal work in a nearby city or to attend school. Nearly one-third of these return migrants had lived in Panama City and its environs. Many were specialized workers; others were peasants unable to find permanent employment in the city; still others were children sent home to be cared for by kin.

Those people who migrated were, as a whole, young. In the 1970s nearly 75 percent of them were under 35 years of age; among rural-urban migrants, the percentage rose to more than 80 percent. School-age migrants represented a significant group in the migration stream. Although many simply accompanied their parents on moves, a significant minority were sent by their rural families for education in nearby cities. Men formed the majority among rural-urban migrants to Colón; women, however, accounted for a slight majority of all rural-urban migrants. This tendency was most marked in migration of women to cities in the interior but was also found among migrants to Panama City. In general, observers attributed the high rate of female migration to the metropolitan region to the opportunities for employment available for young women there. Unemployment was lower among urban females than among their rural counterparts, whereas the reverse was true for males.

Urban Society

Since the 1950s, Panama has been in the midst of massive urban expansion. In 1960 slightly more than one-third of the total population was classified as urban; by the early 1980s, the figure had risen to 55 percent. Between 1970 and 1980, overall population increased by 2.5 percent per year, urban population by 2.8 percent, and the metropolitan population surrounding Panama City by 3.7 percent. Regional cities shared in the general urban expansion: the number of people in Santiago grew at 4.1 percent annually; David, 3.7 percent; and Chitré, 3.3 percent. Economically depressed Colón lagged with an annual increase of less than 0.5 percent. Economic activity and population density in Panama were concentrated along two main axes: the Pan-American Highway (also known as the the Inter-American Highway) on the Pacific corridor from La Chorrera to Tocumen and the Trans-isthmian Highway from Panama City to Colón (see fig. 8).

Far and away the most significant focus of urban development was the path following the former Canal Zone that stretches from Colón on the Atlantic coast to Panama City on the Pacific. In the mid-1980s, the region accounted for more than half the total

population of the country and over two-thirds of all those classified as inhabitants of cities. It also included most nonagricultural
economic activity: 76 percent of manufacturing, 85 percent of construction, 95 percent of transportation, and 84 percent of communications. Growth was not spread evenly throughout the region,
and since the 1950s, Panama City and its environs had eclipsed
Colón. Colón remained the only significant urban center on Panama's Atlantic coast, but by the early 1980s, substantial numbers
of that city's business and professional community had emigrated
in response to Panama City's expanding economy.

In terms of sheer numbers, most of the urban expansion was
concentrated in slum tenements and, since the 1950s, in squatter
settlements around the major cities. As was the case in most urban
trends, Panama City led the way. In 1958 there were 11 identifiable slums or squatter settlements housing 18,000 people associated
with the city; by the mid-1970s, there were some 34 slum communities, and their population had mushroomed more than five-fold.
Surveys indicated that 80 percent of slum and squatter settlement
inhabitants were migrants to the city.

Many of the tenements took the form of two-story frame houses
built as pre-World War I temporary housing for the canal labor
force. They continued to be occupied, although in the early 1980s
they were in an advanced state of decay. When one part of a building collapsed, slum dwellers continued to live in those sections of
the building that remained standing. The structures were frequently
condemned, which merely added to their attractiveness for impoverished city dwellers because the rent therefore dropped to nothing. Squatter settlements offered their own inducements. If squatters
were able to maintain their claims to land, the settlements tended
to improve and gained amenities over time. Because they were
essentially rent-free, they gave their inhabitants considerable advantages over costly and over-crowded, if more centrally located, tenements. A substantial portion of the squatters settled on government
land, and there were numerous programs to permit them to purchase their housing sites. The Torrijos regime allocated funds for
low-income housing projects, and there were efforts to upgrade the
amenities available to the urban poor. By the 1980s, about 96 percent of the urban population had access to potable water and nearly
70 percent had electricity. Despite indications of some slowing in
the rate of rural-urban migration in the 1980s, migrants represented
a major strain on public services and the economy's ability to generate employment.

Although rural society was relatively homogeneous and simple
in the social distinctions it made, urban Panama was not. It was

ethnically and socially diverse and highly stratified. City dwellers took note of ethnic or racial heritage, family background, income (and source of income), religion, culture, education, and political influences as key characteristics in classifying individuals.

But, in the late 1980s, the boundaries among the elite, the middle class, and the lower class were neither especially well defined nor impervious. The ambitious and lucky city dweller could aspire to better significantly his or her social and economic status. Neither were the distinctions between rural and urban inhabitants absolute. City and countryside were linked in numerous ways; given the frequency with which migrants moved, this year's urban worker was last year's and (not uncommonly) next year's peasant. There was considerable social mobility, principally from the lower to the middle class and generally on an individual rather than a group basis. Wealth, occupation, education, and family affiliation were the main factors affecting such mobility.

The Elite

Urban society in the late 1980s included virtually all members of the elite. Centered mainly in the capital, this class was composed of old families of Spanish descent and a few newer families of immigrants. All elite families were wealthy, but the assets of the immigrant families were more tightly linked with commerce and Panama's twentieth-century development as a transit zone. Older families were inclined to think of themselves an aristocracy based on birth and breeding. Newer families, lacking such illustrious antecedents, had less prestige and social status. Until the advent of Torrijos, whose power base was the National Guard, an oligarchy of older elite families virtually controlled the country's politics under the auspices of the Liberal Party (see Organizing the New Republic; the Oligarchy under Fire, ch. 1).

The upper class was a small, close-knit group that had developed strong ties of association and kinship over the years. Prominent family names recurred frequently in the news of the nation: Arias, Arosemena, Alemán, Chiari, Goytía, and de la Guardia. People without a claim to such a family background could gain acceptance, at least for their children, by marriage into an elite family.

Since colonial times, education had been recognized as a mark of status; hence, almost all men of elite status received a university education. Most attended private schools either at home or abroad, and many studied a profession, with law and medicine the most favored. The practice of a profession was viewed not as a means of livelihood, but as a status symbol and an adjunct to a political career. The elite maintained a dual cultural allegiance, because

Panama City skyline
Courtesy Embassy of Panama

families usually sent their sons to Western Europe or the United States to complete their education. Increasing numbers of women also attended college, but most families did not see such education as essential.

Politics was the quintessential career for a young man of elite background. The old, aristocratic families had long provided the republic's presidents, its cabinet ministers, and many members of the legislatures. Young women were increasingly finding employment in public administration and commerce in the 1980s.

Older elite families were closely interrelated and were careful to avoid racially mixed unions. Antillean blacks enjoyed little success in attaining elite status, although a wealthy, Spanish-speaking, Roman Catholic black could gain acceptance. There was an increasing degree of admixture with mestizo and more recent immigrant elements. Many such families entered the elite and intermarried with members of the older families. In a sense, commercial success had in large measure become a substitute for an illustrious family background. "Money whitens everyone" was a popular saying describing the phenomenon.

The Middle Class

The middle class was predominantly mestizo, but it included such diverse elements as the children and grandchildren of Antillean

109

blacks, the descendants of Chinese laborers on the railroad, Jews, more recent immigrants from Europe and the Middle East, and a few former elite families fallen on hard times. Like the elite, the middle class was largely urban, although many small cities and towns of the interior had their own middle-class families. The middle class encompassed small businessmen, professionals, managerial and technical personnel, and government administrators. Its membership was defined by those who, by economic assets or social status, were not identifiably elite but who were still markedly better off than the lower class. As a whole, the middle class benefited from the economic prosperity of the 1960s and early 1970s, as well as the general expansion in educational opportunities in the late twentieth century.

Members of the middle class who had held such status for any length of time were rarely content to remain fixed on the social scale. Emulating elite norms and attitudes, they exerted great effort to continue their climb up the social ladder. They were aware of the importance of education and occupation in determining status and the compensatory role these variables could play in the absence of family wealth or social background. Middle-class parents made great sacrifices to send their children to the best schools possible. Young men were encouraged to acquire a profession, and young women were steered toward office jobs in government or business. In contrast with the elite, the middle class viewed teaching as an appropriate occupation for a young woman.

Nationalist sentiment served to unify the diverse elements of the middle class in the decades following World War II. University students, who were predominantly middle class in family background, typified both the intense nationalism and the political activism of the middle class. Political observers noted a sharp class cleavage in the political consciousness of the Spanish-speaking natives and the more recent, unassimilated immigrant families. Middle-class immigrants tended to be preoccupied with commercial pursuits and largely conservative or passive in their politics.

The Lower Class

The lower class constituted the bulk of the country's urban population. As a group, it was stratified by employment and race. In terms of livelihood it was made up of unskilled or semiskilled workers, including artisans, vendors, manual laborers, and servants. The basic cleavages were between those who were wage earners and the self-employed, and those employed in the former Canal Zone, who constituted a "labor elite" earning twice the average of the metropolitan region as a whole.

Self-employment offered a precarious existence to most who pursued it, but served as an alternative for those unable to find other work when the economy contracted in the late 1970s and 1980s. Unemployment ran in excess of 10 percent in the late 1970s and early 1980s, and much of it was concentrated in the metropolitan region, which accounted for approximately four-fifths of the country's jobless. In poorer neighborhoods, the rate ran closer to 25 percent, and among low-income families, roughly 40 percent were unemployed (see Human Resources and Income, ch. 3).

Because the majority of rural-urban migrants to the metropolitan region were women, women outnumbered men in many larger urban areas. Many came in search of work as domestics. Young, single mothers constituted a significant proportion of the urban population; in Colón, for example, they represented one-third of all families. Women suffered higher unemployment rates than did men, and their earnings, when they were employed, averaged less than half those of males.

Ethnically, the lower class had three principal components: mestizo migrants from the countryside, children and grandchildren of Antillean blacks, and Hispanicized blacks—descendants of former slaves. The split between Antillean blacks and the rest of the populace was particularly marked. Although there was some social mixing and intermarriage, religious and cultural differences isolated the Antilleans. They were gradually becoming more Hispanicized, but the first generation usually remained oriented toward its Caribbean origins, and the second and third generations were under North American influence through exposure to United States citizens in the former Canal Zone where most were employed. Although some Antillean blacks were middle class, most remained in the lower class.

Increasing numbers of urban lower-class parents were sending their children to school. A secondary-school diploma, in particular, served as a permit to compete for white-collar jobs and elevation to middle-class status. This kind of mobility was on the rise throughout the 1960s and 1970s. Mestizos were better able to take advantage of these opportunities than most, but Antilleans who were educated and conformed to Hispanic cultural norms enjoyed considerable mobility as well. The National Guard, and later the FDP, have been an avenue of advancement for both Hispanic and Antillean blacks. A substantial portion of the enlisted personnel have come from the ranks of the black urban poor and, increasingly, the rural mestizo population. Enlisted personnel could hope to advance to the officer corps. Under the Torrijos regime, many troop commanders were promoted from the ranks.

Religion

The Constitution prescribes that there shall be no prejudice with respect to religious freedom, and the practice of all forms of worship is authorized. However, the Constitution recognizes that the Roman Catholic faith is the country's predominant religion and contains a provision that it be taught in the public schools. Such instruction or other religious activity is not, however, compulsory.

The Constitution does not specifically provide for the separation of church and state, but it implies the independent functioning of each. Members of the clergy may not hold civil or military public office, except such posts as may be concerned with social welfare or public instruction. The Constitution stipulates that senior officials of the church hierarchy in Panama must be native-born citizens.

The majority of Panamanians in the late 1980s were at least nominal Roman Catholics. The Antillean black community, however, was largely Protestant. Indians followed their own indigenous belief systems, although both Protestant and Catholic missionaries were active among the various tribes. Roman Catholicism permeated the social environment culturally as well as religiously. The devout regarded church attendance and the observance of religious duties as regular features of everyday life, and even the most casual or nominal Roman Catholics adjusted the orientation of their daily lives to the prevailing norms of the religious calendar. Although some sacraments were observed more scrupulously than others, baptism was almost universal, and the last rites of the church were administered to many who during their lives had been indifferent to the precepts of the faith or its religious rituals.

In the mid-1980s, when nearly 90 percent of the population was Roman Catholic, there were fewer than 300 priests in the country. Virtually every town had its Roman Catholic church, but many did not have a priest in residence. Many rural inhabitants in the more remote areas received only an occasional visit from a busy priest who traveled among a number of isolated villages.

Religious attitudes, customs, and beliefs differed somewhat between urban and rural areas, although many members of the urban working class, often recent migrants from rural regions, presumably retained their folk beliefs. According to one anthropologist, the belief system of the campesinos centered on God, the Devil, the saints, and the Virgin. Christ was viewed as more or less the chief saint, but as peripheral to the lives of men. The Virgin Mary served as an inspiration and model to women, but there was no comparable model for men.

The Golden Altar in the Church of San José, Panama City

Although the campesinos believed that each individual "is born with a destiny set by God," they also believed that the destiny could be altered if the individual succumbed to the constant blandishments and enticements of the Devil. The rural dwellers possessed a clear sense of reward and punishment that centered on All Souls' Day. On that day all who died during the previous year are summoned to judgment before God and the Devil. The life record of each person is recited by Saint Peter, and the good and bad deeds are weighed out on a Roman balance scale, thus determining the person's afterlife.

Throughout the society, birth and death were marked by religious rites observed by all but a very few. One of the first social functions in which newly born members of the family participated was the sacrament of baptism, which symbolized their entry into society and brought them into the church community. In the cities, church facilities were readily available, but in rural areas families often had to travel some distance to the nearest parish center for the ceremony. The trip was considered of great importance and was willingly undertaken. In fact, baptism was generally considered the most significant religious rite.

If the family lived near a church that had a priest in regular attendance, children received an early exposure to the formal teachings of the church and were usually taken to mass regularly by their mothers. As they grew older, they took an increasing part in church liturgy and by the age of ten were usually full participants in such activities as catechism classes, communion, and confession. As they approached manhood, boys tended to drift away from the church and from conscientious observation of church ritual. Few young men attended services regularly, and even fewer took an active part in the religious life of the community, although they continued to consider themselves Roman Catholics.

Girls, on the other hand, were encouraged to continue their religious devotions and observe the moral tenets of their faith. Women were more involved in the church than men, and the community and clerics accepted this as a basic axiom. There was social pressure on women to become involved in church affairs, and most women, particularly in urban areas, responded. As a rule, they attended mass regularly and took an active part in church and church-sponsored activities. Religious gatherings and observances were among the principal forms of diversion for women outside the home, and to a great extent these activities were social as much as devotional.

Education

Public education began in Panama soon after independence from Colombia in 1903. The first efforts were guided by an extremely paternalistic view of the goals of education, as evidenced in comments made in a 1913 meeting of the First Panamanian Educational Assembly, "The cultural heritage given to the child should be determined by the social position he will or should occupy. For this reason education should be different in accordance with the social class to which the student should be related." This elitist focus changed rapidly under United States influence.

By the 1920s, Panamanian education subscribed to a progressive educational system, explicitly designed to assist the able and ambitious individual in search of upward social mobility. Successive national governments gave a high priority to the development of a system of (at least) universal primary education; in the late 1930s, as much as one-fourth of the national budget went to education. Between 1920 and 1934, primary-school enrollment doubled. Adult illiteracy, more than 70 percent in 1923, dropped to roughly half the adult population in scarcely more than a decade.

By the early 1950s, adult illiteracy had dropped to 28 percent, but the rate of gain had also declined and further improvements were slow in coming. The 1950s saw essentially no improvement; adult illiteracy was 27 percent in 1960. There were notable gains in the 1960s, however, and the rate of adult illiteracy dropped 8 percentage points by 1970. According to 1980 estimates, only 13 percent of Panamanians over 10 years of age were illiterate (see table 5, Appendix A). Men and women were approximately equally represented among the literate. The most notable disparity was between urban and rural Panama; 94 percent of city-dwelling adults were literate, but fewer than two-thirds of those in the countryside were—a figure that also represented continued high illiteracy rates among the country's Indian population (see Indians, this ch.).

From the 1950s through the early 1980s, educational enrollments expanded faster than the rate of population growth as a whole and, for most of that period, faster than the school-aged population. The steepest increases came in secondary and higher educational enrollments, which increased ten and more than thirty times, respectively (see table 6, Appendix A). By the mid-1980s, primary-school enrollment rates were roughly 113 percent of the primary-school-aged population. Male and female enrollments were relatively equal overall, although there were significant regional variations.

Enrollments at upper levels of schooling had increased strikingly both in relative and absolute terms since 1960. Between 1960 and the mid-1980s, secondary-school enrollments expanded some four-and-a-half times and higher education, nearly twelve-fold. In 1965 fewer than one-third of children of secondary school age were in school and only 7 percent of people aged 20 to 24 years. In the mid-1980s, almost two-thirds of secondary-school-aged children were enrolled, and about 20 percent of individuals aged 20 to 24 years were in institutions of higher education.

School attendance was compulsory for children from ages six through fifteen years, or until the completion of primary school. A six-year primary cycle was followed by two types of secondary-school programs: an academic-oriented program and a vocational-type program. The academic program, which represented nearly three-quarters of all secondary-school enrollment, involved two three-year cycles. The lower cycle was of a general or exploratory nature, with a standard curriculum that included Spanish, social studies, religion, art, and music. The upper cycle consisted of two academic courses of study: in arts and sciences, leading to entrance to the university, or a less rigorous course of study, representing the end of a student's formal education (fewer than 4 percent of students pursued this course of studies in the mid-1980s).

In addition to the academic program, there was a vocational-type secondary-school program that offered professional or technical courses aimed specifically at giving students the technical skills needed for employment following graduation. In the mid-1980s, roughly one-quarter of all secondary students pursued this type of course. Like the more academic-oriented secondary-school program, the vocational-type program was divided into two cycles. Students could choose their studies from a variety of specializations, including agriculture, art, commerce, and industrial trades.

Admission to the university normally required the *bachillerato* (graduation certificate or baccalaureate), awarded on completion of the upper cycle of the academic course of studies, although the University of Panama had some latitude in determining admissions standards. The *bachillerato* was generally considered an essential component of middle-class status. Public secondary schools that offered the baccalaureate degree also offered the lower cycle. They were generally located in provincial capital cities. The oldest, largest, and most highly regarded of these was the National Institute in Panama City. The University of Panama grew out of it, and the school had produced so many public figures that it was known as the Nest of Eagles (Nido de Aguilas). It tended to draw its student body from upwardly mobile rather than long-established elements of the elite. Its students were well known for their political activism.

School in Antón, Coclé Province
Courtesy Agency for International Development

Higher education on the isthmus dates from the founding of a Jesuit university in 1749; that institution closed with the order's expulsion from the New World in 1767. Another college, the Colegio del Istmo, was started early in the nineteenth century, but the school did not prosper, and Panamanians who wished to pursue a higher education were required to go abroad or to Colombia until 1935, when the University of Panama was founded. In the mid-1980s, most postsecondary schooling took place within the university. Other institutions, such as the School of Nursing and the Superior Center for Bilingual Secretaries, accounted for less than 3 percent of enrollment at this educational level.

Nearly three-quarters of all university students attended the University of Panama in the 1980s. The university had, as well, a number of regional centers and extensions representing a small portion of the school's enrollment and faculty. The University of Santa María la Antigua, a private Roman Catholic institution established in 1965, enrolled another 5,000 to 6,000 students in the 1980s. A third university, the Technical University, was founded in 1981. It accounted for approximately 7,000 students. A substantial portion of the well-to-do continued to study abroad.

Most education was publicly funded and organized. In addition to the University of Santa María la Antigua, there were some private primary and secondary schools. Typically located in cities and considered very prestigious, they accounted for 5 to 7 percent of primary-school enrollment and approximately 25 percent of secondary-school students in the mid-1980s.

Education continued to claim a large share of government budgets. It represented 15 to 20 percent of the national government's expenditures in the early to mid-1980s (see table 7, Appendix A). Most funding went to primary schooling, although both secondary and higher education received proportionately higher funding per student. Primary schools received roughly one-third of government education spending, secondary and higher education approximately 20 percent each (see table 8, Appendix A). Budgets from 1979 through 1983 allocated on average B220 per primary school student, B274 per secondary school student, and B922 per university student (for value of the balboa—see Glossary).

The growth in enrollment was accompanied by a concomitant (if not always adequate) expansion in school facilities and increase in teaching staff. Teacher education was a high priority in the 1970s and 1980s, a reflection of the generally poor training teachers had received in the past. Schools increased at every level during the early 1980s; secondary schools made the most notable gains, more than doubling (see table 9, Appendix A). Pupil-teacher ratios for all levels were in the range of nineteen to twenty-six pupils per teacher in the mid-1980s.

Health and Welfare

The Ministry of Health bore primary responsibility for public health programs in the late 1980s. At the district and regional levels, medical directors were responsible for maintaining health-care services at health-care centers and hospitals and monitoring outreach programs for the communities surrounding these facilities. The Social Security Institute also maintained a medical fund for its members and ran a number of health-care facilities, which members could use for free and others for a nominal fee. In practice there was a history of conflict between Social Security Institute and Ministry of Health personnel at the district and regional levels. Since 1973 the Social Security Institute and the Ministry of Health had attempted—with limited success—to coordinate what were in essence two public health-care systems, in an effort to eliminate redundancy.

Despite the bureaucratic conflicts, a number of health indicators showed significant improvement. Life expectancy at birth in 1985 was seventy-one years—an increase of nearly ten years since 1965 (see table 10, Appendix A). Infant mortality rates in 1984 were less than one-third their 1960 levels, and the childhood death

JUSTO AROSEMENA
1817–1896

University of Panama
Courtesy Organization of American States

rate stood at less than 20 percent of the 1960 level. The number of physicians per capita had nearly tripled.

The Department of Environmental Health was charged with administering rural health programs and maintaining a safe water supply for communities of fewer than 500 inhabitants—roughly one-third of the total population. The National Water and Sewage Institute and the Ministry of Public Works shared responsibility for urban water supplies.

By 1980 approximately 85 percent of the population had access to potable water and 89 percent to sanitation facilities. In rural Panama in the early 1980s, roughly 70 percent of the population had potable water and approximately 80 percent had sanitation facilities. The quality of water and sewage disposal varied considerably, however. Water transmission was less than reliable on the fringes of urban centers. In rural areas, much depended on the community's dedication to maintaining sanitation facilities and an operating water system. Many water treatment facilities were poorly maintained and overloaded, because of the intense urban growth the country had experienced since the end of World War II. In rural Panama, latrines and septic tanks tended to be over-used and under-maintained. The system as a whole stood in need of substantial renovation and repair in the late 1980s.

Public health, especially for rural Panamanians, was a high priority. Under the slogan "Health for All by the Year 2000," in the early 1970s the government embarked on an ambitious program to improve the delivery of health services and sanitation in rural areas. The program aimed at changing the emphasis from curative, hospital-based medical care to community-based preventive medicine. The 1970s and early 1980s saw substantial improvements in a wide variety of areas. Village health committees attempted to communicate the perceived needs of the villagers to health-care officials. The program enjoyed its most notable successes in the early 1970s with the construction of water delivery systems and latrines in a number of previously unserved rural areas. Village health committees also organized community health-education courses, immunization campaigns, and medical team visits to isolated villages. They were assisted by associations or federations of these village health committees at the district or regional level. These federations were able to lend money to villages for the construction of sanitation facilities, assist them in contacting Ministry of Health personnel for specific projects, and help with the financing for medical visits to villages.

Village health committees were most successful in regions where land and income were relatively equitably distributed. The regional medical director was pivotal; where he or she assigned a high priority to preventive health care, the village communities continued to receive adequate support. However, many committees were inoperative by the mid-1980s. In general, rural health-care funding had been adversely affected by government cutbacks. Facilities tended to be heavily used and poorly maintained.

In the early 1980s, there continued to be marked disparities in health care between urban and rural regions. Medical facilities, including nearly all laboratory and special-care facilities, were concentrated in the capital city. In 1983 roughly 87 percent of the hospital beds were in publicly owned and operated institutions, mostly located in Panama City; one-quarter of all hospitals were in the capital (see table 11, Appendix A). Medical facilities and personnel were concentrated beyond what might reasonably be expected, even given the capital city's share of total population. Panama City had roughly 2.5 times the national average of hospital beds and doctors per capita and nearly 3 times the number of nurses per capita (see table 12, Appendix A). The effect of this distribution was seen in continued regional disparities in health indicators. Rural Panama registered disproportionately high infant and maternal mortality rates. Rural babies were roughly 20 percent more likely to die than their urban counterparts; childbearing was 5 times more likely to be fatal in rural Panama than in cities (see table 13, Appendix A). In the early 1980s, the infant mortality rate of Panamá Province was one-third that of Bocas del Toro and one-fourth that of Darién.

Panama's social security system covered most permanent employees. Its principal disbursements were for retirement and health care. Permanent employees paid taxes to the Social Security Institute; the self-employed contributed on the basis of income as reported on income tax returns. Agricultural workers were generally exempted. Changes in 1975 lowered the age at which workers could retire and altered the basis on which benefits were calculated. The general effect of the changes was to encourage the retirement of those best paid and best covered. It did little to benefit the most disadvantaged workers.

*　*　*

There are a number of useful works on Panamanian society. John and Mavis Biesanz's *The People of Panama,* although dated, remains the most complete treatment of Panamanian society in its entirety. Stephen Gudeman's *The Demise of a Rural Economy* looks at the changing situation of small farmers and describes mestizo life in the countryside. There is extensive literature on Panama's principal Indian tribes. Of particular use to the general reader are *Ngawbe* by Philip D. Young (on the Guaymí), as well as his article co-authored with John R. Bort, "Politicization of the Guaymí," and *The Kuna Gathering* (about the Cuna) by James Howe. Statistical information on a wide variety of topics is available from the Panamanian government's *Panamá en Cifras.* (For further information and complete citations, see Bibliography.)

Chapter 3. The Economy

Cuna Indian mola *design of a San Blas inter-island boat at dock*

SEVERAL DISTINCTIVE FEATURES characterized Panama's economy in the late 1980s; the most striking was its internationally oriented services sector, which in 1985 accounted for over 73 percent of the gross domestic product (GDP—see Glossary), the highest such percentage in the world. That distinctiveness was best symbolized by the Panama Canal, which has dominated the country's economy in the twentieth century. The scope of the services sector has expanded and broadened through increased government services and initiatives such as the Colón Free Zone (CFZ—see Glossary), a trans-isthmian oil pipeline, and the International Financial Center.

Another distinguishing feature was Panama's paper currency, the United States dollar. The local currency, the balboa, was tied to the United States dollar but was available only in coins. Panama's money supply was determined by the United States Federal Reserve System; therefore, the country could neither print money nor devalue the currency. Because its monetary instruments are limited, Panama has avoided the cycle of exchange-rate devaluations and the accelerating inflation that have typified most Latin American economies. The balboa has remained on par with the United States dollar, and Panama has enjoyed the lowest average annual rate of inflation in Latin America—7.1 percent in the 1970s, and only 3.7 percent between 1980 and 1985.

The third economic distinction is that the Panamanians have one of the highest levels of per capita income in the developing world. Construction of the Panama Canal across the isthmus in the early 1900s and expanding world commerce have combined to foster rapid economic growth in the country throughout the twentieth century. By 1985 per capita gross national product (GNP—see Glossary) reached US$2,100, twice the average in Central American countries, greater than all South American countries except for Venezuela (US$3,080) and Argentina (US$2,130), and on a level with Mexico (US$2,080). Panamanians, however, have not shared equally in the rising living standards, because the distribution of income has been highly skewed.

The military leaders who seized control of the government in 1968 under the leadership of General Omar Torrijos Herrera instituted economic policies that aimed at greater equity as well as integration of various facets of the country's fragmented economy. By the time of Torrijos's death in July 1981, they had achieved some remarkable results, but at the expense of a low rate of private investment, increased urban unemployment, continued rural poverty, and growing external public debt. A document entitled *Towards a More Human Economy* was published in 1985 by Panama's Archbishop Marcos Gregorio McGrath, revealing a society in which 38 percent of the families lived in poverty and in which 22 percent of the population failed to earn at least US$200 a month—the minimum amount considered necessary to purchase a basic basket of goods. The document went on to criticize many measures taken by the Torrijos government in the 1970s. At the same time, however, the publication recognized that remarkable progress had been made in other areas, such as a decline in infant mortality rates, a rise in the literacy rate, and social security coverage for 60 percent of the population as compared with only 12 percent in 1960. Indeed, the economic policies instituted by the Torrijos regime (1968–81) were pivotal in Panama's history, but the results were mixed.

Growth and Structure of the Economy

Since the early 1500s, Panamanians have relied on the country's comparative advantage—its geography. Exploitation of this advantage began soon after the Spanish arrived, when the conquistadors used Panama to transship gold and silver from Peru to Spain (see The Conquest, ch. 1). Ports on each coast and a trail between them handled much of Spain's colonial trade from which the inhabitants of the port cities prospered. This was the beginning of the country's historical dependence on world commerce for prosperity and imports. Agriculture received little attention until the twentieth century, and by the 1980s had—for much of the population—barely developed beyond indigenous Indian techniques. Industry developed slowly because the flow of goods from Europe and later from North America created a disincentive for local production.

Panama has been affected by the cyclical nature of international trade. The economy stagnated in the 1700s as colonial exchange via the isthmus declined. In the mid-1800s, Panama's economy boomed as a result of increased cargo and passengers associated with the California gold rush. A railroad across the isthmus, completed in 1855, prolonged economic growth for about fifteen years until completion of the first transcontinental railroad in the United States caused trans-isthmian traffic to decline. France's efforts to construct a canal across the isthmus in the 1880s and efforts by the United States in the early 1900s stimulated the Panamanian economy.

The United States completed the canal in 1914, and canal traffic expanded by an average of 15 percent a year between 1915 and 1930. The stimulus was strongly felt in Panama City and Colón, the terminal cities of the canal. The world depression of the 1930s reduced international trade and canal traffic, however, causing extensive unemployment in the terminal cities and generating a flow of workers to subsistence farming. During World War II, canal traffic did not increase, but the economy boomed as the convoy system and the presence of United States forces, sent to defend the canal, increased foreign spending in the canal cities. The end of the war was followed by an economic depression and another exodus of unemployed people into agriculture. The government initiated a modest public works program, instituted price supports for major crops, and increased protection for selected agricultural and industrial products.

The postwar depression gave way to rapid economic expansion between 1950 and 1970, when GDP increased by an average of 6.4 percent a year, one of the highest sustained growth rates in the world. All sectors contributed to the growth. Agricultural output rose, boosted by greater fishing activities (especially shrimp), the development of high-value fruit and vegetable production, and the rapid growth of banana exports after disease-resistant trees were planted. Commerce evolved into a relatively sophisticated wholesale and retail system. Banking, tourism, and the export of services to the Canal Zone grew rapidly. Most importantly, an increase in world trade provided a major stimulus to use of the canal and to the economy.

In the 1970s and 1980s, Panama's growth fluctuated with the vagaries of the world economy. After 1973 economic expansion slowed considerably as the result of a number of international and domestic factors (see Recent Economic Performance, this ch.). Real GDP growth averaged 3.5 percent a year between 1973 and 1979. In the early 1980s, the economy rebounded with GDP growth rates of 15.4 percent in 1980, 4.2 percent in 1981, and 5.6 percent in 1982. The acute recession in Latin America after 1982, however, wreaked havoc on Panama's economy. GDP growth in 1983 was a mere 0.4 percent; in 1984 it was negative 0.4 percent. In 1985 Panama experienced economic recovery with 4.1-percent GDP growth; the corresponding figure for 1986 was estimated to be 2.8 percent.

Changing Structure of the Economy

The structure of Panama's economy in the twentieth century has been characterized by the dichotomy of a large internationally

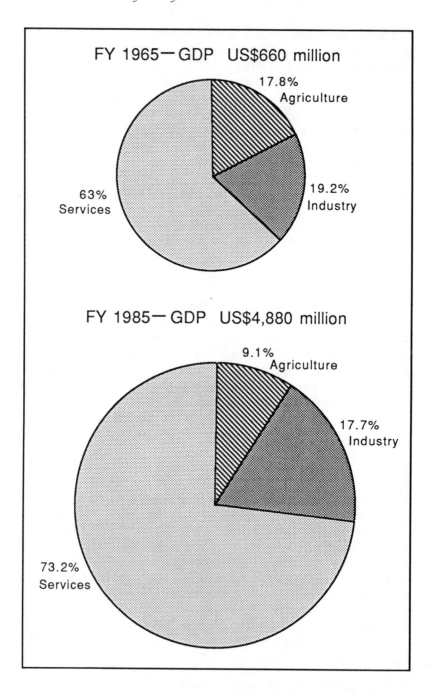

Figure 7. Gross Domestic Product by Sector, 1965 and 1985

oriented services sector and a small inward-looking goods sector. The major change in that structure has been the rapid growth of the services sector. In 1950 services accounted for about 57 percent of GDP; that share rose to 63 percent in 1965 and to over 73 percent in 1985 (see fig. 7). Given Panama's geographic location, modern infrastructure, and an educated population trained in commercial and financial activity, services will likely remain the leading sector of the economy.

In contrast, the goods sector has declined in relative terms. Although efforts have been made to stimulate agriculture and industry—and both registered substantial growth—their share of GDP has fallen as that of the services sector has risen. In the late 1980s, one of the greatest challenges facing Panamanian policymakers was that of using the services sector as a springboard for growth, primarily in industry but also in agriculture.

During the Torrijos administration, the economy was stimulated in several areas. The principal stimulus to the services sector was banking, particularly offshore banking (see Glossary). Transportation also increased rapidly, along with expansion of the road network. Substantial investments were made in the communications system in an effort to meet international standards expected by the extensive network of foreign businesses. Storage and warehousing grew rapidly in response to the economy's own needs and particularly to the foreign business conducted in the CFZ.

Industrialization progressed rapidly after 1950, with industrial production rising from 10 percent of GDP in 1950 to 19 percent in 1965. This expansion was based primarily on import substitution. Industry continued to grow at an average annual rate of 5.9 percent from 1965 through 1980, but registered negative 2.2-percent average annual growth between 1980 and 1985.

As a result of the lack of growth as well as the rapid rise of the services sector, industrial production had dropped slightly as a percentage of GDP in 1985—to just under 18 percent. Manufacturing accounted for about half of the industrial sector, followed by construction, energy, and mining. Given the small size of the domestic market, observers believed that future industrial growth would rely primarily on foreign markets. Success, therefore, would depend to a large extent on Panama's ability to make its industry internationally oriented and competitive.

Although the agricultural sector continued to expand and to employ the largest number of workers, its share of GDP declined substantially, from 29 percent in 1950 to 18 percent in 1965 and about 9 percent in 1985. This sector grew at a respectable average annual rate of 2.4 percent between 1965 and 1980, and 2.7 percent between 1980 and 1985, but it could not keep pace with the rapid growth rate of the services sector. Bananas, shrimp, and sugar continued to lead the list of export items. The expansion of the agricultural sector hinged on exports and product diversification.

Recent Economic Performance

The Torrijos era (1968–81) stands as a dividing point in Panama's economic history. Under Torrijos, the state took a more active role in the economy and initiated ambitious social projects. The public sector expanded to an unprecedented degree, as did the fiscal deficit and the external debt. In the 1980s, Panama was forced to address some of the excesses of the 1970s and to adjust its policies, often under the aegis of the International Monetary Fund (IMF—see Glossary) and the World Bank (see Glossary).

In the 1960s, Panama experienced buoyant growth in virtually all areas of the economy as a result of the boom in canal-related activities and the growth in private investment. GDP expanded at an average of 8 percent per year. Employment grew at 3.5 percent per year, well above the population growth of about 3 percent a year. Most of the new jobs were generated by the private sector.

In the 1970s, Panama's average annual growth rate of GDP fell to 3.4 percent. Many factors contributed to the decline. In the international arena, reduced canal use (especially after the Vietnam war), rising oil prices, international inflation, and recession in the major industrial countries had a negative impact on Panama's economy. Domestically, investment fell in response to government policies of agrarian reform, expropriation of private power companies, creation of state industries, protection of labor, controls on housing, subsidies, and high support prices. In addition, the prolonged negotiations between the United States and Panama over the canal adversely affected investor confidence. The government sought to regain private investment by investing in large infrastructure projects and by expanding or acquiring productive enterprises. Two-thirds of the new jobs created in the 1970s were in the public sector. The public-sector deficit expanded, and the government was forced to borrow money from abroad. By 1980 the external debt had reached 80 percent of GDP.

In 1982 Panama, like most of Latin America, felt the impact of the world recession. Once again, the government sought to remedy the declining private-sector investment through increased public expenditures. In the same year, the public-sector deficit reached 11 percent of GDP. In 1983 and 1984, the government imposed a severe austerity program, which had the imprimatur of the IMF. Public investment was reduced by 20 percent in 1983 and by a further 8 percent in 1984. The public deficit was also cut, to about 6 percent of GDP in both years. In addition, the government undertook structural adjustment measures in the areas of industry and agriculture and instituted changes to streamline the public sector. The simultaneous recession and reduction in public expenditures caused GDP to fall in 1984, the first decline in more than twenty years. In the following years, however, Panama, avoiding the economic slump that plagued most Latin American countries, experienced moderate growth.

Role of Government

The government has played a limited role in economic matters throughout most of Panama's history, restricting its activities to infrastructural development and creating a climate conducive to private investment. The government's role expanded dramatically after 1968, when the National Guard, now called the Panama Defense Forces (Fuerzas de Defensa de Panamá—FDP), took control of the government under Torrijos's leadership. Members of the National Guard tended to be provincial, racially mixed, and lower- or middle-class in background and thus provided an outlook different from that of the urban-oriented elite that had dominated Panamanian politics in the twentieth century (see The Government of Torrijos and the National Guard, ch. 1).

The National Guard implemented policies that attempted to reduce the most glaring discrepancies between the urban and rural economies. In 1968 economic activity was heavily concentrated in the two provinces of Panamá and Colón, which accounted for over two-thirds of GDP and an even larger share of the country's manufacturing, construction, trade, transport, and communications (see fig. 1). Residents of the metropolitan areas had access to relatively well-developed education, health, and other services. Their consumption pattern was closer to that of affluent developed countries; they owned most of the country's cars, refrigerators, telephones, and television sets. Their tastes and aspirations were patterned on those of United States citizens in the Canal Zone and the many international visitors. In contrast, rural residents had access to far fewer services, and their living conditions were substantially below those of urbanites (see Rural Society, ch. 2). The majority of the population in the countryside had incomes of less than one-third of those in Panama City and Colón, and many had little more than one-tenth. The economic policies of the military leaders aimed at continued high growth of the urban economy, from which resources could be channeled to the poorer elements of the society to bring about greater economic and social integration.

High growth of service industries in the terminal cities was considered essential because of several constraints: canal-related activities were not expected to provide much of a growth stimulus; import substitution opportunities in manufacturing had been largely exhausted; and expansion of banana exports appeared limited by international conditions. Panama became a regional financial center after 1970, when the government created the International Financial Center. Tourism was bolstered by construction of additional airports, a convention center, new hotels, and resorts. The CFZ was upgraded, and transportation and warehousing facilities were also improved.

Under Torrijos the government became more active in the goods sectors. In agriculture, land reform was accelerated, and cooperative farming was promoted. In industry, state-owned companies expanded, most notably in sugar refining, cement production, and electric power. Torrijos intervened more forcefully in other areas of the economy, such as in the setting of wages and prices; a 1972 labor code increased job security and promoted union organization.

These measures created a more equitable society, but often at the expense of efficiency and overall growth. Government expenditure rose sharply, and the public sector became bloated with a proliferation of new government agencies. In the services sector, construction declined in the mid-1970s, in part because of the disincentive created by rent controls. In agriculture, considerable improvements in social conditions were not accompanied by increased incomes. Moreover, greater government participation and prolonged canal negotiations created difficulties and uncertainties for private investors, and private investment declined precipitously.

After 1975 the government became more pragmatic and modified its programs to stimulate economic activity. Incentives to investors were increased. The 1972 labor code was modified in 1976 to meet some of the objections by employers. A freeze on collective bargaining agreements was established that in effect prohibited wage increases. Government-set prices were raised to encourage production.

Under a structural adjustment program in 1983 and 1984, Panama reduced the scope of the public sector in the economy. In March 1986, and as preconditions for two structural adjustment loans from the World Bank, the government passed several major laws that revised its labor code, removed protective tariffs, changed the price structure for agricultural goods, and encouraged foreign investment. In August 1986 the government launched a privatization program and proposed the sale of state assets worth US$13 million.

Monetary Policy

Panama's monetary system is unique. United States dollar notes serve as the paper currency and are legal tender in Panama. The local currency is the balboa, which, since its creation in 1904, has remained tied to and equal to the United States dollar. Panama issues only coins corresponding in size and metallic content to United States coins. No foreign exchange restrictions existed in Panama in the mid-1980s.

With no need for a bank to issue and protect the paper currency, Panama did not have a central bank. The National Bank of Panama (Banco Nacional de Panamá—BNP), a state-owned commercial bank, was responsible for nonmonetary aspects of central banking. The BNP was assisted by the National Banking Commission, which was created along with the country's International Financial Center, and was charged with licensing and supervising banks. In 1985 the level of M1 (currency and demand deposits) was US$410 million, while M2 (M1 plus time deposits) was US$1.95 billion.

In a sense, Panama could not have a monetary policy, because it lacked the instruments to implement such a policy, such as money creation and exchange-rate manipulation. In effect, Panama's money supply was determined by the balance of payments, by movements in interest rates, and by the United States, which controlled the number of dollars available for the country's international transactions.

Panama's monetary system has benefited the country in numerous ways. The country has enjoyed almost automatic monetary and price stability. International transactions have been facilitated by the use of the United States dollar. No short-term transfer problems are associated with the balance of payments. The foreign exchange constraint felt by most developing countries has been obviated by the dollars circulating in the economy and the ability to borrow.

In the late 1980s, the financial system consisted largely of banking. Panamanian businesses relied relatively little on public stock or bond issues. No formal stock exchange existed; supervised, independent brokers handled the limited trading in regulated financial certificates, stocks, and bonds. In addition, some insurance companies, savings and loan associations, and unregulated consumer-finance companies were formed. The country's social security fund invested in government bonds and various development projects.

Fiscal Policy

Panama's financial stability and international credit standing were determined not by monetary policy, but principally by fiscal policy and balance of payments. Fiscal policy was thus more important for Panama than for most other countries, and as a result, public-sector deficits were especially problematic for the government.

From 1971 through 1975, the annual average for the consolidated public-sector deficit was 6.5 percent of GDP. That figure nearly doubled to 12.9 percent between 1976 and 1980, at the height of government spending on infrastructure and ambitious social programs. In the 1980s, the figure has declined, from 10.8 percent in 1982 to 5.8 percent in 1984 (see table 14, Appendix A). The 1982 figure represented an aberration, brought about by the political uncertainty and lack of fiscal restraint following Torrijos's death. Most impressively, the deficit was reduced to 2.5 percent of GDP in 1985, a figure even lower than the 3.5 percent targeted by the IMF. The reduction was brought about by increased revenues, reduced expenditures, and streamlined administration.

Budget Process

Panama developed an efficient and centralized budgetary system in the mid-1960s. By law, the budget had to balance, so increasing recourse was made to handle some expenditures outside the budget. One such device was the creation of autonomous government agencies. These agencies increased in numbers and importance in the 1960s and 1970s. Their areas of operation included banking, the national electrical system, welfare, tourism, and gambling. Their budgets were excluded from that of the central government, although various transfers were made.

The collection of direct taxes (on income, businesses, and corporations) was relatively efficient in Panama. Direct taxes totalled 7 percent of GDP in 1983. Although this figure is high compared with those of other countries in the region, direct taxes have brought stability to Panama's budget system and avoided the fluctuations that occurred in neighboring countries, which were more dependent on import and sales taxes. In the late 1980s, only a fraction of Panama's revenue was derived from taxes levied on foreign trade.

Revenues

In the first half of the twentieth century, Panama's tax base was narrow, and taxes were regressive. Up to 40 percent of the urban work force was employed in the Canal Zone (including most of

Ship transits Miraflores Locks, Panama Canal
Courtesy Agency for International Development

those with higher wages) where, because of treaty arrangements, their incomes could not be taxed by Panama. The rural population was largely untaxed because of farming's subsistence nature and the high costs of collecting rural taxes. Before the 1940s, over half of the taxes were from imports, mainly consumption goods for urbanites.

A 1955 treaty revision substantially expanded government revenue sources. The treaty permitted taxation of Panamanians working in the Canal Zone; it increased wage scales for those workers. A major tax reform, undertaken in 1964, made individual and corporate income taxes more progressive and improved the procedures for tax collection. By 1968 the tax structure compared favorably with that of other developing countries. Nearly half the tax revenues came from taxes on income and wealth; import duties and excise taxes on nonessential commodities provided an additional 15 percent of tax revenues.

The structure of government current revenue changed in 1979 because of the implementation of the Panama Canal treaties. Total revenue increased from US$477 million in 1979 to US$986 million in 1985. Direct taxation grew as a share of revenue, from 45.2 percent in 1979 to 52.6 percent in 1985. Tax receipts (direct and indirect taxation), as a share of revenue, dropped from 84.9 percent in 1979 to 69.8 percent in 1985. The drop was brought about primarily by the rise in the annual income received from operating the canal, which accounted for about 40 percent of non-tax revenue in 1985. Other sources of non-tax revenue included royalties and taxes from the trans-isthmian oil pipeline and levies on gambling.

Expenditures

In the 1950s and most of the 1960s, the expansion of revenue sources and the growing economy permitted an increase in government expenditures. Spending remained concentrated on the canal, and only a small share went to agriculture, industry, or commerce. Government investments were not large, but revenues financed only a part of them, thereby requiring a substantial increase in the public debt to fund the remainder. Expanding private investment was achieved through a high rate of private savings in spite of a considerable increase in per capita private consumption in the terminal cities.

In the 1970s, government current expenditures expanded dramatically. Most of that increase was a result of the rise in interest payments on the public debt, from 2 percent to 6 percent of GDP. In 1979 expenditures totalled US$554 million, most of which covered administrative costs (52.4 percent) and interest payments (23.6 percent). By 1985 expenditures had risen substantially to US$1.4 billion, but the actual structure of government expenditures changed very little; administrative costs accounted for 56 percent of the budget, followed by interest payments at 32.3 percent.

Between 1972 and 1983, the share of total expenditures fell in the categories of education (from 20.7 percent to 11.0 percent), health (15.1 percent to 13.1 percent), and economic services (24.2 percent to 13.5 percent). The share of expenditures allocated for housing, amenities, social security, and welfare rose during the same period from 10.8 percent to 12.2 percent. The biggest increase, however, was in the "other" category, which rose from 29.1 percent to 50.2 percent, mostly because of a larger debt service share (including interest payments and amortization).

Human Resources and Income

A 1985 World Bank study concluded that in spite of a relatively well-educated work force, unemployment was Panama's "gravest economic and social problem." The unemployment rate climbed steadily, from 8.1 percent in 1978 to 11.8 percent in 1985. The study predicted that the unemployment situation would further deteriorate unless the government took forceful measures to change structural rigidities in the labor code and market. Legislation approved in March 1986 addressed some of the rigidities in the 1972 labor code. Those changes may have been responsible, at least in part, for the lowering of the unemployment rate in 1986 to 10 percent.

Employment

As a result of declining birth rates and stabilizing mortality rates, Panama's overall population growth rate fell from an annual average of 2.6 percent between 1965 and 1980 to 2.2 percent between 1980 and 1985 (see table 2, Appendix A). The working-age population (15 years and over) increased from 1,011,700 in 1978 to 1,256,800 in 1985, at a rate of approximately 4 percent a year. From 1970 through 1984, the rate of job creation was less than half the growth rate of GDP. Analysts have estimated that the economy would have to grow indefinitely by 7.5 percent a year to absorb new entrants into the labor market—a level almost impossible to sustain and far above Panama's average annual growth rates in the past.

Panama's experience suggested that a government's ability to improve the employment situation through direct intervention in the labor market is severely limited. In the 1960s, an average of 13,000 new jobs were created each year. During the recession in the 1970s, unemployment rose dramatically. In late 1977, the government sought to reverse the deteriorating employment situation with an emergency jobs program. As a result, 28,000 new jobs were created within a year—20,000 of which were in the public sector. The employment program drained government resources, however, and in 1980 it was terminated. Only 11,000 jobs were created annually between 1979 and 1982.

In 1985 the sectoral distribution of the labor force reflected shifts that had taken place since the 1960s (see table 15, Appendix A). The services sector, led by financial services, continued to grow and accounted for 57.4 percent of the total labor force in 1985. Agriculture (including forestry and fishing) consistently experienced a relative decline, but still furnished 26.5 percent of the jobs. Industry's share of the labor force grew slightly between 1965 and 1980, but dropped to 16.1 percent in 1985.

The public-sector share of total employment rose slightly from 11 percent in 1963 to 13.1 percent in 1970. With the expansion of the public sector in the 1970s under Torrijos and the Emergency Employment Program in 1977, that share peaked at 25.1 percent in 1979. In 1982 the public sector still accounted for 25 percent of total employment.

Wage Policy and Labor Code

Panama's salaries were high by regional standards in the mid-1980s. In a 1982 study comparing salaries in manufacturing, Costa Rica's average monthly salary was only 41 percent that of Panama's; Guatemala's, 71 percent; and Honduras's, 84 percent. In 1985 the average monthly salary in Panama was US$450, but that figure was influenced by salaries in the canal area, which averaged US$1,300 per month. In 1985 the minimum wage in the metropolitan area was US$0.82 per hour; that wage was adjusted for location and type of industry.

In the 1970s, the government became heavily involved in labor matters and intervened actively to increase wages. Although a labor code had existed for many years, only the minimum wage provisions were consistently enforced. In 1971 two decrees were issued; the first imposed an education tax and the second required employers to pay workers an extra month's wage each year.

In early 1972 a broad labor code, patterned after that of Mexico, substantially changed labor-management relations. Workers' security, benefits, and bargaining power were increased considerably. Collective bargaining and unionization were encouraged and resulted in rapid growth of union membership (see Business, Professional, and Labor Organizations, ch. 4).

Although the 1972 labor code contributed to political stability in the 1970s, it substantially raised costs for employers, especially those in labor-intensive activities. The code also created disincentives to further hiring and private investment. Employers were prohibited from reducing a worker's salary. Therefore, piecework and assembly-type industries could not reward workers on the basis of productivity. As a partial result of these rigidities, Panama's labor costs were among the highest in the Caribbean Basin. According to a 1984 World Bank report, the annual cost of running a textile plant with 500 workers was US$588,300 in Haiti; US$789,800 in Costa Rica; US$919,700 in the Dominican Republic; US$1,048,500 in Colombia; US$1,057,600 in Mexico; and US$1,156,700 in Panama. Only Jamaica's costs were higher (US$1,828,300).

The labor code caused the effective cost of wages to rise, fueling inflation and discouraging private investment. The government, unable to devalue the currency, was forced to address the root of the problem—high labor costs. Law 95, which became effective in 1977, modified provisions of the labor code that related to job security and benefits. Previously, employers could only dismiss workers during their first two years on the job; that term was extended to five years. New provisions inhibited union actions, such as strikes, and imposed a two-year moratorium on collective bargaining agreements, which froze wages.

As a condition for the disbursement of a structural adjustment loan, the World Bank in 1985 recommended making the code more flexible. Panama's then-President Nicolás Ardito Barletta Vallarino (October 1984–September 1985) fully backed the World Bank recommendations. Opposition from unions and from within his own party, the Democratic Revolutionary Party (Partido Revolucionario Democrático—PRD), forced Ardito Barletta to withdraw the proposed changes and contributed to his resignation. His successor, Eric Arturo Delvalle Henríquez, was more successful. In March 1986, the Legislative Assembly approved major reforms in the labor code, in spite of widespread protests and a ten-day work stoppage by the unions. The changes included production-based wages, uniform rates of overtime pay, piecework provisions, removal of protective measures in industry, and flexible agricultural pricing. On the whole, the labor code modifications were aimed at making Panama's industry and agriculture more competitive internationally and expanding employment opportunities. Nonetheless, the economy was deemed likely to continue to experience high unemployment, especially in the metropolitan area, where unemployment rates tended to be much higher than the national average.

Income Distribution

One of Torrijos's major goals was to address the problem of unequal income distribution, which during the 1960s was one of the most skewed in the world. In 1970 the richest quintile (20 percent) of the households received 61.8 percent of the income; in stark contrast, the poorest quintile received only 2 percent of the income. Results of a study conducted in 1983 by the Panamanian government suggested that the Torrijos policies did, in fact, make income distribution more equitable. The income share of the richest quintile fell to nearly 50 percent, while all other income groups increased their share: the fourth quintile (second-to-richest) from 20 percent to 23 percent; the third quintile from 11 percent to 15 percent; the second quintile from 5 percent to 9 percent; and the first (poorest) quintile to 3 percent. Nevertheless, despite the program's success, the 1983 study confirmed a continuing pattern of a relatively prosperous metropolitan area and poor rural provinces.

Panama Canal

The Panama Canal continued to play a central role in world trade and Panama's economy in the mid-1980s. Some 5 percent of the world's trade in goods passed through the canal, contributing 9 percent of Panamanian GDP in 1983. This canal's location at one of the crossroads of international trade has spawned a plethora of other service-oriented activities, such as storage, ship repair, break bulk (the unloading of a portion or all of a ship's cargo), transshipment, bunkering, and distribution and services to ship travelers. The dynamism of the canal also was instrumental in the development of the CFZ, the trans-isthmian pipeline, and offshore financing. Evidence suggests, however, that the canal's relative importance to world trade is likely to continue to experience a small relative decline in the future, which has led Panama, together with the United States and Japan, to study alternatives for improving or replacing the canal.

Role of the Canal from 1903 to 1977

In 1903 the United States secured the right, by treaty, to build a canal across Panama (see The 1903 Treaty and Qualified Independence, ch. 1). The United States rejected plans to build a sea-level canal similar to that attempted by the French and opted instead for a system based on locks. Construction began in 1907 and was facilitated by medical work that largely eradicated yellow fever and reduced the incidence of malaria (see Building the Canal, ch. 1).

Construction of the canal involved damming the Río Chagres to create the huge Gatun Lake in the middle of the isthmus. Channels were dug from each coast, and locks were built to raise and lower ships between sea level and Gatun Lake. Three sets of locks were constructed: Gatun Locks on the Atlantic side and the Pedro Miguel and Miraflores Locks on the Pacific side. The lock chambers were 303 meters long by 33 meters wide, which limited vessel size to approximately 287 meters in length and 32 meters in width. Distance through the canal is eighty-two kilometers, and in 1987 transit took about fifteen hours, nearly half of which was spent in waiting. The canal began commercial operations in 1914.

The United States operated the canal and set tolls from the beginning of operation. Tolls covered operation costs but were kept low to encourage canal use. Direct benefits to Panama were minimal, consisting of annual annuity payments that increased infrequently, usually in response to Panamanian demands. In the 1975 to 1977 period, the annuity payments reached US$2.3 million a year. Indirect benefits to Panama's economy were substantial, however, and included the jobs of its citizens working in the Canal Zone, value of goods and services sold to the Canal Zone and to passing ships, and expenditures by visitors.

Economic Implications of the 1977 Treaties

The 1977 treaties and the related documents, which became effective October 1, 1979, signaled important changes for the Panamanian economy. The most obvious benefit was in receipts from operation of the canal. Under the terms of the treaties, the government of Panama receives from the Panama Canal Commission: a fixed annuity of US$10 million; an annual payment of US$10 million for public services such as police and fire protection, garbage collection, and street maintenance, which Panama provides in the canal operating areas and housing areas covered by the treaties; a variable payment of US$0.30 per Panama Canal net ton (see Glossary) for each vessel transiting the canal (in 1986 this amounted to US$57.6 million); and an additional annuity, not to exceed US$10 million, to be paid only when canal operations produce a profit. In 1986, for example, US$1.1 million was paid; in 1984, on the other hand, canal operations registered a US$4.1-million loss, and no payment was made.

The United States controls the tolls because of its majority (five members) on the nine-member Panama Canal Commission, which will operate the canal until December 31, 1999 (see The 1977 Treaties and Associated Agreements, ch. 1). In order to encourage use of the canal, tolls have remained relatively low, although high enough to cover costs. (Under the United States law that implemented the canal treaties, the canal must be operated on a self-sustaining basis.) Maximum use of the canal is in Panama's interest, because its annuity depends on transit tonnage. Tolls were raised by nearly 30 percent in October 1979 and by an additional 9.8 percent in March 1983.

Under treaty provisions, the canal administrator is an American and his deputy is a Panamanian. In 1989, a Panamanian will become administrator and the deputy an American. In order to prepare Panama to assume operation of the canal in the year 2000, the Panama Canal Commission has encouraged the hiring and training of Panamanians for all types of canal-related work. The commission's work force was approximately 82 percent Panamanian in 1987.

According to the treaty provisions, Panama also received substantial assets in the former Canal Zone, including three large ports (Colón, Cristóbal, and Balboa), the railroad across the isthmus, two airfields, 147,700 hectares of land (including housing, utility systems, and streets), a dry dock, large maintenance and repair shops, and service facilities formerly operated by the Panama Canal Company (see fig. 3). Ownership and operation of the canal ports of Balboa and Cristóbal were transferred to Panama in October 1979, but a portion of these port facilities will continue to be used by the Panama Canal Commission for canal operations until the year 2000. Panama also received housing that belonged to the former Panama Canal Company but will continue to supply housing to the Panama Canal Commission and the United States Department of Defense in decreasing amounts until 2000. Some assets and functions of the government of the former Canal Zone, such as schools and hospitals, are maintained by the United States Department of Defense. The Panama Canal Commission continues to operate utilities in the zone areas that it received under the treaty.

The 1977 treaties had important provisions concerning employment and wages. Panamanians would gradually replace United States citizens in the operation of the canal. Perhaps most important was the provision that former Canal Zone employees who became employees in Panama under the treaties were guaranteed wages and conditions similar to those that their position in the zone had commanded. In 1979 a zone employee received about twice the wages of someone employed in a similar position elsewhere in the economy. The canal areas will therefore continue to exert a pull on other domestic wages, making the country less competitive internationally.

Current Use and Future of the Canal

In both the short and the long term, the impact of the 1977 treaties on the economy will depend to a large extent on canal traffic. Since 1979, when the treaties went into effect, the amount of canal traffic has stagnated. In 1979 the canal was transited by 13,056 ships; by 1984 that number had fallen to 11,230—the lowest number in 2 decades. Cargo tonnage also dropped during the same period, from about 154 million to about 140 million tons. Despite the decline in the number of ships and cargo tonnage, toll revenues expanded over the period from US$208 million to US$298 million because of the toll increase in March 1983.

The decline in canal traffic was in large measure a result of the opening of the trans-isthmian oil pipeline, which carries Alaskan North Slope oil. In 1983 the pipeline diverted 30 million tons of oil from the canal. In terms of Panama's economy, the diversion of oil from the canal to the pipeline did not cause alarm as it was little more than a transfer of services.

Some observers expressed concern that the canal had seen its best days and that it would decline in importance over the long run. Latin American trade, much of which passes through the canal, has stagnated because of prolonged regional recession and balance

Thatcher Bridge over Panama Canal
Courtesy Pan American Union

of payments constraints resulting from the regional debt crisis. Many supertankers and bulk cargo carriers are too big for the canal. Even some smaller vessels sought to avoid the delays associated with transiting the canal. Increased tolls also lowered the demand for canal usage. Many coal and banana producers shunned the canal and shipped to Europe from the Caribbean Basin and to the Pacific Basin from the west coast of Latin America. In addition, the canal faced competition from Mexican and United States land bridges (roads or railroads linking Atlantic and Pacific ports). Standardized cargo containers have made land bridges an increasingly attractive option, even though the distances involved are much greater (the United States land bridge is over 5,600 kilometers long) than across the canal. The concern over the future of the canal was partially allayed by the increase in total canal traffic between 1984 and 1986. In 1986 11,925 ships transited the canal, carrying 139 million long tons of cargo and generating US$321 million in tolls and revenues. In 1987 canal tolls and revenues totaled US$330 million. The increase in 1986 was due in large measure to increased automobile trade.

In 1982 Panama joined the United States and Japan, the two principal users of the canal, in an agreement to establish a tripartite commission aimed at studying improvements in or alternatives to the canal. The US$20-million study was expected to be ready in 1991. One modest proposal, at a cost of US$200 million, was that of widening the canal at the Gaillard Cut, its narrowest channel. The Gaillard Cut measured approximately 100 meters when the canal opened in 1914, and in the 1960s it was broadened to about 165 meters. The proposal called for doubling the width of the Gaillard Cut. A more extensive plan, at a cost of US$500 million, proposed widening the entire canal by 16 meters to allow for uninterrupted 2-way traffic along the waterway. The canal's existing capacity was forty-two vessels a day; the less expensive proposal would accommodate fifty ships. The most ambitious plan, however, was that for a second, sea-level canal, which could handle even the largest supertankers without the use of locks. This plan's estimated cost was US$20 billion, considered prohibitive in the light of foreseeable toll revenues. Alternatives to a second canal included an improved railroad system, an express highway for container traffic, and additional pipelines.

Services

Panama's services sector dwarfed agriculture and industry, and its share of GDP was growing in the late 1980s. In 1965 services accounted for about 63 percent of GDP; by 1985 that share had risen to about 73 percent. In the latter year, transportation contributed 25.3 percent of GDP, followed by financial services (14 percent), government services (13.2 percent), wholesale and retail trade (12.3 percent), and other services (8.1 percent).

Transportation and Communications

Transportation was the single most important contributor to Panama's service-oriented economy. The Panama Canal has given great impetus to other transportation services, and many of those, such as the oil pipeline and the CFZ, have achieved a dynamism of their own. In the area of communications, Panama was served by 213,400 telephones in 1984, in addition to 142 radio stations, 6 television channels, and 6 daily newspapers.

The transportation sector has been further broadened by a network of roads, ocean ports, and airports (see fig. 8). The major roads were the Pan-American Highway and the Trans-isthmian Highway (also known as the Boyd-Roosevelt Highway) between Panama City and Colón. In 1984 Panama had 9,535 kilometers of roads, of which 32 percent were asphalted. Panama had only three railroads: two in the west originating in David and Almirante and extending to the Costa Rican border, and one linking Panama City and Colón. The General Omar Torrijos Herrera International

Airport (commonly known as Tocumen International Airport), located near Panama City, served international airlines.

Panama had fourteen ports, the most important of which were Balboa on the Pacific side and Cristóbal on the Atlantic, located at the entrances to the canal. Together, the two ports served 70 percent of the international ships arriving in Panama in 1983. The two ports, however, have declined in regional importance since the 1970s, in part because of technological change and competition. In their prime, Balboa and Cristóbal were transshipment centers of break-bulk traffic. In the 1970s, containerization became widespread; large ships could break the bulk cargo into containers at any port offering container facilities, at which point the cargo could be stored or transshipped through the canal on a smaller vessel. Miami and Kingston developed sophisticated container facilities and contributed to the precipitous decline (from 145,000 tons in 1969 to 38,707 tons in 1980) in transshipment traffic through Balboa and Cristóbal. In order to compete more effectively, US$18 million was spent on Cristóbal in the early 1980s, making it the first container port in Panama. Later plans call for upgrading eight other ports as well.

Oil Pipeline

The trans-isthmian oil pipeline served as a transshipment point for Alaskan North Slope oil en route to the east coast of the United States. The pipeline, completed in October 1982, was 81 kilometers long and had a capacity to move 850,000 barrels of oil a day. The pipeline joined two terminals owned by Petroterminales de Panamá, a joint venture between the Panamanian government and a United States company, Northville Industries.

In 1982 the pipeline generated US$69 million, a figure that rose to US$138.8 million in 1986. The pipeline accounted for 7.4 percent of Panama's GDP in 1985, when value added peaked at US$158.7 million; in 1986 its share of GDP fell to 6 percent. In fact, the pipeline's net contribution to GDP has been small. Despite the increase in activity since 1982, the pipeline has never reached capacity; its daily throughput in mid-1987 was 575,000 barrels. Moreover, if the pipeline had not been built, the transportation of oil across the isthmus could still be accommodated by the canal. The pipeline did, however, free up the canal and was expected to make a greater net contribution to GDP.

Panama's oil pipeline faced competition from the All American Pipeline, which extended from Santa Barbara, California, to McCarney, Texas, where it connected with other pipelines that led to the east coast of the United States and to the Gulf of Mexico.

Figure 8. Transportation System, mid 1980.

146

Nearly completed in 1987, the new pipeline, owned by Celeron Oil Company, was the longest in the United States. Whether the American pipeline would be able to compete effectively with Panama remained uncertain; overland pipeline transport was generally more expensive than sea transport in large tankers.

Colón Free Zone

The CFZ has grown rapidly to become the second largest free zone in the world, after Hong Kong. The CFZ, in existence since 1953, was a base for 460 companies in the late 1980s. Goods from foreign countries were landed and stored or repackaged there and shipped onward without being subject to Panama's customs duties. Among the CFZ services offered were commercial intermediation, break bulk, warehousing, assembly, and transshipment. In addition to its excellent location, foreign firms were attracted to the CFZ because of good transport, communications, and banking services. A state-owned corporation operated the free zone, providing the necessary infrastructure and services.

The CFZ has contributed greatly to Panama's economy. In 1983 the CFZ provided direct employment for 6,000 workers. CFZ earnings in export services were second only to the canal. In 1985 CFZ imports and re-exports totalled US$3.3 billion, down from a peak of US$4.3 billion in 1981; value added in the CFZ made a net contribution of 2.8 percent to GDP. The declining figures reflected the Latin American recession and the concomitant fall in regional trade. The CFZ linked producers in industrialized countries, which in 1984 supplied 60 percent of CFZ imports, primarily with Latin American countries, and accounted for 59 percent of CFZ exports. Since 1983 Japan's exports to the CFZ have surpassed those of the United States; in that year, Japan exported 21 percent of the goods entering the CFZ, followed by the United States (15.5 percent), Taiwan (10 percent), and Hong Kong (9.3 percent).

Observers believed that dependence on the Latin American markets might limit the growth potential of the CFZ. Other constraints to growth included competition from Miami and the tendency of Latin American countries to circumvent the CFZ through bilateral transactions. The greatest potential for CFZ growth lay in expanding manufactured exports, especially to the United States, under the terms of the Caribbean Basin Initiative (CBI). Until the mid-1980s, the value added for manufacturing in the CFZ was rather small; transport, storage, and warehousing contributed the largest share. CFZ activities declined between 1982 and 1984, but stabilized in 1985 and expanded by 15 percent in 1986.

Finance

Panama was considered the most important international banking center in Latin America in the late 1980s. In 1970 only 28 banks operated in Panama's international banking center; by 1987 there were 120, with assets of nearly US$39 billion. The growth in Panama's Eurocurrency (see Glossary), or offshore banking, has contributed to the country's relative prosperity and accentuated the importance of the services sector in the economy. As an example of offshore banking, the Central Bank of India established an office in Panama in the late 1970s to finance its trade with Brazil.

The idea of opening Panama up to international banking was the brainchild of Ardito Barletta, who, as Torrijos's minister of planning in 1969, sought to diversify Panama's economy away from the canal and the CFZ. His timing could not have been better; Panama benefited greatly from the recycling of petrodollars after the 1973 and 1979 oil price hikes. Panama also became a center for flight capital from Latin America and tax evasion dollars from the United States and other countries.

Panama's success in attracting offshore banking has been attributed to the political stability of the Torrijos years, the dollar-based economy, the country's tradition as a trade and business center, and a policy of low taxes on deposits and income. Most importantly, however, Panama's success has been a result of its stringent secrecy laws. In 1970 banking laws were liberalized, secrecy was guaranteed, currency controls were abolished, and few restrictions were imposed on bank transactions. Panama's banking commission had the sole right to conduct general inspections of bank records, and banks were not allowed to disclose information concerning their customers. Ardito Barletta once claimed that Panama's secrecy laws were stricter than those of Switzerland.

Observers disagreed on the benefits derived from offshore banking. Banks were required to maintain offices in Panama, where they generated employment for 10,000 Panamanians, slightly more than the number of jobs associated with the canal. Approximately US$200 million has been injected into the domestic economy each year through loans. Some critics have charged, however, that the offshore banking has "denationalized" Panama's economy. According to this line of thought, offshore banking limits a nation's political and economic autonomy because the government must maintain a favorable investment climate. International capital is highly fungible and is subject to flight in the event of major political or economic disturbances, as occurred in the latter part of 1987.

Panama City street
Courtesy Organization of American States

149

Total deposits in the offshore banks peaked at US$47 billion at the end of 1982 and then fell, primarily as a reflection of Latin America's financial crisis. In 1984 numerous United States banks reduced their Panamanian assets, such as Citibank (by 70 percent) and Bank of America (50 percent). Some banks (Chase Manhattan and Citibank) also reduced their operations within Panama, while others (Security Pacific and Libra Bank International, a London-based consortium) actually left Panama. This drain, however, was partially offset by the increased exposure of other United States banks, such as First National Bank of Chicago, and by the influx of Japanese banks, many of which have made Panama their Latin American banking headquarters. Also, "narcodollars" (income derived from the sale of illegal drugs) reportedly were transferred to Panama from Caribbean havens that were placed under closer scrutiny.

In 1985 the largest banks in Panama's International Financial Center were First National Bank of Chicago (assets worth US$3.6 billion); Banco de la Nación Argentina (US$2.8 billion); American Express Bank (US$2.4 billion); BNP (US$1.4 billion); Deutsche Sudamerikanische Bank (US$1.3 billion); Crédit Lyonnais, Sanwa Bank, Bank of Tokyo, and Sumimoto Bank (US$1.2 billion); and Banco do Brasil (US$1.1 billion).

The foreign share of total deposits in the International Financial Center declined from 94 percent in 1979 to 85 percent in 1985. The assets of 14 Panamanian banks remained virtually constant, at US$5.5 billion from 1982 through 1984; their relative share of total deposits increased from 10 percent in 1982 to 15 percent in 1985 as a result of the reduction of foreign deposits. Founded in 1904, the BNP was the country's most important bank. It served as the government's depository and fiscal agent in addition to being the largest commercial bank with forty-seven branches throughout the country and an agency in New York. The other major state-owned financial institutions were a savings bank (established 1934), a mortgage bank (1973), an agricultural development bank (1973), and a development finance company (1975). The latter two institutions were founded to provide longer-term credit for agricultural and industrial development than was generally available from the commercial banks.

Panama's offshore banking confronted severe challenges in the late 1980s. Firstly, it faced charges that it had become the center for laundering drug money. Given the secretive nature of Panama's banking legislation, substantiating such charges was difficult. According to the United States Department of the Treasury, an estimated US$600 million in drug-related money is laundered through Panama's offshore banking system annually. Since 1985 the United States has pressured Panama to sign the Mutual Legal Assistance Treaty (MLAT), which lifts banking confidentiality. A similar treaty has been signed by the Cayman Islands, the Netherlands Antilles, the Turks and Caicos Islands, Switzerland, Turkey, and Italy. Although Panama has resisted any changes in its banking secrecy regulations, fearing negative repercussions on its International Financial Center, it did make major concessions in a law passed on December 26, 1986. The new law had three basic provisions: penalties for drug trafficking were made more severe; extradition procedures were established; and money-laundering was made a crime. The measures fell short of those established in the MLAT, but they were expected to deflect United States criticism, at least in the short term (see Other Aspects of Panamanian-United States Relations, ch. 4; Involvement in Political and Economic Affairs, ch. 5).

A second major challenge to offshore banking in Panama was that of political instability. The political turmoil of mid-1987 damaged Panama's reputation as a safe haven. International banks were a major target for attacks by progovernment groups seeking to blame foreign elements for the political disturbances. In June the government further shattered investor confidence when it suspended interest payments on its debt to foreign governments, a de facto default. One international bank lowered Panama's rating on the political risk scale, and First National Bank of Chicago closed its Panama branch. Perhaps one-tenth of the estimated US$40 million in deposits left the country as capital flight, creating a liquidity crisis for the country.

Tourism

Panama offered a wide range of tourist attractions and gambling facilities. In 1983 the National Tourism Council was founded to coordinate national tourism in conjunction with the Panamanian Tourism Institute. The number of tourists peaked in 1980 at 377,600 and declined to 302,400 in 1984. Despite the reduction, the expenditures by visitors (in addition to tourists, this category includes travel that is related to business and education) remained virtually unchanged, at about US$130 million per year from 1979 to 1983. During the same period, travelers in transit (including those only changing planes and those who remained in Panama up to 48 hours) injected an additional US$38 million per year into the economy.

Agriculture

For centuries agriculture was the dominant economic activity for most of Panama's population. After construction of the canal, agriculture declined; its share of GDP fell from 29 percent in 1950 to just over 9 percent in 1985. Agriculture has always employed a disproportionate share of the population because of its labor-intensive nature. Nevertheless, the percentage of the labor force in agriculture has also dropped, from 46 percent in 1965 to 26 percent in 1984.

In 1985 crops accounted for 63.3 percent of value added in agriculture, followed by livestock (29.5 percent), fishing (4.3 percent), and forestry (2.9 percent). Despite its relative decline, agriculture was the main supplier of commodities for export, accounting for over 54 percent of total export earnings in 1985. The agricultural sector satisfied most of the domestic demand. The principal food imports were wheat and wheat products, because climatic conditions precluded wheat cultivation. In 1985 the value of food imports was US$108.7 million (8.8 percent of total imports), only half that of food exports.

Between 1969 and 1977, the government undertook agrarian reform and attempted to redistribute land. The expanded role of the state in agriculture improved social conditions in rural areas, but long-term economic effects of the agrarian reform were modest. In the early and mid-1980s, the government sought to reverse the decline of agriculture by diversifying agricultural production, lowering protection barriers, and reducing the state's role in agriculture. In March 1986, the government instituted major changes in the agricultural incentives law and removed price controls, trade restrictions, farm subsidies, and other supports.

Land Use

Panama's land area totals approximately 7.7 million hectares, of which forests account for 4.1 million hectares, followed by pasture land (1.2 million hectares) and permanently cultivated fields (582,000 hectares). About 2 percent of the land was used for roads and urban areas. Nearly all of the cultivated and pasture land was originally forested. A large amount of virgin land has been opened up for cultivation by the Pan-American Highway.

Panama's climate and geology impose major constraints on the development of agriculture. Heavy rainfall throughout the year prevents cultivation of most crops on the Atlantic side of the continental divide (see Regions of Settlement, ch. 2). The Pacific side has a dry season (December to April) and accounts for most of the cultivated land (see fig. 9). The mountainous terrain also restricts cropping. In addition, the country does not have high-quality soils. Most of the areas classified as cultivable are so considered on the assumption that farmers will practice conservation measures, but many do not. The topsoil is thin in most areas, and erosion is a serious problem. Most of the nearly level areas conducive to cultivation are in the provinces of Los Santos, Coclé, Veraguas, and Chiriquí.

A further constraint on production is the practice of slash-and-burn cultivation, in which trees, brush, and weeds are cut and then burned on the patch of ground selected for cultivation. Indians utilized the slash-and-burn method for centuries, and the Spanish made few changes in techniques. In the 1980s, most farmers practiced a slash-and-burn type of shifting cultivation. The thin and poor-quality topsoil yielded an initially good harvest, followed by a smaller harvest the second year. Typically, the land was cultivated for only two years, and then the farmer repeated the process on another plot, allowing the first plot to rest ten years before refarming.

Much of the farming was of a subsistence nature and accomplished with a minimum of equipment. Plowing was generally not practiced on subsistence farms; the seeds were placed in holes made by a stick. Tree cutting, land clearing, weeding, and harvesting were accomplished with a few kinds of knives, principally the machete and the axe, which comprised the major farm implements.

Land Tenure and Agrarian Reform

Before the 1950s, land was readily available to anyone who was willing to clear and plant a plot. The cutting and clearing of forests greatly accelerated as the population increased. By the 1960s, subsistence farmers sometimes reduced the rest period of cleared plots from ten years of fallow to as few as five years because of the unavailability of farm land. The reduced fallow period diminished soil fertility and harvests. Consequently, cropped acreage peaked during the 1960s. The hard life and low income of farmers accelerated the exodus of workers from the countryside to the cities (see Rural Society and Migration, ch. 2).

The long period when new land was easily obtainable contributed to a casual attitude toward land titles. In 1980 only 32.9 percent of the 151,283 farms had such titles. The decline in available agricultural land has made land titling more necessary. Moreover, insecure tenure has been a particularly severe constraint to improved techniques and to commercial crop production. The cost of titling a piece of land, however, has been too high for most subsistence farmers.

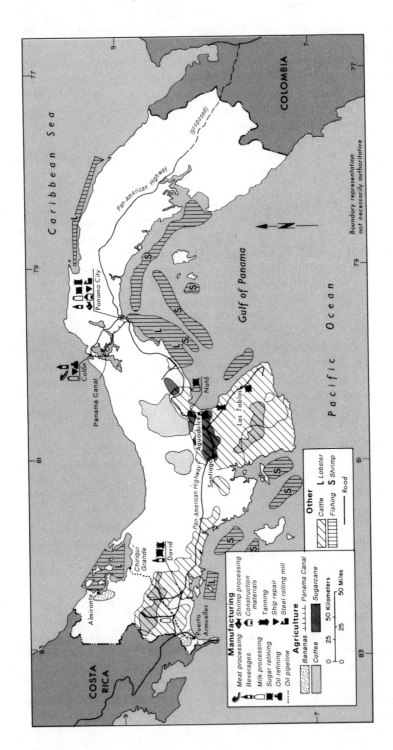

Figure 9. Location of Major Economic Activity

Between 1969 and 1977, the government attempted to redistribute land. In the late 1980s, however, the distribution of land and farm incomes remained very unequal. In 1980 58.9 percent of farms had an annual income below US$200. The issue of unequal land distribution, however, has not been as explosive in Panama as in many other Latin American countries. This was because of the service-oriented nature of the economy and because about half of the population lived in or near Panama City. Also, about 95 percent of all farm land was owner-operated, and virtually all rural families owned or occupied a plot.

In an effort to redistribute land, the government acquired 500,000 hectares of land and expropriated an additional 20 percent of the land. About three-quarters of the land acquired was in the provinces of Veraguas and Panamá. By 1978 over 18,000 families (about 12 percent of rural families in the 1970 census) had access to either individual plots or collectively held land as a result of the redistribution. The land acquisition created uncertainty, however, and adversely affected private investment in agriculture, slowing production in the 1970s.

As part of its agrarian reform, the government placed heavy emphasis on organizing farmers into collectives for agricultural development. Several organizational forms were available, the two most important being *asentamientos* (settlements) and *juntas agrarias de producción* (agrarian production associations). The distinctions between the two were minor and became even more blurred with time. Both encouraged pooling of land and cooperative activity. In some instances, land was worked collectively. Other organizational forms included marketing cooperatives, state farms, and specialized producers' cooperatives for milk, chickens, or pigs. Growth of these agricultural organizations slowed by the mid-1970s, and some disbanded, as emphasis shifted to consolidation.

The cost of agrarian reform was high. The government channeled large amounts of economic aid to organized farmers. Rural credit was greatly increased; farm machinery was made available; improved seeds and other inputs were supplied; and technical assistance was provided. Cooperative farm yields increased, but these higher yields were not impressive, considering the level of investment. Despite the high costs of the government programs, incomes of cooperative farmers remained low. After the mid-1970s, the government changed its policy toward cooperatives and stressed efficiency and productivity instead of equity.

Although the economic results of agrarian reform were disappointing, the social conditions of most farmers improved. The number of rural residents with access to safe water increased by

50 percent between 1970 and 1978. Improved sewerage facilities, community health programs, and rural clinics reduced mortality rates considerably. Major expansion of educational facilities, including education programs for rural residents, helped rural Panamanians become better educated and more mobile.

Crops

The crops category is the largest within agriculture, but its share has fallen slightly, from 66.1 percent in 1980 to 63.3 percent in 1985. During that period, crop production was erratic, and annual growth averaged a mere 1.7 percent. The major crops and foreign exchange earners were bananas and sugar. In the 1980s, however, crop production became increasingly diversified. The production of corn, coffee, beans, and tobacco has increased, as has that of such nontraditional products as melons and flowers. Fruits (especially citrus), cacao (the bean from which cocoa is derived), plantains, vegetables, and potatoes were produced on a minor scale; nevertheless, they were important cash crops for small farms.

Bananas were the leading export item, and in 1985 accounted for 23 percent (US$78 million) of total exports. In that year, the Chiriquí Land Company, a subsidiary of United Brands (formerly United Fruit Company), produced 70 percent of all bananas, followed by private Panamanian producers (25 percent) and the state-owned Corporación Bananera del Atlántico (5 percent). The volume of bananas produced in Panama peaked in 1978 and slowly declined in the 1980s. Observers doubted that United Brands would expand its production in Panama because bananas could be produced more cheaply in Costa Rica and Ecuador.

The history of banana production in Panama virtually coincides with that of United Brands, which has been in Panama since 1899. The company built railroads, port facilities, and storage areas for the processing and export of bananas. In the 1930s, a disease seriously curtailed banana production. In the 1950s, disease-resistant plants were developed, and production increased rapidly. In the early 1970s, a ''banana war'' erupted when banana-producing countries disagreed among themselves and with United Brands about an export tax on bananas. Panama threatened to take over United Brands' plantations. An agreement was reached in 1976 to tax banana exports. In that year, the tax provided the government with US$10 million, nearly 4 percent of all revenues. In addition, United Brands sold all 43,000 hectares of land that it owned in Panama to the government; payment was in tax credits. The government leased back to United Brands over 15,000 hectares for banana production and export operations. Part of the

Harvesting bananas
Courtesy Organization of American States

excess land went to the government's newly established banana companies.

Sugar has traditionally been Panama's second largest crop in terms of production and export value. Panama consumed about half its sugar output and exported most of the rest to the United States. The production of sugar in Panama increased during the 1970s, peaked in 1982 at 260,000 tons, and fell to 165,000 tons in 1986. The dramatic decline after 1982 was because of low world prices and the rapid reduction in the United States quota from 81,200 tons in 1983 to 26,390 tons in 1987. Annual sugar exports earned an average US$40 million from 1975 through 1981 but fell steadily from US$41.3 million in 1983 to US$33 million in 1984, US$27.3 million in 1985, and US$22 million in 1986.

The state has been heavily involved in Panama's sugar production. Under the 1983-84 structural adjustment program, however, the state has privatized, closed, and tried to sell numerous sugar mills. Nonetheless, of the six major sugar mills in Panama, four were still under state control in 1987. The largest was the Corporación Azucarera La Victoria, which in 1985 accounted for 64 percent of total sugar production. Several small mills operated throughout the country, but their output was for domestic consumption only.

The production of coffee has steadily expanded, from 7,000 tons in 1981 to 11,000 tons in 1985. Coffee was Panama's third-largest crop export earner. In 1985 it earned US$15.6 million, which was 4.6 percent of total export earnings.

Rice and corn production also increased in the early 1980s. Panama imported rice in the 1970s but by the mid-1980s experienced a surplus, as a result of the expansion of production in the early 1980s, from 178,000 tons in 1982 to 200,000 tons in 1985. Panama produced 75,000 tons of corn in 1985, but in the same year it imported about 40 percent of the corn it consumed, some of which was used for poultry feed. The government granted incentives to increase corn production.

Livestock

Panama was virtually self-sufficient in livestock production, which included cattle, pigs, chickens, eggs, and milk. Beef was by far the most important product, and output was growing slowly in the 1980s. Between 1981 and 1985, the number of cattle slaughtered rose from 239,000 to 295,000; during the same period, the total stock of cattle increased only slightly, from 1.43 million head to 1.44 million head. Milk production remained steady between 1981 and 1985, averaging 89,140,400 liters a year.

Cattle raising for both meat and milk was common on land on the Pacific watershed and was concentrated in the provinces of Chiriquí, Los Santos, and Veraguas. Most ranches produced both meat and milk, although some specialized in dairy farming. The majority of ranches had fewer than 100 hectares. Cattle were almost entirely grass fed. The grasslands were not particularly productive, lacking added nutrients and other improvements; on average, more than one hectare is required for each head of cattle. Low government credits, competition from regional cattle producers (especially Colombia), and United States market restrictions have hindered the growth of Panama's cattle production.

From 1982 to 1985, poultry production grew rapidly, from 4.5 million chickens to 6.1 million. During the same period, annual egg production also increased, from 28,859 dozen to 31,205 dozen. Pork production has remained steady; the number of pigs in 1985 totalled 210,000.

Fishing and Forestry

Fishing was more important to Panama's economy than forestry, supplying the domestic market and providing substantial export earnings. The waters of the two oceans afforded a variety of fish and crustaceans. Shrimp provided 84 percent of the total value of fishing, and their share of total export earnings increased from 16 percent in 1983 (US$51.4 million) to 18 percent in 1985 (US$60 million). Fish production increased from 117 million kilograms in 1981 to 127 million kilograms in 1985. The most important fish products were anchovies and herring, which were processed into fish meal and oil. Lobster accounted for a minuscule share of fishing products.

Large portions of the country's forests are commercially exploited. Forestry production remained virtually constant in the early 1980s, when the annual forestry output averaged 2,047 cubic meters. The government has implemented a program of reforestation, but the pace of depletion has exceeded that of replanting. Deforestation was most pronounced along the canal, posing a long-term threat to the canal's water level.

Industry

Industrial development has been uneven in Panama. Between 1965 and 1980, industry grew at an average annual rate of 5.9 percent; between 1980 and 1985, that rate was negative 2.2 percent. In 1985 industry accounted for nearly 18 percent of GDP. Within the industrial sector, manufacturing (based primarily on the processing of agricultural products) and mining contributed 9.1 percent to GDP, followed by construction (4.7 percent) and energy (3.4 percent).

Several factors contributed to the rapid expansion of industry between 1950 and 1970. A 1950 law granted liberal incentives and protection from imports to investors, including those in manufacturing. An agreement in 1955 phased out a number of manufacturing activities in the Canal Zone and opened a market for such Panamanian products as bakery goods, soft drinks, meats, and bottled milk. Foreign investment went into relatively large plants for oil refining, food processing, and utilities. The government invested in the infrastructure, especially in roads and the power supply. A building boom increased the demand for construction materials and furniture, further stimulating manufacturing. Management gained experience during the period, and labor productivity increased.

The stagnation in industrial growth during the 1970s resulted from external and internal causes that reduced private investment. Externally, the rise of oil prices, recession in the industrialized countries, and uncertainty relating to the future status of the canal clouded the investment climate. Domestically, a recession reduced construction activity and lowered the demand for manufactured goods. The government built cement and sugar mills to compete with privately owned mills; it also implemented an agrarian reform program, instituted a liberal labor code, and enforced rent control laws. These measures created apprehension on the part of investors, and although the government granted tax holidays, export incentives, and protection from imports, private investment declined. A key goal of the structural adjustment program of the mid-1980s was to increase private investment in industry and to make Panama's industry competitive internationally.

Manufacturing

In 1984 the value added in manufacturing totaled US$344 million, distributed approximately as follows: food and agriculture, 42 percent; textiles and clothing, 11 percent; chemicals, 8 percent; machinery and transport equipment, 1 percent; and other manufacturing, 37 percent. Manufacturing was almost completely oriented toward the domestic market; manufactured goods accounted for a mere 2.5 percent of the value of exports of goods and nonfactor services. Production was concentrated in Panama City (over 60 percent of establishments), with smaller industrial centers at David (10 percent) and Colón (5 percent).

Industrial development has faced the serious constraints of the small size of the domestic market, lack of economies of scale, high labor and unit costs, and government policies of high protection

Field-workers harvest pineapples
Courtesy Inter-American Development Bank

against imports. The greatest growth in manufacturing occurred in response to import-substitution industrialization in the 1960s and 1970s. By the 1980s, however, the "easy phase" of import-substitution industrialization was over; a second phase, that of industrial deepening, was more difficult to carry out in such a small economy. The economy's obvious limitations in manufacturing have been partially offset by an educated labor force, highly developed internal and external transport and communication links, extensive financial facilities, the country's centralized location, and relatively few restrictions on foreign investment. The Panama Canal treaties provided additional space for expanding the CFZ, an ideal location for light industry and assembly plants.

During the 1970s, the public sector took the lead in manufacturing by building a cement plant, sugar mills, and iron and steel works. The structural adjustment program of the mid-1980s sought to reduce the state's role in the economy and to make the private sector the engine of manufacturing growth. The industrial incentives legislation of March 1986 encouraged manufacturers to be export-oriented by removing tax exemptions for those firms that produced for the domestic market. The legislation also provided for maintaining tax exemptions on imported inputs, income, sales, and capital assets for those firms that produced exports. The legislation also lowered import barriers over a period of five years in

161

an effort to increase the productivity and competitiveness of local manufacturing. In addition, new companies were given tariff reductions of up to 60 percent for the first 7 years and 40 percent thereafter.

Since the early 1970s, industrial expansion and job creation have lagged behind the growth of the labor force. In the 1960s, an average of 2,400 jobs was created each year in manufacturing. The rigidities of the industrial incentives law in 1970 and the labor code in 1972 contributed to a decline in manufacturing employment; an average of only 530 new jobs was created each year in manufacturing during the 1970s. The changes introduced in the labor code in March 1986 sought to reverse the antiemployment bias in manufacturing. The slight reduction in the overall unemployment rate in 1986 may be partially attributed to the labor code revisions.

Despite government measures to stimulate manufacturing, Panama's becoming a major industrial center seemed unlikely. Under the CBI, some potential arose for the development of twin-plant operations, especially in association with firms in Puerto Rico, where labor costs were higher than in Panama. In general, however, Panama was unable to compete effectively with Mexico, given the latter country's low labor costs and proximity to the United States market. Also, the possibility existed that industries from East Asia, especially clothing manufacturers, might increasingly relocate to Panama, in an attempt to circumvent United States quotas. This possibility was limited by uncertainty over the United States response. The United States Department of Commerce had called for the reduction of United States imports from Panama, precisely in those products manufactured by Asian investors.

Mining

Despite the variety of mineral deposits and the potential of copper production, the contribution of mining to GDP was negligible, accounting for only US$2.5 million in 1985, down from a 1982 peak of US$4.1 million (both figures at 1970 market prices). The production was restricted to the extraction of limestone, clays, and sea salt. A state company, Cemento Bayano, produced limestone and clay and operated a cement plant with an annual capacity of 330,000 tons.

In the 1970s, several copper deposits were discovered. The largest was Cerro Colorado, in Chiriquí, which if developed would be one of the largest copper mines in the world. Commercial development of the Cerro Colorado project was in the hands of the state-owned Corporación de Desarrollo Minero Cerro Colorado, which had a 51-percent stake in the operation, and of Río Tinto-Zinc,

High-rise condominiums and office buildings in Panama City
Courtesy Inter-American Development Bank

with 49 percent. In the 1970s, ore reserves at Cerro Colorado were estimated at nearly 1.4 billion tons (0.78 copper content). In the late 1970s, the cost of developing the mines was estimated at US$1.5 billion, nearly equal to total GDP at that time. Commercial exploitation was postponed because of low copper prices on the world market but could be undertaken if copper prices rose substantially.

Construction

Construction boomed in the 1970s as a result of government spending on infrastructure and housing. In the early 1980s, with the building of the trans-isthmian oil pipeline and the Edwin Fábrega Dam and associated hydroelectric plant, construction continued to grow, from US$124.3 million in 1980 to US$154.7 million in 1982. Construction fell dramatically in 1983 to US$106.4 million, when the government cut expenditures, and continued to decline in 1984 (US$94.4 million) and 1985 (US$93.4 million). In 1986 the decline was finally reversed, as the sector registered 5-percent growth, generated primarily by private residential building. Thus, the structural adjustment program of 1983 and 1984 achieved its goal of shifting construction activity from the public to the private sector. Nonetheless, the state continued to play a significant role in construction. The government planned to build 2,500 houses and service facilities for low-income families in Panama

City. The construction sector benefited from liberal tax incentives, which included preferential interest rates on mortgages and exemption from capital gains tax on sales of urban real estate through 1988. In the immediate aftermath of the political turmoil of mid-1987, the rate of construction lowered dramatically as credit available to the private sector declined.

Energy

Energy is generally considered a part of industry, to the extent that it is an intermediate input in the production process. In Panama, however, the largest shares of energy are sold to the consumer and to commerce. Therefore, a significant portion of energy used in Panama should be considered a part of the services sector; for the sake of this analysis, however, energy is placed under industry, following conventional practice.

Panama's energy production has increased substantially, from an average annual growth rate of 6.9 percent between 1965 and 1980 to 11.1 percent between 1980 and 1985. The expansion of hydroelectric generating capability has been responsible for most of the growth. Per capita energy consumption has increased, from 576 kilograms of oil equivalent in 1965 to 634 kilograms in 1985. This figure is higher than that of Nicaragua (259 kilograms) and Costa Rica (534 kilograms) but lower than that of Colombia (755 kilograms) and Mexico (1,290 kilograms).

Panama depended on petroleum for 80 percent of its domestic energy needs in the late 1980s. Petroleum exploration has been underway since 1920, but without success; as a result, the country is dependent on imported petroleum. Saudi Arabia and Venezuela were the primary suppliers until 1981, when Mexico replaced Saudi Arabia and joined Venezuela in the San José Agreement of 1980, under which the two countries supply oil to Caribbean Basin countries on concessionary terms. Panama nearly halved its imports of oil between 1977 (20.5 million barrels) and 1983 (11.8 million barrels) in response to rising oil prices. Oil imports have declined as a share of the total value of imports, from 33 percent in 1977 to 19 percent in 1985; in the latter year, the value of oil imports was US$19.2 million.

The country's only oil refinery, near Colón, has a capacity of 100,000 barrels per day. Since 1976 it has been operating far below capacity, because greater use has been made of hydroelectricity. Refinery products supplied the domestic fuel for thermal power plants, most of the transportation system, and other minor uses. In 1977 about 64 percent of the imported crude was reexported after refining, mostly to ships' bunkers; by 1983 that figure had fallen to 35 percent. The government has approved the construction of a second refinery, also near Colón, with a capacity of 75,000 barrels per day.

Hydroelectricity accounted for 10 percent of energy consumption and was the country's main domestic energy resource in the late 1980s. Panama has been substituting hydroelectric power generation for petroleum-based thermal generation since the late 1970s. By 1980 some 30 sites had been identified on the country's numerous rivers, which, if developed, could generate 1,900 megawatts of power. The capacity for generating electricity was 300 megawatts in 1979; in 1984 it had increased to 980 megawatts, of which 650 megawatts was hydroelectric and 330 megawatts was thermal. The increase was due in large measure to the Edwin Fábrega Dam, on the Río Chiriquí, which began operation in 1984 with a generating capacity of 300 megawatts.

In 1985 the Institute of Hydraulic Resources and Electrification, responsible for power generation and distribution, initiated a five-year program to expand Panama's electrical generating capacity. At the time, there were 275,429 electricity consumers. A major goal of the program was to increase the distribution of electricity to an additional 12,000 people in rural areas.

Other energy sources, such as bagasse, charcoal, and wood, accounted for the remainder of energy demand. Firewood supplied half of the country's energy requirements as late as the 1950s but declined rapidly thereafter, partly because of the deforestation it engendered. Bagasse was used as fuel at sugar mills. Coal reserves were discovered in the Bocas del Toro region in the 1970s, near the border with Costa Rica. If commercially exploitable, the coal in the region could be used for generating electricity. In August 1985, the government announced plans to explore the reserves, with funding from the United States Agency for International Development and the United States Geological Survey.

Foreign Economic Relations

In the 1980s, Panama has struggled to adjust to the constraints imposed on its economy by a high external debt. To compensate for a deficit in the capital account, its current account has registered a surplus since 1983, because the services sector has maintained a surplus. Debt has remained high in per capita terms, but the actual debt burden has fallen.

Trade

The value of Panama's merchandise exports has always lagged behind imports. The level of imports relative to the size of the economy has remained large. Panama's consumption standards have been high for a developing country. In the early 1900s, nearly everything consumed in the metropolitan areas was imported because little agricultural surplus and virtually no manufacturing existed. By the mid-1980s, the country was largely self-sufficient in foods except for wheat, temperate-zone fruits and vegetables, and oils and fats. Domestic manufacturing provided a growing share of consumer goods, but the country still imported a wide range of commodities.

With the decline of commodity prices on world markets in the 1980s, the terms of trade (see Glossary) have steadily moved against Panama. Based on a terms of trade index of 100 in 1980, Panama's index stood at 82 in 1985, meaning that it had to export considerably more in order to import the same value of goods it had previously imported.

Panama controlled trade by issuing import and export licenses. Since 1983 tariffs have gradually replaced quantitative restrictions on imports. Taxes were levied on some imports, and incentives were given to nontraditional exports through tax credit certificates.

In 1985 merchandise exports totalled US$414.50 million (excluding reexports from the CFZ), down from US$526.10 million in 1980 (see table 16, Appendix A). Refined petroleum topped the list of export items, at US$100.60 million, but its net contribution to the trade balance was much smaller, given that Panama's crude oil is imported. Bananas, traditionally the largest export item, accounted for US$78.1 million in exports, followed by shrimp (US$53.4 million), manufactured goods (US$45 million), sugar (US$33.3 million), coffee (US$15.6 million), and clothing (US$11.5 million).

About 75 percent of Panama's exports went to industrial countries; Latin America received the other 25 percent. The United States was by far the largest single market, and in 1985 received 60.5 percent of Panama's exports. Most of the remaining exports went to Costa Rica (7.5 percent), the Federal Republic of Germany (West Germany) (5.5 percent), Belgium (4.9 percent), and Italy (4.5 percent). The CBI was expected to increase Panama's exports to the United States. The CBI seeks to provide long-term trade, aid, and investment incentives to promote the economic revitalization of the Caribbean Basin. The most significant incentive is twelve-year, duty-free access of most goods to the United States market. Some omitted goods were footwear, textiles, leather and general apparel, canned tuna, petroleum and petroleum products, rubber and plastic gloves, luggage, and handbags. In addition, special rules limited the eligibility of sugar for duty-free treatment. Twenty countries, including Panama, were granted this access in

January 1984. In 1987 judging the long-term CBI benefits for Panama was premature. Critics charged that few new trade benefits would accrue from the CBI beyond those under the Generalized System of Preferences, which already accommodated 87 percent of Caribbean Basin exports to the United States. In the initial years of CBI implementation, the share of Panama's exports going to the United States remained unchanged.

In 1985 Panama's merchandise imports amounted to US$1.34 billion, or about 30 percent of GDP. In that year, manufactured goods were the largest import item (US$348.6 million), followed by crude oil (US$271.8 million), machinery and transport equipment (US$266.7 million), chemicals (US$158.0 million), and food products (US$142.6 million). Crude oil has traditionally been the largest import item, but in the 1980s its share of imports fell as petroleum prices declined and hydroelectric energy capacity increased.

About one-third of Panama's imports came from the United States, another third from other industrial countries, and one-third from Latin America. In 1985 Panama's imports came from the United States (30.8 percent), Japan (8.9 percent), Mexico (8.2 percent), Venezuela (6.8 percent), and Ecuador (7.2 percent). Mexico and Venezuela supplied 70 percent of Panama's crude oil under the San José Agreement.

Balance of Payments

Because of its domestic use of the United States dollar, Panama had no short-term transfer problem and no foreign exchange constraint. Capital flows and changes in the banking system's foreign assets were less dependent on the current account than was the case in other countries; these items responded mostly to the government's fiscal situation and to conditions affecting international banking.

Panama's balance of payments has always been characterized by a large negative imbalance in its merchandise trade. In the 1970s, this imbalance grew almost uninterruptedly, to a large degree because of rising international prices for crude oil. In the 1980s, the merchandise trade balance continued to be negative; in 1985 merchandise imports exceeded exports by US$904 million (see table 17, Appendix A).

Panama's current account balance has been negative since the 1970s because of large deficits in merchandise trade. In 1982 the current account balance registered a negative US$405.4 million, and the merchandise trade deficit was US$973.8 million. Since 1983, Panama has had to adjust to its heavy external obligations, and the current account, though still negative, improved to a negative US$172.6 million in 1985. The current account has benefited from the large surpluses in services (US$1.02 billion in 1985), which have nearly compensated for the deficits in merchandise trade. Transportation contributed the largest share to the services surplus—US$384 million in 1985. Other sources of services income included official transactions in the canal area, banking, insurance, and shipping. One of the largest drains on the current account was interest payments on the foreign debt.

In 1985 Panama experienced a net capital inflow of US$32.2 million and negative errors and omissions of US$136 million. The foreign reserves in the banking system declined by US$134.7 million. Direct foreign investment in Panama fluctuated in the early 1980s; in 1985 it totalled US$68 million. Panama was open to foreign investment, although it restricted activities in retailing, broadcasting, and mining.

External Debt

One of the major legacies of the Torrijos government was a large external debt. In the 1970s, the government relied increasingly on loans, essentially from abroad, to finance capital investments. The external public debt increased from US$150 million at the beginning of 1970 to US$774 million at the end of 1975. External factors, such as the rise in oil prices, were partly to blame for the larger debt. By the end of 1978, Panama's external debt was nearly US$1.9 billion, about 80 percent of GDP—one of the highest ratios in the world.

In 1985 the external debt reached US$3.6 billion, or 73.5 percent of GDP, which on a per capita basis (US$1,636) was one of the largest in the world (see table 18, Appendix A). Most of the debt (US$3.27 billion) was long-term in its maturity structure; US$2.13 billion was owed to private creditors and US$1.14 billion to official creditors (US$741 million to multilateral agencies and US$403 million to bilateral sources).

Despite the high level of debt, the debt burden, as measured by the ratio of total interest to GDP, fell from 8.0 percent in 1982 to 6.6 percent in 1985. Several factors helped Panama lower its debt burden. These included the drop in world oil prices and the decline in the average interest rate from a high of 11.4 percent in 1982 to 8.5 percent in 1985. In 1983 the government implemented an economic adjustment program, which, from 1982 to 1985, slowed the annual rate of foreign debt accumulation from 16.4 percent to 6.7 percent and cut the private creditors' share of long-term debt from 72 percent to 65 percent.

Panama has rescheduled its loans from international bank creditors in 1983, 1985, and 1987. In September 1985, the Paris Club (a financial consortium of Western financiers and governments) also agreed to restructure US$19 million in principal repayments. An estimated US$1.2 billion was due between 1987 and 1990. Although the debt was still high in per capita terms, the lowered debt burden enhanced the country's chances of successfully rescheduling its loans.

*   *   *

The World Bank's *Panama: Structural Change and Growth Prospects* is an in-depth analysis of Panama's economy, with an emphasis on policy formulation. For comparative studies, see John Weeks's *The Economies of Central America* and issues of the Economist Intelligence Unit's *Country Profile: Nicaragua, Costa Rica, and Panama*. For annual updates of economic activity in Panama, see the Inter-American Development Bank's *Economic and Social Progress in Latin America,* the International Monetary Fund's *Balance of Payments Statistics Yearbooks,* and the World Bank's *World Development Reports*. (For further information and complete citations, see Bibliography.)

Chapter 4. Government and Politics

Cuna Indian mola *design of a winged figure*

IN LATE 1987, PANAMA'S political system was unable to respond to the problems confronting the nation. Protests over the role in the government played by the Panama Defense Forces (Fuerzas de Defensa de Panamá—FDP) and their commander, General Manuel Antonio Noriega Moreno, had produced economic disruption and the appearance of political instability and had contributed to serious strains in relations with the United States. With no immediate resolution of the conflict likely, Panama appeared to be in its most severe political crisis since the 1968 coup, which had made the military the dominant political force in the nation.

The October 1968 coup marked the third time that the military had ousted Arnulfo Arias Madrid from the presidency of Panama. It differed from previous coups, however, in that it installed a military regime that promoted a mixture of populist and nationalist policies, while at the same time assiduously courting international business. Led, until his death in 1981, by the charismatic General Omar Torrijos Herrera, the military used limited but effective repression to prevent civilian opposition groups from returning to power. Torrijos also created the Democratic Revolutionary Party (Partido Revolucionario Democrático—PRD), which became the official ruling party.

The death of Torrijos, in an airplane crash on July 31, 1981, precipitated a prolonged struggle for power. In a little more than four years Panama had three FDP commanders and five civilian presidents. At the same time, both domestic and international pressures for a return to civilian rule increased steadily. Constitutional revisions in 1983, followed by presidential and legislative elections in 1984, were supposed to promote this process. The elections, however, were tainted by widespread allegations of fraud. Whatever credibility the newly installed civilian government had was undermined further in September 1985, when President Nicolás Ardito Barletta Vallarino was forced out of office by General Noriega and the FDP. In the following two years, political tensions continued to increase, fueled by negative publicity abroad, by the murder of a prominent opposition political figure, Dr. Hugo Spadafora, by the open break between General Noriega and his most prominent rival within the military, Colonel Roberto Díaz Herrera, and by serious economic problems, notably a major international debt burden and major capital flight.

The era of military rule had not been without its positive accomplishments. Most notable was the successful negotiation of the 1977 Panama Canal treaties with the United States. These treaties, which went into effect on October 1, 1979, ended the separate territorial status of the Panama Canal Zone and provided for Panama's full control over all canal operations at the end of the century. Under the military, Panama also had emerged as a major international banking center, had become a more prominent actor in world affairs, exemplified by its position as one of the original "Core Four" mediators (along with Mexico, Venezuela, and Colombia) in the Contadora negotiating process seeking to mediate the conflicts in Central America, and had implemented numerous social reforms, raising the standard of living for many of its citizens. In late 1987, however, many of these accomplishments appeared jeopardized by the continuing crisis in civil-military relations and the inability of the Panamanian government to maintain a peaceful evolution toward a more open, democratic political system.

The Constitutional Framework

In 1987 Panama was governed under the Constitution of 1972 as amended by the Reform Acts of 1978 and the Constitutional Act of 1983. This was Panama's fourth constitution, previous constitutions having been adopted in 1904, 1941, and 1946. The differences among these constitutions have been matters of emphasis and have reflected the political circumstances existing at the time of their formulation.

The 1904 constitution, in Article 136, gave the United States the right to "intervene in any part of Panama, to reestablish public peace and constitutional order." Reflecting provisions of the Hay-Bunau-Varilla Treaty, this confirmed Panama's status as a de facto protectorate of the United States (see The United States Protectorate, ch. 1). Article 136, along with other provisions of the Hay-Bunau-Varilla Treaty, such as that giving the United States the right to add additional territory to the Canal Zone whenever it believed this was necessary for defensive purposes, rankled Panamanian nationalists for more than three decades.

In 1939 the United States abrogated its right of intervention in internal Panamanian affairs with the ratification of the Hull-Alfaro Treaty. The 1941 constitution, enacted during Arnulfo Arias's first, brief presidential term, not only ended Panama's constitutionally mandated protectorate status, but also reflected the president's peculiar political views (see The War Years, ch. 1). Power was concentrated in the hands of the president, whose term, along with that of members of the legislature, was extended from four to six years. Citizenship requirements were added that discriminated against the nation's English-speaking black community and other non-Hispanic minorities (see Ethnic Groups, ch. 2).

In October 1941, President Arias was deposed by the National Police (the predecessor of the National Guard and FDP), and the presidency was assumed by Ricardo Adolfo de la Guardia. In 1946 President de la Guardia promulgated a new constitution, which was basically a return to the 1904 document without the offensive Article 136. The 1946 constitution lasted for twenty-six years. Following the 1968 military coup, eleven constitutional guarantees, including freedom of speech, press, and travel, were suspended for several months, and some were not restored fully until after the adoption of the 1972 Constitution. The 1972 Constitution was promulgated by General Torrijos and reflected the dominance of the political system by the general and the military (see The Government of Torrijos and the National Guard, ch. 1).

Article 277 of the 1972 Constitution designated Torrijos as the "Maximum Leader of the Panamanian Revolution," granting him extraordinary powers for a period of six years, including the power to appoint most government officials and to direct foreign relations. On October 11, 1978, this and other temporary provisions of the 1972 Constitution expired, and a series of amendments, ratified by the Torrijos-controlled National Assembly of Municipal Representatives, became law. These amendments called for a gradual return to democratic political processes between 1978 and 1984 and were designed, in part, to assuage United States concerns over the undemocratic nature of the Panamanian political system (see Torrijos Government Undertakes "Democratization," ch. 1).

In 1983 a commission representing various political parties was created to amend further the Constitution in preparation for the 1984 elections. The sixteen-member commission changed nearly half of the Constitution's articles, producing several significant alterations. Article 2 had given the military a special political role, but all mention of this was omitted in the revised draft. The legislature was also revamped. The National Legislative Council was eliminated, and the unwieldy, government-controlled National Assembly of Municipal Representatives, which had 505 representatives, one from each *corregimiento* (municipal subdistrict), became the Legislative Assembly, with 67 members apportioned on the basis of population and directly elected. The independence of the judiciary and the Electoral Tribunal were strengthened, the term of the president was reduced to five years, and two vice presidents were to be elected. Guarantees of civil liberties were strengthened, and official support for candidates in elections was, at least in theory, severely restricted.

The amended Constitution contains 312 articles. Power emanates from the people and is exercised by the three branches of government, each of which is "limited and separate," but all of which, in theory, work together in "harmonious collaboration." The national territory is defined as "the land area, the territorial sea, the submarine continental shelf, the subsoil, and air space between Costa Rica and Colombia." Any ceding, leasing, or other alienation of this territory to any other state is expressly forbidden. Spanish is the country's national language.

Citizenship may be acquired by birth or naturalization. Articles 17 through 50 guarantee a broad range of individual rights, including property rights, but Article 51 gives the president power to suspend many of these by declaring a "state of emergency." Articles 52 through 124 establish the role of the state in protecting the family, regulating labor conditions, promoting education and culture, providing assistance for health and other areas of social security, promoting agriculture, and protecting the environment.

After the elaboration of the composition, powers, and duties of the various organs of the governmental system, the Constitution ends with descriptions of the state's responsibilities with respect to the national economy, public administration, and national security. Engaging in economic activities, for example, is primarily the function of private individuals, but the state will "orient, direct, regulate, replace, or create according to social necessities . . . with the object of increasing national wealth and to ensure its benefits for the largest possible number of the nation's inhabitants." Article 308 provides for amending the Constitution, either through approval of amendments without modification by an absolute majority of two successive elected assemblies or approval with modifications by two assemblies and subsequent ratification of the modified text by a national referendum.

Panama's successive constitutions have been respected in varying degrees by the republic's governments. Since the 1968 coup, opponents of various governments have accused them of violating the spirit and, at times, the letter of the Constitution and of invoking the state of emergency provisions for purely political purposes. Creating public confidence in the rule of law established by the Constitution presented the government with one of its major challenges in the late 1980s.

The Governmental System

The Executive

As is the case throughout most of Latin America, constitutional power in Panama—although distributed among three branches of government—is concentrated in the executive branch. The 1978 and 1983 amendments to the Constitution decreased the powers of the executive and increased those of the legislature, but the executive branch of government remains the dominant power in the governmental system as defined by the Constitution.

The executive organ is headed by the president and two vice presidents. They, together with the twelve ministers of state, make up the Cabinet Council, which is given several important powers, including decreeing a state of emergency and suspending constitutional guarantees, nominating members of the Supreme Court, and overseeing national finances, including the national debt. These officials, together with the FDP commander, attorney general, solicitor general, president of the Legislative Assembly, directors general of various autonomous and semiautonomous state agencies, and president of the provincial councils, make up the General Council of State, which has purely advisory functions.

The president and the two vice presidents, who must be native-born Panamanians and at least thirty-five years of age, are elected to five-year terms by direct popular vote. Candidates may not be related directly to the incumbent president or have served as president or vice president during the two preceding terms. Should the president resign or be otherwise removed from office, as was the case with President Ardito Barletta in 1985, he is replaced by the first vice president, and there is no provision for filling the vacancy thus created in the vice presidential ranks.

Under the Constitution, the president has the exclusive right to appoint or remove ministers of state, maintain public order, appoint one of the three members of the Electoral Tribunal, conduct foreign relations, and veto laws passed by the Legislative Assembly. In theory a veto may be overridden by a two-thirds majority vote of the assembly. In addition, many powers are exercised by the president jointly with the appropriate individual cabinet member, including appointing the FDP high command, appointing and removing provincial governors, preparing the budget, negotiating contracts for public works, appointing officials to the various autonomous and semiautonomous state agencies, and granting pardons. The president's power to appoint and remove cabinet members would seem to make the requirement for operating with the consent of the cabinet largely a formality, but the FDP and its allies in the PRD frequently have dictated the composition of the cabinet, using this as a means to exercise control over the president.

The two vice presidencies are relatively powerless positions, but since three vice presidents have succeeded to the presidency during the 1980s, the posts are not insignificant. The first vice president acts as chief executive in the absence of the president, and both have votes in the Cabinet Council.

The ministers of state include the ministers of agriculture, commerce and industries, education, finance, foreign relations, government and justice, health, housing, labor and social welfare, planning and economic policy, the presidency, and public works. There is no ministry directly representing or having jurisdiction over the FDP (see Missions and Organization of the Defense Forces, ch. 5). Nevertheless, the minister of government and justice has nominal authority over the FDP's police functions, along with control over prisons, civil aviation, and internal communications, making this one of the most powerful cabinet posts. This ministry also supervises local government in the Comarca de San Blas as well as in the nine provinces, thus exerting central government control over local affairs.

The Legislature

The 1983 amendments to Panama's Constitution created a new legislative organ, the Legislative Assembly, a unicameral body with sixty-seven members, each of whom has an alternate. Members and alternates are elected for five-year terms that run concurrently with those of the president and vice presidents. To be eligible for election, an individual must be at least twenty-one years of age and be a Panamanian citizen either by birth or by naturalization with fifteen years of residence in Panama subsequent to naturalization. The legislature holds two four-month sessions each year and may also be called into special session by the president.

In theory, the assembly has extensive powers. It can create, modify, or repeal laws, ratify treaties, declare war, decree amnesty for political offenses, establish the national currency, raise taxes, ratify government contracts, approve the national budget, and impeach members of the executive or judicial branches. There are, however, significant limitations on these powers, both in law and in practice. Members are nominated for election by parties, and the parties may revoke their status as legislators. This gives the official government party, the PRD, and its allies the power to ensure conformity with government policy and prevent defections from its ranks. Moreover, there are no provisions for legislative control over the military. The legislature also is severely limited in its ability to control the budget. Under Article 268 of the Constitution, the assembly is prohibited from adding to the budget submitted by the executive without the approval of the Cabinet Council. It may not repeal taxes included in the budget unless, at the same time, it creates new taxes to make up any revenue lost.

Legislative Palace, Panama City
Courtesy Embassy of Panama

Differences in practice are also important. Since its creation, the assembly has never rejected an executive nomination for a government post, refused to ratify a treaty, or turned down an executive request for grants of extraordinary powers or for the establishment or prolongation of a state of emergency. The opposition, which held twenty-two seats in late 1987, has used the assembly as a forum to attack government policies and to criticize the role played in the administration by the FDP, but it has been unable to block or even seriously delay any government project. Assembly debates normally are broadcast live, but during the disturbances of June 1987, speeches by opposition members frequently were not carried on the radio.

The lack of institutional independence also has inhibited the development of local or special interest representation within the assembly. The parties' tight control over the selection of candidates and their subsequent performance as legislators works against such representation, as does the dominance of the executive branch. This control is further strengthened by the fact that elections are held only every five years and occur in conjunction with presidential elections.

Should political conditions change in Panama and the dominant role of the military be significantly reduced, the Legislative Assembly has the potential to emerge as a significant participant in the national political process, but its powers would still be less extensive than those exercised by the executive branch. Under the circumstances existing in late 1987, it lacked both the power and the will to block, or even significantly modify, government projects and served largely as a public debating forum for government supporters and opponents.

The Judiciary

The Constitution establishes the Supreme Court as the highest judicial body in the land. Judges must be Panamanian by birth, be at least thirty-five years of age, hold a university degree in law, and have practiced or taught law for at least ten years. The number of members of the court is not fixed by the Constitution. In late 1987, there were nine justices, divided into three chambers, for civil, penal, and administrative cases, with three justices in each chamber. Judges (and their alternates) are nominated by the Cabinet Council and subject to confirmation by the Legislative Assembly. They serve for a term of ten years. Article 200 of the Constitution provides for the replacement of two judges every two years. The court also selects its own president every two years.

The Constitution defines the Supreme Court as the guardian of "the integrity of the Constitution." In consultation with the attorney general, it has the power to determine the constitutionality of all laws, decrees, agreements, and other governmental acts. The court also has jurisdiction over cases involving actions or failure to act by public officials at all levels. There are no appeals from decisions by the court.

Other legislation defines the system of lower courts. The nation is divided into three judicial districts: the first encompasses the provinces of Panamá, Colón, and Darién; the second, Veraguas, Los Santos, Herrera, and Coclé; the third, Bocas del Toro and Chiriquí (see fig. 1). Directly under the Supreme Court are four superior tribunals, two for the first judicial district and one each for the second and third districts. Within each province there are two circuit courts, one for civil and one for criminal cases. The lowest regular courts are the municipal courts located in each of the nation's sixty-five municipal subdivisions. In the tribunals, the judges are nominated by the Supreme Court, while lower judges are appointed by the courts immediately above them.

The Constitution also creates a Public Ministry, headed by the attorney general, who is assisted by the solicitor general, the district and municipal attorneys, and other officials designated by law. The attorney general and the solicitor general are appointed in the same way as Supreme Court justices, but serve for no fixed term.

Lower-ranking officials are appointed by those immediately above them. The functions of the Public Ministry include supervising the conduct of public officials, serving as legal advisers to other government officials, prosecuting violations of the Constitution and other laws, and arraigning before the Supreme Court officials over whom the Court "has jurisdiction." This provision pointedly excludes members of the FDP.

Several constitutional provisions are designed to protect the independence of the judiciary. These include articles that declare that "magistrates and judges are independent in the exercise of their functions and are subject only to the Constitution and the law"; that "positions in the Judicial Organ are incompatible with any participation in politics other than voting"; that judges cannot be detained or arrested except with a "written order by the judicial authority competent to judge them"; that the Supreme Court and the attorney general control the preparation of the budget for the judicial organ; and that judges "cannot be removed, suspended, or transferred from the exercise of their functions except in cases and according to the procedures prescribed by law."

The major defect in the judicial system lies in the manner in which appointments are made to the judiciary. Appointments of judges and of the attorney general are subject to the approval of the Legislative Assembly, but that body has functioned as a rubber stamp for candidates selected by the executive. Lower-level appointments, made by superiors within the judicial organ, are not subject to assembly approval. In addition, the first two Supreme Court justices appointed after the 1984 elections were both former attorneys general, closely associated with the government and even involved in some of its most controversial actions, such as the investigation of the murder of opposition leader Spadafora. As a result, the opposition has regularly denounced the judicial system for being a political organ controlled by the FDP and the PRD. Numerous external observers, including the Inter-American Commission on Human Rights of the Organization of American States (OAS), the United States Department of State, and various human rights organizations, also have criticized the lack of independence of the Panamanian judiciary and of the Public Ministry (see Administration of Justice, ch. 5).

State Agencies and the Regulation of Public Employees

In addition to the three branches of government, the state apparatus includes numerous independent or quasi-independent agencies and institutions that function in a variety of ways. The most important of these is the three-member Electoral Tribunal. The

Constitution provides that the executive, legislative, and judicial branches of government will each select one of the members of this body. The tribunal is charged with conducting elections, tabulating and certifying their results, regulating, applying, and interpreting electoral laws, and passing judgment on all allegations of violations of these laws. The tribunal also conducts the registration of voters and the certification of registered political parties and has jurisdiction over legal disputes involving internal party elections. Its decisions are final and may be appealed only in cases where the tribunal is charged with having violated constitutional provisions. Although the tribunal may pass judgment on charges of violations of electoral laws and procedures, the prosecution of those charged with such violations is in the hands of the electoral prosecutor, an individual independent of the tribunal who is appointed by the president for a single term of ten years.

While autonomous in theory, in practice the Electoral Tribunal has consistently followed the dictates of the government and the FDP. This was exemplified most clearly in the decision to certify the results of the 1984 elections, dismissing all charges of fraud and other irregularities. The position of the electoral prosecutor is even more subject to administrative control. The opposition parties consistently have attacked the lack of independence of the tribunal and the prosecutor and have refused to participate in tribunal-controlled projects aimed at reforming the electoral code in preparation for the 1989 elections. President Eric Arturo Delvalle Henríquez urged broad participation in such efforts and promised to appoint a member of the opposition to the tribunal, but such actions did not satisfy the opposition. The tribunal, itself, has declared that it is not provided adequate funds for the tasks with which it is charged.

The Constitution also provides for an independent comptroller general who serves for a term equal to that of the president and who may be removed only by the Supreme Court. The comptroller is charged with overseeing government revenues and expenditures and investigating the operations of government bodies. Although independent in theory, in practice holders of this office have virtually never challenged government policy.

Quasi-independent governmental commissions and agencies include the National Bank of Panama; the Institute of Hydraulic Resources and Electrification, which is in charge of the nation's electrical utility; the Colón Free Zone; and the University of Panama. Other state agencies and autonomous and semiautonomous agencies function in various capacities within the social and economic system of the nation.

Public employees, defined by the Constitution as "persons appointed temporarily or permanently to positions in the Executive, Legislative, or Judicial Organs, the municipalities, the autonomous and semiautonomous agencies, and in general those who collect remuneration from the State," are all to be Panamanian citizens and are governed by a merit system. The Constitution prohibits discrimination in public employment on the basis of race, sex, religion, or political affiliation. Tenure and promotion, according to Article 295, are to "depend on their competence, loyalty, and morality in service." Several career patterns relating to those in public service are outlined and standardized by law. The Constitution also identifies numerous individuals, including high political appointees, the directors and subdirectors of autonomous and semiautonomous agencies, secretarial personnel, and temporary employees, who are exempted from these regulations. In addition, the Constitution stipulates that a number of high government officials, including the president and vice presidents, Supreme Court justices, and senior military officials, must make a sworn declaration of their assets on taking and leaving office. In practice, these provisions often are ignored or circumvented. Public employment is characterized by favoritism, nepotism, and a tendency to pad payrolls with political supporters who do little if any actual work.

Provincial and Municipal Government

The nine provincial governments are little more than administrative subdivisions of the central government. Article 249 of the Constitution states that "in each province there shall be a Governor freely appointed and removed by the Executive who shall be the agent and representative of the President within his jurisdiction." In addition, each province has a body known as the Provincial Council, composed of district (*corregimiento*) representatives. The governor, mayors, and additional individuals "as determined by the law" also take part in each council, but without voting rights. The powers of these councils are largely advisory, and they lack actual legislative responsibility. The Comarca de San Blas, inhabited largely by Cuna Indians, has a distinct form of local government headed by caciques, or tribal leaders (see Indians, ch. 2).

In contrast, the nation's sixty-five municipal governments are "autonomous political organizations." Although closely tied to the national government, municipal officials, under Article 232 of the Constitution, may not be removed from office by the national administration. In each municipality, mayors, the directors of municipal administration, and their substitutes (*suplentes*) are directly elected for five-year terms. There is, however, an additional constitutional provision that the Legislative Assembly may pass laws requiring that officials in some or all municipalities are to be appointed by the president rather than elected. In 1984 municipal officials were elected in a separate election, held on short notice after the election of the president and the legislature. Opposition parties protested the timing and conditions of these elections, but participated. The great majority of offices, including those in the capital, were won by pro-government candidates, but opposition parties did gain control of a few municipalities, notably in David, capital of Chiriquí Province.

Municipalities are divided further into districts, from each of which a representative is elected to the Municipal Council. Should a town have fewer than five districts, five council members are chosen in at-large elections. These districts, in turn, have their own form of local government, headed by a *corregidor,* and including a *junta communal* made up of the *corregidor,* the district's representative to the Municipal Council, and five other residents "selected in the form determined by law."

The major concern of municipal and district officials is the collection and expenditure of local revenues. These local politicians have some control over public works, business licenses, and other forms of local regulations and improvements, but many functions that fall within the jurisdiction of local governments in other nations, such as educational, judicial, and police administration, are left exclusively to the jurisdiction of the central government. Local administrations do contribute to the cost of schools, but the amount of their contribution is determined at the national level, based on their population and their state of economic and social development.

Nationalism, Populism, and Militarism: The Legacy of Omar Torrijos

From 1968 until his death in an airplane crash in 1981, General Torrijos dominated the Panamanian political scene. His influence, greater than that of any individual in the nation's history, did not end with his death. Since 1981 both military and civilian leaders have sought to wrap themselves in the mantle of Torrijismo, claiming to be the true heirs of the general's political and social heritage. As of the late 1980s, none had been particularly successful in this effort.

Before 1968 Panama's politics had been characterized by personalism (*personalismo*), the tendency to give one's political loyalties to an individual, rather than to a party or particular ideological platform (see The Oligarchy under Fire, ch. 1). The dominant force had been the traditional elite families, known as the *rabiblancos*

Political rally with poster of Torrijos
Courtesy National Archives

(white tails), concentrated in Panama City. They manipulated
nationalist sentiment, largely directed against United States control over the Canal Zone, the National Guard, and various political parties in order to maintain their control. The most dominant
individual in the pre-1968 period was Arnulfo Arias, a charismatic,
right-wing nationalist who was both feared and hated by the
National Guard's officers. His overthrow in 1968 marked the third
time that he had been ousted from the presidency, never having
been allowed to finish even half of the term for which he had been
elected.

It soon became apparent that the 1968 coup differed fundamentally from those that preceded it. Torrijos actively sought to add
lower- and middle-class support to the power base provided by his
control over the military, using a mixture of nationalism and
populism to achieve this goal. He cultivated laborers, small farmers, students, and even the communists, organized in Panama as
the People's Party (Partido del Pueblo—PdP). He excluded the
traditional elites from political power, although he left their economic power base largely untouched. Political parties were banned,
and the legislature was dissolved (until replaced in 1972 by the
National Assembly of Municipal Representatives, 505 largely
government-selected representatives of administrative subdistricts
supposedly elected on a nonpartisan basis). Torrijos justified his

185

policies as being required by the pressing social needs of the population and by the overriding need to maintain national unity in order to negotiate a treaty with the United States that would cede sovereignty over the Canal Zone and ultimately give control of the Panama Canal to Panama.

In the early 1970s, the strength of the populist alliance forged by Torrijos was impressive. He had reduced the traditional antagonism between the National Guard and the students, purging disloyal elements within both in the process. The loyalty of the middle classes was procured through increased public-sector employment. Major public housing projects, along with expanded health, education, and other social service programs, helped maintain support in urban areas. Labor leaders were cultivated through the adoption of a much more favorable labor code, and a constant emphasis on the necessity of gaining control over the canal undercut the nationalist appeal of Arnulfo Arias. By 1976, however, rising inflation, increased unemployment, and the continued failure to negotiate a canal treaty had begun to undermine the general's popularity.

The 1977 signing of the Panama Canal treaties, giving Panama full control over the canal in the year 2000, actually added to the problems confronting Torrijos. There was considerable opposition in Panama to some provisions of the treaties, and it took all of the general's prestige to secure the needed two-thirds majority for ratification in an October 1977 national plebiscite. Resentment further increased when the government acceded to several amendments passed by the United States Senate after the plebiscite (see The 1977 Treaties and Associated Agreements, ch. 1). At the same time, in order to facilitate United States ratification of the treaties, Torrijos found it necessary to promise to restore civilian rule and return the military to the barracks.

The 1978 amendments to the Constitution were the first step in the process of restoring civilian rule. That same year, the government allowed exiled political opponents to return, permitted the re-emergence of political parties, and promised to hold legislative elections in 1980 and presidential elections in 1984. Only parties that could register 30,000 members, however, would gain official recognition. Torrijos and his supporters used the new system to create their own political party, the PRD, which tried to combine the old elements of the Torrijos coalition into a single political structure. Torrijos also appointed a new civilian president, Aristides Royo, and announced that he was relinquishing the special powers he had exercised since 1972.

Opponents argued that the pace of democratization was too slow and called for immediate, direct election of both the president and a representative legislature. Ultimately, however, most sought to achieve legal status for their parties. A major exception was Arnulfo Arias's Panameñistas, who initially boycotted the entire process. In the 1980 elections for nineteen of the fifty-seven seats in the legislature, the principal parties to emerge were the PRD, with twelve seats, and the opposition National Liberal Party (Partido Liberal Nacional—PLN), with five seats, and Christian Democratic Party (Partido Demócrato Cristiano—PDC), with one seat.

Political Developments in the Post-Torrijos Era

The death of General Torrijos in a July 1981 airplane crash represented a major break in the pattern of Panamanian politics (see The Post-Torrijos Era, ch. 1). The next several years saw considerable turmoil both in the National Guard and among the political leadership, as various individuals jockeyed to fill the void created by Torrijos's untimely death. Command of the National Guard was initially assumed by Colonel Florencio Florez Aguilar, but in March 1982, a struggle for power among the officers resulted in his replacement by Colonel Rubén Darío Paredes, who promptly promoted himself to general and, four months later, forced President Royo to resign. In December further changes in the National Guard's command structure saw the emergence of Colonel Noriega as chief of staff and the likely successor to Paredes.

On April 24, 1983, nearly 88 percent of the voters in a national referendum approved further amendments to the Constitution designed to set the stage for the 1984 presidential and legislative elections. Much of the rest of the year was devoted to maneuverings by Paredes and other potential presidential candidates, seeking to gain support for their ambitions and to form coalitions with other political groups and parties, in order to further enhance their prospects. By September 13 parties had gained the 30,000 signatures necessary for official registration. These included the Panameñistas, as Arnulfo Arias reversed his longstanding boycott of the political process. Nominated by the PRD and several other parties, Paredes resigned from his post as the National Guard's commander to pursue his presidential ambitions. Nevertheless, after Noriega was promoted to general and took over command of the National Guard, he quickly moved to undercut Paredes, leading to a sudden announcement of Paredes's withdrawal as a presidential candidate in September.

Paredes's withdrawal led to considerable confusion in the political process. Ultimately, two major coalitions emerged and presented candidates for president. (Although the parties united behind their

187

presidential candidates, they nevertheless ran separate slates for seats in the legislature.)

The National Democratic Union (Unión Nacional Democrática—UNADE) was formed by six parties: the PRD; the Labor and Agrarian Party (Partido Laborista Agrario—PALA), frequently referred to simply as the Labor Party; the PLN; the Republican Party (PR—Partido Republicano); the Panameñista Party (Partido Panameñista—PP), a small faction that broke away from the majority of Panameñistas, who continued to follow Arnulfo Arias; and the Broad Popular Front (Frente Amplio Popular—FRAMPO). UNADE's presidential candidate was Nicolás Ardito Barletta, an international banker with little political experience. PR leader Eric Arturo Delvalle and PLN veteran Roderick Esquivel received the vice presidential nominations. UNADE's principal competition was the Democratic Opposition Alliance (Alianza Democrática de Oposición—ADO), which encompassed three major parties: the majority of Panameñistas organized in the Authentic Panameñista Party (Partido Panameñista Auténtico—PPA), the PDC, and the National Liberal Republican Movement (Movimiento Liberal Republicano Nacional—MOLIRENA). A number of smaller parties also joined the coalition. ADO's presidential candidate was eighty-three-year-old Arnulfo Arias. Carlos Francisco Rodríguez and Christian Democratic leader Ricardo Arias Calderón were its vice presidential candidates.

Five minor candidates also entered the race. They included General Paredes, who reentered the field as the candidate of the Popular Nationalist Party (Partido Nacionalista Popular—PNP); Carlos Iván Zúñiga of the Popular Action Party (Partido de Acción Popular—PAPO); and the candidates of three small, far-left parties.

The campaign and election were marred by violence and repeated charges by Arnulfo Arias and other opposition candidates that the Guard was using force, fraud, and intimidation to promote Ardito Barletta's candidacy. Official counting of the vote was delayed for several days and the Electoral Tribunal appeared divided, but ultimately the government certified Ardito Barletta as president, declaring that he had won with 300,748 votes to 299,035 for Arias. None of the minor candidates won more than 16,000 votes. All parties outside the major alliances plus the smallest members of the UNADE coalition (FRAMPO and the PP) lost their legal status by failing to receive 3 percent of the total vote. Supporters of Arnulfo Arias charged that Ardito Barletta's victory was the result of massive government fraud and organized several protest demonstrations, but to no avail. Charges of fraud also were launched against the winners of several legislative seats. In these races, official returns gave a large majority to members of the government coalition; the PRD won thirty-four seats, the PPA fourteen, PALA seven, the PDC five, the PR and MOLIRENA three each, and the PLN one.

Disturbances continued for weeks after the announcement of Ardito Barletta's victory, contributing to a decision to postpone scheduled municipal elections. The disturbances also aggravated an already deteriorating economic situation, fueled by a massive debt and a rising budget deficit. In November 1984, shortly after his inauguration, Ardito Barletta attempted to implement an austerity program and to reduce the budget deficit through increased taxes. These measures led to a wave of strikes and public demonstrations, and the president was forced to back off on some of his proposals.

Conditions continued to deteriorate in 1985. Elements of the government coalition joined in protests against Ardito Barletta's economic policies, and pressures from the National Guard and the PRD forced the president to agree to changes in several key cabinet posts. Both business and labor confederations withdrew from government-sponsored meetings to discuss the situation, and labor disturbances increased. In August Noriega publicly criticized the government.

Rumors of a coup were spreading when, on September 14, 1985, the headless body of a prominent critic of Noriega, Dr. Hugo Spadafora, was found in Costa Rica. This discovery unleashed another round of protest demonstrations. Noriega and the National Guard denied any involvement in the murder, but they refused to allow an independent investigation. When Ardito Barletta seemed to indicate some willingness to do so, he was hurriedly recalled from a visit to the United Nations (UN) and, on September 28, forced to resign. Vice President Delvalle became the fifth president in less than four years.

The ousting of Ardito Barletta failed to calm the situation. Protests over Spadafora's murder and over the economic situation continued. In October the government was forced to close all schools for several days. Rising tensions also began to affect relations with the United States, which had opposed the ousting of Ardito Barletta, and even created problems within the major pro-government party, the PRD, which underwent a shake-up in its leadership.

The new administration initially attempted to reverse the rising tide of discontent by returning to the populist policies of the Torrijos era. Prices of milk, rice, and petroleum were lowered, and President Delvalle announced that any agreement with the International Monetary Fund (IMF—see Glossary) would be based on negotiations with labor and with the private sector. Economic realities, however, soon forced the government to impose an austerity program remarkably similar to that advocated by Ardito Barletta and to introduce, over strong objections from the unions, sweeping reforms in the labor code, designed to make Panama more attractive for foreign and domestic investment (see Wage Policy and Labor Code, ch. 3). A national strike protesting the new policies failed when Noriega and the FDP supported Delvalle. The new policies produced some economic improvement but did nothing to resolve mounting political problems.

Panama's domestic problems were paralleled by growing criticism abroad, notably in the United States. In March 1986, the Subcommittee on Western Hemisphere Affairs of the United States Senate Committee on Foreign Relations began holding hearings on the situation in Panama, and the following month hearings also began in the House of Representatives. In June a series of articles by Seymour Hersh alleging involvement by Panamanian officials in narcotics trafficking, the murder of Spadafora, and the passing of sensitive intelligence to Cuba were published in the *New York Times* (see Involvement in Political and Economic Affairs, ch. 5). Both within and outside Panama, the increased criticism focused attention on the military and on General Noriega. Delvalle's civilian government found it increasingly difficult to contend with the perception that it was little more than a pliant tool of the military. These perceptions were further strengthened in October 1986, when the president, despite open protests, was forced to dismiss four cabinet ministers and appoint their replacements from a list prepared by the PRD.

Tensions also increased between the government and opposition media within Panama in 1986. Roberto Eisenman, Jr., editor of *La Prensa,* took refuge in the United States, alleging that there was a government plot to kill him. Radio Mundial, owned by opposition political leader Carlos Iván Zúñiga, was ordered closed. But despite increased protests and international pressures, the government's hold on power seemed unshaken.

The situation changed abruptly in June 1987. A long-time power struggle within the FDP between Noriega and his chief of staff, Colonel Roberto Díaz Herrera, led to the forced retirement of Díaz Herrera on June 1. Six days later, the colonel responded by a series of public denunciations, accusing Noriega of involvement in the deaths of Torrijos and Spadafora and of using massive fraud to ensure the victory of Ardito Barletta in the 1984 elections. The result was widespread rioting. The opposition demanded that both Noriega and Delvalle resign, and numerous civic and business groups formed the National Civic Crusade (Cruzada Civilista

Nacional—CCN) to press for changes in the government. As demonstrations spread, the government declared a state of emergency, suspending constitutional rights and instituting censorship (see Administration of Justice; National Security, ch. 5). The CCN responded by calling a national strike that paralyzed the economy for several days. Violent actions by government forces and anti-government demonstrators further polarized public opinion. The leadership of Panama's Roman Catholic Church joined in criticism of the government but urged a peaceful solution to the national crisis. Such calls were ignored by the government, which, instead, threatened to arrest those involved in the protests and seize the property of businesses that joined in the strike, closed the schools, and unleashed a virulent propaganda campaign accusing its opponents of being linked with United States interests that wanted to abort the Panama Canal treaties.

The general strike collapsed after a few days, but protests did not end. Periodic protests, strikes, and demonstrations continued throughout the summer and fall of 1987. Relations with the United States deteriorated rapidly as the government charged the United States embassy with supporting the opposition and bitterly protested a United States Senate resolution calling for an investigation of the charges made by Díaz Herrera. An attack on the embassy by a mob and the arrest of United States diplomatic and military personnel by the FDP led to a suspension of military assistance by the United States. At the end of 1987, relations were more strained than at any time since the 1964 riots.

The continued civil strife also badly damaged Panama's economy. The future of the banking sector seemed especially imperiled if the deadlock between the government and its opponents should be prolonged.

In late 1987, it seemed clear that the CCN and the opposition political parties could not, by themselves, force a change in either the military or civilian leadership. Indeed, their efforts may have solidified military support behind Noriega and Delvalle. But it was equally clear that the incumbent leadership could neither restore business confidence nor stop the steady flight of capital from the country. Efforts to portray the conflict as a class struggle or as part of a United States plot to retain control of the canal only exacerbated the situation. Restoring order, rebuilding the economy, and creating faith in the political system were formidable tasks that became more difficult with each passing month. Panama, in late 1987, was a society in crisis, with a political system that could not function effectively, but the government appeared determined to resist any effort to produce fundamental changes.

Political Forces

During the first decades of independence, Panamanian politics were largely dominated by traditional, upper-class families in Panama City. By the 1940s, however, the populist nationalism of Arnulfo Arias and the growing strength of the National Police (later the National Guard and then the FDP) had begun a steady process of reducing the oligarchy's ability to control events. Following World War II, students and, to a lesser extent, labor groups became more active in national politics. The 1968 military coup, which brought Torrijos to power, represented both the ascendancy of the military as the preeminent political force in Panama and a further diminution in the influence of traditional political parties and elite families. At the same time, the growth of the Panamanian economy gave business and professional organizations greater importance and potential influence.

From the 1964 riots until the 1978 ratification of the Panama Canal treaties, the issue of United States control over the Panama Canal dominated the national political scene (see The 1964 Riots, ch. 1). When treaty ratification largely removed that issue, the focus shifted back to internal political conditions, and pressures, both domestic and international, for a return to civilian rule mounted steadily. Internal political dynamics had changed fundamentally, however, during the Torrijos era. His death in 1981 unleashed a struggle for power within the military, between the military and civilians, and among civilians, which has continued and intensified in subsequent years.

Political Parties

Panama inherited the traditional political parties of Colombia—the Liberal Party and the Conservative Party—which vied against one another from 1903 until the 1920s (see Organizing the New Republic, ch. 1). This proved to be an unnatural party alignment: the Conservatives had never identified strongly with the independence movement and were not able to develop a mass following. The dominant political focus was rather on divisions within the Liberal Party. In time, the Liberals split into factions clustered around specific personal leaders who represented competing elite interests. The emergence of Arnulfo Arias and the Panameñistas provided a major challenge to the factionalized Liberals. The creation of a military-linked party in the 1950s, the National Patriotic Coalition (Coalición Patriótica Nacional—CPN), further reduced the Liberals' strength. Liberals (the PLN) did win the 1960 and 1964 presidential elections, but lost in 1968 to Arnulfo Arias, who

*Opposition march in
Panama City, August 1987
Courtesy Picture Group
(Bill Gentile)*

*General Manuel Antonio
Noriega Moreno, August 1987
Courtesy Picture Group
(Bill Gentile)*

was ousted promptly by the military. In the aftermath of that coup, the military declared political parties illegal. Despite this edict, the PLN and the PPA survived the period of direct military rule and other parties, such as the PDC, actually gained strength during this period.

The first party to register after political parties were legalized in late 1978 was the PRD. Designed to unify the political groups and forces that had supported Torrijos, the PRD, from its inception, was linked closely with and supported by the military. Proclaiming itself the official supporter and upholder of Torrijismo, the vaguely populist political ideology of Torrijos, the PRD included a broad spectrum of ideologies ranging from extreme left to right of center. The prevailing orientation was left of center. Like the ruling Institutional Revolutionary Party (Partido Revolucionario Institucional—PRI) in Mexico, the PRD has managed to co-opt much of the Panamanian left, thereby limiting and undermining the strength of avowedly Marxist political parties. Unlike the PRI, however, the PRD has never been able to separate itself from the military or to gain majority popular support. At times the PRD also has claimed a social-democratic orientation, and in 1986 it acquired the status of a ''consulting member'' in the Socialist International.

According to its declaration of principles, in the late 1980s the PRD was a multi-class, revolutionary, nationalistic, and independent party. Its structure included organizations for workers, peasants, women, youth, government employees, and professionals. It consistently had sought, with some success, to cultivate close ties with organized labor. The PRD had 205,000 registered members in 1986. It won approximately 40 percent of the votes in the 1980 elections, but gained only 27.4 percent of the vote in 1984, losing its place as the nation's largest party to the PPA. The PRD did, however, win thirty-four of the sixty-seven seats in the legislature.

Because of its inability to muster majority support, the PRD has sought electoral alliances with other parties. At first it was allied with FRAMPO and the PdP, the orthodox, pro-Moscow communist party that had earlier supported Torrijos. The PRD later cut its ties with the PdP and, together with FRAMPO, joined the PLN, PALA, PP, and PR to form the UNADE coalition, which supported the 1984 presidential candidacy of Ardito Barletta. FRAMPO won only 0.8 percent of the vote in 1984 and lost its legal status, as did the PP, but the coalition of the other 4 parties— PRD, PLN, PALA, and PR—remained officially in place in the late 1980s.

In the late 1980s, the PLN was only a shadow of its former self. It had split repeatedly, including a rift in late 1987 when Vice

President Esquivel began criticizing the policies of President Delvalle and was, in turn, ousted from control of the party by a faction headed by Rodolfo Chiari. Affiliated with the Liberal International, the party won 4.4 percent of the vote in 1984 and gained 1 seat in the legislature. Its ideology was generally right of center.

The PALA was the second largest party in UNADE. PALA won 7.1 percent of the vote and 7 seats in the legislature in 1984. The party's secretary general, Ramón Sieiro Murgas, is Noriega's brother-in-law. Despite its title, the party generally has adopted a right-of-center, pro-business position. The party experienced considerable turmoil in 1987, with founder Carlos Eleta Almarán being ousted as party president. In addition, one of its seven legislators, Mayin Correa, denounced the government's actions during the June disturbances, leading, in turn, to efforts to expel her from PALA.

The PR was a right-of-center party dominated by the aristocratic Delvalle and Bazan families. In return for joining UNADE, Delvalle was given one of the vice presidential nominations and became president following the forced resignation of Ardito Barletta. The party won 5.3 percent of the popular vote and gained 3 seats in the legislature in the 1984 elections.

The principal opposition party was the PPA, which won 34.5 percent of the votes in the 1984 elections, the largest percentage gained by any party. Since its founding in the 1940s, the Panameñista Party had served as the vehicle for the ambitions and populist ideas of Arnulfo Arias. After a party split in 1981, the great majority of Panameñistas stayed with Arias and designated themselves as Arnulfistas, and their party became known as the PPA. The smaller faction adopted Partido Panameñista (PP) as its name. Strongly nationalist, the PPA was anticommunist and antimilitary and advocated a populist nationalism that would restrict the rights of Antillean blacks and other immigrant groups.

Arias turned eighty-six in 1987 and could no longer exercise the leadership or muster the popular support he enjoyed in the past. He remained politically active, however, and his party was officially committed to installing him as president. With fourteen seats, it controlled the largest opposition bloc in the legislature, but its future, given the age and growing infirmity of its leader, was highly uncertain.

In 1984 the PPA had joined with several other parties in the ADO, which supported the presidential candidacy of Arnulfo Arias. The most important of these parties was the Christian democratic PDC, which won 7.3 percent of the 1984 vote but secured only 5 seats in the legislature. Its leader, Ricardo Arias Calderón, was a vice presidential candidate on the Arnulfo Arias ticket and emerged in 1987 as the most visible spokesman of the political opposition. The party was an active member of both the Latin American and world organizations of Christian democratic parties. The party was anticommunist and was generally located in the center of the political spectrum, advocating social reforms and civilian control over the military.

MOLIRENA also joined ADO and won 4.8 percent of the vote and 3 seats in the legislature in 1984. It was a pro-business coalition of several center-to-right political movements including dissident factions of the PLN. Its supporters worked closely with the PDC.

In addition to the seven principal parties that each won more than 3 percent of the 1984 vote, thereby gaining representation in the legislature and maintaining their legal status as registered parties, there were numerous other, smaller political parties and organizations that lacked this legal status. They included the Authentic Liberal Party (Partido Liberal Auténtico—PLA), a dissident Liberal faction that supported ADO in 1984, and the PP, a small group that broke with Arnulfo Arias and supported UNADE in 1984. There were also several groups on the far left, including the Moscow-oriented PdP, the Socialist Workers Party, and the Revolutionary Workers Party. All were Marxist, all ran presidential candidates in 1984, and each won less than 1 percent of the vote.

The PAPO was an independent group with a social democratic orientation. It had ties to the leading opposition newspaper, *La Prensa,* and was a constant critic of the government and of the FDP. It ran Carlos Iván Zúñiga for president in 1984 but gained only 2.2 percent of the vote, thus forfeiting its legal status.

The Panama Defense Forces

Although Panama's Constitution expressly prohibits military intervention in party politics, there was general agreement in the late 1980s that the FDP and its commander, General Noriega, controlled the internal political process. The PRD and, to a lesser extent, PALA, were seen as vehicles for military influence in politics. Presidents served at the pleasure of the military, and elections were widely viewed as subject to direct manipulation by the FDP. The officer corps had virtually total internal autonomy, including control over promotions and assignments and immunity from civil court proceedings. The military was supposed to have begun a turnover of power to civilians in 1978, but in 1986 Professor Steve Ropp noted that "the system of government, established by General Torrijos, which allows the Defense Forces high command to rule through the instrument of the Democratic Revolutionary Party, remains largely intact."

If anything, the influence and power of the FDP increased after 1978. The force expanded from a total of 8,700 in 1978 to nearly 15,000 by the end of 1987. The military retained direct control of all police forces and expanded its influence in such areas as immigration, railroads, ports, and civil aviation. Three presidents were forced to resign, and the military itself changed commanders several times without consulting the president or the legislature.

The small size and pyramidical rank structure of the FDP's officer corps helped maintain unity and concentrated effective power in the hands of the commander. This situation facilitated communications and consultations among senior officers, inhibited dissent, and made any effort to defy the wishes of the commander both difficult and dangerous. The total failure of the efforts of former Colonel Díaz Herrera to gain support from within the officer corps, following his forced retirement in June 1987, illustrated both the cohesion of this body and the ability of its commander to dominate subordinate officers. Internal discipline within the officer corps was very strong, pressures to support existing policies were constant, and any deviation from these norms was likely to be fatal to an officer's hopes for future advancement.

The gap between the FDP and the civilian population was great and probably widening in the late 1980s. Part of this distance was the result of a deliberate policy by the high command, which actively promoted institutional identity defined in terms of resisting any external efforts to reduce the military's power or privileges or to gain any degree of control over its internal affairs. In this context, any criticisms of the FDP's commander, of the FDP's role in politics or the economy, and any charges of corruption have been viewed as attacks on the institution, and mass meetings of junior officers have been held to express total support for the high command.

Although there was no ideological unity within the officer corps, there was a consensus in favor of nationalism (often defined as suspicion of, if not opposition to, United States influence), developmentalism, and a distrust of traditional civilian political elites. There was also an overwhelming consensus against allowing Arnulfo Arias to return to power. The FDP was very proud of its extensive civic-action program, which it has used to gain political support in rural areas. It also saw itself as the promoter and guarantor of the populist political heritage of Torrijos.

Business, Professional, and Labor Organizations

Traditionally, sectoral interest groups have played a minor role in Panamanian politics. Commercial and industrial interests were

197

expressed largely within the extended family systems that constituted the oligarchy. A heavy reliance on government jobs inhibited the development of professional organizations that could reflect middle-class interests. The slow rate of industrial development, the major role of the United States as an employer of Panamanians in the Canal Zone, and fragmentation and infighting within the labor movement all contributed to keeping that sector chronically weak. Nevertheless, the absence of political parties during most of the 1970s, accompanied by economic expansion, led to a growing importance for sectoral groups as vehicles for the expression of political interests. Frustrations over the failures of the political process and the evident inability of political parties to control the military gave this trend further impetus during the 1980s. As a result, sectoral groups emerged during the 1987 upheavals as major political actors, mounting a significant challenge to military domination of the political process.

In the late 1980s, Panamanian businesses and professions were organized into numerous specialized groups, such as the Bar Association, the National Union of Small and Medium Enterprises, the Panamanian Banking Association, and the National Agricultural and Livestock Producers. Two of the most important organizations were the Chamber of Commerce, Industries, and Agriculture of Panama and the Panamanian Business Executives Association. These and numerous other organizations were included in the National Free Enterprise Council (Consejo Nacional de la Empresa Privada—CONEP). The various groups within CONEP have often disagreed on issues, making it difficult to present a position of common interest. On two issues, however, protection from government encroachments on the private sector and the maintenance of their position vis-à-vis labor, members of CONEP consistently have found a unified position. Moreover, sentiment has grown increasingly within CONEP and many of its affiliated organizations that the problems facing the private sector extend beyond specific issues to growing problems within the political system as a whole. Resentment over continued military domination of the political system, a perception of increased corruption and inefficiency within the government, and a feeling that political conditions were increasingly unfavorable for business all combined to make many business leaders willing to join, and even lead, open opposition to the government when the June 1987 crisis erupted.

During the June 1987 crisis, business groups played a key role in the organization and direction of the CCN, which spearheaded protests against the regime. Many of the major bodies within CONEP, such as the Chamber of Commerce and Panamanian

Business Executives Association, became formal members of the CCN. A total of more than 130 business, professional, civic, and labor groups joined the crusade, which undertook the task of organizing, directing, and coordinating the campaign to force Noriega out of power and to reduce the role of the military in government. The crusade deliberately excluded political parties from its membership and active politicians from its leadership. The presidents of CONEP and of the Chamber of Commerce took major leadership roles within the crusade, which emphasized peaceful demonstrations, economic pressures, and boycotts of government enterprises as means of forcing change on the government. The FDP responded with a campaign of measured violence and intimidation against the crusade's leaders and supporters. By the fall of 1987, most of the original leadership had been driven into exile, and the effort appeared to have lost much of its impetus. The economic pressures continued, however; exiled leaders undertook a major international propaganda campaign against the government, and business groups within Panama kept up economic pressures, which began to have a serious impact on the economy and on government revenues. In December 1987, Delvalle offered an amnesty to most of the exiled crusade leaders, but this action neither appeased the opposition among the business and professional classes nor in any way responded to the causes that had created the crusade.

Although at the end of 1987 the crusade had not been able to force basic change on the government and the military, neither had the government and the FDP been able to end the campaign of civic opposition. How long the CCN would endure and what ultimate success it might enjoy remained unanswered questions, but the role and power of business and professional organizations within the Panamanian political structure had undergone fundamental change.

The Panamanian labor movement traditionally had been fragmented and politically weak. The political weakness of labor was exacerbated further by the fact that Panamanians working in the Canal Zone belonged to United States rather than Panamanian labor unions. The 1977 Panama Canal treaties made provisions for the collective bargaining and job security of these workers, and it was likely that Panamanian unions would replace United States unions when Panama assumed full control over the canal, but in the late 1980s, most canal workers remained with the original unions.

Labor organizations grew significantly in size and importance under Torrijos, who actively supported this trend. Major labor federations included the relatively moderate Confederation of Workers of the Republic of Panama, which had approximately 35,000 members, and the somewhat smaller, leftist, antibusiness National Workers' Central, which had ties with the Moscow-oriented PdP. There was also the Isthmian Workers' Central, a small confederation linked to the PDC. In 1972 these three bodies created the National Council of Organized Workers (Consejo Nacional de Trabajadores Organisados—CONATO) to give them a more unified voice and greater influence on issues of interest to organized labor. Other unions, including the important National Union of Construction and Related Workers, have since joined CONATO, increasing its affiliates to 12 with a claimed combined membership of 150,000. The diverse labor alliance in CONATO was an uneasy one, but the council succeeded in generating greater unity and militancy than had its component unions individually. A 1985 general strike called by CONATO forced the government to suspend plans to amend the labor code. Ultimately, however, the code was amended, reducing workers' job security. A March 1986 strike protesting these changes failed. CONATO reacted by urging its members to resign from parties that supported the government.

Despite the 1985–86 problems, labor generally was more supportive of the government than of the political opposition. This situation, however, was strained by the disturbances that began in June 1987. A few smaller labor groups joined the civic crusade, but CONATO did not. The government's problems, however, were compounded by a series of strikes by the public employees' union, the National Federation of Associations and Organizations of Public Employees (Federación Nacional de Asociaciones y Sindicatos de Empleados Públicos—FENASEP). The leadership of FENASEP even went so far as to threaten to respond to any government effort to dismiss government workers by publishing lists of all those on the government payroll ''who do not go to work.'' CONATO was also critical of many government actions, demanding that closed newspapers and radio stations be reopened and that the government open a dialogue to end the continuing crisis. Whereas labor's influence in Panamanian politics remained limited, it was increasing steadily and was something that neither the government nor its political opposition could control or take for granted.

Students

University and secondary school students have long played a leading role in Panama's political life, often acting as advocates of the interests of the lower and middle classes against the oligarchy and the military. Students also played a leading role in demonstrations against United States control over the Canal Zone. Using a combination of force and rewards, the Torrijos government largely co-opted the students at the University of Panama, gaining considerable influence over the Federation of Panamanian Students (Federación de Estudiantes Panameños—FEP), the largest of several student federations. But relations between the government and student groups began to deteriorate in 1976, and a variety of competing student federations developed, notably the Federation of Revolutionary Students (Federación de Estudiantes Revolucionarios—FER), a group on the far left. Student groups were leaders in the opposition to ratification of the Panama Canal treaties, objecting largely to the continued presence of United States military bases in Panama.

Students and some teachers' groups played a major role in the 1987 protests. At least one university student was killed by the FDP, and the government closed the University of Panama twice and closed all secondary schools during the June protests. Periodic student protests took place throughout the year, frequently producing violent confrontations with the security forces. Although most student organizations were not part of the CCN, their growing opposition to the political role of the FDP and the policies of the government made the task of restoring order and stability even more difficult.

The Roman Catholic Church

Although Panama was nearly 90 percent Roman Catholic in the late 1980s, the church had a long tradition of noninvolvement in national politics (see Religion, ch. 2). Weak organization and a heavy dependence on foreign clergy (only 40 percent of the nation's priests were native-born Panamanians) inhibited the development of strong hierarchical positions on political issues. As a result, Panamanian politics largely avoided the anticlericalism that was so prevalent in much of Latin America. Church concern over social issues increased notably in the 1960s and 1970s, and there were conflicts between the hierarchy and the Torrijos government, especially following the disappearance in 1971 of a prominent reform priest, Father Héctor Gallegos.

In the late 1980s, the church hierarchy was headed by Archbishop Marcos Gregorio McGrath, a naturalized Panamanian citizen and a leader among the Latin American bishops. McGrath and the other bishops strongly supported Panama's claims to sovereignty over the Canal Zone and urged ratification of the Panama Canal treaties. Nevertheless, the church leadership also criticized the lack of democracy in Panama and urged a return to elected civilian rule. In 1985, as political tensions began to mount, the archbishop called for an investigation into the murder of Dr. Hugo Spadafora and urged both the government and the opposition to enter into a national dialogue. When the 1987 disturbances began, the church stepped up its criticism of the government, accusing the military of having "beaten civilians without provocation" and of using "tactics to humiliate arrested individuals." Priests were frequently present at CCN rallies and demonstrations, and masses downtown became a focal point for some CCN activities. Priests also stayed with Díaz Herrera in his house after he issued his June 1987 charges against Noriega and the government, and when the house was stormed by the FDP and Díaz Herrera arrested, the bishops demanded his release and denounced government restrictions on the press. But the church stopped short of endorsing the CCN or calling for specific changes in the government and the FDP. Instead, it stressed the need for dialogue and reconciliation. The archbishop's insistence on pursuing a moderate, neutral course in the conflict did not satisfy all of the church leadership. In November two assistant bishops and a large number of clergy issued their own letter, denouncing government actions and urging changes in the conduct of the military. In late 1987, the church was becoming more active but was finding it difficult to agree on the manner and nature of that activity.

The Communications Media

The press, radio, and, more recently, the television of Panama have a history of strong political partisanship and rather low standards of journalistic responsibility. The government has subsidized some news outlets and periodically censored others. During most of the Torrijos era, the press and radio were tightly controlled but, following the ratification of the Panama Canal treaties, a significant degree of press freedom was restored. It was at this time that the most significant opposition paper, *La Prensa,* was founded.

Throughout the 1980s, conflicts between the government and the opposition media, notably *La Prensa,* escalated. The government and the FDP blamed *La Prensa* and its publisher, Roberto Eisenmann, Jr., for much of the negative publicity they received in the United States. The paper was attacked, its writers were harassed, and in 1986 Eisenmann fled to the United States, charging that his life had been threatened.

Events in 1987 increased the level of conflict between the government and the media. Strict censorship was instituted over all newspapers and radio and television news broadcasts. In response, three opposition papers suspended publication. Publication was resumed in late June, but in July the government closed *La Prensa* and the two other papers, as well as two radio stations. The English-language *Panama Star and Herald,* the nation's oldest newspaper, was forced out of business. The government pressured remaining stations and newspapers to engage in self-censorship and attempted to crack down on foreign press coverage, expelling several correspondents. In October President Delvalle sent to the legislature a proposed press law that would have made the publishing of "false, distorted, or inexact news" a crime for which individual journalists would be held responsible. Even the pro-government media attacked this proposal, which the legislature rejected. Although there were indications that the opposition media would be allowed to re-open in 1988, it seemed unlikely that government efforts to control news coverage would cease.

Foreign Relations

Panama's strategic location, the traditional domination of both the economy and the political agenda by the canal, and the strong influence exerted by the United States throughout most of Panama's independent history have combined to magnify the importance of foreign policy in the nation's political life. From the signing of the Hay-Bunau-Varilla Treaty in 1903 until the ratification of the Panama Canal treaties in 1978, Panama's overriding concern, both domestically and internationally, was to gain sovereignty over the Canal Zone and control over the canal itself. Determined to obtain sovereignty over its entire national territory, but aware of the limitations posed by its weakness in comparison with the United States, Panama sought the support of other nations, particularly in multilateral forums, in its efforts to renegotiate the canal treaties. In pursuing this end, Panama gained an international visibility much greater than that of most nations of similar size.

Traditionally, all other foreign policy matters were subordinated to Panama's concern with the canal issue. Secondary emphasis was given to commercial interests in dealings with other nations. Vehicles of international trade, such as the Colón Free Zone, international banking, and shipping, were central factors in Panama's foreign economic relations. In the 1980s, the issue of the mounting foreign debt also had become the focus of increasing attention and concern.

The experience and visibility gained in the long effort to obtain international support for Panama's stance in the canal negotiations were carried over into the years following the signing of the new treaties, as exemplified by Panama's role in the 1978–79 Nicaraguan civil conflict and its participation in the Contadora peace process (see Glossary). Panama also has tried, with limited success, to appeal to the same Latin American and Third World sentiments that won it support for its efforts to renegotiate the Panama Canal treaties to gain support in subsequent disputes with the United States. Although foreign policy concerns were not as dominant in the 1980s as in previous decades, they occupied a high priority for Panama's government and still centered on relations with the United States. This pattern was likely to persist until at least the year 2000.

Relations with the United States: The Panama Canal

United States and Panamanian relations on issues connected to the control, operation, and future of the canal were conducted within the framework of the 1977 Panama Canal treaties. The negotiation of these treaties took several years and aroused domestic political controversies within both nations (see The Treaty Negotiations; The 1977 Treaties and Associated Agreements, ch. 1). Negotiations were finally concluded in August 1977, and the following month the treaties were signed in Washington.

The treaties were ratified in Panama by slightly more than two-thirds of the voters in a national plebiscite. Ratification by the United States Senate was much more difficult and controversial and was not completed until April 1978. During the ratification process, the Senate added several amendments and conditions, notably the DeConcini Condition, which declared that if the canal were closed or its operations impaired, both the United States and Panama would "have the right to take such steps as each deems necessary . . . including the use of military force in the Republic of Panama, to reopen the canal or restore the operations of the canal." Despite an additional amendment, which specifically rejected any United States "right of intervention in the internal affairs of the Republic of Panama or interference with its political independence or sovereign integrity," the Senate's changes were met with strong protests from Panama, which never ratified the new amendments. Formal ratifications, however, were exchanged in June, and the treaties came into force on October 1, 1979.

To implement the provisions of the treaties establishing the new Panama Canal Commission, to regulate the conditions for canal employees, and to provide for the handling and disbursement of canal revenues, the United States Congress enacted Public Law (PL) 96–70, the Panama Canal Act of 1979. Several provisions of this act immediately became a focus for ongoing controversy between the two nations. Panamanians objected to provisions for the use of canal revenues to pay for early retirements for United States employees, to finance travel for education by the dependents

A ship passes through the Panama Canal near the Culebra Cut
Courtesy Inter-American Development Bank

of United States employees, and to provide subsidies to make up for any loss of earning power when, as required under the treaties, United States employees lost access to United States military commissaries. By 1986 Panamanian authorities were claiming that such provisions had cost their nation up to US$50 million. The claim was largely based on the fact that Panama had not been receiving the up to US$10 million annual contingency payment from Panama Canal Commission profits provided for by the treaties. The commission explained that this was because the surplus simply did not exist, a fact that Panama, in turn, attributed to provisions of PL 96–70.

The level of Panamanian complaints about PL 96–70 and the intensity of government charges of noncompliance by the United States in other areas were often influenced by the overall state of relations between the two nations. As tensions increased during 1986 and 1987, Panamanian complaints became more frequent and passionate. United States executive and congressional pressures and the suspension of aid that followed the June 1987 disturbances were portrayed by the government and its supporters as part of a United States plot to block implementation of the 1977 treaties and/or to maintain the United States military bases in Panama beyond the year 2000. In the months that followed, the government stepped up this campaign, attempting to link the opposition with elements in the United States Congress who allegedly were trying to overturn the treaties. Such charges, however, seemed more an effort to influence domestic opinion than a reflection of actual concerns over the future of the treaties.

Article XII of the Panama Canal Treaty provides for a joint study of ''the feasibility of a sea-level canal in the Republic of Panama.'' In 1981 Panama formally suggested beginning such a study. After some discussion, a Preparative Committee on the Panama Canal Alternatives Study was established in 1982, and Japan was invited to join the United States and Panama on this committee. The committee's final report called for the creation of a formal Commission for the Study of Alternatives to the Panama Canal, which was set up in 1986. Although there was a general perception that the costs of such a canal would outweigh benefits, the commission was still studying the problem in late 1987, and further action in this area would await the conclusion of its labors.

One continuing bone of contention related to the treaties was the presence and function of United States military bases in Panama (see United States Forces in Panama, ch. 5). United States military forces in Panama numbered slightly under 10,000. The United States military also employed 8,100 civilians, 70 percent of whom were Panamanian nationals. In addition to the units directly involved in the defense of the canal, the United States military presence included the headquarters of the United States Southern Command, responsible for all United States military activities in Central and South America, the Jungle Operations Training Center, the Inter-American Air Forces Academy, which provided training for Latin American air forces, and the Special Operations Command-South. Until 1984 Panama also was home to the United States Army School of the Americas, which trained Latin American army officers and enlisted personnel, but the facility housing that institution reverted to Panama in 1984, and when negotiations with Panama over the future of the school broke down, the United States Army transferred the operation to Fort Benning, Georgia.

Issues involving the United States military presence included the possible retention of some bases beyond the year 2000, the use of the bases for activities not directly related to the defense of the canal, most notably allegations of their use in support of operations directed against Nicaragua's government, and, since June 1987, charges by the United States of harassment and mistreatment of United States military personnel by Panamanian authorities. There were also problems relating to joint manuevers between United States and Panamanian forces, exercises designed to prepare Panama to assume responsibility for the defense of the canal (see Canal Defense, ch. 5). These manuevers were suspended in 1987, in part because of a United States congressional prohibition on the use of government funds for "military exercises in Panama" during 1988.

Despite such problems, the implementation of the 1977 treaties has continued on schedule and the United States has stated repeatedly its determination to adhere to the provisions and transfer full control of the canal to Panama in the year 2000. An October 1987 effort to amend the fiscal year (FY) 1988 foreign relations authorization act to include a sense of the Senate resolution that the United States should not have ratified the treaties and that they should be voided if Panama refused to accept the DeConcini Condition within six months was defeated by a vote of fifty-nine to thirty-nine. Barring a much higher level of turmoil in Panama that would directly threaten canal operations, it appeared highly likely that the canal would become fully Panamanian in the year 2000.

Other Aspects of Panamanian-United States Relations

Panamanian relations with the United States, in areas other than those related to the canal, have undergone increasing strains since the 1985 ouster of President Ardito Barletta. The United States protested this action by reducing economic assistance to Panama and began pressuring Panama to reform its banking secrecy laws, crack down on narcotics trafficking, investigate the murder of Spadafora, and reduce the FDP's role in the government. When these points were raised by United States ambassador-designate to Panama Arthur Davis in his confirmation hearings, Panamanian officials issued an official complaint, claiming that they were the victim of a "seditious plot" involving the United States Department of State, Senator Jesse Helms, and opposition politicians in Panama.

Additional problems continued to arise throughout 1986 and early 1987. In April 1987, the United States Senate approved a nonbinding resolution calling for a 50-percent reduction in assistance to Panama because of alleged involvement by that nation's officials in narcotics trafficking. The Panamanian legislature responded with a resolution of its own, calling for the withdrawal of Panama's ambassador in Washington. Hearings on Panama held by Senator Helms produced further controversy, especially when a Senate resolution called on the United States Central Intelligence Agency to investigate narcotics trafficking in Panama. Again Panama protested. The FDP issued a resolution accusing Helms of a "malevolent insistence on sowing discord," and the Panamanian representative to the Nonaligned Movement's meeting in Zimbabwe charged that the United States was not fulfilling the Panama Canal treaties.

Continued United States pressure in such areas as human rights, political reform, narcotics trafficking, and money laundering, as well as conflicts over economic matters, including a reduction in Panama's textile quota, kept relations tense during the first months of 1987. In March Panama issued an official protest, charging the United States with exerting "political pressures damaging to Panama's sovereignty, dignity, and independence." This, however, did not deter Senate passage, a few days later, of a nonbinding resolution rejecting presidential certification of Panamanian cooperation in the struggle against the drug trade. President Ronald Reagan's certification that Panama was cooperating in the struggle against drug trafficking was based on some Panamanian concessions on bank secrecy laws and a highly publicized narcotics and money-laundering sting operation (see Finance, ch. 3; Involvement in Political and Economic Affairs, ch. 5).

The deterioration in relations accelerated following the outbreak of disturbances in June 1987. United States calls for a full investigation of the allegations made by Díaz Herrera and for movement toward "free and untarnished elections" led to Panamanian charges of United States interference in its internal affairs.

The Legislative Assembly adopted a resolution demanding the expulsion of the United States ambassador, and the head of the PRD charged that United States pressures were part of a plot "not to fulfill the obligations of the Carter-Torrijos Treaties" and were also designed "to get Panama to withdraw from the Contadora Group." Panama took its protest over United States policy and the Senate resolution to the Organization of American States (OAS), which on July 1 adopted, by a vote of seventeen to one with eight abstentions, a resolution criticizing the Senate resolution and calling for an end to United States interference in Panama's internal affairs. On June 30 a government-organized mob attacked the United States embassy, inflicting over US$100,000 in damages. The United States responded by suspending economic and military assistance until the damage was paid for. Panama apologized for the attack and, at the end of July, paid for the damage, but the freeze on United States assistance remained in effect as a demonstration of United States displeasure with the internal political situation.

Relations between the two nations failed to improve during the balance of 1987. Attacks on United States policies by pro-government politicians and press in Panama were almost constant. The actions of the United States ambassador were an especially frequent target, and there were suggestions that he might be declared persona non grata. There was also a growing campaign of harassment against individual Americans. In September the economic officer of the United States embassy was arrested while observing an antigovernment demonstration. The following month, nine American servicemen were seized and abused under the pretext that they had been participating in such demonstrations. United States citizens driving in Panama were repeatedly harassed by the Panamanian police. Restrictions also were increased on United States reporters in Panama.

For its part, the United States kept up pressure on Panama. In August 1987, the secretary of state announced that the freeze on United States aid would remain in effect, despite Panama's having paid for the damage done to the embassy. In November the United States cancelled scheduled joint military exercises with Panama. In December Congress adopted a prohibition on economic and military assistance to Panama, unless the United States president certified that there had been "substantial progress in assuring civilian control of the armed forces," "an impartial investigation into allegations of illegal actions by members of the Panama Defense

Forces,'' agreement between the government and the opposition on "conditions for free and fair elections," and "freedom of the press." The same bill suspended Panama's sugar quota until these conditions were met (see Crops, ch. 3). Panama responded by ordering all personnel connected with the United States Agency for International Development mission out of the country.

At the end of 1987, United States-Panamanian relations had reached their worst level since at least 1964. On the United States side, there was a high degree of agreement between the executive branch and the Congress that fundamental changes in both the domestic and international behavior of Panama's government were needed. There was little sign of movement toward resolving any of the basic issues that divided the two nations, and it appeared that this deadlock would continue until there was a change in the Panamanian leadership's position or composition.

Relations with Central America

Although it is part of the same geographic region as the countries of Central America (see Glossary), Panama historically has lacked strong political and economic ties with the five nations immediately to its north. Panama was not a member of either the Central American Common Market or the Central American Defense Council, although it did have observer status with the latter body. Under the rule of Torrijos, however, Panama actively sought to expand its contacts with Central America. At first, much of this was related to the effort to gain support in negotiations with the United States over a new canal treaty. During the Nicaraguan civil conflict of 1978–79, Torrijos gave political and military support to the Sandinista guerrillas seeking to overthrow the dictatorship of Anastasio Somoza. At the June 1979 OAS foreign ministers meeting on Nicaragua, Panama allowed the foreign minister-designate of the Sandinista-organized provisional government to sit with the Panamanian delegation. After the Sandinistas took power, Torrijos offered to train their military and police forces. But the Panamanian mission soon found itself reduced to training traffic police, and Torrijos, frustrated by growing Cuban influence in Nicaragua, withdrew his advisers. Since then, Panamanian relations with Nicaragua have been of lessened importance. Panamanian leaders have criticized United States efforts directed against the Sandinistas, but they also have criticized Sandinista policies. Nevertheless, during the June 1987 crisis in Panama, Nicaraguan President Daniel Ortega visited Panama, and the Nicaraguan government expressed strong support for Delvalle and Noriega.

Torrijos also had attempted to influence internal events in El Salvador, where he supported the reform efforts of Colonel Adolfo Majano, a military academy classmate of his, who had been named to the ruling junta in 1979. But Majano was removed from power in 1980 while visiting Panama, largely ending Panamanian influence in that nation.

Relations with Costa Rica were cool for several decades, following a 1921 settlement of the border dispute between the two nations, a settlement that Panama viewed as largely unfavorable to its interests. The opening of the Pan-American Highway between the two nations led to an increase in commercial ties and contributed to a steady strengthening of bilateral relations in the 1960s and 1970s. During the 1978–79 Nicaraguan civil conflict, Panama offered to help defend Costa Rica's northern border from incursions by Nicaraguan forces, and, during the war's last months, then Costa Rican president Rodrigo Carazo and Torrijos worked closely together to facilitate the flow of supplies to the Sandinista insurgents. Cordial relations were maintained with Carazo's successor, Luis Alberto Monge, but numerous problems have emerged since Oscar Arias became president of Costa Rica in 1986. These began with the discovery, in Costa Rican territory, of the mutilated body of leading Panamanian critic Spadafora. Commercial disputes also began to disrupt trade. Early in 1987, the two nations signed an agreement to regulate commerce in the border region, but a few days later, Panama closed the border, claiming that Costa Rica was violating the agreement. The border was reopened after a few days, and in March presidents Delvalle and Arias signed an agreement designed to deal with commercial problems and to promote cooperation in areas such as health and education. Costa Rican press criticism of Panamanian government policy following the June disturbances, however, led to a cooling in relations. In December the Panamanian ambassador to Costa Rica charged that United States and Costa Rican officials were plotting to organize an invasion of Panama and to assassinate Noriega. Costa Rica rejected the charges, for which no supporting evidence was produced. Although this issue soon faded, relations between the two nations at the end of 1987 were less cordial than they had been in preceding years.

Reflecting both the growth of Panamanian involvement in Central American affairs and the expanded international role that the nation has sought was Panama's participation in the Contadora peace process (see Glossary). In January 1983, Panama invited the foreign ministers of Mexico, Venezuela, and Colombia to meet at the island resort of Contadora to discuss ways of mediating the

211

conflicts in Central America. The result was the formation of the Contadora Group, a four-nation effort to promote a peaceful resolution of Central American conflicts. Although Panama's role in the mediating process was not so prominent as that of some of the other nations, it did give Panama increased visibility and prestige in international relations. Panama was also the site for many of the group's meetings with Central American representatives. Although the Contadora peace process failed to produce the hoped-for peace treaty, and, since 1987, has taken a backseat to the peace proposals of Costa Rica's president Arias, the Contadora Group still exists and, under the Arias Plan, could play a significant role in dealing with security issues involving Central American states.

Bilateral Relations with Other Nations

The number of nations with which Panama maintains formal diplomatic relations expanded during the 1970s, in part because of the campaign to renegotiate the canal treaties and in part because of its role as a commercial, banking, and trading center. During the 1980s, economic difficulties contributed to slowing, but not reversing this trend toward expanded international contacts. In most cases, the focus on bilateral relations was on economic issues, with political matters more frequently addressed through multilateral forums.

Relations with Cuba have been a subject of some controversy, both within Panama and in Panama's relations with the United States. Panama broke relations with Cuba in the 1960s, but re-established them in the early 1970s, and by the end of the decade, Cuba's diplomatic mission in Panama City was second only to that of the United States in the number of its personnel. Torrijos openly solicited Cuban support during the canal negotiations, but Cuban-Panamanian relations generally have been based more on commercial than political grounds. During the 1970s, Cuba made extensive use of the Colón Free Zone to obtain materials that the United States trade embargo of Cuba made it difficult to obtain directly.

Relations with Cuba have been a side issue in disputes between Panama and the United States. Cuba has openly supported Noriega and attempted to portray criticisms of the general as part of a United States plot to sabotage the Panama Canal treaties. The United States, for its part, has accused Panama of participating in the illegal shipment of American high-technology equipment to Cuba.

Panama's relations with its southern neighbor, Colombia, have never been close since Panama broke away from Colombia and declared its independence (see The 1903 Treaty and Qualified Independence, ch. 1). Part of this coolness was a function of poor communications; the border area is wild and thinly populated and represents the last gap in the Pan-American Highway system (see fig. 8). Relations have been strained by Panamanian concerns that Colombian settlers and guerrillas were moving into areas on the Panamanian side of the border and by the prevalent belief in the Colombian military that Panama was supporting Colombian guerrilla groups.

Relations with other states of Latin America and the Caribbean were of lesser importance in the late 1980s. There was some strengthening of ties with Venezuela in the 1970s, spurred by the economic resources available to Venezuela as a result of the rise in oil prices. But the precipitous fall in oil prices in the mid-1980s damaged the Venezuelan economy and reduced the Panamanian incentive to seek any further expansion of existing ties. Panama sought to expand its ties with the smaller Caribbean states in the late 1970s and early 1980s. It even undertook the training of police in Grenada. But the more active United States presence in the area, signaled by the Caribbean Basin Initiative and the 1984 Grenada intervention, undercut this effort, which, in any case, was limited by economic, cultural, political, and linguistic factors.

Relations between Panama and Canada, Western Europe, and Japan were largely commercial in nature. Relations with Western Europe were somewhat complicated by ties between West European political parties and opposition groups in Panama. These links have been an increasing problem in relations with the Federal Republic of Germany (West Germany), whose Christian Democratic Party maintained close ties with Panama's opposition Christian Democrats. Relations with Japan have assumed growing importance, in part because of Japan's participation on the Commission for the Study of Alternatives to the Panama Canal.

Panama has long maintained close ties with Israel and, in 1987, Delvalle made a state visit to that nation. Nevertheless, late in 1987 Panama indicated an interest in expanding contacts with Libya, with which it had no formal diplomatic relations, and some officials expressed the hope that Libya could become a major source of financial assistance. It was, however, unclear whether this was a serious proposal or simply a tactic in Panama's ongoing dispute with the United States.

Panama had no formal diplomatic relations with the Soviet Union or China. In the case of China, this situation was because of Panama's maintenance of diplomatic relations with the government on Taiwan. Interest in expanded ties with socialist and communist nations has, however, increased, fueled by the fact that the Soviet Union has become the third largest user of the canal. In March

1987, Panama and Poland initiated a broad program of educational, scientific, and cultural cooperation. That same month, the president of Panama's Legislative Assembly visited the Soviet Union, but Panama denied that this was a prelude to establishing diplomatic relations. In December Panama gave the Soviet airline Aeroflot permission to begin regular flights to Panama, but once again denied that it was planning to open formal diplomatic relations.

Multilateral Relations

Panama has long emphasized the role of multilateral forums and bodies in its foreign relations, using them to enhance its prestige, secure economic assistance, and marshall support for its dealings with the United States. In 1973 the UN Security Council held a meeting in Panama to discuss the canal issue, and the Panama Canal treaties were signed in a special ceremony at the OAS.

Panama has been an active member of the OAS since its inception. It repeatedly has used this forum to criticize United States policies, especially those regarding the canal, and to seek Latin American support for its positions. That this trend has continued was demonstrated by the 1987 OAS resolution criticizing United States interference in Panama's internal affairs.

The UN provided Panama with a platform from which it was able to address a broader audience. In 1985 Panama's vice president, Jorge Illueca Sibauste, served as president of the UN General Assembly. Within the UN, Panama frequently adopted a position on economic matters similar to that of other small, Third World nations. On political matters, it generally took a position closer to that of the United States, but it did break with the United States over the Falkland/Malvinas Islands issue in 1982 and was openly critical of United States Central American policy. In both cases, Panama sponsored resolutions in the UN Security Council that were at variance with United States policy. Over time, the trend has been to move slowly away from the positions held by the United States and toward those of the Nonaligned Movement.

Panama was an active member of the Nonaligned Movement and acted in it much as it did in the UN. Other multilateral organizations in which Panama maintained an active participation were the General Agreement on Tariffs and Trade and the United Nations Conference on Trade and Development.

Dealings with international financial organizations and problems connected with Panama's debt formed a major part of Panama's foreign policy agenda. In 1987 Panama took part, with seven larger Latin American nations, in a major economic summit in Acapulco,

Mexico. Efforts to use this forum to win support in its conflicts with the United States were largely unsuccessful, but Panama did contribute to the discussion of the debt crisis and supported the group's resolutions, which were highly critical of Western economic policies. Panama has borrowed extensively from the World Bank (see Glossary), the IMF, and the Inter-American Development Bank, a practice that may be jeopardized by its dispute with the United States. Panama's 1985–87 agreement with the IMF has expired, and the World Bank has suspended payments on a major structural adjustment loan because of Panama's failure to comply with a mandated austerity program.

Foreign Policy Decision Making

Article 179 of Panama's Constitution gives the president, with the participation of the minister of foreign relations, the power to "direct foreign relations, to negotiate treaties and public conventions, which will then be submitted to the consideration of the Legislative Organ, and to accredit and receive diplomatic and consular agents." In practice, however, the president's role in foreign policy was circumscribed by several factors. The most significant was the dominant influence of the FDP and its commander. No major foreign policy initiatives were possible without FDP approval. Torrijos began the practice, continued by Noriega, of direct military involvement in foreign policy matters without going through, or even necessarily consulting, the civilian political structure. The official party, the PRD, also played a role, both in selecting the foreign minister and in the Legislative Assembly, where it held an absolute majority. There, resolutions frequently were passed on matters of foreign policy. Although such resolutions lacked the force of law, their passage complicated the policy process.

The foreign ministry had a core of professional, career employees, but the post of foreign minister and most of the key ambassadorial appointments were filled by political appointees. The ministry itself played largely an administrative, rather than a decision-making, role in the policy process. Its authority was somewhat greater in commercial matters than in political matters. Internally, it was organized into a number of directorates for various world regions plus one for international organizations. In the past, various interests groups, such as CONEP and university students, were able to exercise some influence over foreign policy, but growing internal political polarization largely negated their influence.

*   *   *

215

The debate over the Panama Canal treaties generated a large body of literature on the canal and on United States-Panamanian relations, but little of this deals with internal Panamanian affairs. Panama's national politics remain among the least studied of any Latin American nation. Basic documents include the *Constitución Política de la República de Panamá de 1972: Reformada por los Actos Reformatorios de 1978 y por el Acto Constitucional de 1983* and the *Codigo Electoral de la República de Panamá y Normas Complementarias* as well as the 1977 *Panama Canal Treaty* and the associated *Treaty Concerning the Permanent Neutrality and Operation of the Panama Canal* (for text of treaties, see Appendix B). A first-person account of the negotiation and ratification of the treaties is William J. Jorden's *Panama Odyssey*, while a more analytical study is provided by William L. Furlong and Margaret E. Scranton in *The Dynamics of Foreign Policymaking*. The best studies of internal Panamanian politics are those of Steve Ropp. Rapidly changing events have made his 1982 book *Panamanian Politics: From Guarded Nation to National Guard* somewhat dated, but his subsequent articles in *Current History* fill in some of the gaps. Also useful are Thomas John Bossert's "Panama" in *Confronting Revolution,* edited by Morris J. Blachman, William M. Leogrande, and Kenneth Sharpe, and the 1987 *Report on Panama: Findings of the Study Group on United States-Panamanian Relations* published by the Johns Hopkins University School of Advanced International Studies. Opposition views of recent events are available in articles by Guillermo Sanchez Borbón and Ricardo Arias Calderón. The United States Congressional hearings on Panama held in 1986 and 1987 also provide valuable information, as does the annual "Political Risk Report: Panama," produced by Frost and Sullivan of New York. (For further information and complete citations, see Bibliography).

Chapter 5. National Security

Cuna Indian mola *design of a United States Air Force airplane*

ACCORDING TO the 1983 amended version of the 1972 Constitution of the Republic of Panama, the national defense and public security of the country are the responsibility of the Panama Defense Forces (Fuerzas de Defensa de Panamá—FDP). Before the FDP was created in 1983, a paramilitary organization called the National Guard had handled national security functions. After the 1968 military coup that brought General Omar Torrijos Herrera to power, the National Guard became the dominant political institution in the country. This legacy of military involvement in politics continued after Torrijos's death in 1981, even though the political system was ostensibly transformed from a military dictatorship into a civilian democracy, and the National Guard replaced by the FDP.

Negotiation of the Panama Canal treaties during the late 1970s led to changes in Panama's national security system. When the Canal Zone was integrated into the republic, people began to think of their country as a single territorial entity. This changed attitude was reflected in the military segments of the National Guard, which moved to make the institution less a police force and more a true national army capable of defending the expanded national territory. The implementation agreements of the treaties referred to the "Panamanian Armed Forces," rather than to "Panama's police force" or "Panama's paramilitary force," as had been done in the past. Transformation of the National Guard into a national army was accomplished in 1983, when legislation was passed creating the FDP.

The treaties also stimulated creation of a national army by reducing United States responsibility in Panama. Since the early 1900s, the armed forces of the United States had provided the primary defense of the Canal Zone and, in effect, of Panama itself. The treaties mandate cooperation and coordination in the protection and defense of the canal until December 31, 1999, when the United States is to withdraw its troops. After 1999 Panama will be fully responsible for the operation, but the United States will continue to share responsibility for the defense of the canal.

By the mid-1980s, the strength of the FDP was estimated at around 15,000, including the Ground Forces, composed of infantry battalions and companies equivalent in size to a small army or United States infantry brigade. Other major segments were the Panamanian Air Force, National Navy, Police Forces, and National Guard. The FDP was theoretically administered through the Ministry of Government and Justice; there was no ministry of defense.

Internal security problems, however, grew in the 1980s. By 1987 widespread concern over the lack of democratic institutions had generated major challenges to government authority. The integrity of the Panamanian system of justice was broadly questioned as well as the personal ethics of highly placed government officials. Newspapers in Panama and the United States reported widespread drug trafficking within the country and implicated the FDP. Panama was alleged to be both a transshipment point for the movement of drugs from South America to North America and a banking haven for laundering funds. The volume of such activity was not documented, however. In response to a general strike and widespread public disturbances, the government declared a state of emergency (subsequently lifted) and temporarily suspended articles of the Constitution guaranteeing basic rights such as freedom of speech and assembly.

Historical Background

On November 18, 1903, Secretary of State John Hay, representing the United States, and Special Envoy Philippe Bunau-Varilla, representing the Republic of Panama, signed an agreement that became known as the Hay-Bunau-Varilla Treaty. According to Article I of that treaty, the United States guaranteed Panamanian independence (see The 1903 Treaty and Qualified Independence, ch. 1). With that kind of insurance, the rulers of the new republic did not need to be concerned about developing armed forces.

When the country gained its independence, an oversized battalion of former Colombian troops under the command of General Estéban Huertas became the Panamanian army. Huertas and his soldiers had favored the independence movement and had switched their allegiance from Colombia to Panama. The general was named commander in chief of the small army and became one of Panama's most prominent citizens; however, when he tried to give orders to the new republic's first president, Manuel Amador Guerrero, the general was forced into retirement, and the army was demobilized. Although Huertas failed in his attempt to use the armed force as a political instrument, he established a precedent for such attempts.

To replace the disbanded army, the Corps of National Police was formed in December 1904 and for the next forty-nine years functioned as the country's only armed force. The government decree establishing the National Police authorized a force of 700, and the tiny provincial (formerly Colombian) police force that had been operating since independence was incorporated into the new organization. The corps was deployed territorially, and by 1908 its overall strength had risen to 1,000. The heaviest concentration of forces was (and has continued to be) in the Panama City area. For many years strength fluctuated, but generally remained close to 1,000 depending on budgetary allowances. There were, however, massive turnovers of personnel as new political regimes came to power and used positions in the police corps as patronage plums. By the 1940s some stability had been achieved, but it was not until the presidency of José Antonio Remón in the early 1950s that institutionalization of the corps took place, and the National Police was designated the National Guard.

The emergence of the National Guard and its successor institution, the FDP, as powerful actors in domestic politics is inextricably intertwined with the professional military career of Colonel Remón. Born in 1908 to a middle-class family, he studied at the then prestigious National Institute, which served as the training ground for sons of wealthy families. Upon graduation, he received a scholarship to attend the Mexican Military Academy, and he graduated from there in 1931. Because few Panamanian police officers at that time had academy training of any sort, he entered the National Police as a captain. By 1947 he had become commandant of police.

Remón's ability to convert the police into an important political force resulted not only from his personal and professional skills but also from the nature of Panamanian politics during the late 1940s and early 1950s (see The National Guard in Ascendance, ch. 1). As a military academy graduate, Remón realized the limitations of a police force both as an organization commanding national respect and as an instrument for wielding political power. In 1953, therefore, he created the National Guard.

During the 1950s and 1960s, the National Guard was militarized and professionalized, largely with United States aid under the Mutual Security Act. This trend away from the police roots and toward increased military status accelerated during the 1960s, as a result of the perceived threat from Fidel Castro's Cuba. More Panamanian officers and enlisted personnel were trained at United States facilities in the Canal Zone, and military assistance increased dramatically during the 1960s.

Remón was assassinated in 1955, but the legacy of militarization that he passed on to his successor, General Bolívar Vallarino, had culminated by the late 1960s in the formation of a National Guard that was increasingly sure of its professional identity and no longer averse to becoming involved in politics. Total force strength reached 5,000 with an officer corps of 465; an increasing number of officers had received academy training. Although police work still predominated and many officers were promoted from the ranks of "street cops," middle-ranking officers such as Torrijos were increasingly drawn from the small but growing band of academy graduates. Within the National Guard, there were more positions requiring officers with formal military training. For instance, a special public-order force was created in 1959, in response to an amphibious invasion launched from Cuba by a small group of armed Panamanians. New rifle companies were formed during this same period, the prototypes of the contemporary FDP combat battalions formed in the 1980s.

In spite of all these changes in Panama's military institution, it was not until the coup of 1968 and the political ascendancy of Torrijos that the National Guard began to make a lasting imprint on the socioeconomic structure of the country. With the death of Remón in 1955, the role of the armed forces in mobilizing the lower classes against the urban commercial elite had been curtailed, and politics were once again controlled by the oligarchy. Torrijos changed that, introducing a populist brand of politics as well as further expanding and professionalizing the National Guard (see The Government of Torrijos and the National Guard, ch. 1).

During the Torrijos years (1968–81), rank structure within the National Guard allowed control by a single military leader in the tradition of Remón and Vallarino. This phenomenon of a single institutional leader may have resulted because the police and National Guard had traditionally been institutions with low esteem and few links to the national political system. Regardless of the reason, Torrijos was the only general, the positions on the general staff being occupied by lieutenant colonels. Torrijos controlled the National Guard through a highly centralized administrative structure. Although there were by now a number of light infantry companies and other units with some combat potential, Torrijos managed to exercise independent control over all of the infantry companies and all officer assignments. During the Torrijos years, the National Guard was still small enough for Torrijos to maintain a close and personal working relationship not only with members of the officer corps but also with enlisted personnel.

From 1968 until Torrijos's death in 1981, the National Guard continued the expansion, militarization, and professionalization that had begun under Remón in the late 1940s. Furthermore, dramatic changes took place in officer recruitment and training. During the 1950s and 1960s, most academy-trained officers entering the National Guard were members of the lower-middle class who had received their military training in Mexico and other countries in Central America; Torrijos himself was schooled in El Salvador.

Brigadier General Omar Torrijos Herrera

During the 1970s, more junior officers attended South American academies, such as those in Brazil, Peru, Chile, Venezuela, and Argentina.

Since World War II, Panama had maintained close security ties to the United States, and that country had assisted in the development of Panama's military institutions. Panama had been one of the twenty original signatories to the 1945 Act of Chapultepec, binding the countries of Latin America and the United States to a mutual defense agreement by which all were to respond to an external attack against any one. Two years later, most of the same countries (including Panama) signed the Inter-American Treaty of Reciprocal Assistance (Rio Treaty), which also provided for mutual defense against external attack, but further bound the signers to peaceful arbitration of disputes arising among member states. In 1948 the charter of the Organization of American States (OAS) incorporated the provisions of the Rio Treaty. Panama also signed the Treaty for the Prohibition of Nuclear Weapons in Latin American (Tlatelolco Treaty) in 1967, an agreement that prohibited the deployment of nuclear weapons in Latin America. A bilateral military assistance pact existed between the United States and Panama and, under the Panama Canal treaties, the two countries pledged themselves to the joint defense of the Panama Canal.

Missions and Organization of the Defense Forces

On September 29, 1983, a new law—Law 20—created the FDP as the successor institution to the National Guard. The law simultaneously repealed all previous legislation relating to the organization, mission, and functions of the Panamanian armed forces, including Law 44 of December 23, 1953, and Law 50 of November 30, 1958. Opposition parties strongly criticized the new law, claiming that it "implies the militarization of national life, converts Panama into a police state, makes the members of the armed forces privileged citizens, and gives the commander of the National Guard authoritarian and totalitarian power." However, the Defense Forces' commander in chief, General Manuel Antonio Noriega Moreno, claimed that the change in the law was necessary in order to confront the deteriorating security situation in Central America and to prepare the military for its growing role in defending the Panama Canal.

The functions of the FDP stated in the organic law were very broad, giving it an increasing role and bringing other organizations under its control. Major functions included protecting the life and property of Panamanians and foreigners living in Panama; cooperating with civilian authorities to guarantee individual rights in the republic; preventing crime; defending the Panama Canal in cooperation with the United States as specified under terms of the treaties; regulating traffic; and cooperating with civilian authorities in the areas of drug trafficking, contraband, and illegal immigration.

The new organizational structure established by the 1983 law created a "public force" that brought a broad array of institutions under a single operational command. The FDP encompassed the General Staff, Military Regions and Zones, Ground Forces, Panamanian Air Force, National Navy, Police Forces, and National Guard. In addition, the FDP would include any institution created in the future that might perform functions similar to the institutions listed above. One effect of these changes was to reduce the National Guard to only one of a number of co-equal military institutions within the FDP structure that was bound together, as the Guard had been, through a single command and commander in chief (see fig. 10).

Although the Constitution designates the president of the republic as the supreme chief of the FDP, this role is largely symbolic. The law specifies that he "will exercise his command by means of orders, instructions, resolutions, and regulations which will be transmitted through the commander in chief." The FDP enjoyed administrative autonomy that in effect allowed it to determine its own internal procedures in regard to personnel policies, disciplinary sanctions against FDP members, organizations created to further the social welfare of members, and recommendations for the defense budget.

Since there was no role for civilian officials in determining FDP policy and the organization was under a single military command, the law itself provided the only parameters for the commander in chief's role. The duties of the commander in chief were very broad and sometimes simply restated duties assigned to the FDP as a whole. The commander in chief was charged, for example, with adopting "measures needed to guarantee the security of inhabitants and their property and the preservation of the public order and social peace." The commander in chief was also required to keep the president abreast of any developments in the area of national security and to participate in all modifications of the law that would affect the FDP.

Within the FDP, the commander in chief was responsible for promotions, transfers, and awarding military decorations. He supervised disciplinary measures and was to improve "the moral and material condition of the institution as well as the cultural and intellectual condition of its members." The president of the republic could replace the FDP's top officer in case of retirement, death,

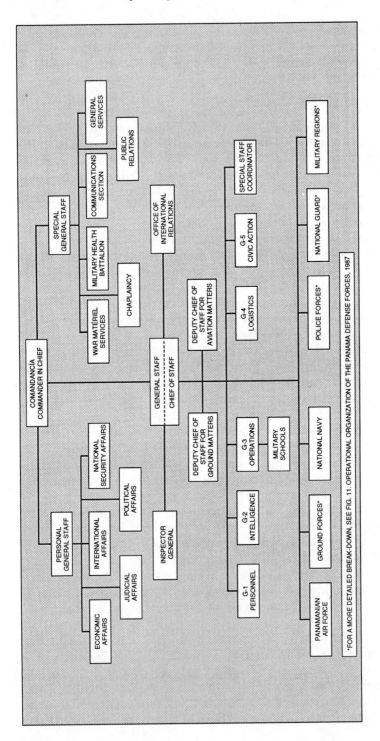

Figure 10. Organization of the Panama Defense Forces, 1987

disobedience of orders that were supported by constitutional provisions, and personal incapacity.

The General Staff

Article 36 of the 1983 law stated that "The commander in chief of the Defense Forces . . . will have an advisory body comprised of officers with the rank of general, colonel, and lieutenant colonel." This advisory body was called the General Staff, and its members were appointed by the commander in chief. The primary task assigned to the General Staff was to help the commander in chief with planning in the areas of military operations, training, and administration.

The structure of the General Staff of the FDP was inherited from its predecessor, the National Guard. The General Staff was structured in approximately the same way as a United States Army staff at division level or above. The basic similarity was in the section breakdown, that is, G–1, Personnel; G–2, Intelligence; G–3, Operations; G–4, Logistics; and G–5, Civic Action. There were a chief of staff and two deputy chiefs of staff, who obviously occupied positions of extreme importance within this highly centralized command structure. In June 1987, the position of vice chief of staff was spilt into two new positions: the deputy chief of staff for ground matters, who served concurrently as G–3, and the deputy chief of staff for aviation matters, who also occupied the G–5 position. The chief of staff, deputy chiefs of staff, and assistant chiefs were all full colonels.

In addition to the General Staff, there were two other structures at the level of the general command. There was a Special General Staff that incorporated the War Matériel Services, Military Health Battalion, Communications Section, General Services, Chaplaincy, and Public Relations. There was also a Personal General Staff supplying advice to the commander in chief on an "as needed" basis. The Personal General Staff included five sections: Economic Affairs, Judicial Affairs, International Affairs, Political Affairs, and National Security Affairs. The Personal General Staff seemed to institutionalize the involvement of the FDP in a wide range of civilian policy matters—an involvement that can be traced back to the days when Torrijos commanded the National Guard. Noriega commented that the new staff structure initiated with passage of the 1983 law furthered the goal of "performing our mission more effectively and realistically in conformance with the geopolitical situation from which Panama cannot escape . . . ." and pointed to "the formation of a new Personal General Staff of the Commander . . . ." This staff functioned in essence as an in-house National Security Council.

Military Zones

Organizational descriptions of the Defense Forces included a structure of four military regions within which the military zones operated (see fig. 11). In 1987, however, these regions existed only on paper. Noriega had referred to the military regions as areas ''which constitute the strategic triangles of national security,'' but their eventual activation was thought to be linked to the further elaboration and expansion of Panama's four combat battalions.

During the 1950s and 1960s, when the National Guard was still primarily a police force, the military zones together with the General Staff were the heart of the institution. Commanders of the ten military zones into which the country was then divided were powerful figures who often served as de facto provincial governors. Usually holding the rank of major, they could expect their next assignment to be command of another zone or a position on the General Staff, then largely composed of lieutenant colonels. When the National Guard gave way to the FDP, the zone commanders' role remained significant even though the 1983 law made no specific provision for military zones; it simply stated, ''The internal regulations of the Defense Forces . . . can divide the territory . . . into regions, military zones, detachments, districts, or any other form of division suitable for the better exercise of institutional functions . . . .''

In the mid-1980s, zone commanders continued to be regarded as the most powerful individuals in the provinces, surpassing by far the importance of the provincial governors. They controlled political, military, and economic affairs in the zones, and they rather than the governors settled labor disputes and strikes. Within the FDP, the zone commanders, generally holding the rank of major, were also significant. They were personally selected by the FDP commander and were directly responsible to him. Military units headquartered within the zones, including the emergent combat battalions, appeared to be fully integrated into the zones and thus firmly under the control of the zone commanders. The Fifth Military Zone, for example, was the home base of the Peace Battalion, whose commander reported directly to the zone commander.

There were twelve military zones in 1987, the most recent having been created in 1986 in the Comarca de San Blas (see fig. 1). This area had traditionally exercised considerable territorial autonomy as the home of the Cuna Indians (see Indians, ch. 2). Their traditional suspicion of the Guard (and their attempt to insulate themselves from Hispanic politico-military influence) was partially overcome in the 1980s, when more Indians entered the military, and as a result of increased encroachment on their territory by

Colombians and settlers from other parts of Panama. Nevertheless, the creation of the Twelfth Military Zone became acceptable to the Cuna only after lengthy FDP lobbying and the granting of various concessions.

Ground Forces

Panama's Ground Forces, officially the Ground Forces for Defense and National Security (Fuerzas Terrestres de Defensa y Seguridad Nacional), constituted a critical element within the FDP in the late 1980s. Their primary mission appeared to be to develop the capability to defend the canal after the year 2000. However, these forces had developed historically in response to other needs. Before the 1931 coup d'état that removed President Florencio H. Arosemena, the United States had frequently intervened militarily to oversee elections and quell riots (see United States Intervention and Strained Relations, ch. 1). The United States' decision not to use troops in 1931 to prevent the coup precipitated a change in the Panamanian military. It was now clearly up to the national police to guarantee internal security through the formation of a troop contingent.

Proposals were made to create a militarily trained police reserve unit of battalion strength to respond quickly to serious disorders, but political fears and budgetary limitations prevented action on the proposals. Renewed efforts through the years met with the same lack of success. The 1959 amphibious landing of Panamanian dissidents demonstrated that the National Guard, which was still primarily a police organization, lacked the training and the capability to repulse even a small-scale attack. Plans were then made to create a Public Order Company (Compañía de Orden Público) that could serve as a field force as well as a police reserve.

A police detachment stationed at Panamá Viejo (Old Panama, a suburb of Panama City) was used as a cadre in forming the new Public Order Company, which was to quell public disturbances and rebellions; to assist on special occasions, such as sporting events, parades, and ceremonies; to maintain order during natural disasters; to accomplish rescues in the jungles and mountains and at sea; to furnish raiding parties for police actions; and to act by virtue of its existence as a deterrent to social disorder. Many of the company's original personnel were sent for special training to United States Army schools in the Canal Zone.

The Public Order Company was the precursor of the eight infantry companies (*compañías de infantería*) that in the late 1980s constituted the major portion of Panama's Ground Forces. These companies had been established individually as necessary to perform a wide variety of tasks in addition to those mentioned above.

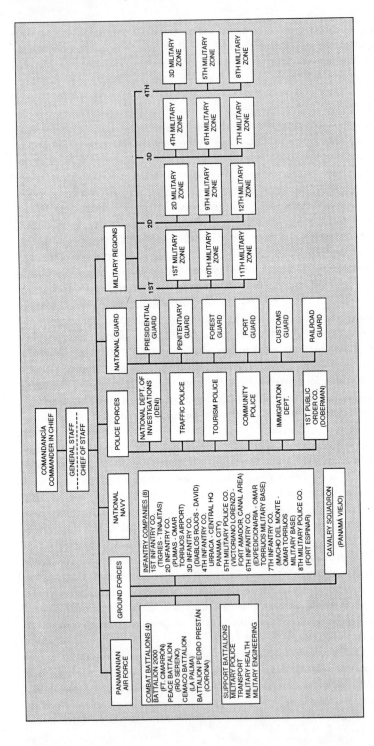

Figure 11. Operational Organization of the Panama Defense Forces, 1987

The eight infantry companies, sometimes referred to as combat companies (*compañías de combate*) or rifle companies (*compañías de fusileros*), were generally patterned on the standard infantry rifle company of the United States Army, although the Panamanians did not have the wide range of equipment available to their United States counterparts. The infantry companies were usually commanded by captains who had lieutenants as executive officers and platoon leaders. Squads were led by sergeants. Directly subordinate to the office of the commander (*comandancía*), the infantry companies were deployed at the discretion of the commander in chief. Although they had on occasion been used as quick-reaction, antiriot forces, the establishment of a special unit within the Police Forces (the First Public Order Company—Doberman) had preempted their use for such purposes. The strength of the infantry companies was estimated to average 200 personnel each. As of the mid-1980s, the FDP had sixteen V–150 and twelve to thirteen V–300 armored personnel carriers.

Infantry units were traditionally garrisoned within a thirty-kilometer radius of Panama City, with the exception of one rifle company at David and two at Omar Torrijos Military Base (formerly Río Hato). This deployment changed, however, with the creation of new combat battalions. In the late 1980s, the First Infantry Company, an airmobile company called the Tigres, was stationed at Tinajitas. The Second Infantry Company (Pumas) guarded General Omar Torrijos International Airport (more commonly known as Tocumen International Airport). The Third Infantry Company (Diablos Rojos) was located in David, the capital of Chiriquí Province, near the Costa Rican border. The Fourth Infantry Company (Urraca) was stationed at the Central Headquarters in Panama City to protect the General Staff and *comandancía*. The Fifth Military Police Company (Victoriano Lorenzo) was headquartered at Fort Amador in the canal area. The Sixth Infantry Company (Expedicionaria) and Seventh Infantry company (Macho del Monte) were headquartered at Omar Torrijos Military Base; these two companies, which controlled some of the country's light armored vehicles, once in essence represented Torrijos's private army. Finally, the Eighth Military Police Company was stationed at Fort Espinar on the Atlantic side of the isthmus.

Another component of the Ground Forces was the Cavalry Squadron (Escuadrón de Caballería), stationed at Panamá Viejo. Although primarily a ceremonial unit, it was called upon to perform crowd-control duties when situations warranted. Cavalrymen assumed routine police duties when not employed in their mounted roles. The Cavalry Squadron has a long and colorful history. A mounted unit in the national police force dates back to the early days of the republic, when a frontier atmosphere prevailed and mounted troopers pursued cattle rustlers and other bandits. Through the years the unit underwent various reorganizations and changes in deployment, eventually leaving its rural posts for Panama City. Despite its name, the mounted unit in the mid-1980s bore little organizational resemblance to the old-time, battalion-sized cavalry squadron. The unit was actually similar to an infantry company in that the squadron commander was a captain, his executive officer was a lieutenant, and the platoons and squads were led by lieutenants and sergeants, respectively.

The new mission assumed by the armed forces in the 1980s—defense of the canal—prompted the creation of four new combat battalions. The need for such battalions was premised on the belief that defense of the canal until the year 2000 and thereafter required the ability to defend not only the immediate environs of the waterway but also the various approaches to it. Fearing that conflicts elsewhere in Central America might spill over into Panama, the nation wanted to protect its borders with Colombia and Costa Rica. Of the four battalions envisioned (Battalion 2000, Peace Battalion, Cemaco Battalion, and Pedro Prestán Battalion), Battalion 2000 was by far the most fully developed by the mid-1980s. It was headquartered at Fort Cimarrón and commanded by a major who had a captain as his chief executive officer. The heart of Battalion 2000's combat potential consisted of an airmobile company, an airborne company, a mechanized company, and an infantry company; the First Rifle Company at Tinajitas provided fire support. The Peace Battalion, commanded by a captain, was headquartered in the town of Río Sereno near the Costa Rican border. In theory, the Cemaco Battalion, also commanded by a captain, was to be headquartered in Darién Province at La Palma near the Colombian border. Nevertheless, as of late 1987 its status was uncertain. It appeared to be only a company-sized element despite its designation as a battalion, and its actual location had not been finalized. When established, the Pedro Prestán Battalion was to be headquartered in Corona. In late 1987, it had not yet taken shape, however.

Also attached to the Ground Forces were a number of battalions supplying support services: the Military Police Battalion (Batallón de Policía Militar), composed of the Fifth and Eighth Military Police Companies; the Military Health Battalion (Batallón de Salud Militar); the Transport Battalion (Batallón de Transporte y Mantenimiento); and the Military Engineering Battalion (Batallón de Ingenería Militar). The Military Health Battalion was commanded by a captain and the others by majors.

Panamanian Air Force and National Navy

Before conversion of the National Guard into the FDP, the Panamanian military did not have separate service branches. Even in 1987, the six groups into which the FDP was divided (Ground Forces, Panamanian Air Force, National Navy, Police Forces, National Guard, and Military Zones) were referred to as "entities" (*entidades*) rather than service branches. Prior to 1983, the air force and navy were under the direct jurisdiction of the G-3 (Operations). Although not granted autonomy from the General Staff by the 1983 law, they seemed to have assumed more of a separate identity in the late 1980s.

Establishment of the Panamanian air capability came in 1964, when a Cessna 185 airplane was purchased from the United States. When Torrijos became commander in chief, he began building up the air arm, officially establishing the Panamanian Air Force (Fuerza Aérea Panameña) in January 1970, in recognition of not only its military utility but also its political potential. Airplanes and later helicopters allowed Torrijos to tour outlying areas of the country, areas where he could establish a political base that could neutralize the influence of historically powerful urban groups. The first officers to enter the air force were mostly civilian pilots and thus did not really constitute an officer corps as such. Also, there was little opportunity for an independent air force identity to emerge because pilots were regularly rotated to other positions within the National Guard, a practice that still prevailed in the FDP in the late 1980s. The most significant development affecting the air force during the Torrijos years, then, was not the development of an independent service identity, but the rapid growth of the air arm. There were only twenty-three officer pilots in 1969, but by 1978 there were sixty.

Although in 1987 the air force did not have any combat aircraft, there had been a steady buildup in other equipment, particularly helicopters. As of 1987, regular aircraft included three CASA C-212s, one DHC-3 Otter, two DHC-6 Twin Otters, one Short Skyvan, one Islander, one Boeing 727, and two Cessnas. In addition, there were nine Bell and six UH helicopters and one Super Puma. Personnel and airplanes were primarily based at the Tocumen Air Base, which is collocated with Tocumen International Airport near Panama City, and at Albrook Air Force Base in the canal area.

Panama's navy (officially, the National Navy—Marina Nacional) was formed at approximately the same time as the air force (1964). Known at that time as the Department of Marine Operations

(Departamento de Operaciones Marinas), it was a small organization involved primarily in coastal patrol operations under the direction of the G–3. In the late 1980s, the navy was equipped with two large rough-water patrol craft, two utility coastal patrol boats, about five small patrol and harbor craft, and three or four former United States Navy amphibious landing ships. The two large craft were the GC10 *Panquiaco* and the GC11 *Ligia Elena,* both constructed by Vosper Thornycroft in Portsmouth, England, in 1970. Each measured about 30 meters in length and was armed with 2 20mm guns; the manning level called for 23 officers and enlisted men. The 2 utility patrol craft each measured about 19 meters in length, mounted a pair of 12.7mm machineguns, and carried a complement of 10 people. The craft had been transferred to Panama from the United States Coast Guard in the mid-1960s. Two of the smaller coastal patrol craft were twelve-meter boats transferred to Panama from the United States Navy under the Military Assistance Program in the early 1960s. Each mounted a single 12.7mm machinegun and carried a crew of 4 enlisted personnel.

Because of the age and the limited capabilities of many of their naval craft, Panamanian officials sought to purchase more modern vessels that would allow the navy to defend the canal approaches and also enhance its coastal patrol capabilities. In the 1980s Panama took delivery of two swift ships, the MN GC–201 *Comandante Torrijos* and MN GC–202 *Presidente Porras,* which were constructed in the United States.

With this continued increase in the navy's vessels, there has been a concomitant expansion in personnel. In 1983 the navy moved to new headquarters at Fort Amador at the Pacific terminus of the canal. The commanding officer in the mid-1980s was a navy commander.

Police Forces

The Police Forces (Fuerzas de Policía) in the mid-1980s included a number of major units and several smaller ones performing relatively minor functions. Most important was the National Department of Investigations (Departamento Nacional de Investigaciones—DENI), which has historically been viewed by many Panamanians as a kind of secret police. For most of its history, Panama has had organizations similar to the DENI. The undercover police began with the decree-law, issued by President José D. Obaldía in 1909, establishing a ten-man section in the Panama City Police and a five-man section in Colón to engage exclusively in undercover police investigations. In effect, Obaldía created a detective organization supervised by the commander of the National Police.

In 1941, during the presidency of Arnulfo Arias Madrid, the enlarged detective agency became the National Secret Police and was removed from the jurisdiction of the police commander, although it remained under the Ministry of Government and Justice. According to the decree establishing it, the National Secret Police was to be the investigative agency dealing with infractions of the law as well as with conspiracies against the state or against national security.

In May 1960, President Ernesto de la Guardia, with the approval of the cabinet and the Permanent Legislative Commission, issued a decree-law that created the DENI to replace the National Secret Police. The new agency was removed from the Ministry of Government and Justice and placed in the Public Ministry under the direction of the attorney general. DENI powers were carefully delineated in the 1960 law; primarily an investigatory agency, it acquired broader authority that made it the Panamanian counterpart of the United States Federal Bureau of Investigation. Besides investigating crime, DENI was to maintain surveillance on known political extremists and potential subversives. DENI agents were authorized to maintain surveillance of hotels, pensions, and boarding houses in Panamanian cities in order to follow the movements of transients who might be potential violators of the law. The agency was also charged with administering a national identity bureau and with keeping records of all criminals and criminal activities. A fingerprint file was established by recording the prints of each citizen who applied for the national identity card (*cédula*).

DENI became a member of the International Organization of Criminal Police (Interpol). Sometime after the coup d'état of 1968, it was subordinated to the G–2 of the National Guard's General Staff. In the mid-1980s, the DENI was commanded by a major and headquartered in Ancón near Panama City. The overall strength of this organization and location of its agents were not publicized; however, it was generally assumed that Panama City, Colón, and David were its main areas of activity.

The Police Forces also included the Traffic Police (Dirección Nacional de Tránsito Terrestre), which was founded as a separate entity in 1969. Headquartered in Panama City, the Traffic Police regulated and controlled traffic throughout the country. Units were stationed in the cities and suburbs as well as on the back roads and highways, including the Pan-American Highway (see fig. 8). In performing its countrywide duties, the Traffic Police coordinated with other FDP personnel in the posts and stations of eleven of the twelve military zones; coordination was not possible in the Twelfth Military Zone, located in the Comarca de San Blas, because of the lack of roads. Responsibilities of the Traffic Police included issuing, renew-ing, and revoking drivers' licenses and vehicle registrations; investigating accidents and infractions of the vehicle laws; inspecting vehicles for safety hazards; and developing training programs for safe driving. In the late 1980s, the force was commanded by a major.

The Police Forces also included small police units called the Tourism Police (Policía de Turismo) and Community Police (Policía Comunitaria), both commanded by lieutenants. The Immigration Department and the First Public Order Company (Doberman) first came under the control of the Police Forces in 1983. The Immigra-tion Department was staffed by civilians but was fully integrated into the FDP; its head reported directly to the FDP commander. The First Public Order Company, commanded by a captain, was charged with riot control and was the primary instrument used for this purpose in the 1980s.

National Guard

The last of the six major entities making up the Defense Forces was the National Guard (Guardia Nacional). As reconstituted, the National Guard was scarcely a shadow of its former self. As of late 1987, it had neither a commander nor a staff element and func-tioned primarily as a paper entity encompassing the Presidential Guard (Guardia Presidencial), Penitentiary Guard (Guardia Peni-tenciaría), Forest Guard (Guardia Forestal), Port Guard (Guardia Portuaria), Customs Guard (Guardia Aduanera), and Railroad Guard (Guardia Ferroviaria). The Presidential Guard was a spe-cially selected unit charged with guarding the president and the presidential palace. The unit, which was quartered on the palace grounds, was believed to be similar to an infantry company in organization; although used as a ceremonial honor guard, its per-sonnel were also trained in the use of weapons and in security tech-niques. On parade or when mustered to greet foreign dignitaries, the Presidential Guard presented an impressive appearance in tailored white uniforms, white helmets, boots with white laces, and white belts and rifle slings. The Presidential Guard wore a variety of other uniforms as well, including a dark blue uniform with black cap and a solid gray uniform with white helmet and white belt. The unit was commanded by a major or a captain who answered directly to the *comandancía*.

Other small units of the National Guard protected specific areas or facilities. The Port Guard, Railroad Guard, and Forest Guard all were formed to handle functions and responsibilities turned over to Panama by the 1978 treaties. The Forest Guard, for example, dealt with the increasingly serious problem of deforestation in the basin drained by the canal.

Administration and Operations of the Defense Forces
Manpower

Service in the FDP and its predecessor organizations had been voluntary since Panama gained its independence, but a law provided for conscription if necessary. If there were a perceived threat to national sovereignty, the Defense Forces were charged with managing conscription. Naturalized citizens were exempted from participation in cases where they would have to fight against their country of origin. (As of the mid-1980s, however, no emergency since independence had necessitated activation of the law.)

Government officials reported through the years that there had always been more recruits for the Defense Forces than available spaces. Even the possibility of increased manning levels to meet additional requirements under the Panama Canal treaties did not seem to exhaust the pool of recruits. In the mid-1980s, Panamanians aspiring to military service generally reported to Omar Torrijos Military Base at Río Hato, where they took a series of physical and mental examinations. Those accepted were issued uniforms and received some basic training before being sent to the Military Training Center (Centro de Instrucción Militar—CIM) at Fort Cimarrón. There was no set schedule for basic training courses, but they occurred two to three times each year. All Panamanians who enjoyed ". . . their civilian and political rights, who have not been sentenced for crimes against property, or sanctioned by the judicial branch with a sentence depriving them of freedom for committing a crime against the public administration . . ." could apply for admission to the Defense Forces.

The commander in chief made all promotions and used the following criteria to determine whether a promotion was merited: "(1) Verification of service rendered in the lower rank and proof of seniority, (2) Exhibition of optimal physical condition . . ., (3) Demonstration of a positive moral attitude . . ., and (4) Exhibition of intellectual attitude and competence . . . ." If a member of the Defense Forces were found guilty of insubordination or some other violation of military discipline, the right to promotion could be suspended for up to three years. In October 1985, Noriega promoted the largest number of officers and enlisted personnel ever promoted at one time in the history of the armed forces (some 1,200). This occurred as a result of both the rapid expansion of the Defense Forces and the anticipated need for more senior officers and enlisted men as the year 2000 approached. Noriega's action further altered the rank structure by creating more high-level officer billets and strengthened his position within the Defense Forces.

Statistics were not maintained on the ethnic and racial backgrounds of Defense Forces personnel, but there was no apparent discrimination. In fact, since the National Police and its successor institutions had been among the few bureaucratic organizations in Panama not to discriminate on the basis of race, many black Panamanians found their way into military service. Enlisted personnel historically came mostly from the urban transit area, since the National Police served primarily as policemen in that area. After the creation of new infantry units during the 1960s and 1970s, there has been some indication that recruitment shifted to rural areas. Most officers had traditionally come from the urban lower-middle class, but increasing numbers were drawn from the rural middle and lower classes in the 1950s and 1960s.

Although there had always been a few women in the Panamanian armed forces, their numbers greatly increased in the 1980s. Part of this increase resulted from the creation of the FDP in 1983, when women in bureaucracies such as the Immigration Department were brought under the armed forces. However, it was also a reflection of changing policy and the military five-year plan implemented in the early 1980s. This plan called for the eventual creation of a separate administrative office for the women's component of the armed forces known as the Female Force (Fuerza Feminina). As of the mid-1980s, there were 1,824 women on active duty. In 1986 the School for Women's Training (Escuela de Formación Feminina) was established with a female captain as its commander. The first graduating class of twenty had received twelve weeks of instruction in a variety of military subjects.

Article 24 of the September 1983 Law 20 on the Defense Forces of the Republic of Panama states that the professional classification of military ranks within the FDP will be as follows: "(1) general of the forces, (2) corps general, (3) division general, (4) brigadier general, (5) colonel, (6) lieutenant colonel, (7) major, (8) captain, (9) lieutenant, (10) second lieutenant, (11) first sergeant, (12) second sergeant, (13) first corporal, (14) second corporal, (15) agent, (16) aid, and (17) orderly. Posts in the military ranks mentioned above will be filled in accordance with institutional needs." The commander in chief is traditionally the only active-duty officer to hold the rank of general. The rank of general came into use in the mid-1960s with Vallarino. Previously, colonel was the highest rank except for Remón's posthumous promotion to general, approved by the National Assembly after his assassination. In the late 1980s, the FDP's commander, General Noriega, held the four-star general rank (see fig. 12).

The most common uniforms in the mid-1980s were either green fatigue or khaki-colored short-sleeved shirts and trousers. Officers sometimes wore short-sleeved khaki shirts with dark green trousers or various (white or dark green) dress uniforms. Both the fatigue uniforms and khaki uniforms also had long-sleeved versions. Headgear varied, including a variety of helmets or helmet liners, berets of various colors, the stiff-sided visored fatigue cap, and the visored felt garrison caps similar to those worn by United States Army officers. Field-grade officers and the one general officer wore gold braid on their visored caps. Combat boots were the most common footwear, but officers frequently wore low-quarter shoes. Officer rank insignia consisted of gold bars or stars. The noncommissioned officer (NCO) ranks were designated by chevrons similar to those worn by some NCOs in the United States Army. Distinctive unit shoulder patches were worn by all ranks on the right shoulder of their uniforms (see fig.13). On the left shoulder, all ranks wore the familiar blue, white, and red shield of the FDP showing crossed rifles bisected by an upright saber.

Training

Until the 1950s, systematic training had been at best sporadic and at worst nonexistent. During the construction of the canal, United States instructors in police methods were frequently hired, but none stayed more than a few months, and the turnover hurt the already inefficient police force. In 1917 Albert R. Lamb was hired as an instructor for the National Police, and within two years he had been promoted to the post of inspector general. Even after a Panamanian was named commander in 1924, Lamb remained as an inspector and continued to exert an important influence on the police. He was credited with having created a relatively efficient force, but discipline, training, and efficiency declined after he left in 1927.

Police officials during the 1930s and 1940s periodically recommended the establishment of a police training center, but lack of funds always prevented action on such recommendations. In 1946 the National Assembly created the Police School (Escuela de Policía), but even after that decree and even with Remón as commander, the police had difficulties securing sufficient funds to operate a school. As president, Remón was instrumental in arranging for a Venezuelan military mission to advise and assist in establishing the National Guard School (Escuela de Formación de Guardias Nacionales), forerunner of the present-day CIM and the Police Training Academy (Academía de Capacitación Policial—ACAPOL).

COMMISSIONED OFFICERS

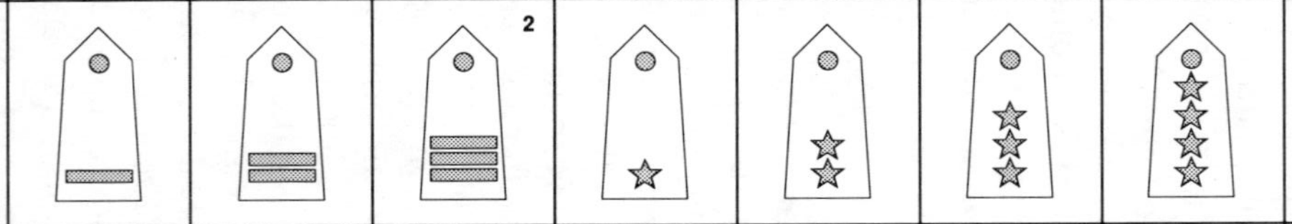

PANAMA RANK	SUBTENIENTE	TENIENTE	CAPITÁN [2]	MAYOR	TENIENTE CORONEL	CORONEL	GENERAL DE BRIGADA	GENERAL DE DIVISIÓN	GENERAL DE CUERPO	GENERAL DE LAS FUERZAS
DEFENSE FORCES	(insignia)	(insignia)	(insignia)	(insignia)	(insignia)	(insignia)	(insignia)	INSIGNIA NOT KNOWN	INSIGNIA NOT KNOWN	INSIGNIA NOT KNOWN
U.S. RANK TITLES [1]	2D LIEUTENANT	1ST LIEUTENANT	CAPTAIN	MAJOR	LIEUTENANT COLONEL	COLONEL	BRIGADIER GENERAL	MAJOR GENERAL	LIEUTENANT GENERAL	GENERAL
U.S. NAVY RANK TITLES	ENSIGN	LIEUTENANT JUNIOR GRADE	LIEUTENANT							

ENLISTED PERSONNEL

PANAMA RANK	SOLDADO RASO / MARINERO [3]	CABO SEGUNDO	CABO PRIMERO	SARGENTO DE SEGUNDA	SARGENTO DE PRIMERA
DEFENSE FORCES	NO INSIGNIA	INSIGNIA NOT KNOWN	(insignia)	(insignia)	(insignia)
U.S. ARMY RANK TITLES	BASIC PRIVATE	PRIVATE 1ST CLASS	CORPORAL	SERGEANT	SERGEANT 1ST CLASS
U.S. AIR FORCE RANK TITLES	AIRMAN BASIC	AIRMAN 1ST CLASS	SERGEANT	STAFF SERGEANT	MASTER SERGEANT
U.S. NAVY RANK TITLES	SEAMAN RECRUIT	SEAMAN	PETTY OFFICER 3D CLASS	PETTY OFFICER 2D CLASS	CHIEF PETTY OFFICER

NOTE- [1]Army and Air Force   [2]No Panama Navy rank above Capitán   [3]Navy

Figure 12. Ranks and Insignia of the Panama Defense Forces, 1987

Under the leadership of General Torrijos, training for both officers and enlisted men improved considerably. In the 1970s, officer training shifted from Central to South America, resulting in a significant upgrading in the quality of professional education received. Although many officers were still promoted from the ranks, the percentage of those with academy training gradually increased. By 1979 some 315 of 700 officers were academy graduates.

Since the early 1950s, approximately 5,000 Panamanian officers and enlisted men have been trained by the United States. Although some of these students were sent to the United States, the majority attended United States facilities located in the former Canal Zone, including the United States Army School of the Americas, the Inter-American Air Forces Academy at Albrook Air Force Base, and the Small Craft Instruction and Training School at the Naval Support Facility near the Pacific end of the canal. Although in the late 1980s some FDP personnel still received training at United States facilities, their numbers were reduced because the School of the Americas moved to Fort Benning, Georgia, in 1984. Nevertheless, for the majority of Panamanian officers, the command and staff course given at the School of the Americas remained the final rung on the educational ladder.

One of the FDP's most important training facilities was the CIM located near Panama City at Fort Cimarrón. It housed the Airborne School and offered a parachute-rigging course in addition to its responsibility for the basic training of recruits and the refresher training of all military personnel in subjects such as patrolling, first aid, and map reading. Besides providing regular teaching and field training, the facility assisted in the development of new courses of instruction designed to keep the organization abreast of innovations and current methods of military operation. Its commandant, usually a major or captain, was assisted by an executive officer and a staff and faculty consisting of officers and sergeants.

Another Panamanian school, the General Tomás Herrera Military Institute (Instituto Militar General Tomás Herrera), was located at Omar Torrijos Military Base in Río Hato. Established in 1974 on the model of a Peruvian military high school, it offered training for young people who might some day choose to pursue a military career. It also provided the Defense Forces with technically trained personnel proficient in developmental fields such as agronomy. As of 1986, ten classes had been graduated from the institute and many of its students were receiving scholarships to various military academies throughout Latin America.

The José Domingo Espinar Educational Center was an FDP training facility that replaced the United States Army School of the

1st Infantry Company
Airmobile

2d Infantry Company
Air Transportable

3d Infantry Company

4th Infantry Company

5th Military Police
Company

6th Infantry Company

7th Infantry Company

National Navy

Panamanian Air Force

Source: Based on information from *Defensa*, Panama City, December 1979, 5.

Figure 13. Selected Unit Insignia of the Panama Defense Forces, 1987

Americas. Located near Colón, this center was named after the Panamanian patriot who first declared territorial independence from Colombia. It had a number of different faculties and offered a variety of courses on subjects such as basic criminal investigations, basic intelligence, English language, and radio communications. It also offered a promotion course for future noncommissioned officers. The ACAPOL, which offered basic police training, was housed in this facility. The academy offered a wide variety of courses to both officers and enlisted personnel and high-level seminars dealing with national problems. The importance of this facility within the educational structure of the Defense Forces was indicated by the fact that its commander in the mid-1980s was a lieutenant colonel.

Other FDP training facilities included the Benjamín Ruíz School for Noncommissioned Officers (Escuela de Suboficiales Benjamín Ruíz), the Command and Special Operations School (Escuela de Comando y Operaciones Especiales), and the Pana-Jungla School (Escuela Pana-Jungla). The School for Noncommissioned Officers was established in 1986 at Omar Torrijos Military Base. It was primarily a training facility designed to identify prospective second lieutenants. Secondary school graduates went through a two-year training program and were awarded the rank of first sergeant. Following two years of ''on-the-job training'' and additional courses, the best of the group became second lieutenants. The Command and Special Operations School was a facility for training members of the infantry companies in various types of special activities. Graduates were mostly sergeants with more than ten years of military service. The Pana-Jungla School was located in Bocas del Toro Province along the Río Teribe and near the Costa Rican border. Commanded by a major, it offered training in jungle survival skills to both Panamanian soldiers and military personnel from other countries.

Foreign Military Assistance

Ever since the early post-World War II period, Panama has been the recipient of some annual military aid under various programs established by the United States government (see table 19, Appendix A). In a diplomatic message accompanying the Panama Canal treaties, the United States agreed (pending congressional approval) to provide up to US$50 million in credits under the Foreign Military Sales (FMS) program. The credits were to be spread over the first ten years of the treaty period.

In fact, FMS deliveries to Panama have risen dramatically in the 1980s, from a mere US$187,000 in fiscal year (FY) 1980 to over US$12 million in FY 1986. Assistance under the International Military Education and Training Program also has registered a steady increase from US$270,000 in FY 1980 to US$575,000 in FY 1985, with a slight drop to US$507,000 in FY 1986.

In late 1987, however, it remained to be seen whether and under what circumstances Panama would continue to receive United States military aid. The United States suspended all military and economic aid to Panama in the summer of 1987, in response to

Panama's failure to take steps toward a democratic, civilian-ruled government, in accordance with conditions associated with the Panama Canal treaties.

Canal Defense

Some observers have held that the Panama Canal cannot be defended. Even as early as 1953, a simulated nuclear strike during exercises near Miraflores Locks demonstrated the locks' extreme vulnerability to such attack (see fig. 3). Four years later in "Operation Caribbean," United States war gamers found the canal's defenses inadequate and asked the government of Panama for missile sites outside the Canal Zone. The Panamanians, however, feared that United States missile sites would only make their country more of a target for someone else's missiles; in addition, they did not want to give up any more territory to the United States. Years later, testimony before committees of the United States Congress during treaty hearings pointed out the vulnerability of the locks to various kinds of sabotage, such as placement of an explosive in the hydraulic system.

Vulnerability to attack or sabotage notwithstanding, the canal is mandated to be defended by the combined military efforts of Panama and the United States. With this fact as a basic assumption, the drafters of the Panama Canal treaties spelled out the modus operandi for joint defense in the Treaty Concerning the Permanent Neutrality and Operation of the Panama Canal and projected the possibility of United States military assistance to Panama even into the twenty-first century (see Appendix B). Among the five binational bodies established by Panama and the United States to handle all matters concerning the canal until December 31, 1999, two—the Combined Board and the Joint Committee—were set up to take care of defense affairs. The Combined Board consisted of an equal number of senior military representatives from each country, who consulted and cooperated on all matters dealing with defense and planned "actions to be taken in concert for that purpose." Specifically, the board was charged with coordinating such matters as the preparation of canal defense contingency plans and the planning and execution of combined military exercises. The board was further charged with reviewing defense needs and making recommendations to the respective national governments and assessing at five-year intervals the resources provided by the two countries for their defense commitments.

The Joint Committee, which also consisted of senior military officers and their deputies, looked after the day-to-day contacts and cooperation between the two defense forces. The United States half

U.S.S. Tarawa *enters Pedro Miguel Locks,*
Panama Canal, July 1976
Courtesy Agency for International Development

of the committee also dealt with United States military personnel and civilian employees and their dependents under the status-of-forces agreements. The Agreement in Implementation of Article IV of the Panama Canal Treaty spelled out the complex responsibilities and functions of the Joint Committee in detail. To accomplish its numerous and varied tasks, the committee was divided into subcommittees, each having several sections. Because neither the Combined Board nor the Joint Committee had decision making or command authority, deadlocked issues had to be referred to their respective governments.

Between 1979 and 1985, at least sixteen joint military exercises involving Panamanian and United States forces took place, testing combined capabilities to defend the canal. Beginning in 1982, a series of exercises called "Kindle Liberty" were conducted. These exercises practiced the rapid movement of support troops from the United States, evaluated operational terrain, and tested joint troop coordination and performance. Generally, Kindle Liberty exercises involved Panamanian companies from Battalion 2000 and the Peace Battalion and United States forces from the 193d Infantry Brigade stationed in the canal area and from Fort Bragg, North Carolina. Combined troop participation normally ranged from 3,000 to 5,000. A series of operations called "Black Fury" were also conducted between 1979 and 1981 in the canal area. Their primary purpose was to simulate defending the canal from an attack by guerrilla forces by mobilizing troops in both Panama and the United States. Black Fury training exercises involved approximately 5,000 United States troops, including some from various state national guards.

Joint military exercises held in the mid-1980s were larger than those held previously. "Minuteman II" in 1985, for example, involved 10,000 United States troops from various national guard units in Puerto Rico, Florida, Texas, Alabama, Missouri, and Louisiana in addition to 5,000 members of the FDP. These exercises also dealt more with scenarios of guerrilla or low-intensity conflict. For example, in early 1986 a joint exercise called "Donoso 86" was held on a remote portion of the Atlantic coast west of the terminus of the canal. The scenario called for a large band of guerrillas operating with extensive foreign backing to have gained the support of the local population. The primary Panamanian forces involved in this exercise came from Battalion 2000, and the main United States contingent was from the 193d Infantry Brigade. In early 1987, a joint exercise called "Candela 87" was conducted on the border with Costa Rica using various tactical units of the FDP, including the Peace Battalion. The future of these exercises was uncertain in late 1987, however. After the United States Congress prohibited the use of FY 88 funds for military exercises in Panama, all such joint ventures were suspended.

Involvement in Political and Economic Affairs

Panama's security forces have changed dramatically since independence. Originally established as a police force after the national army was abolished, these forces evolved toward a paramilitary configuration during the 1950s and 1960s. In the late 1970s, they began to evolve once more as Panama assumed responsibility for defending the canal. During each successive stage, prior functions and missions were not abandoned; rather, new ones were added. These three different stages of institutional development were associated with three distinct types of military participation in politics. During the earliest period when the security forces performed a police role, the institution merely reflected the interests of the dominant civilian elite. Thus, they were used to keep the peace and to prevent the urban masses from challenging the elite through strikes and other socially disruptive types of activity.

With the adoption of a paramilitary role, the newly formed National Guard began to act politically to further its own interests and those of the commander in chief. The Guard not only began to serve as the court of last resort for settling feuds among the

Queen Elizabeth 2 *transits Miraflores Locks,*
Panama Canal, March 1977
Courtesy Agency for International Development

civilian elite, but eventually seized political power in its own name.
Under the leadership of Torrijos, the National Guard and its General Staff fashioned a "civilian" political regime in their own image, but real power remained in the hands of the military (see The Panama Defense Forces, ch. 4). In 1983 Panama implemented constitutional changes aimed at restoring direct presidential elections, but it was clear that even Torrijos's death would not force the military to give up its central role in politics. Despite the Constitution's assertion that the ultimate political authority in Panama was the will of the people, the civilian government that expressed this will was expected to rely heavily on the advice of the military. According to the Constitution, "Power emanates from the people and is exercised by the government through a distribution of functions among the executive, legislative, and judicial branches acting in harmonic collaboration with the National Guard."

The central role played by the FDP during the 1980s was the logical outgrowth of both the historical evolution of Panama's security forces and changes in the civilian sector. Before the National Guard was created in the early 1950s, officers in the National Police did not have enough social standing or sufficient institutional support to play a significant role in politics. By the 1970s, however, officers had emerged with enhanced social status, an enlarged

247

institutional power base, and growing links with marginalized civilian groups. As the "spokesman" for these groups during the 1970s and 1980s, the military worked to implement social and economic policies viewed as being both in the interest of these groups and of benefit to the military itself.

In the economic sphere, the National Guard and the Defense Forces have sought to have civilian technocrats whose views were similar to those of the military appointed to key decision-making positions. During the 1970s, for example, Torrijos worked with a small group of professionals from the reform wing of the National Liberal Party, placing them in key government positions. And in supporting the presidential candidacy of Nicolás Ardito Barletta Vallarino (a former vice president of the World Bank) in 1984, the Defense Forces once again demonstrated their penchant for working with like-minded civilian professionals.

Top FDP officers were also alleged to have been engaged in a wide variety of legal and illegal business activities. A series of articles published in the *New York Times* in 1986 suggested that the FDP commander was deeply involved in both drug transactions and arms smuggling. Panama's alleged role in the drug business had never historically been related to production activities (although some marijuana was supposedly grown there) but rather to transshipment and the laundering of illicitly obtained funds. The articles went so far as to suggest that the FDP commander in chief was not only aware of these activities but played an active role in encouraging them. Subsequently, additional credible evidence of FDP involvement in drug-trafficking and money-laundering activities continued to surface.

The Defense Forces have at times cooperated with the United States government in some activities related to drug enforcement, such as making arrests, extraditing traffickers, and seizing boats carrying drug cargoes. In response to a United States request, Panama made drug money-laundering illegal in 1986 and agreed to give United States authorities access to certain bank records in drug investigations. "Operation Pisces," a drugs and money-laundering sting launched by the Drug Enforcement Administration in 1987 against cocaine traffickers, received extensive support from Panamanian authorities. Nevertheless, observers increasingly believed that such cooperation was an expedient ploy to sacrifice lower-level operations and personnel in order to safeguard more significant illegal activities.

United States Forces in Panama

United States military forces have been present in Panama since that nation broke away from Colombia at the beginning of the twentieth century. Indeed, the presence of the U.S.S. *Nashville* and the U.S.S. *Dixie* had influenced the outcome of Panama's revolt. Even before completion of the canal, United States soldiers or marines occasionally intervened in Panamanian affairs, usually at the request of local officials and in compliance with the 1903 treaty that gave the United States government broad discretionary powers. United States intervention took a new turn in 1918, when the United States unilaterally intervened to restore stability during a Panamanian political crisis. Most United States forces withdrew after elections were held and the crisis eased; however, a detachment of marines remained in Chiriquí Province for about two years for the purpose of maintaining public order.

Even though the National Police had been somewhat professionalized under the leadership of Albert R. Lamb, police authority dissolved in 1925 in the face of a renters' strike in Panama City. High rents charged for workers' housing by the urban oligarchy caused the strike, which turned violent and resulted in many deaths during two days of rioting. Panamanian authorities requested aid, and 600 United States Army troops carrying rifles with fixed bayonets entered the city to restore order. The rioters were dispersed, and for twelve days United States soldiers patrolled the streets keeping order and guarding government officials and property. Similar rent strikes recurred in 1932 but with the National Police restoring order. Intervention or the threat of intervention from United States forces continued to be an irritant to the Panamanian people and a cause célèbre for Panamanian politicians over the next several years. In 1936 negotiations between the two countries resulted in an agreement that prohibited United States intervention in Panamanian civil affairs (see A New Accommodation, ch. 1).

During and immediately after World War II, the United States military presence in the Canal Zone underwent a metamorphosis corresponding to broad hemispheric developments. When Nazi activities in Latin America became widespread, and to counteract German influence, interest in some kind of joint defense revived. Shortly before the United States entered the war in December 1941, the United States had begun to establish military missions in the capital cities of the Latin American republics. The missions served as liaison agencies between the military establishment of the United States and those of the Latin American countries, and mission personnel became advisers to the Latin American military. After the war, canal defense continued to be the primary United States mission, but the United States Caribbean Command in Panama retained responsibility for United States security interests throughout Latin America and administered the aid and advisory programs for the entire area. In 1963 the Caribbean Command was redesignated the United States Southern Command (SOUTHCOM), retaining the same functions and responsibilities.

Transfer of control of the Canal Zone to Panama in 1979 did not substantially alter the mission of SOUTHCOM because the United States retained primary responsibility for defense; as a result, observers expected SOUTHCOM or a similar successor organization to remain in place until United States obligation under the Panama Canal treaties is fulfilled at the end of the century. SOUTHCOM is what is known in common military parlance as a unified command, that is, one in which all services operate under, and are responsible to, a single commander. Because the army has historically been the principal component of United States forces in Panama, SOUTHCOM has been under the command of an army general.

The primary missions of SOUTHCOM remained much as they had been during previous decades: to defend the Panama Canal, to administer programs of military assistance to Latin American military institutions, to coordinate United States participation in joint military exercises in the region, and to help with disaster relief. Major SOUTHCOM installations included the general headquarters at Quarry Heights, Fort Clayton, Fort Davis, Fort Sherman, Rodman Naval Base, Fort Amador, and Howard Air Force Base. Fort Clayton served as headquarters for the most important United States military unit in the area, the 193d Infantry Brigade. The Brigade consisted of two infantry battalions, one special forces battalion, and a combat support battalion, in addition to other specialized units. Overall SOUTHCOM military strength in the mid-1980s was approximately 9,400 men and women of the army, navy, and air force. By the terms of the Panama Canal treaties, the United States pledged to maintain its armed forces at a peacetime manning level, that is, not in excess of the number that were present in the zone just before the treaty became effective.

A Status-of-Forces Agreement (SOFA) between the United States and Panama was combined with the Base Rights Agreement as part of the Panama Canal treaties. The SOFA details the legal rights and obligations of United States military personnel and their dependents residing in Panama and stipulates crimes over which the United States military or the Panamanian courts have jurisdiction.

Administration of Justice

For the first several years of its existence, Panama depended on the legal code inherited from Colombia. The first Panamanian codes, promulgated in 1917, were patterned on those of Colombia and other Latin American states that had earlier broken away from the Spanish Empire; therefore, Panama's legal heritage was based on Roman law as passed on through Spain and its colonies. Nevertheless, several features of Anglo-American law have also been accepted in Panama. Habeas corpus, a feature of Anglo-American legal procedure that is not found in many Latin American codes, has been constitutionally guaranteed in Panama. Judicial precedent, another Anglo-American practice, has also made some headway; however, judges and magistrates usually have had little leeway in matters of procedure, delays, and degrees of guilt.

The Public Ministry provided for in the Constitution has defended the interest of the state; fostered the enforcement and execution of laws, judicial decisions, and administrative orders; supervised the official conduct and the performance of duty of public officials; prosecuted offenses of constitutional or legal provisions; and served as legal adviser to administrative officials. The functions of the Public Ministry were fulfilled by the attorney general of the republic, the solicitor general, the district attorneys, and the municipal attorneys. There were two alternates for each official of the ministry; all were appointive positions. The attorney general, the solicitor general, and their alternates were executive appointees; district attorneys and municipal attorneys were appointed by their immediate superiors in the judicial system. They in turn appointed subordinate personnel in their own offices.

In addition to the stipulations of "free, prompt, and uninterrupted" administration of justice and the establishment of the Public Ministry, the Constitution has several other statements about the application of laws, the treatment of citizens under the law, and the handling of prisoners. Article 21 guarantees freedom from arbitrary arrest, and Article 22 provides for habeas corpus. Article 29 prohibits the death penalty. Article 42 provides that "In criminal matters, a law favorable to the accused always has priority and retroactivity, even though the judgement may have become final." Article 163 gives the president power to grant pardons for political offenses, to reduce sentences, and to grant parole. Article 187 states that a person convicted of an offense against public order may not hold any judicial office in the future. Article 197 establishes trial by jury.

Under a section of the Constitution headed "Individual and Social Rights and Duties," private citizens are assured that they can be prosecuted by government authorities only for violations of the Constitution or the law. The procedure for arrests is also described, stating that arrests may result from response to complaints made to the police or from direct action on the part of police or DENI agents at the scene of the crime or disturbance. The validity of citizen's arrest is recognized: "An offender surprised flagrante delicto may be apprehended by any person and must be delivered immediately to the authorities." No person may be held for more than twenty-four hours by the police without being brought before competent authority. The Constitution forbids arrest or detention for violation of purely civil obligations or for debts.

During the course of an investigation, the accused and all witnesses are questioned, the latter under oath. The Constitution guarantees that no accused person may be forced to incriminate himself or herself, and the authorities are forbidden to force testimony from any close relative, whether related by blood or marriage, that is, "within the fourth degree of consanguinity or the second degree of affinity." Investigators may enter a person's home only with consent or a written order (search warrant) from a competent authority or to assist victims of crime or natural disaster. In general, all testimony must be presented in written form and be signed by investigators, accused, and witnesses. If a case warrants prosecution, it is referred to the appropriate court. Although bail is permissible in some cases, it is a privilege subject to many restrictions and may be denied at the request of the prosecutor if a judge concurs.

There was considerable evidence that many of these constitutional provisions were not realized in the daily lives of Panamanian citizens in the late 1980s. The most striking example was the case of Dr. Hugo Spadafora. Spadafora was a former senior government official, who had criticized the role of the Defense Forces in politics and the alleged role of Noriega in drug trafficking. Spadafora's headless body was found in Costa Rica near the border of Panama in September 1985 after reports that he had been taken into custody by members of the Defense Forces. There also were allegations that Dr. Mauro Zúñiga, head of an opposition group called the National Civilian Coordinating Committee (Coordinador Civilista Nacional—COCINA), was abducted and beaten.

Although the Constitution provides for habeas corpus and the prompt and uninterrupted administration of justice, several incidents suggested that these principles were sometimes violated. It should also be noted that various articles of the Constitution guaranteeing basic rights were suspended during the temporary state of emergency declared in 1987. Moreover, the government responded with excessive brutality to popular marches and demonstrations in Panama in mid-1987. According to a December 1987 United States Senate staff report on Panama, over 1,500 persons were arrested between June and September 1987. Credible evidence suggests that many of them were subjected to cruel and inhuman treatment while in jail.

Criminal Justice

The Criminal Code and the Administrative Code, respectively, defined crimes against public order, public security, public trust, decency, the person, and property as felonies (*delitos*) or misdemeanors (*faltas*), depending on the seriousness of the crime. Although sentences also were prescribed according to the seriousness of the crime, in nearly all cases the codes established upper and lower limits within which a court had discretion in sentencing. In crimes of violence against government officials, more severe sentences were prescribed.

Capital and corporal punishments were prohibited. The most severe penalty permitted for a single offense was a twenty-year imprisonment, and prison sentences were differentiated as to place of confinement. All prisoners could be required to perform prison labor whether or not it was included in a sentence. The most severe sentence, a specific type of imprisonment (*reclusión*), included the place of confinement—Coiba Penal Colony on the Isla de Coiba—and the manner of serving—hard labor. A sentence of *reclusión* could range from thirty days to twenty years. The sentence of simple imprisonment (*prisión*) could range from thirty days to eighteen years, but serving in Coiba was not inherent in the sentence. Depending on the seriousness of their crimes, prisoners sentenced to *reclusión* could be eligible for parole after three-quarters of the term had been served, and those sentenced to *prisión* could be eligible after serving two-thirds of the term.

Detention (*arresto*) was a penalty assessed for less serious offenses and could extend to eighteen months, usually served in a local jail. A punishment without physical restraint (*confinamiento*) limited the offender to a specified place of residence that had to be at least thirty kilometers from the scene of the crime and from where the victim resided. The period of the *confinamiento* was at the discretion of the court unless prescribed in law. Fines (*multas*) were the least severe penalties and in some cases were added to jail sentences. If an offender failed to pay or defaulted on payments, a *multa* was convertible to *arresto* in a ratio of money to time prescribed by law.

Conditional penalty (*condena condicional*) was a suspended sentence used at the discretion of a court in the sentencing of a first offender, except on a major felony charge. The sentence required residing at a fixed address and reporting any change, frequent visits to the court, and checks by the police on the offender's conduct. Many misdemeanors were punished by suspended sentences, fines, or short periods in jail. Sentences of public labor without confinement could also be adjudged at the discretion of a court.

Provisions for appeal existed in the system, and many categories of cases required automatic review in a higher court. Time limits were set on the preparation of appeals and court action on them, as well as on the time taken for automatic review. Few cases could be appealed to the Supreme Court, an appeal usually requiring that an error be shown in the handling by a lower court. Prosecutors also had the right of appeal.

The cases of minors were handled in a special system designed to combat juvenile delinquency and to keep young offenders from contact with hardened criminals. The Guardianship Court for Minors (Tribunal Tutelar de Menores), established in 1951, worked closely with the Defense Forces, DENI, and various social agencies to handle the cases of young offenders and to provide them with guidance and assistance if possible. Cases involving persons under age eighteen were not made public.

Although trial by jury is established by Article 197 of the Constitution, the same article stipulates that ''the law will determine the cases to be decided by this system.'' In practice, most criminal cases, except for those heard in the night courts of Panama City and Colón, were conducted by deposition, and the accused was not present during the proceedings. Only the most serious criminal cases, that is, those involving homicide or other heinous crimes, were heard by juries in the presence of the accused. Decisions were usually made by judges or magistrates after consideration of depositions from defense attorneys and prosecutors. Defendants and their attorneys were entitled to be fully informed of charges and the evidence on which charges were brought, and they could appeal the charges or later appeal the sentence.

One of the continuing sources of complaints concerning the system of criminal justice has centered around use of the night courts in Panama City and Colón. Judges, operating from 6:00 P.M. until 6:00 A.M., have been accused of dispensing justice in an arbitrary and summary manner. Some offenders have found themselves serving a sentence (of up to one year) without ever having been allowed to consult an attorney. The independence of the judiciary has also been called into question because of executive interference and, more particularly, because of interference from the G–2 of the Defense Forces, which has assumed de facto right of review in criminal cases.

The Penal System

Article 27 of the Constitution declares that the prison system is based on the principles of security, rehabilitation, and the protection of society. Provisions have been made to establish training programs designed to teach skills and trades that will afford prisoners the opportunity of reentering society as useful citizens after they complete their sentence. The same article also prohibits physical, mental, and moral abuse of prisoners. Juvenile offenders who were sentenced by a court were cared for in a special system that provided protection and education and attempted to rehabilitate minors before they came of age. Women were also segregated in the penal system.

The Department of Corrections was established in 1940 to administer the country's penal system for the Ministry of Government and Justice. Operation of the prisons had previously been a direct function of the National Police. The intention of the government officials who established the Department of Corrections was to end the inherent abuses in the system, but the new department was never properly staffed, and police had to be used as jailers. The same situation continued in the mid-1980s; because of understaffing in the Department of Corrections, most jails were staffed by members of the Defense Forces, and the prison system was still considered an entity of the FDP. Other abuses apparently also continued. Major complaints expressed about the penal system concerned overcrowding, poor sanitation facilities, and lack of adequate medical attention.

The Isla de Coiba has been the site of the Coiba Penal Colony, Panama's most severe prison, since 1919. Although most of its prisoners were sentenced by courts to specified terms, sometimes persons were sent to Coiba while awaiting the results of pretrial investigation or awaiting sentencing, a violation of judicial regulations, if, as indicated in the criminal code, Coiba was the most severe regime in the prison system. The prisoners were housed in a main camp and in several small camps scattered about the island, but there was no indication that pretrial detainees were segregated from prisoners serving sentences. In the main camp, there were some facilities for rehabilitation training and a small school; however, many of the inmates had little or no access to those facilities because they lived some distance from the main camp. Work was required of all prisoners, including those awaiting trial or awaiting sentencing. Labor was unremunerated for the majority of prisoners, most of whom were engaged in farming and animal husbandry in areas that they or former prisoners had cleared of jungle growth. Some mechanics and other skilled craftsmen received small wages for their labor.

Another major prison, the Model Jail (Cárcel Modelo), in Panama City was built in 1920; over the years, however, it acquired a reputation that belied its name. Its biggest problem, one not unique to the Model Jail or to Panama, was overcrowding. Cells intended to house three inmates were frequently found to have as many as fifteen; this severe overcrowding may have accounted for the large number of pretrial detainees that were sent to Coiba. First offenders confined to the Model Jail were not always segregated from hardened criminals, a pattern that prevailed throughout most of the prison system. Prisoners awaiting trial were often confined for extended periods before their cases appeared on a court docket, and there were complaints that rights to habeas corpus had been violated by holding some offenders incommunicado.

There was a jail in each provincial capital. The same complaints of overcrowding and abuse of rights were reported from the outlying provinces.

In contrast to the conditions under which male prisoners served sentences and awaited trial, women received much better care. The Women's Rehabilitation Center (Centro Feminino de Rehabilitación) in Panama City appeared to be an ideal prison. The center was under the supervision of the Department of Corrections, as were all prisons in Panama, but it was operated by nuns who had established a reputation for discipline tempered by humaneness and decency. Few complaints were reported from prisoners at the women's center. When first arrested, however, women were sometimes held overnight or for several nights at the Model Jail where, even though segregated, women experienced conditions that differed little from those described for men.

Incidence of Crime

The number of persons arrested for felonies and misdemeanors rose from 18,491 in 1980 to 20,073 in 1983 or from 9.5 per 1,000 inhabitants in 1980 to 9.6 per 1,000 inhabitants in 1983. When figures were broken down according to province, the greatest number of arrests in 1983 were found in the most populous province, Panamá, which accounted for approximately 50 percent of the total. Chiriquí and Colón ranked second and third in number of arrests, and in each case the principal cities (David and Colón) accounted for very high percentages of the totals. The statistics gave no details concerning the crimes for which the listed arrests were made.

Crimes by juveniles (persons under eighteen) increased during the early 1980s. The number of cases handled by the Guardianship Court for Minors rose from 2,923 in 1980 to 3,136 in 1983. Although juvenile offenses ran the gamut from homicide (17 in 1983) to traffic infractions serious enough to be taken to court

(275 in 1983), the largest increases were in the categories of property damage, attacks against persons, and fights.

National Security

As perceived by the Defense Forces, threats to national security were of two basic types: those arising from domestic insurgency and those of foreign origin. Although the FDP has conducted military exercises to deal with the contingency of guerrilla activity, there was no such activity in Panama through the mid-1980s.

To understand the military's perception of internal threat, it is important to note that the Defense Forces were closely identified with the formation of the political regime in existence in the late 1980s. This regime was formed in 1968 when Torrijos and the National Guard seized power through a coup d'état. For two decades, the military served as the ultimate guarantor of this political regime, whether headed as it was in the early 1970s by Torrijos or later by a succession of civilian presidents. Given this history of close military association with the existing political regime, there has been a tendency to view any domestic political challenge to it (democratic or otherwise) as a threat to national security.

The belief by members of opposition political parties that the direct elections for president held in 1984 had been rigged by the FDP led them to challenge the legitimacy of Ardito Barletta's government. When he was removed by the Defense Forces in 1985 and replaced by Eric Arturo Delvalle Henríquez, political opposition groups became even more vociferous in their charges of military interference in politics. Charges of electoral fraud and FDP involvement in perpetrating it were rendered even more credible in 1986, when articles in the *New York Times* cited high United States government officials as having proof that the electoral results had been rigged.

Responses by the Defense Forces to these charges of electoral fraud demonstrated the relationship they saw as existing between domestic political opposition and national security. In April 1986, following a period in which United States congressmen and Panamanian political parties openly criticized the Defense Forces, 400 lieutenants issued a statement that was read by one of their number on national television. The "Lieutenants' Declaration" suggested that foreign and domestic groups were attacking the FDP in an effort to destroy its national cohesion and undermine national security: "For the first time in our republican history . . . political groups—although they consider themselves to be democratic and idealistic—have adopted an open position of selling out the national interest and have opened up the embarrassing possibility of foreign intervention."

The FDP viewed this threat to national security as also emanating from the links between the domestic political opposition and certain United States congressional leaders opposed to the existing regime. President Delvalle and the FDP suggested that there was a "seditious plot" involving the United States Department of State and certain "bad Panamanians" aiming not only to have the president removed from office but also to roll back the clock to the 1960s, when the oligarchy dominated the political arena.

Troops of the Defense Forces, particularly the First Public Order Company (Doberman), have been used on occasion to quell domestic rioting viewed as a threat to national security. Most public demonstrations and riots during the mid-1980s resulted from deteriorating economic conditions related to the global recession. In 1986 the National Council of Organized Workers called a forty-eight-hour general strike that eventually resulted in some random violence and one death. The most extensive use of military forces to quell domestic violence came in 1987, following accusations about Noriega's involvement in electoral fraud and narcotics trafficking made by the forcibly retired former chief of staff, Colonel Roberto Díaz Herrera.

Whereas the Panamanian military's role as a police force had traditionally conditioned it to concentrate on internal threats to national security, the FDP has increasingly turned its attention to the external environment. The crises affecting several of the countries in Central America, coupled with the FDP's assumption of the new military mission of defending the canal, have led to a serious concern with security policy in the broadest sense. New units such as the Peace Battalion were specifically charged with defending the border and preventing illegal immigration from countries such as Nicaragua and El Salvador. Battalion 2000's participation in United States-Panamanian military field exercises was intended to make it capable of rebuffing threats to the canal from guerrilla groups supported by a foreign power.

To the extent that Panamanian foreign policy is a reflection of opinion within the FDP, it suggests that the military thinks geo-strategically about the security of the canal in the context of a volatile regional situation. Panama, as one of the original "Core Four" mediators (along with Mexico, Venezuela, and Colombia) in the Contadora peace process (see Glossary), has been an active participant in the search for negotiated peace settlements in Central America. However, the Panamanians have argued, often through Noriega, that any peace treaty for Central America with no military "teeth" would not bring true peace. In addition, Noriega has often stated that the region's military leaders must be actively involved in the peace process. The FDP's view appears to be that the security of Panama and the canal demands a strong regional military structure capable of ensuring treaty compliance. From the above, it can be gathered that the FDP has come to view questions of national security in much the same light as they have traditionally been viewed by other Latin American armies.

* * *

The magazine *Defensa,* published by the G-3 of the Defense Forces, is an indispensable source of information concerning military developments in Panama. It contains articles on organizational structure, military exercises, and political orientation. For a broad understanding of the historical evolution of the military since independence, two books are useful: Renato Pereira's *Panamá: fuerzas armadas y política* and Steve C. Ropp's *Panamanian Politics: From Guarded Nation to National Guard.* The Panama Canal treaties, implementation agreements, and records of congressional hearings on the treaties are essential as sources of information on Panamanian security affairs and the future United States role in those affairs. The administration of justice as well as a range of matters affecting United States-Panamanian security relations were treated at length in the hearings on ''The Situation in Panama'' held by the United States Senate in March and April 1986. (For further information and complete citations, see Bibliography.)

Appendix A

Table 1. Metric Conversion Coefficients and Factors

When you know	Multiply by	To find
Millimeters	0.04	inches
Centimeters	0.39	inches
Meters	3.3	feet
Kilometers	0.62	miles
Hectares (10,000 m²)	2.47	acres
Square kilometers	0.39	square miles
Cubic meters	35.3	cubic feet
Liters	0.26	gallons
Kilograms	2.2	pounds
Metric tons	0.98	long tons
....	1.1	short tons
....	2,204	pounds
Degrees Celsius	9	degrees Fahrenheit
(Centigrade)	divide by 5 and add 32	

Table 2. Population and Annual Growth Rates, Census Years 1911–80

Census Year	Population	Years Covered	Average Annual Growth Rate (in percentage)
1911	336,742	n.a.	n.a.
1920	446,098	1911–20	3.17
1930	467,459	1920–30	0.47
1940	622,576	1930–40	2.76
1950	805,285	1940–50	2.56
1960	1,075,541	1950–60	2.94
1970	1,428,082	1960–70	3.06
1980	1,831,399	1970–80	2.52

n.a.—not applicable.

Source: Based on information from Panama, Directorate of Statistics and Census, *Panamá en Cifras: Años 1979-1983,* Panama City, November 1984, 38-39.

Table 3. Annual Population Growth Rates, by Province, 1970–80

Province	Annual Growth Rate (in percentage)
Bocas del Toro	3.07
Coclé	1.78
Colón	2.11
Chiriquí	2.37
Darién	2.17
Herrera	1.74
Los Santos	0.48
Panamá	3.49
Veraguas	1.63

Source: Based on information from Panama, Directorate of Statistics and Census, *Estadística Panameña,* No. 970, Panama City, March 1985, 6–7.

Table 4. Indigenous Population, by Province or Territory, 1980 [1]

Province or Territory	Total	Indigenous Population	Percent Indigenous
Bocas del Toro	53,487	17,468	33.00
Chiriquí	287,350	30,862	11.00
Comarca de San Blas	28,621	27,588	96.00
Darién	26,524	8,924	34.00
Panamá	831,048	2,294	0.30
Veraguas	173,245	5,955	3.00
PANAMA [2]	1,831,399	93,091	5.00

[1] Provinces of Colón, Coclé, Los Santos, and Herrera do not contain significant numbers of Indians, and statistics were not available for those provinces.
[2] Total is for all nine provinces and the Comarca de San Blas.

Source: Based on information from Panama, Directorate of Statistics and Census, *Panamá en Cifras: Años 1979–1983,* Panama City, November 1984, 48–49.

Table 5. Illiteracy Rates for Population over Ten Years of Age, by Sex, 1970 and 1980

	1970	1980
Male	101,931	84,515
Female	101,351	89,610
TOTAL	203,282	174,125
Percentage of Total Population ...	21	13

Source: Based on information from Panama, Directorate of Statistics and Census, *Panamá en Cifras: Años 1979–1983,* Panama City, November 1984, 252.

Table 6. *Educational Enrollment, Selected Years, 1950–83*

	1950	1960	1970	1975	1979	1980	1981	1982	1983
Preprimary	n.a.	n.a.	n.a.	18,677	18,136	22,616	24,656	25,843	25,843
Primary	110,059	161,800	255,287	325,394	373,823	337,522	335,239	336,740	335,950
Secondary [1]	17,519	38,964	78,466	125,745	137,816	171,273	174,078	174,791	176,916
Postsecondary	1,519	4,030	8,159	22,581	38,865	41,311	43,964	47,592	47,131
Other [2]	n.a.	n.a.	n.a.	n.a.	13,085	14,458	9,905	12,611	8,653
TOTAL	129,097	204,794	341,912	473,720	582,266	582,700	585,802	596,390	594,493

n.a.—not available.

[1] Includes both technical and academic programs.

[2] Includes special education and vocational courses of less than three years.

Sources: Based on information from Panama, Directorate of Statistics and Census, *Panamá en Cifras: Años 1973-1977*, Panama City, November 1978, 176–80; and Panama, Directorate of Statistics and Census, *Panamá en Cifras: Años 1979-1983*, Panama City, November 1984, 261–62.

Table 7. Education Budgets, 1979–84

| | Ministry of Education | | University of Panama | |
	Amount*	Percentage of Total Budget	Amount*	Percentage of Total Budget
1979	85,037	18.4	16,681	3.6
1980	110,913	15.3	17,332	2.4
1981	120,153	15.2	21,455	2.7
1982	133,862	12.1	22,801	2.1
1983	145,927	12.7	26,665	2.3
1984	217,840	18.3	32,294	2.7

*In thousands of balboas; for value of the balboa—see Glossary.

Source: Based on information from Panama, Directorate of Statistics and Census, *Panamá en Cifras: Años 1979–1983,* Panama City, November 1984, 266.

Table 8. Government Spending for Education, by Level of Instruction, 1979–83 (in thousands of balboas)*

	1979	1980	1981	1982	1983
Primary	63,441	74,254	70,760	68,502	74,605
Secondary	32,177	33,644	37,441	47,161	48,525
University	19,769	24,316	31,897	41,105	43,442
Adult education	866	126	1,523	1,161	845
Other	39,394	49,773	53,412	56,238	61,708
TOTAL	155,647	182,113	195,033	214,167	229,125

*For value of the balboa—see Glossary.

Source: Based on information from Panama, Directorate of Statistics and Census, *Panamá en Cifras: Años 1979–1983,* Panama City, November 1984, 268.

Table 9. Schools, Classrooms, and Teachers, Selected Years, 1950–83

Year	Primary	Secondary	Postsecondary
1950			
Schools	950	78	1
Classrooms	n.a.	n.a.	n.a.
Teachers	3,415	959	n.a.
1960			
Schools	1,298	127	2
Classrooms	n.a.	n.a.	n.a.
Teachers	5,309	1,704	191
1970			
Schools	1,784	192	2
Classrooms	n.a.	n.a.	n.a.
Teachers	1,784	3,784	448
1975			
Schools	2,171	209	2
Classrooms	n.a.	n.a.	n.a.
Teachers	10,685	5,670	869
1980			
Schools	2,306	301	2
Classrooms	11,280	3,763	318
Teachers	12,361	8,138	1,310
1981			
Schools	2,316	307	2
Classrooms	11,508	3,947	370
Teachers	12,393	8,610	1,586
1982			
Schools	2,347	313	3
Classrooms	11,726	3,973	451
Teachers	12,853	8,928	1,705
1983			
Schools	2,376	321	3
Classrooms	11,289	4,011	506
Teachers	12,613	9,249	1,766

n.a.—not available.

Sources: Based on information from Panama, Directorate of Statistics and Census, *Panamá en Cifras: Años 1973-1977,* Panama City, November 1978, 176–80; and Panama, Directorate of Statistics and Census, *Panamá en Cifras: Años 1979-1983,* Panama City, November 1984, 256–59.

Table 10. Life Expectancy at Birth, by Sex, 1965 and 1985

	1965	1985
Male	62	69
Female	64	73

Sources: Based on information from Panama, Directorate of Statistics and Census, *Panamá en Cifras: Años 1979–1983*, Panama City, November 1984, 76; and World Bank, *World Development Report 1986*, New York, 1986, 233.

Table 11. Medical Facilities, by Location, 1983

	Hospitals	Medical Centers	Local Clinics
Cities			
Panama City	12	20	n.a.
Colón	2	5	n.a.
Provinces			
Bocas del Toro	3	4	56
Chiriquí	6	31	98
Coclé	3	17	46
Colón	3	17	47
Darién	3	5	32
Herrera	5	11	23
Los Santos	4	11	14
Panamá	16	53	63
Veraguas	3	17	51
Indigenous Territory			
Comarca de San Blas	4	4	13

n.a.—not available.

Source: Based on information from Panama, Directorate of Statistics and Census, *Panamá en Cifras: Años 1979–1983*, Panama City, November 1984, 221.

Table 12. *Medical Personnel and Facilities, per 10,000
Inhabitants, by Location, 1983*

	Hospital Beds	Doctors	Nurses
Cities			
Panama City	91	21.8	28.1
Colón	48	12.5	15.4
Provinces			
Bocas del Toro	31	4.1	6.5
Chiriquí	25	6.1	5.9
Coclé	24	4.4	4.1
Colón	24	8.2	8.3
Darién	25	3.6	3.2
Herrera	42	5.6	5.6
Los Santos	67	6.1	6.1
Panamá	45	13.9	14.4
Veraguas	17	2.6	3.2
Indigenous Territory			
Comarca de San Blas	22	2.3	1.1
PANAMA	36	9.0	9.4

Source: Based on information from Panama, Directorate of Statistics and Census, *Panamá
en Cifras: Años 1979-1983,* Panama City, November 1984, 223-26.

Table 13. Birth and Death Rates, per 1,000 Inhabitants, 1979-83

	1979	1980	1981	1982	1983
Live Births					
Urban	26.1	25.5	25.1	25.9	25.7
Rural	30.2	28.9	28.9	27.4	26.6
Panama	28.2	27.2	27.0	26.7	26.2
Mortality					
All deaths					
Urban	4.2	4.1	4.0	4.2	4.4
Rural	4.5	4.2	3.9	3.7	3.8
Panama	4.4	4.2	4.0	4.0	4.1
Infant*					
Urban	21.5	19.4	19.7	17.1	18.8
Rural	27.7	23.9	24.7	22.6	22.1
Panama	24.6	21.7	22.2	19.9	20.5
Maternal					
Urban	0.4	0.2	0.4	0.5	0.2
Rural	1.0	1.1	0.8	1.2	1.0
Panama	0.7	0.7	0.6	0.9	0.6

*Aged less than one year.

Source: Based on information from Panama, Directorate of Statistics and Census, *Panamá en Cifras: Años 1979-1983,* Panama City, November 1984, 61.

Table 14. Central Government Budgets, 1981-85
(in millions of balboas) [1]

	1981	1982	1983	1984	1985 [2]
Consolidated public sector					
Revenues	1,169.0	1,264.5	1,385.5	1,424.6	1,531.8
Expenditures	1,383.7	1,726.5	1,650.2	1,699.0	1,654.8
Balance	-214.7	-462.0	-264.7	-274.4	-123.0
Unconsolidated public-sector balance [3]	6.6	-2.0	17.4	8.0	12.0
Total public-sector borrowing requirement	208.1	464.0	247.3	266.4	121.0
As percentage of GDP [4]	5.4	10.8	5.7	5.8	2.5

[1] For value of the balboa—see Glossary.
[2] Estimate.
[3] To which no transfers are made.
[4] GDP—gross domestic product—see Glossary.

Source: Based on unpublished data provided by the Controloría General de la República de Panamá, 1987.

Table 15. *Distribution of Labor Force by Sector, Selected Years, 1965-85*
(in percentage)

Sector	1965	1973	1980	1985
Agriculture	46.3	38.6	31.8	26.5
Industry	15.8	17.8	18.1	16.1
Services	37.9	43.6	50.1	57.4
TOTAL	100.0	100.0	100.0	100.0

Source: Based on unpublished data provided by the Controloría General de la República de Panamá, 1987.

Table 16. *External Trade, 1980-85*
(in millions of United States dollars at current prices)

	1980	1981	1982	1983	1984	1985 [1]
Exports						
Bananas	61.6	69.2	66.0	75.0	74.7	78.1
Petroleum	233.3	209.1	166.6	131.2	134.4	100.6
Shrimp	43.7	42.7	52.9	51.4	46.7	53.4
Sugar	65.8	52.6	23.7	41.3	42.6	33.3
Manufactures	31.5	31.4	38.7	29.3	34.5	45.0
Other	90.2	88.9	140.9	109.9	94.0	104.1
Total exports f.o.b. [2] ..	526.1	493.9	488.8	438.1	426.9	414.5
Imports						
Food	123.0	115.4	124.1	130.0	127.8	142.6
POL [3] and other energy sources	424.4	426.1	408.6	384.0	350.2	271.8
Other consumer goods	162.5	195.0	203.2	196.5	206.9	197.8
Other intermediate goods ..	373.4	413.6	404.5	360.6	392.8	439.7
Capital goods	258.7	319.8	355.6	280.8	264.4	288.2
Total imports c.i.f. [4] ..	1,342.0	1,469.9	1,496.0	1,351.9	1,342.1	1,340.1

[1] Preliminary.
[2] f.o.b.—free on board.
[3] POL—Petroleum, oil, and lubricants.
[4] c.i.f.—Cost, insurance, and freight.

Source: Based on unpublished data provided by the Controloría General de la República de Panamá, 1987.

Table 17. Balance of Payments, 1980–85
(in millions of United States dollars at current prices)

	1980	1981	1982	1983	1984	1985*
Exports of goods and non-factor services (NFS)	1,644.6	1,734.3	1,769.3	1,774.4	1,742.4	1,819.6
Imports of goods and NFS	-1,697.6	-1,854.6	-1,870.5	-1,697.0	-1,679.7	-1,705.3
RESOURCE BALANCE	-53.0	-120.3	-101.2	77.4	62.7	114.3
Net factor income	-283.0	-271.2	-349.8	-324.2	-375.8	-370.2
Net current transfers ..	14.4	31.2	45.6	44.3	89.6	83.3
CURRENT ACCOUNT BALANCE	-321.6	-360.3	-405.4	-202.5	-223.5	-172.6
Capital Long-term capital inflow	131.6	402.0	492.1	386.0	250.4	130.6
Total other items (net)	186.1	-5.1	-85.4	-95.4	1.7	-24.9
Net short-term capital	-90.4	37.7	-125.8	-177.5	-80.3	-229.1
CAPITAL ACCOUNT BALANCE	227.3	434.6	280.9	113.1	171.8	-123.4
Net errors and omissions	-276.5	42.8	-40.4	-82.1	-67.6	-136.4
Change in net reserves	3.9	-36.6	-1.3	-88.1	-14.2	134.7

*Preliminary.

Source: Based on unpublished data provided by the Controlaría General de la República de Panamá, 1987.

Table 18. External Capital and Debt, 1980–85
(in millions of United States dollars at current prices)

	1980	1981	1982	1983	1984	1985 [1]
Public and publicly guaranteed						
external debt	2,283.4	2,441.3	2,926.7	3,146.5	3,229.7	3,275.6
Official creditors	581.2	682.2	830.5	1,006.0	1,078.9	1,144.3
Multilateral	327.5	358.8	432.3	558.3	660.4	741.0
Bilateral	253.7	323.4	398.2	447.7	418.5	403.3
Private creditors	1,702.2	1,759.1	2,096.2	2,140.5	2,150.8	2,131.3
Suppliers	35.7	29.2	29.1	27.1	50.1	42.5
Financial markets	1,666.5	1,729.9	2,067.1	2,113.4	2,100.7	2,088.8
IMF credit [2]	23.1	93.6	84.0	192.8	271.1	311.2
TOTAL EXTERNAL						
DEBT	2,306.5	2,534.9	3,010.7	3,339.3	3,500.8	3,586.8
Percentage of total long-term						
debt on concessional						
terms	12.2	12.8	11.8	11.5	11.7	12.1
(with variable interest rates)	52.2	51.1	55.9	57.0	57.7	59.5

[1] Estimate.
[2] IMF—International Monetary Fund.

Source: Based on unpublished data provided by the Controloría General de la República de Panamá, 1987.

Table 19. United States Military Aid and Sales to Panama, Fiscal Years 1980–86
(in thousands of United States dollars)

Fiscal Year	FMS Deliveries [1]	Commercial Arms Sales	MAP [2]	IMETP [3]
1980	187	29,241	3	270
1981	154	752	n.a.	328
1982	360	1,000	1	359
1983	481	1,504	n.a.	466
1984	546	1,800	n.a.	453
1985	2,124	594	n.a.	575
1986	12,488	560	n.a.	507

n.a.—not available.
[1] FMS—Foreign Military Sales.
[2] MAP—Military Assistance Program.
[3] IMETP—International Military Education and Training Program.

Source: Based on information from United States, Department of Defense, Security Assistance Agency, *Foreign Military Sales, Foreign Military Construction Sales, and Military Assistance Facts,* Washington, 1986.

Appendix B

Panama Canal Treaty

The United States of America and the Republic of Panama, *Acting* in the spirit of the Joint Declaration of April 3, 1964, by the Representatives of the Governments of the United States of America and the Republic of Panama, and of the Joint Statement of Principles of February 7, 1974, initialed by the Secretary of State of the United States of America and the Foreign Minister of the Republic of Panama, and *Acknowledging* the Republic of Panama's sovereignty over its territory, *Have decided* to terminate the prior Treaties pertaining to the Panama Canal and to conclude a new Treaty to serve as the basis for a new relationship between them and, accordingly, have agreed upon the following:

ARTICLE I

Abrogation of Prior Treaties and Establishment of a New Relationship

1. Upon its entry into force, this Treaty terminates and supersedes:

(a) The Isthmian Canal Convention between the United States of America and the Republic of Panama, signed at Washington, November 18, 1903;

(b) The Treaty of Friendship and Cooperation signed at Washington, March 2, 1936, and the Treaty of Mutual Understanding and Cooperation and the related Memorandum of Understandings Reached, signed at Panama, January 25, 1955, between the United States of America and the Republic of Panama;

(c) All other treaties, conventions, agreements, and exchanges of notes between the United States of America and the Republic of Panama concerning the Panama Canal, which were in force prior to the entry into force of this Treaty; and

(d) Provisions concerning the Panama Canal, which appear in other treaties, conventions, agreements, and exchanges of notes between the United States of America and the Republic of Panama, which were in force prior to the entry into force of this Treaty.

2. In accordance with the terms of this Treaty and related agreements, the Republic of Panama, as territorial sovereign, grants to the United States of America, for the duration of this Treaty, the rights necessary to regulate the transit of ships through the Panama Canal, and to manage, operate, maintain, improve, protect, and defend the Canal. The Republic of Panama guarantees to the United States of America the peaceful use of the land and water areas which it has been granted the rights to use for such purposes pursuant to this Treaty and related agreements.

3. The Republic of Panama shall participate increasingly in the management and protection and defense of the Canal, as provided in this Treaty.

4. In view of the special relationship established by this Treaty, the United States of America and the Republic of Panama shall cooperate to assure the uninterrupted and efficient operation of the Panama Canal.

ARTICLE II

Ratification, Entry Into Force, and Termination

1. The Treaty shall be subject to ratification in accordance with the constitutional

procedures of the two Parties. The instruments of ratification of this Treaty shall be exchanged at Panama at the same time as the instruments of ratification of the Treaty Concerning the Permanent Neutrality and Operation of the Panama Canal, signed this date, are exchanged. This Treaty shall enter into force, simultaneously with the Treaty Concerning the Permanent Neutrality and Operation of the Panama Canal, six calendar months from the date of the exchange of the instruments of ratification.

2. This Treaty shall terminate at noon, Panama time, December 31, 1999.

ARTICLE III

Canal Operation and Management

1. The Republic of Panama, as territorial sovereign, grants to the United States of America the rights to manage, operate, and maintain the Panama Canal, its complementary works, installations, and equipment and to provide for the orderly transit of vessels through the Panama Canal. The United States of America accepts the grant of such rights and undertakes to exercise them in accordance with this Treaty and related agreements.

2. In carrying out the foregoing responsibilities, the United States of America may:

(a) Use for the aforementioned purposes, without cost except as provided in this Treaty, the various installations and areas (including the Panama Canal) and waters, described in the Agreement in Implementation of this Article, signed this date, as well as such other areas and installations as are made available to the United States of America under this Treaty and related agreements, and take the measures necessary to ensure sanitation of such areas;

(b) Make such improvements and alterations to the aforesaid installations and areas as it deems appropriate, consistent with the terms of this Treaty;

(c) Make and enforce all rules pertaining to the passage of vessels through the Canal and other rules with respect to navigation and maritime matters, in accordance with this Treaty and related agreements. The Republic of Panama will lend its cooperation, when necessary, in the enforcement of such rules;

(d) Establish, modify, collect, and retain tolls for the use of the Panama Canal, and other charges, and establish and modify methods of their assessment;

(e) Regulate relations with employees of the United States Government;

(f) Provide supporting services to facilitate the performance of its responsibilities under this Article;

(g) Issue and enforce regulations for the exercise of the rights and responsibilities of the United States of America under this Treaty and related agreements. The Republic of Panama will lend its cooperation, when necessary, in the enforcement of such rules; and

(h) Exercise any other right granted under this Treaty, or otherwise agreed upon between the two Parties.

3. Pursuant to the foregoing grant of rights, the United States of America shall, in accordance with the terms of this Treaty and the provisions of United States law, carry out its responsibilities by means of a United States Government agency called the Panama Canal Commission, which shall be constituted by and in conformity with the laws of the United States of America.

(a) The Panama Canal Commission shall be supervised by a Board composed of nine members, five of whom shall be nationals of the United States of America, and four of whom shall be Panamanian nationals proposed by the Republic of Panama for appointment to such positions by the United States of America in a timely manner.

(b) Should the Republic of Panama request the United States of America to remove a Panamanian national from membership on the Board, the United States of America shall agree to such request. In that event, the Republic of Panama shall propose another Panamanian national for appointment by the United States of America to such position in a timely manner. In case of removal of a Panamanian member of the Board on the initiative of the United States of America, both Parties will consult in advance in order to reach agreement concerning such removal, and the Republic of Panama shall propose another Panamanian national for appointment by the United States of America in his stead.

(c) The United States of America shall employ a national of the United States of America as Administrator of the Panama Canal Commission, and a Panamanian national as Deputy Administrator, through December 31, 1989. Beginning January 1, 1990, a Panamanian national shall be employed as the Administrator and a national of the United States of America shall occupy the position of Deputy Administrator. Such Panamanian nationals shall be proposed to the United States of America by the Republic of Panama for appointment to such positions by the United States of America.

(d) Should the United States of America remove the Panamanian national from his position as Deputy Administrator, or Administrator, the Republic of Panama shall propose another Panamanian national for appointment to such position by the United States of America.

4. An illustrative description of the activities the Panama Canal Commission will perform in carrying out the responsibilities and rights of the United States of America under this Article is set forth at the Annex. Also set forth in the Annex are procedures for the discontinuance or transfer of those activities performed prior to the entry into force of this Treaty by the Panama Canal Company or the Canal Zone Government which are not to be carried out by the Panama Canal Commission.

5. The Panama Canal Commission shall reimburse the Republic of Panama for the costs incurred by the Republic of Panama in providing the following public services in the Canal operation areas and in housing areas set forth in the Agreement in Implementation of Article III of this Treaty and occupied by both United States and Panamanian citizen employees of the Panama Canal Commission: police, fire protection, street maintenance, street lighting, street cleaning, traffic management, and garbage collection. The Panama Canal Commission shall pay the Republic of Panama the sum of ten million United States dollars (US$10,000,000) per annum for the foregoing services. It is agreed that every three years from the date that this Treaty enters into force, the costs involved in furnishing said services shall be reexamined to determine whether adjustment of the annual payment should be made because of inflation and other relevant factors affecting the cost of such services.

6. The Republic of Panama shall be responsible for providing, in all areas comprising the former Canal Zone, services of a general jurisdictional nature such as customs and immigration, postal services, courts, and licensing, in accordance with this Treaty and related agreements.

7. The United States of America and the Republic of Panama shall establish a Panama Canal Consultative Committee, composed of an equal number of high-level representatives of the United States of America and the Republic of Panama, and which may appoint such subcommittees as it may deem appropriate. This Committee shall advise the United States of America and the Republic of Panama on matters of policy affecting the Canal's operation. In view of both Parties' special interest in the continuity and efficiency of the Canal operation in the future, the Committee shall advise on matters such as general tolls policy, employment and training policies to increase the participation of Panamanian nationals in the operation of the Canal, and international policies on matters concerning the Canal. The Committee's recommendations shall be transmitted to the two Governments, which shall give such recommendations full consideration in the formulation of such policy decisions.

8. In addition to the participation of Panamanian nationals at high management levels of the Panama Canal Commission, as provided for in paragraph 3 of this Article,

there shall be growing participation of Panamanian nationals at all other levels and areas of employment in the aforesaid commission, with the objective of preparing, in an orderly and efficient fashion, for the assumption by the Republic of Panama of full responsibility for the management, operation, and maintenance of the Canal upon the termination of this Treaty.

9. The use of the areas, waters, and installations with respect to which the United States of America is granted rights pursuant to this Article, and the rights and legal status of United States Government agencies and employees operating in the Republic of Panama pursuant to this Article, shall be governed by Agreement in Implementation of this Article, signed this date.

10. Upon entry into force of this Treaty, the United States Government agencies known as the Panama Canal Company and the Canal Zone Government shall cease to operate within the territory of the Republic of Panama that formerly constituted the Canal Zone.

ARTICLE IV

Protection and Defense

1. The United States of America and the Republic of Panama commit themselves to protect and defend the Panama Canal. Each Party shall act, in accordance with its constitutional processes, to meet the danger resulting from an armed attack or other actions which threaten the security of the Panama Canal or of ships transiting it.

2. For the duration of this Treaty, the United States of America shall have primary responsibility to protect and defend the Canal. The rights of the United States of America to station, train, and move military forces within the Republic of Panama are described in the Agreement in Implementation of this Article, signed this date. The use of areas and installations and the legal status of the armed forces of the United States of America in the Republic of Panama shall be governed by the aforesaid Agreement.

3. In order to facilitate the participation and cooperation of the armed forces of both Parties in the protection and defense of the Canal, the United States of America and the Republic of Panama shall establish a Combined Board comprised of an equal number of senior military representatives of each Party. These representatives shall be charged by their respective governments with consulting and cooperating on all matters pertaining to the protection and defense of the Canal, and with planning for actions to be taken in concert for that purpose. Such combined protection and defense arrangements shall not inhibit the identity or lines of authority of the armed forces of the United States of America or the Republic of Panama. The Combined Board shall provide for coordination and cooperation concerning such matters as:

(a) The preparation of contingency plans for the protection and defense of the Canal based upon the cooperative efforts of the armed forces of both Parties;

(b) The planning and conduct of combined military exercises; and

(c) The conduct of United States and Panamanian military operations with respect to the protection and defense of the Canal.

4. The Combined Board shall, at five-year intervals throughout the duration of this Treaty, review the resources being made available by the two Parties for the protection and defense of the Canal. Also, the Combined Board shall make appropriate recommendations to the two Governments respecting projected requirements, the efficient utilization of available resources of the two Parties, and other matters of mutual interest with respect to the protection and defense of the Canal.

5. To the extent possible consistent with its primary responsibility for the protection and defense of the Panama Canal, the United States of America will endeavor to maintain its armed forces in the Republic of Panama in normal times at a level

not in excess of that of the armed forces of the United States of America in the territory of the former Canal Zone immediately prior to the entry into force of this Treaty.

ARTICLE V

Principle of Non-Intervention

Employees of the Panama Canal Commission, their dependents, and designated contractors of the Panama Canal Commission, who are nationals of the United States of America, shall respect the laws of the Republic of Panama and shall abstain from any activity incompatible with the spirit of this Treaty. Accordingly, they shall abstain from any political activity in the Republic of Panama as well as from any intervention in the internal affairs of the Republic of Panama. The United States of America shall take all measures within its authority to ensure that the provisions of this Article are fulfilled.

ARTICLE VI

Protection of the Environment

1. The United States of America and the Republic of Panama commit themselves to implement this Treaty in a manner consistent with the protection of the natural environment of the Republic of Panama. To this end, they shall consult and cooperate with each other in all appropriate ways to ensure that they shall give due regard to the protection and conservation of the environment.

2. A Joint Commission on the Environment shall be established with equal representation from the United States and the Republic of Panama, which shall periodically review the implementation of this Treaty and shall recommend as appropriate to the two Governments ways to avoid or, should this not be possible, to mitigate the adverse environmental impacts which might result from their respective actions pursuant to the Treaty.

3. The United States of America and the Republic of Panama shall furnish the Joint Commission on the Environment complete information on any action taken in accordance with this Treaty which, in the judgment of both, might have a significant effect on the environment. Such information shall be made available to the Commission as far in advance of the contemplated action as possible to facilitate the study by the Commission of any potential environmental problems and to allow for consideration of the recommendation of the Commission before the contemplated action is carried out.

ARTICLE VII

Flags

1. The entire territory of the Republic of Panama, including the areas the use of which the Republic of Panama makes available to the United States of America pursuant to this Treaty and related agreements, shall be under the flag of the Republic of Panama, and consequently such flag always shall occupy the position of honor.

2. The flag of the United States of America may be displayed, together with the flag of the Republic of Panama, at the headquarters of the Panama Canal Commission, at the site of the Combined Board, and as provided in the Agreement in Implementation of Article IV of this Treaty.

3. The flag of the United States of America also may be displayed at other places and on some occasions, as agreed by both Parties.

ARTICLE VIII

Privileges and Immunities

1. The installations owned or used by the agencies or instrumentalities of the United States of America operating in the Republic of Panama pursuant to this Treaty and related agreements, and their official archives and documents, shall be inviolable. The two Parties shall agree on procedures to be followed in the conduct of any criminal investigation at such locations by the Republic of Panama.

2. Agencies and instrumentalities of the Government of the United States of America operating in the Republic of Panama pursuant to this Treaty and related agreements shall be immune from the jurisdiction of the Republic of Panama.

3. In addition to such other privileges and immunities as are afforded to employees of the United States Government and their dependents pursuant to this Treaty, the United States of America may designate up to twenty officials of the Panama Canal Commission who, along with their dependents, shall enjoy the privileges and immunities accorded to diplomatic agents and their dependents under international law and practice. The United States of America shall furnish to the Republic of Panama a list of the names of said officials and their dependents, identifying the positions they occupy in the Government of the United States of America, and shall keep such list current at all times.

ARTICLE IX

Applicable Laws and Law Enforcement

1. In accordance with the provisions of this Treaty and related agreements, the law of the Republic of Panama shall apply in the areas made available for the use of the United States of America pursuant to this Treaty. The law of the Republic of Panama shall be applied to matters or events which occurred in the former Canal Zone prior to the entry into force of this Treaty only to the extent specifically provided in prior treaties and agreements.

2. Natural or juridical persons who, on the date of entry into force of this Treaty, are engaged in business or non-profit activities at locations in the former Canal Zone may continue such business or activities at those locations under the same terms and conditions prevailing prior to the entry into force of this Treaty for a thirty-month transition period from its entry into force. The Republic of Panama shall maintain the same operating conditions as those applicable to the aforementioned enterprises prior to the entry into force of this Treaty in order that they may receive licenses to do business in the Republic of Panama subject to their compliance with the requirements of its law. Thereafter, such persons shall receive the same treatment under the law of the Republic of Panama as similar enterprises already established in the rest of the territory of the Republic of Panama without discrimination.

3. The rights of ownership, as recognized by the United States of America, enjoyed by natural or juridical private persons in buildings and other improvements to real property located in the former Canal Zone shall be recognized by the Republic of Panama in conformity with its laws.

4. With respect to buildings and other improvements to real property located in the Canal operating areas, housing areas, or other areas subject to the licensing procedure established in Article IV of the Agreement in Implementation of Article III of this Treaty, the owners shall be authorized to continue using the land upon which their property is located in accordance with the procedures established in that Article.

5. With respect to buildings and other improvements to real property located in areas of the former Canal Zone to which the aforesaid licensing procedure is not applicable, or may cease to be applicable during the lifetime or upon termination of this Treaty, the owners may continue to use the land upon which their property is

located, subject to the payment of a reasonable charge to the Republic of Panama. Should the Republic of Panama decide to sell such land, the owners of the buildings or other improvements located thereon shall be offered a first option to purchase such land at a reasonable cost. In the case of non-profit enterprises, such as churches and fraternal organizations, the cost of purchase will be nominal in accordance with the prevailing practice in the rest of the territory of the Republic of Panama.

6. If any of the aforementioned persons are required by the Republic of Panama to discontinue their activities or vacate their property for public purposes, they shall be compensated at fair market value by the Republic of Panama.

7. The provisions of paragraphs 2–6 above shall apply to natural or juridical persons who have been engaged in business or non-profit activities at locations in the former Canal Zone for at least six months prior to the date of signature of this Treaty.

8. The Republic of Panama shall not issue, adopt, or enforce any law, decree, regulation, or international agreement or take any other action which purports to regulate or would otherwise interfere with the exercise on the part of the United States of America of any right granted under this Treaty or related agreements.

9. Vessels transiting the Canal, and cargo, passengers, and crews carried on such vessels shall be exempt from any taxes, fees, or other charges by the Republic of Panama. However, in the event such vessels call at a Panamanian port, they may be assessed charges thereto, such as charges for services provided to the vessel. The Republic of Panama may also require the passengers and crew disembarking from such vessels to pay such taxes, fees, and charges as are established under Panamanian law for persons entering its territory. Such taxes, fees, and charges shall be assessed on a nondiscriminatory basis.

10. The United States of America and the Republic of Panama will cooperate in taking such steps as may from time to time be necessary to guarantee the security of the Panama Canal Commission, its property, its employees and their dependents, and their property, the Forces of the United States of America and the members thereof, the civilian component of the United States Forces, the dependents of members of the Forces and civilian component, and their property, and the contractors of the Panama Canal Commission and of the United States Forces, their dependents, and their property. The Republic of Panama will seek from its Legislative Branch such legislation as may be needed to carry out the foregoing purposes and to punish any offenders.

11. The Parties shall conclude an agreement whereby nationals of either State, who are sentenced by the courts of the other State, and who are not domiciled therein, may elect to serve their sentences in their State of nationality.

ARTICLE X

Employment With the Panama Canal Commission

1. In exercising its rights and fulfilling its responsibilities as the employer, the United States of America shall establish employment and labor regulations which shall contain the terms, conditions, and prerequisites for all categories of employees of the Panama Canal Commission. These regulations shall be provided to the Republic of Panama prior to their entry into force.

2. (a) The regulations shall establish a system of preference when hiring employees, for Panamanian applicants possessing the skills and qualifications required for employment by the Panama Canal Commission. The United States of America shall endeavor to ensure that the number of Panamanian nationals employed by the Panama Canal Commission in relation to the total number of its employees will conform to the proportion established for foreign enterprises under the law of the Republic of Panama.

(b) The terms and conditions of employment to be established will in general be no less favorable to persons already employed by the Panama Canal Company or Canal Zone Government prior to the entry into force of this Treaty, than those in effect immediately prior to that date.

3. (a) The United States of America shall establish an employment policy for the Panama Canal Commission that shall generally limit the recruitment of personnel outside the Republic of Panama to persons possessing requisite skills and qualifications which are not available in the Republic of Panama.

(b) The United States of America will establish training programs for Panamanian employees and apprentices in order to increase the number of Panamanian nationals qualified to assume positions with the Panama Canal Commission, as positions become available.

(c) Within five years from the entry into force of this Treaty, the number of United States nationals employed by the Panama Canal Commission who were previously employed by the Panama Canal Company shall be at least twenty percent less than the total number of United States nationals working for the Panama Canal Company immediately prior to the entry into force of this Treaty.

(d) The United States of America shall periodically inform the Republic of Panama, through the Coordinating Committee, established pursuant to the Agreement in Implementation of Article III of this Treaty, of available positions within the Panama Canal Commission. The Republic of Panama shall similarly provide the United States of America any information it may have as to the availability of Panamanian nationals claiming to have skills and qualifications that might be required by the Panama Canal Commission, in order that the United States of America may take this information into account.

4. The United States of America will establish qualification standards for skills, training, and experience required by the Panama Canal Commission. In establishing such standards, to the extent they include a requirement for a professional license, the United States of America, without prejudice to its right to require additional professional skills and qualifications, shall recognize the professional licenses issued by the Republic of Panama.

5. The United States of America shall establish a policy for the periodic rotation, at a maximum of every five years, of United States citizen employees and other non-Panamanian employees, hired after the entry into force of this Treaty. It is recognized that certain exceptions to the said policy of rotation may be made for sound administrative reasons, such as in the case of employees holding positions requiring certain non-transferable or non-recruitable skills.

6. With regard to wages and fringe benefits, there shall be no discrimination on the basis of nationality, sex, or race. Payments by the Panama Canal Commission of additional remuneration, or the provision of other benefits, such as home leave benefits, to United States nationals employed prior to entry into force of this Treaty, or to persons of any nationality, including Panamanian nationals who are thereafter recruited outside of the Republic of Panama and who change their place of residence, shall not be considered to be discrimination for the purpose of this paragraph.

7. Persons employed by the Panama Canal Commission or Canal Zone Government prior to the entry into force of this Treaty, who are displaced from their employment as a result of the discontinuance by the United States of America of certain activities pursuant to this Treaty, will be placed by the United States of America, to the maximum extent feasible, in other appropriate jobs with the Government of the United States in accordance with United States Civil Service regulations. For such persons who are not United States nationals, placement efforts will be confined to United States Government activities located within the Republic of Panama. Likewise, persons previously employed in activities for which the Republic of Panama

assumes responsibility as a result of this Treaty will be continued in their employment to the maximum extent feasible by the Republic of Panama. The Republic of Panama shall, to the maximum extent feasible, ensure that the terms and conditions of employment applicable to personnel employed in the activities for which it assumed responsibility are not less favorable than those in effect immediately prior to the entry into force of this Treaty. Non-United States nationals employed by the Panama Canal Company or Canal Zone Government prior to the entry into force of this Treaty who are involuntarily separated from their positions because of the discontinuance of an activity by reason of this Treaty, who are not entitled to an immediate annuity under the United States Civil Service Retirement System, and for whom continued employment in the Republic of Panama by the Government of the United States of America is not practicable, will be provided special job placement assistance by the Republic of Panama for employment in positions for which they may be qualified by experience and training.

8. The Parties agree to establish a system whereby the Panama Canal Commission may, if deemed mutually convenient or desirable by the two Parties, assign certain employees of the Panama Canal Commission, for a limited period of time, to assist in the operation of activities transferred to the responsibility of the Republic of Panama as a result of this Treaty or related agreements. The salaries and other costs of employment of any such persons assigned to provide such assistance shall be reimbursed to the United States of America by the Republic of Panama.

9. (a) The right of employees to negotiate collective contracts with the Panama Canal Commission is recognized. Labor relations with employees of the Panama Canal Commission shall be conducted in accordance with forms of collective bargaining established by the United States of America after consultation with employee unions.

(b) Employee unions shall have the right to affiliate with international labor organizations.

10. The United States of America will provide an appropriate early optional retirement program for all persons employed by the Panama Canal Company or Canal Zone Government immediately prior to the entry into force of this Treaty. In this regard, taking into account the unique circumstances created by the provisions of this Treaty, including its duration, and their effect upon such employees, the United States of America shall, with respect to them:

(a) determine that conditions exist which invoke applicable United States law permitting early retirement annuities and apply such law for a substantial period of the duration of the treaty;

(b) seek special legislation to provide more liberal entitlement to, and calculation of, retirement annuities than is currently provided for by law.

ARTICLE XI

Provisions for the Transition Period

1. The Republic of Panama shall reassume plenary jurisdiction over the former Canal Zone upon entry into force of this Treaty and in accordance with its terms. In order to provide for an orderly transition to the full application of the jurisdictional arrangements established by this Treaty and related agreements, the provisions of this Article shall become applicable upon the date this Treaty enters into force, and shall remain in effect for thirty calendar months. The authority granted in this Article to the United States of America for this transition period shall supplement, and is not intended to limit, the full application and effect of the rights and authority granted to the United States of America elsewhere in this Treaty and in related agreements.

2. During this transition period, the criminal and civil laws of the United States of America shall apply concurrently with those of the Republic of Panama in certain

of the areas and installations made available for the use of the United States of America pursuant to this Treaty, in accordance with the following provisions:

(a) The Republic of Panama permits the authorities of the United States of America to have the primary right to exercise criminal jurisdiction over United States citizen employees of the Panama Canal Commission and their dependents, and members of the United States Forces and civilian component and their dependents, in the following cases:

(i) for any offense committed during the transition period within such areas and installations, and

(ii) for any offense committed prior to that period in the former Canal Zone.

The Republic of Panama shall have the primary right to exercise jurisdiction over all other offenses committed by such persons, except as otherwise agreed.

(b) Either Party may waive its primary right to exercise jurisdiction in a specific case or category of cases.

3. The United States of America shall retain the right to exercise jurisdiction in criminal cases relating to offenses committed prior to the entry into force of this Treaty in violation of the laws applicable in the former Canal Zone.

4. For the transition period, the United States of America shall retain police authority and maintain a police force in the aforementioned areas and installations. In such areas, the police authorities of the United States of America may take into custody any person not subject to their primary jurisdiction if such person is believed to have committed or to be committing an offense against applicable laws or regulations, and shall promptly transfer custody to the police authorities of the Republic of Panama. The United States of America and the Republic of Panama shall establish joint police patrols in agreed areas. Any arrests conducted by a joint patrol shall be the responsibility of the patrol member or members representing the Party having primary jurisdiction over the person or persons arrested.

5. The courts of the United States of America and related personnel, functioning in the former Canal Zone immediately prior to the entry into force of this Treaty, may continue to function during the transition period for the judicial enforcement of the jurisdiction to be exercised by the United States of America in accordance with this Article.

6. In civil cases, the civilian courts of the United States of America in the Republic of Panama shall have no jurisdiction over new cases of a private civil nature, but shall retain full jurisdiction during the transition period to dispose of any civil cases, including admiralty cases, already instituted and pending before the courts prior to the entry into force of this Treaty.

7. The laws, regulations, and administrative authority of the United States of America applicable in the former Canal Zone immediately prior to the entry into force of this Treaty shall, to the extent not inconsistent with this Treaty and related agreements, continue in force for the purpose of the exercise by the United States of America of law enforcement and judicial jurisdiction only during the transition period. The United States of America may amend, repeal, or otherwise change such laws, regulations, and administrative authority. The two Parties shall consult concerning procedural and substantive matters relative to the implementation of this Article, including the disposition of cases pending at the end of the transition period and, in this respect, may enter into appropriate agreements by an exchange of notes or other instrument.

8. During this transition period, the United States of America may continue to incarcerate individuals in the areas and installations made available for the use of the United States of America by the Republic of Panama pursuant to this Treaty and related agreements, or to transfer them to penal facilities in the United States of America to serve their sentences.

ARTICLE XII

A Sea-Level Canal or a Third Lane of Locks

1. The United States of America and the Republic of Panama recognize that a sea-level canal may be important for international navigation in the future. Consequently, during the duration of this Treaty, both Parties commit themselves to study jointly the feasibility of a sea-level canal in the Republic of Panama, and in the event they determine that such a waterway is necessary, they shall negotiate terms, agreeable to both Parties, for its construction.

2. The United States of America and the Republic of Panama agree on the following:

(a) No new interoceanic canal shall be constructed in the territory of the Republic of Panama during the duration of this Treaty, except in accordance with the provisions of this Treaty, or as the two Parties may otherwise agree; and

(b) During the duration of this Treaty, the United States of America shall not negotiate with third States for the right to construct an interoceanic canal on any other route in the Western Hemisphere, except as the two Parties may otherwise agree.

3. The Republic of Panama grants to the United States of America the right to add a third lane of locks to the existing Panama Canal. This right may be exercised at any time during the duration of this Treaty, provided that the United States of America has delivered to the Republic of Panama copies of the plans for such construction.

4. In the event the United States of America exercises the right granted in paragraph 3 above, it may use for that purpose, in addition to the areas otherwise made available to the United States of America pursuant to this Treaty, such other areas as the two Parties may agree upon. The terms and conditions applicable to Canal operating areas made available by the Republic of Panama for the use of the United States of America pursuant to Article III of this Treaty shall apply in a similar manner to such additional areas.

5. In the construction of the aforesaid works, the United States of America shall not use nuclear excavation techniques without the previous consent of the Republic of Panama.

ARTICLE XIII

Property Transfer and Economic Participation by the Republic of Panama

1. Upon termination of this Treaty, the Republic of Panama shall assume total responsibility for the management, operation, and maintenance of the Panama Canal, which shall be turned over in operating condition and free of liens and debts, except as the two Parties may otherwise agree.

2. The United States of America transfers, without charge, to the Republic of Panama all right, title, and interest the United States of America may have with respect to all real property, including non-removable improvements thereon, as set forth below:

(a) Upon the entry into force of this Treaty, the Panama Railroad and such property that was located in the former Canal Zone but that is not within the land and water areas the use of which is made available to the United States of America pursuant to this Treaty. However, it is agreed that the transfer on such date shall not include buildings and other facilities, except housing, the use of which is retained by the United States of America pursuant to this Treaty and related agreements, outside such areas;

(b) Such property located in an area or a portion thereof at such time as the use by the United States of America of such area or portion thereof ceases pursuant to agreement between the two Parties.

(c) Housing units made available for occupancy by members of the Armed Forces of the Republic of Panama in accordance with paragraph 5(b) of Annex B to the

Agreement in Implementation of Article IV of this Treaty at such time as such units are made available to the Republic of Panama.

(d) Upon termination of this Treaty, all real property and non-removable improvements that were used by the United States of America for the purposes of this Treaty and related agreements and equipment related to the management, operation, and maintenance of the Canal remaining in the Republic of Panama.

3. The Republic of Panama agrees to hold the United States of America harmless with respect to any claims which may be made by third parties relating to rights, title, and interest in such property.

4. The Republic of Panama shall receive, in addition, from the Panama Canal Commission a just and equitable return on the national resources which it has dedicated to the efficient management, operation, maintenance, protection, and defense of the Panama Canal, in accordance with the following:

(a) An annual amount to be paid out of Canal operating revenues computed at a rate of thirty hundredths of a United States dollar (US$0.30) per Panama Canal net ton, or its equivalency, for each vessel transiting the Canal after the entry into force of this Treaty, for which tolls are charged. The rate of thirty hundredths of a United States dollar (US$0.30) per Panama Canal net ton, or its equivalency, will be adjusted to reflect changes in the United States wholesale price index for total manufactured goods during biennial periods. The first adjustment shall take place five years after entry into force of this Treaty, taking into account the changes that occurred in such price index during the preceding two years. Thereafter, successive adjustments shall take place at the end of each biennial period. If the United States of America should decide that another indexing method is preferable, such method shall be proposed to the Republic of Panama and applied if mutually agreed.

(b) A fixed annuity of ten million United States dollars (US$10,000,000) to be paid out of Canal operating revenues. This amount shall constitute a fixed expense of the Panama Canal Commission.

(c) An annual amount of up to ten million United States dollars (US$10,000,000) per year, to be paid out of Canal operating revenues to the extent that such revenues exceed expenditures of the Panama Canal Commission including amounts paid pursuant to this Treaty. In the event Canal operating revenues in any year do not produce a surplus sufficient to cover this payment, the unpaid balance shall be paid from operating surpluses in future years in a manner to be mutually agreed.

ARTICLE XIV

Settlement of Disputes

In the event that any question should arise between the Parties concerning the interpretation of this Treaty or related agreements, they shall make every effort to resolve the matter through consultation in the appropriate committees established pursuant to this Treaty and related agreements, or, if appropriate, through diplomatic channels. In the event the Parties are unable to resolve a particular matter through such means, they may, in appropriate cases, agree to submit the matter to conciliation, mediation, arbitration, or such other procedure for the peaceful settlement of the dispute as they may mutually deem appropriate.

DONE at Washington, this 7th day of September, 1977, in duplicate, in the English and Spanish languages, both texts being equally authentic.

ANNEX

Procedures for the Cessation or Transfer of Activities Carried Out by the Panama Canal Company and the Canal Zone Government and Illustrative List of the Functions That May Be Performed by the Panama Canal Commission

1. The laws of the Republic of Panama shall regulate the exercise of private economic activities within the areas made available by the Republic of Panama for the use of the United States of America pursuant to this Treaty. Natural or juridical persons who, at least six months prior to the date of signature of this Treaty, were legally established and engaged in the exercise of economic activities in accordance with the provisions of paragraphs 2–7 of Article IX of this Treaty.

2. The Panama Canal Commission shall not perform governmental or commercial functions as stipulated in paragraph 4 of this Annex, provided, however, that this shall not be deemed to limit in any way the right of the United States of America to perform those functions that may be necessary for the efficient management, operation, and maintenance of the Canal.

3. It is understood that the Panama Canal Commission, in the exercise of the rights of the United States of America with respect to the management, operation, and maintenance of the Canal, may perform functions such as are set forth below by way of illustration:

a. Management of the Canal enterprise.

b. Aids to navigation in Canal waters and in proximity thereto.

c. Control of vessel movement.

d. Operation and maintenance of the locks.

e. Tug service for the transit of vessels and dredging for the piers and docks of the Panama Canal Commission.

f. Control of the water levels in Gatun, Alajuela (Madden), and Miraflores Lakes.

g. Non-commercial transportation services in Canal waters.

h. Meteorological and hydrographic services.

i. Admeasurement.

j. Non-commercial motor transport and maintenance.

k. Industrial security through the use of watchmen.

l. Procurement and warehousing.

m. Telecommunications.

n. Protection of the environment by preventing and controlling the spillage of oil and substances harmful to human or animal life and of the ecological equilibrium in areas used in operation of the Canal and the anchorages.

o. Non-commercial vessel repair.

p. Air conditioning services in Canal installations.

q. Industrial sanitation and health services.

r. Engineering design, construction, and maintenance of Panama Canal Commission installations.

s. Dredging of the Canal channel, terminal ports, and adjacent waters.

t. Control of the banks and stabilizing of the slopes of the Canal.

u. Non-commercial handling of cargo on the piers and docks of the Panama Canal Commission.

v. Maintenance of public areas of the Panama Canal Commission, such as parks and gardens.

w. Generation of electric power.

x. Purification and supply of water.

y. Marine salvage in Canal waters.

z. Such other functions as may be necessary or appropriate to carry out, in conformity with this Treaty and related agreements, the rights and responsibilities of the United States of America with respect to the management, operation, and maintenance of the Panama Canal.

4. The following activities and operations carried out by the Panama Canal Company and the Canal Zone Government shall not be carried out by the Panama Canal Commission, effective upon the dates indicated herein:

(a) Upon the date of entry into force of this Treaty:

    (i) Wholesale and retail sales, including those through commissaries, food stores, department stores, optical shops, and pastry shops;

    (ii) The production of food and drink, including milk products and bakery products;

    (iii) The operation of public restaurants and cafeterias and the sale of articles through vending machines;

    (iv) The operation of movie theaters, bowling alleys, pool rooms, and other recreational and amusement facilities for the use of which a charge is payable;

    (v) The operation of laundry and dry cleaning plants other than those operated for official use;

    (vi) The repair and service of privately owned automobiles or the sale of petroleum or lubricants thereto, including the operation of gasoline stations, repair garages, and tire repair and recapping facilities, and the repair and service of other privately owned property, including appliances, electronic devices, boats, motors, and furniture;

    (vii) The operation of cold storage and freezer plants other than those operated for official use;

    (viii) The operation of freight houses other than those operated for official use;

    (ix) The operation of commercial services to and supply of privately owned and operated vessels, including the constitution of vessels, the sale of petroleum and lubricants, and the provision of water, tug services not related to the Canal or other United States Government operations, and repair of such vessels, except in situations where repairs may be necessary to remove disabled vessels from the Canal;

    (x) Printing services other than for official use;

    (xi) Maritime transportation for the use of the general public;

    (xii) Health and medical services provided to individuals, including hospitals, leprosariums, veterinary, mortuary, and cemetery services;

    (xiii) Educational services not for professional training, including schools and libraries;

    (xiv) Postal services;

    (xv) Immigration, customs, and quarantine controls, except those measures necessary to ensure the sanitation of the Canal;

    (xvi) Commercial pier and dock services, such as the handling of cargo and passengers; and

    (xvii) Any other commercial activity of a similar nature, not related to the management, operation, or maintenance of the Canal.

(b) Within thirty calendar months from the date of entry into force of this Treaty, governmental services such as:

    (i) Police;

    (ii) Courts; and

    (iii) Prison system.

5. (a) With respect to those activities or functions described in paragraph 4 above, or otherwise agreed upon by the two Parties, which are to be assumed by the Government of the Republic of Panama or by private persons subject to its authority, the two Parties shall consult prior to the discontinuance of such activities or functions by the Panama Canal Commission to develop appropriate arrangements for the orderly transfer and continued efficient operation or conduct thereof.

(b) In the event that appropriate arrangements cannot be arrived at to ensure the continued performance of a particular activity or function described in paragraph 4 above which is necessary to the efficient management, operation, or maintenance of the Canal, the Panama Canal Commission may, to the extent consistent with the other provisions of this Treaty and related agreements, continue to perform such activity or function until such arrangements can be made.

United States Senate Modifications (Incorporated Into the June 1978 Instruments of Ratification)

(a) RESERVATIONS

(1) Pursuant to its adherence to the principle of nonintervention, any action taken by the United States of America in the exercise of its rights to assure that the Panama Canal shall remain open, neutral, secure, and accessible, pursuant to the provisions of the Panama Canal Treaty, the Treaty Concerning the Permanent Neutrality and Operation of the Panama Canal, and the resolutions of ratification thereto, shall be only for the purpose of assuring that the Canal shall remain open, neutral, secure, and accessible, and shall not have as its purpose or be interpreted as a right of intervention in the internal affairs of the Republic of Panama or interference with its political independence or sovereign integrity.

(2) The instruments of ratification of the Panama Canal Treaty to be exchanged by the United States of America and the Republic of Panama shall each include provisions whereby each Party agrees to waive its rights and release the other Party from its obligations under paragraph 2 of Article XII of the Treaty.

(3) Notwithstanding any provision of the Treaty, no funds may be drawn from the Treasury of the United States of America for payments under paragraph 4 of Article XIII without statutory authorization.

(4) Any accumulated unpaid balance under paragraph 4(c) of Article XIII of the Treaty at the date of termination of the Treaty shall be payable only to the extent of any operating surplus in the last year of the duration of the Treaty, and nothing in such paragraph may be construed as obligating the United States of America to pay, after the date of the termination of the Treaty, any such unpaid balance which shall have accrued before such date.

(5) Exchange of the instruments of ratification of the Panama Canal Treaty and of the Treaty Concerning the Permanent Neutrality and Operation of the Panama Canal shall not be effective earlier than March 31, 1979, and such Treaties shall not enter into force prior to October 1, 1979, unless legislation necessary to implement the provisions of the Panama Canal Treaty shall have been enacted by the Congress of the United States of America before March 31, 1979.

(6) After the date of entry into force of the Treaty, the Panama Canal Commission shall, unless otherwise provided by legislation enacted by the Congress of the United States of America, be obligated to reimburse the Treasury of the United States of America, as nearly as possible, for the interest cost of the funds or other assets directly invested in the Commission by the Government of the United States of America and for the interest cost of the funds or other assets directly invested in the predecessor Panama Canal Company by the Government of the United States of America and not reimbursed before the date of entry into force of the Treaty. Such reimbursement for such interest costs shall be made at a rate determined by the Secretary of the Treasury of the United States of America and at annual intervals to the extent earned, and if not earned, shall be made from subsequent earnings. For purposes of this reservation, the phrase "funds or other assets directly invested" shall have the same meaning as the phrase "net direct investment" has under section 62 of title 2 of the Canal Zone Code.

(b) UNDERSTANDINGS

(1) Before the first day of the three-year period beginning on the date of entry into force of the Treaty and before each three-year period following thereafter, the two Parties shall agree upon the specific levels and quality of services, as are referred to in paragraph 5 of Article III of the Treaty, to be provided during the following three-

year period and, except for the first three-year period, on the reimbursement to be made for the costs of such services, such services to be limited to such as are essential to the effective functioning of the Canal operating areas and the housing areas referred to in paragraph 5 of Article III. If payments made under paragraph 5 of Article III for the preceding three-year period, including the initial three-year period, exceed or are less than the actual costs to the Republic of Panama for supplying, during such period, the specific levels and quality of services agreed upon, then the Panama Canal Commission shall deduct from or add to the payment required to be made to the Republic of Panama for each of the following three years one-third of such excess or deficit, as the case may be. There shall be an independent and binding audit, conducted by an auditor mutually selected by both Parties, of any costs of services disputed by the two Parties pursuant to the reexamination of such costs provided for in this understanding.

(2) Nothing in paragraph 3, 4, or 5 of Article IV of the Treaty may be construed to limit either the provisions of the first paragraph of Article IV providing that each Party shall act, in accordance with its constitutional processes, to meet danger threatening the security of the Panama Canal, or the provisions of paragraph 2 of Article IV providing that the United States of America shall have primary responsibility to protect and defend the Canal for the duration of the Treaty.

(3) Nothing in paragraph 4(c) of Article XIII of the Treaty shall be construed to limit the authority of the United States of America, through the United States Government agency called the Panama Canal Commission, to make such financial decisions and incur such expenses as are reasonable and necessary for the management, operation, and maintenance of the Panama Canal. In addition, toll rates established pursuant to paragraph 2(d) of Article III need not be set at levels designed to produce revenues to cover the payment to the Republic of Panama described in paragraph 4(c) of Article XIII.

(4) Any agreement concluded pursuant to paragraph II of Article IX of the Treaty with respect to the transfer of prisoners shall be concluded in accordance with the constitutional processes of both Parties.

(5) Nothing in the Treaty, in the Annex or Agreed Minute relating to the Treaty, or in any other agreement relating to the Treaty obligates the United States of America to provide any economic assistance, military grant assistance, security supporting assistance, foreign military sales credits, or international military education and training to the Republic of Panama.

(6) The President shall include all reservations and understandings incorporated by the Senate in this resolution of ratification in the instrument of ratification to be exchanged with the Government of the Republic of Panama.

TREATY CONCERNING THE PERMANENT NEUTRALITY AND OPERATION OF THE PANAMA CANAL

The United States of America and the Republic of Panama have agreed upon the following:

ARTICLE I

The Republic of Panama declares that the Canal, as an international transit waterway, shall be permanently neutral in accordance with the regime established in this Treaty. The same regime of neutrality shall apply to any other international waterway that may be built either partially or wholly in the territory of the Republic of Panama.

ARTICLE II

The Republic of Panama declares the neutrality of the Canal in order that both in time of peace and in time of war it shall remain secure and open to peaceful transit by the vessels of all nations on terms of entire equality, so that there will be no discrimination against any nation, or its citizens or subjects, concerning the conditions or charges of transit, or for any other reason, and so that the Canal, and therefore the Isthmus of Panama, shall not be the target of reprisals in any armed conflict between other nations of the world. The foregoing shall be subject to the following requirements:

(a) Payment of tolls and other charges for transit and ancillary services, provided they have been fixed in conformity with the provisions of Article III (c);

(b) Compliance with applicable rules and regulations, provided such rules and regulations are applied in conformity with the provisions of Article III;

(c) The requirement that transiting vessels commit no acts of hostility while in the Canal; and

(d) Such other conditions and restrictions as are established by this Treaty.

ARTICLE III

1. For purposes of the security, efficiency, and proper maintenance of the Canal, the following rules shall apply:

(a) The Canal shall be operated efficiently in accordance with conditions of transit through the Canal, and rules and regulations that shall be just, equitable, and reasonable, and limited to those necessary for safe navigation and efficient, sanitary operation of the Canal;

(b) Ancillary services necessary for transit through the Canal shall be provided;

(c) Tolls and other charges for transit and ancillary services shall be just, reasonable, equitable, and consistent with the principles of international law;

(d) As a pre-condition of transit, vessels may be required to establish clearly the financial responsibility and guarantees for payment of reasonable and adequate indemnification, consistent with international practice and standards, for damages resulting from acts or omissions of such vessels when passing through the Canal. In the case of vessels owned or operated by a State or for which it has acknowledged responsibility, a certification by that State that it shall observe its obligations under international law to pay for damages resulting from the act or omission of such vessels when passing through the Canal shall be deemed sufficient to establish such financial responsibility;

(e) Vessels of war and auxiliary vessels of all nations shall at all times be entitled to transit the Canal, irrespective of their internal operation, means of propulsion, origin, destination, or armament, without being subjected, as a condition of transit, to inspection, search, or surveillance. However, such vessels may be required to certify that they have complied with all applicable health, sanitation, and quarantine regulations. In addition, such vessels shall be entitled to refuse to disclose their internal operation, origin, armament, cargo, or destination. However, auxiliary vessels may be required to present written assurances, certified by an official at a high level of the government of the State requesting the exemption, that they are owned or operated by that government and in this case are being used only on government non-commercial service.

2. For the purposes of this Treaty, the terms "Canal," "vessel of war," "auxiliary vessel," "internal operation," "armament," and "inspection" shall have the meanings assigned them in Annex A to this Treaty.

ARTICLE IV

The United States of America and the Republic of Panama agree to maintain the regime of neutrality established in this Treaty, which shall be maintained in order that the Canal shall remain permanently neutral, notwithstanding the termination of any other treaties entered into by the two Contracting Parties.

ARTICLE V

After the termination of the Panama Canal Treaty, only the Republic of Panama shall operate the Canal and maintain military forces, defense sites, and military installations within its national territory.

ARTICLE VI

1. In recognition of the important contributions of the United States of America and of the Republic of Panama to the construction, operation, maintenance, and protection and defense of the Canal, vessels of war and auxiliary vessels of those nations shall, notwithstanding any other provisions of this Treaty, be entitled to transit the Canal irrespective of their internal operation, means of propulsion, origin, destination, armament, or cargo carried. Such vessels of war and auxiliary vessels will be entitled to transit the Canal expeditiously.

2. The United States of America, so long as it has responsibility for the operation of the Canal, may continue to provide the Republic of Colombia toll-free transit through the Canal for its troops, vessels, and materials of war. Thereafter, the Republic of Panama may provide the Republic of Colombia and the Republic of Costa Rica with the right of toll-free transit.

ARTICLE VII

1. The United States of America and the Republic of Panama shall jointly sponsor a resolution in the Organization of American States opening to accession by all nations of the world the Protocol to this Treaty whereby all the signatories will adhere to the objective of this Treaty, agreeing to respect the regime of neutrality set forth herein.

2. The Organization of American States shall act as the depositary for this Treaty and related instruments.

ARTICLE VIII

This Treaty shall be subject to ratification in accordance with the constitutional procedures of the two Parties. The instruments of ratification of this Treaty shall be exchanged at Panama at the same time as the instruments of ratification of the Panama Canal Treaty, signed this date, are exchanged. This Treaty shall enter into force, simultaneously with the Panama Canal Treaty, six calendar months from the date of the exchange of the instruments of ratification.

DONE at Washington, this 7th day of September, 1977, in the English and Spanish languages, both texts being equally authentic.

ANNEX A

1. "Canal" includes the existing Panama Canal, the entrances thereto, and the territorial seas of the Republic of Panama adjacent thereto, as defined on the map annexed hereto (Annex B),[1] and any other interoceanic waterway in which the United States of America is a participant or in which the United States of America has participated in connection with the construction or financing, that may be operated wholly or partially within the territory of the Republic of Panama, the entrances thereto, and the territorial seas adjacent thereto.

---

[1] Not printed here.

2. "Vessel of war" means a ship belonging to the naval forces of a State, and bearing the external marks distinguishing warships of its nationality, under the command of an officer duly commissioned by the government and whose name appears in the Navy List, and manned by a crew which is under regular naval discipline.

3. "Auxiliary vessel" means any ship, not a vessel of war, that is owned or operated by a State and used, for the time being, exclusively on government non-commercial service.

4. "Internal operation" encompasses all machinery and propulsion systems, as well as the management and control of the vessel, including its crew. It does not include the measures necessary to transit vessels under the control of pilots while such vessels are in the Canal.

5. "Armament" means arms, ammunition, implements of war, and other equipment of a vessel which possesses characteristics appropriate for use for warlike purposes.

6. "Inspection" includes on-board examination of vessel structure, cargo, armament, and internal operation. It does not include those measures strictly necessary for admeasurement, nor those measures strictly necessary to assure safe, sanitary transit and navigation, including examination of deck and visual navigation equipment, nor in the case of live cargoes, such as cattle or other livestock, that may carry communicable diseases, those measures necessary to assure that health and sanitation requirements are satisfied.

United States Senate Modifications (Incorporated Into the June 1978 Instruments of Ratification)

(a) AMENDMENTS

(1) At the end of Article IV, insert the following:

"A correct and authoritative statement of certain rights and duties of the Parties under the foregoing is contained in the Statement of Understanding issued by the Government of the United States of America on October 14, 1977, and by the Government of the Republic of Panama on October 18, 1977, which is hereby incorporated as an integral part of this Treaty, as follows:

"Under the Treaty Concerning the Permanent Neutrality and Operation of the Panama Canal (the Neutrality Treaty), Panama and the United States have the responsibility to assure that the Panama Canal will remain open and secure to ships of all nations. The correct interpretation of this principle is that each of the two countries shall, in accordance with their respective constitutional processes, defend the Canal against any threat to the regime of neutrality, and consequently shall have the right to act against any aggression or threat directed against the Canal or against the peaceful transit of vessels through the Canal.

"This does not mean, nor shall it be interpreted as, a right of intervention of the United States in the internal affairs of Panama. Any United States action will be directed at insuring that the Canal will remain open, secure, and accessible, and it shall never be directed against the territorial integrity or political independence of Panama."

(2) At the end of the first paragraph of Article VI, insert the following:

"In accordance with the Statement of Understanding mentioned in Article IV above: The Neutrality Treaty provides that the vessels of war and auxiliary vessels of the United States and Panama will be entitled to transit the Canal expeditiously. This is intended, and it shall so be interpreted, to assure the transit of such vessels through the Canal as quickly as possible, without any impediment, with expedited treatment, and in case of need or emergency, to go to the head of the line of vessels in order to transit the Canal rapidly."

(b) CONDITIONS

(1) Notwithstanding the provisions of Article V or any other provision of the Treaty, if the Canal is closed, or its operations are interfered with, the United States of America and the Republic of Panama shall each independently have the right to take such steps as each deems necessary, in accordance with its constitutional processes, including the use of military force in the Republic of Panama, to reopen the Canal or restore the operations of the Canal, as the case may be.

(2) The instruments of ratification of the Treaty shall be exchanged only upon the conclusion of a Protocol of Exchange, to be signed by authorized representatives of both Governments, which shall constitute an integral part of the Treaty documents and which shall include the following:

"Nothing in the Treaty shall preclude the Republic of Panama and the United States of America from making, in accordance with their respective constitutional processes, any agreement or arrangement between the two countries to facilitate performance at any time after December 31, 1999, of their responsibilities to maintain the regime of neutrality established in the Treaty, including agreements or arrangements for the stationing of any United States military forces or the maintenance of defense sites after that date in the Republic of Panama that the Republic of Panama and the United States of America may deem necessary or appropriate."

(c) RESERVATIONS

(1) Before the date of entry into force of the Treaty, the two Parties shall begin to negotiate for an agreement under which the American Battle Monuments Commission would, upon the date of entry into force of such agreement and thereafter, administer, free of all taxes and other charges and without compensation to the Republic of Panama and in accordance with the practices, privileges, and immunities associated with the administration of cemeteries outside the United States of America by the American Battle Monuments Commission, including the display of the flag of the United States of America, such part of Corozal Cemetery in the former Canal Zone as encompasses the remains of citizens of the United States of America.

(2) The flag of the United States of America may be displayed, pursuant to the provisions of paragraph 3 of Article VII of the Panama Canal Treaty, at such part of Corozal Cemetery in the former Canal Zone as encompasses the remains of citizens of the United States of America.

(3) The President—

(A) shall have announced, before the date of entry into force of the Treaty, his intention to transfer, consistent with an agreement with the Republic of Panama, and before the date of termination of the Panama Canal Treaty, to the American Battle Monuments Commission the administration of such part of Corozal Cemetery as encompasses the remains of citizens of the United States of America; and

(B) shall have announced, immediately after the date of exchange of instruments of ratification, plans, to be carried out at the expense of the Government of the United States of America, for—

(i) removing, before the date of entry into force of the Treaty, the remains of citizens of the United States of America from Mount Hope Cemetery to such part of Corozal Cemetery as encompasses such remains, except that the remains of any citizen whose next of kin objects in writing to the Secretary of the Army not later than three months after the date of exchange of the instruments of ratification of the Treaty shall not be removed; and

(ii) transporting to the United States of America for reinterment, if the next of kin so requests, not later than thirty months after the date of entry into force of the Treaty, any such remains encompassed by Corozal Cemetery and, before the date of entry into force of the Treaty, any remains removed from Mount Hope Cemetery pursuant to subclause (i); and

(C) shall have fully advised, before the date of entry into force of the Treaty, the next of kin objecting under clause (B) (i) of all available options and their implications.

(4) To carry out the purposes of Article III of the Treaty of assuring the security, efficiency, and proper maintenance of the Panama Canal, the United States of America and the Republic of Panama, during their respective periods of responsibility for Canal operation and maintenance, shall, unless the amount of the operating revenues of the Canal exceeds the amount needed to carry out the purposes of such Article, use such revenues of the Canal only for purposes consistent with the purposes of Article III.

(d) UNDERSTANDINGS

(1) Paragraph 1 (c) of Article III of the Treaty shall be construed as requiring, before any adjustment in tolls for use of the Canal, that the effects of any such toll adjustment on the trade patterns of the two Parties shall be given full consideration, including consideration of the following factors in a manner consistent with the regime of neutrality:

(A) the costs of operating and maintaining the Panama Canal;

(B) the competitive position of the use of the Canal in relation to other means of transportation;

(C) the interests of both Parties in maintaining their domestic fleets;

(D) the impact of such an adjustment on the various geographic areas of each of the two Parties; and

(E) the interests of both Parties in maximizing their international commerce. The United States of America and the Republic of Panama shall cooperate in exchanging information necessary for the consideration of such factors.

(2) The agreement "to maintain the regime of neutrality established in this Treaty" in Article IV of the Treaty means that either of the two Parties to the Treaty may, in accordance with its constitutional processes, take unilateral action to defend the Panama Canal against any threat, as determined by the Party taking such action.

(3) The determination of "need or emergency" for the purpose of any vessel of war or auxiliary vessel of the United States of America or the Republic of Panama going to the head of the line of vessels in order to transit the Panama Canal rapidly shall be made by the nation operating such vessel.

(4) Nothing in the Treaty, in Annex A or B thereto, in the Protocol relating to the Treaty, or in any other agreement relating to the Treaty, obligates the United States of America to provide any economic assistance, military grant assistance, security supporting assistance, foreign military sales credits, or international military education and training to the Republic of Panama.

(5) The President shall include all amendments, conditions, reservations, and understandings incorporated by the Senate in this resolution of ratification in the instrument of ratification to be exchanged with the Government of the Republic of Panama.

Bibliography

Chapter 1

Adams, Richard N. *Cultural Surveys of Panama-Nicaragua-Guatemala-El Salvador-Honduras.* (Scientific Publications, No. 33.) Washington: Pan American Sanitary Bureau, 1947.

Aguilar, Alonso. *Pan-Americanism from Monroe to the Present: A View from the Other Side.* New York: Monthly Review Press, 1968.

Anderson, Charles Loftus Grant. *Old Panama and Castilla del Oro.* Washington: Sudwarth, 1911.

Arias de Para, Raúl. *Así Fue el Fraude: Las Elecciones Presidentiales de Panamá, 1984.* Panama City: Edlito, 1984.

Armbrister, Trevor. "Panama: Why They Hate Us," *Saturday Evening Post,* 237, No. 9, March 7, 1964, 75–79.

Austin, Lora (ed.). *Panama Election Factbook: May 12, 1968.* Washington: Institute for the Comparative Study of Political Systems, 1968.

Baxter, Richard R., and Doris Carroll. *The Panama Canal: Background Papers and Proceedings of the Sixth Hammarskjöld Forum.* Published for the Association of the Bar of the City of New York. Dobbs Ferry, New York: Oceana, 1965.

Biesanz, John, and Mavis Biesanz. *The People of Panama.* New York: Columbia University Press, 1955.

Billard, Jules B. "Panama: Link Between Oceans and Continents," *National Geographic,* 137, No. 3, March 1970, 402–40.

Brown, Lady Richmond. *Unknown Tribes, Uncharted Seas.* London: Duckworth, 1924.

Burns, E. Bradford. "Recognition of Panama by the Major Latin America States," *Americas,* 26, No. 6, July 1969, 3–14.

Cameron, Duncan H. "The Panama Canal Policy of the United States," *Midwest Quarterly,* 11, No. 2, January 1970, 141–52.

Chidsey, Donald Barr. *The Panama Canal: An Informal History.* New York: Crown, 1970.

Coker, William. "The Panama Canal Tolls Controversy: A Different Perspective," *Journal of American History,* 53, No. 3, December 1968, 555–64.

Deigh, Robb. "Cover Story: Panama Canal," *Insight,* August 11, 1986, 8–17.

Densmore, Frances. *Music of the Tulé Indians of Panama.* Washington: Smithsonian Institution, 1926.

Dreier, John C. *The Organization of American States and the Hemisphere Crisis.* New York: Harper and Row, 1962.

Drinan, Robert F., Raymond D. Gastil, and Jack H. Vaughn. "The Elections in Panama," *Freedom at Issue,* No. 79, July–August 1981, 32–34, 43–44.

Dubois, Jules. *Danger over Panama.* Indianapolis: Bobbs-Merrill, 1964.

Duval, Miles P., Jr. *And the Mountains Will Move: The Story of the Building of the Panama Canal.* Stanford: Stanford University Press, 1947.

Ealy, Lawrence O. *The Republic of Panama in World Affairs, 1903–1950.* Philadelphia: University of Pennsylvania Press, 1951.

Eisenmann, I. Roberto, Jr. "The Gathering Storm in Panama," *Americas,* June 14, 1986, 485–89.

Falk, Richard A. "Panama Treaty Trap," *Foreign Policy,* No. 30, Spring 1978, 68–82.

Farnsworth, David N., and James W. McKenney. *U.S.-Panama Relations 1903–1978: A Study in Linkage Politics.* Boulder: Westview Press, 1983.

Foreign Policy Association. *Panama: A Great Decision Approaches.* New York: 1977.

Fox, Hugh. "Latin American Report. Panama: The Place Between Places," *North American Review,* 5, No. 6, November–December 1968, 2–4.

García-Mora, Manuel R. "The Panama Canal Controversy," *Vital Speeches of the Day,* 30, No. 13, April 15, 1964, 412–16.

Gause, Frank A., and Charles Carl Carr. *The Story of Panama: The New Route to India.* New York: Arno Press and *New York Times,* 1970.

"General's Death Has Consequences for Whole of Central America," *Latin America Weekly Report* [London], August 7, 1981, 1.

Geyelin, Philip. "The Irksome Panama Wrangle," *Reporter,* 30, No. 8, April 9, 1964, 14–17.

Goldrich, Daniel. "Panama." Pages 150–66 in Martin C. Needler (ed.), *Political Systems of Latin America.* (2d ed.) New York: Van Nostrand, 1970.

Hale, Captain H.C. *Notes on Panama.* Washington: GPO, 1903.

Haring, C.H. *The Spanish Empire in America.* New York: Oxford University Press, 1947.

Harris, Louis K. "Panama." Pages 159–91 in Ben G. Burnett and Kenneth F. Johnson (eds.), *Political Forces in Latin America.* Belmont, California: Wadsworth, 1970.

Herring, Hubert. *A History of Latin America.* (3d ed. rev.) New York: Knopf, 1968.

Howarth, David. *Panama: Four Hundred Years of Dreams and Cruelty.* New York: McGraw-Hill, 1966.

LaFeber, Walter. *The Panama Canal: The Crisis in Historical Perspective.* New York: Oxford University Press, 1979.

Lamberg, Robert F. "Gradual Democratization in Panama," *Swiss Review of World Affairs* [Zurich], 31, No. 3, June 1981, 25–27.

Langley, L.D. "U.S.-Panamanian Relations since 1941," *Journal of Inter-American Studies,* 2, No. 3, July 1970, 339–66.

Lippincott, Aubrey E., and Hartley F. Dame. *A Brief Review of Selected Aspects of the San Blas Cuna Indians.* Washington: Special Operations Research Office, 1964.

Liss, Sheldon B. *The Canal: Aspects of United States-Panamanian Relations.* Notre Dame: University of Notre Dame Press, 1967.

McCullough, David. *The Path Between the Seas: The Creation of the Panama Canal, 1870–1914.* New York: Simon and Schuster, 1977.

Marshall, Jonathan. "The White House Death Squad," *Inquiry,* March 5, 1979, 15–21.

Mecham, J. Lloyd. *The United States and Inter-American Security: 1889–1960.* Austin: University of Texas Press, 1961.

Mellander, G.A. *The United States in Panamanian Politics: The Intriguing Formative Years.* Danville, Illinois: Interstate, 1971.

Methvin, Eugene H. "The Anatomy of a Riot: Panama 1964," *Orbis,* 14, No. 2, Summer 1970, 463–89.

Miner, Dwight Carroll. *The Fight for the Panama Route: The Story of the Spooner Act and the Hay-Herran Treaty.* New York: Columbia University Press, 1940.

Naughton, William A. "The Rails That Linked the Oceans," *Americas,* 17, No. 2, February 1965, 11–17.

Needler, Martin C. "Omar Torrijos: The Panamanian Enigma," *Intellect,* 105, No. 2381, February 1977, 242–43.

Niemeier, Jean Gilbreath. *The Panama Story.* Portland, Oregon: Metropolitan Press, 1968.

Pérez-Venero, Alex. *Before the Five Frontiers: Panama, 1821–1903.* New York: AMS Press, 1978.

Poor, Peggy. "A View from the Canal," *New Republic,* February 22, 1964, 13–14.

Priestley, George A. *Military Government and Popular Participation in Panama: The Torrijos Regime, 1968–1975.* (Westview Special Studies on Latin America and the Caribbean.) Boulder: Westview Press, 1986.

Ropp, Steve C. *Panamanian Politics: From Guarded Nation to National Guard.* New York: Praeger, 1982.

Rosenfeld, Stephen J. "The Panama Negotiations: A Close-Run Thing," *Foreign Affairs,* 54, No. 1, October 1975, 1–13.

Rosenhouse, Harvey. "Terms of the New Treaty for the Panama Canal," *New Republic,* July 22, 1967, 10–11.

"Royo Urged to Call Elections Next Year," *Latin America Weekly Report* [London], 30, July 30, 1982, 5–6.

Schuster, Lynda. "Panama: Struggle for Control Begins," *Wall Street Journal,* August 25, 1982, 3.

Steward, Julian H. (ed.). *Handbook of South American Indians, IV: The Circum-Caribbean Tribes.* Washington: GPO, 1948.

Storrs, K. Larry. *Panama Canal Treaties.* (Library of Congress Congressional Research Service, IB77042.) Washington: 1977.

Stout, David B. *San Blas Cuna Acculturation: An Introduction.* (Viking Fund Publications in Anthropology, No. 9.) New York: Viking Fund, 1947.

"Treaty Negotiations with Republic of Panama," *Congressional Record,* April 1, 1971, S4480–S4487.

"United States and Panama Reestablish Diplomatic Relations" (Statement by President Lyndon B. Johnson), *Department of State Bulletin,* 50, No. 1296, April 27, 1964, 655–56.

United States. Congress. 95th, 1st Session. House of Representatives. Committee on International Relations. *Proposed Panama Canal Treaties.* (Hearings, September 8–October 20, 1978.) Washington: GPO, 1978.

United States. Congress. 95th, 1st Session. Senate. Committee on Foreign Relations. *A Chronology of Events Relating to the Panama Canal.* Washington: GPO, 1977.

_____. *Background Documents Relating to the Panama Canal.* Washington: GPO, 1977.

United States. Congress. 95th, 2d Session. Senate. Committee on Foreign Relations. *Panama Canal Treaties.* (Executive Report No. 95-12.) Washington: GPO, 1978.

United States. Congress. 96th, 1st Session. Senate. Committee on Armed Services. *Panama Canal Treaty Implementing Legislation.* (Hearings, June 26–27, 1979.) Washington: GPO, 1979.

United States. Congress. 96th, 1st Session. Senate. Committee on Foreign Relations. *Senate Debate on the Panama Canal Treaties: A Compendium of Major Statements, Documents, Record Votes, and Relevant Events.* Washington: Library of Congress Congressional Research Service, 1979.

United States. Department of State. Bureau of Public Affairs. *Documents Associated with the Panama Canal Treaties.* (Selected Documents, Inter-American Series, No. 6B.) Washington: September 1977.

_____. *President's Fireside Chat on the Panama Canal Treaties.* (News Release, February 1, 1978.) Washington: 1978.

_____. *Texts of Treaties Relating to the Panama Canal.* (Selected Documents, Inter-American Series, No. 6A.) Washington: September 1977.
United States. Department of State. Embassy in Panama. *Election Data: Panama.* Washington: September 1986.
_____. *1985 Economic Overview for Panama.* Washington: June 1985.
Williams, Mary Wilhelmine. *Anglo-American Isthmian Diplomacy, 1815–1915.* Washington: American Historical Association, 1916.
Wolpin, Miles. *Military Aid and Counterrevolution in the Third World.* Lexington, Massachusetts: D.C. Heath, 1972.

(Various issues of the following publications were also used in the preparation of this chapter: *Facts on File, Yearbook,* 1980–81; Foreign Broadcast Information Service, *Daily Report: Latin America,* September 1983–December 1985; *Keesing's Contemporary Archives* [London], April 1977–November 1985; *Miami Herald,* November 1982–February 1985; *New York Times,* November 1981–December 1982; and *Washington Post,* September 1980–December 1984.)

Chapter 2

Aguilar, Pilar, and Gonzalo Retamal. "Educational Policy and Practice in Panama: A Focus on Adult Education." Pages 79–91 in Colin Brock and Hugh Lawlor (eds.), *Education in Latin America.* London: Croom Helm, 1985.
Arosemena, Agustín Jaén. *Historia de la Iglesia de Coclé.* Panama City: Imprenta Universitaria, 1982.
Biesanz, John, and Mavis Biesanz. *The People of Panama.* New York: Columbia University Press, 1955.
Burkhauser, Richard V. "Social Security in Panama: A Multiperiod Analysis of Income Distribution," *Journal of Development Economics,* 21, No. 1, April 1986, 53–64.
Cobb, Charles E., Jr. "Panama: Ever at the Crossroads," *National Geographic,* 169, No. 4, April 1986, 466–92.
D'Arcy, William G., and Mireya D. Correa A. (eds.). *The Botany and Natural History of Panama.* Saint Louis: Missouri Botanical Garden, 1985.
Gandásegui, Marco A., hijo. *Acumulación y Migraciones Internas en Panamá.* Centro de Estudios Latino Americanos, "Justo Arosemena." Panama City: Government of Panama, 1980.
_____. "Las Migraciones Internas en Panamá." Panama City: Panama, Ministry of Health, Office of Population Studies, November 1978.

Gjording, Chris N. *The Cerro Colorado Copper Project and the Guaymí Indians of Panama.* (Cultural Survival, Occasional Paper No. 3.) Cambridge, Massachusetts: 1981.

Gonzalez, B. "New Trends in Rural Panama," *World Marxist Review,* 18, No. 6, June 1975, 124–29.

Gordon, Burton L. *A Panama Forest and Shore: Natural History and Amerindian Culture in Bocas del Toro.* Pacific Grove, California: The Boxwood Press, 1982.

Gudeman, Stephen. "The *Compradrazgo* as a Reflection of the Natural and Spiritual Person." Pages 459–71 in *Proceedings of the Royal Anthropological Institute for 1971.* London: 1972.

_____. *The Demise of a Rural Economy: From Subsistence to Capitalism in a Latin American Village.* London: Routledge & Kegan Paul, 1978.

_____. "Saints, Symbols, and Ceremonies," *American Ethnologist,* 3, No. 4, November 1976, 709–28.

_____. "Spiritual Relationships and Selecting a Godparent," *Man* [London], 10, No. 2, June 1975, 221–37.

Helms, Mary, and Franklin Loveland (eds.). *Frontier Adaptations in Lower Central America.* Philadelphia: Institute for the Study of Human Issues, 1976.

Howarth, David. *Panama: Four Hundred Years of Dreams and Cruelty.* New York: McGraw-Hill, 1966.

Howe, James. *The Kuna Gathering: Contemporary Village Politics in Panama.* (Latin American Monographs, No. 67.) Austin: Institute of Latin American Studies, University of Texas, 1986.

Keeler, Clyde E. *Cuna Indian Art: The Culture and Craft of Panama's San Blas Islanders.* New York: Exposition Press, 1969.

_____. *Land of the Moon-Children: The Primitive San Blas Culture in Flux.* Athens: University of Georgia Press, 1956.

Kennedy, Dennis (ed.). *Atlas of Central America and the Caribbean.* New York: Macmillan, 1985.

La Forgia, Gerard M. "Fifteen Years of Community Health Organization for Health in Panama: An Assessment of Current Progress and Problems," *Social Science and Medicine,* 21, No. 1, 1985, 55–65.

Lydolf, Paul E. *The Climate of the Earth.* Totowa, New Jersey: Rowman and Allanheld, 1985.

McCullough, David. *The Path Between the Seas: The Creation of the Panama Canal, 1870–1914.* New York: Simon and Schuster, 1977.

Moore, Alexander. "From Council to Legislature: Democracy, Parliamentarianism, and the San Blas Cuna," *American Anthropologist,* 86, No. 1, March 1984, 28–42.

Panama. Directorate of Statistics and Census. *Estadística Panameña.* No. 970. Panama City: March 1985.

_____. *Estadística Panameña, Situación Cultural, 511 (Educación).* Panama City: 1983.

_____. *Panamá en Cifras: Años 1973-1977.* Panama City: November 1978.

_____. *Panamá en Cifras: Años 1979-1983.* Panama City: November 1984.

Panama. Ministry of Public Works. National Geographic Institute. *Atlas Nacional de Panamá.* Panama City: 1975.

_____. *Sintesis Geográfica.* (6th ed.) Panama City: 1980.

Partridge, William L. "The Humid Tropics Cattle Ranching Complex: Cases from Panama Reviewed," *Human Organization,* 43, No. 1, Spring 1984, 76-79.

Paxton, John (ed.). *The Statesman's Yearbook: Statistical and Historical Annual of the States of the World, 1985-1986.* Bungay, Suffolk, United Kingdom: Macmillan, 1986.

Portes, Alejandro, and John Walton. *Urban Latin America: The Political Condition from Above and Below.* Austin: University of Texas Press, 1976.

Priestley, George A. *Military Government and Popular Participation in Panama: The Torrijos Regime, 1968-1975.* (Westview Special Studies on Latin America and the Caribbean.) Boulder: Westview Press, 1986.

Reynolds, Cecil V., and Addison W. Somerville. "Comparative Adolescent Experiences Between the United States and Panama," *Adolescence,* 9, No. 36, Winter 1974, 569-76.

Ropp, Steve C. *Panamanian Politics: From Guarded Nation to National Guard.* New York: Praeger, 1982.

Sahota, Gian S. "The Distribution of the Benefits of Public Expenditure in Panama," *Public Finance Quarterly,* 5, No. 1, April 1977, 203-30.

Smith, David Horton. *Latin American Student Activism: Participation in Formal Volunteer Organizations in Six Latin Countries.* Lexington, Massachusetts: D.C. Heath, 1973.

Stier, Francis. "Modeling Migration: Analyzing Migration Histories from a San Blas Cuna Community," *Human Organization,* 42, No. 1, Spring 1983, 9-22.

Swepston, Lee. "The Indian in Latin America: Approaches to Administration, Integration, and Protection," *Buffalo Law Review,* 27, No. 4, Fall 1978, 715-56.

United States. Department of Commerce. Bureau of the Census. *World Population Profile.* Washington: GPO, 1985.

United States. Department of State. *Report on Human Rights Practices in Countries Receiving U.S. Aid.* Washington: GPO, 1986.

United States. Department of State. Foreign Affairs Information Center. *Panama Post Report: September 1984.* (Series 214.) No. 916. Washington: GPO, 1984.

West, Robert C., and John P. Augelli. *Middle America: Its Lands and Peoples.* (2d ed.) Englewood Cliffs, New Jersey: Prentice-Hall, 1976.

World Bank. *World Development Report, 1986.* New York: Oxford University Press, 1986.

Young, Philip D. *Ngawbe: Tradition and Change Among the Western Guaymí of Panama.* (Illinois Studies in Anthropology, No. 7.) Urbana: University of Illinois Press, 1971.

Young, Philip D., and John R. Bort. "Politicization of the Guaymí," *Journal of the Steward Anthropological Society,* 11, No. 1, Fall 1979, 73–110.

Zaroga, Frank. *La República de Panamá Perfil Ambiental del País: Un Estudio de Campo.* (Country Environmental Profile for United States Agency for International Development Series. English translation.) Washington: International Finance and Technical Institute, 1980.

Chapter 3

Banco Nacional de Panamá. *Memoria Anual 1985: Informe del Gerente General.* Panama City: 1986.

Borrell, J. "Trouble Ahead for the Canal?," *Time,* March 2, 1987, 63.

Crawley, Eduardo. "Panama." Pages 107–10 in Richard Green (ed.), *Latin America and Caribbean Review, 1986.* Saffron Walden, Essex, United Kingdom: World of Information, 1985.

Economist Intelligence Unit. *Country Profile: Nicaragua, Costa Rica, Panama.* No. 71, 1987–88. London: 1987.

_____. *Country Report: Nicaragua, Costa Rica, Panama.* No. 4, 1986. London: September 30, 1986.

Inter-American Development Bank. "Panama." Pages 89–91 in *1986 Annual Report.* Washington: 1987.

_____. "Panama." Pages 296–301 in *Economic and Social Progress in Latin America, 1982 Report.* Washington: 1983.

_____. "Panama." Pages 355–61 in *Economic and Social Progress in Latin America, 1984 Report.* Washington: 1985.

_____. "Panama." Pages 331–34 in *Economic and Social Progress in Latin America, 1986 Report.* Washington: 1987.

International Monetary Fund. *Balance of Payments Statistics: 1986 Yearbook.* 37, Pt. 1. Washington: 1987.

_____. *Balance of Payments Statistics: 1987 Yearbook.* 38, Pt. 1, Washington: 1987.

_____. *International Financial Statistics: 1986 Yearbook.* Washington: 1987.

Koenig, Gunter. "Hard Choices: The Panamanian Economy." Pages 37–42 in *Report on Panama: Findings of the Study Group on United States-Panamanian Relations.* (Central American and Caribbean Program, Occasional Paper No. 13.) Washington: Johns Hopkins University School of Advanced International Studies, April 1987.

Looney, Robert E. *The Economic Development of Panama: The Impact of World Inflation on an Open Economy.* New York: Praeger, 1976.

Moody, J. "Dirty Dollars," *Time,* January 18, 1987, 44–45.

Panama. Directorate of Statistics and Census. *Estadística Panameña: Avance de resultados de la encuesta nacional socioeconómica de 1983.* Panama City: April 14, 1987.

Panama Canal Commission. *Annual Report.* Balboa, Panama: 1987.

Ropp, Steve. "General Noriega's Panama," *Current History,* 85, No. 512, December 1986, 421–24.

Torres A., José E. "Las causas de la crisis actual de la economía panameña," *Tareas* [Panama City], No. 65, January–May 1987, 3–21.

Trivoli, George W. "The Banking System of Panama," *Banker's Magazine,* 5, No. 167, January–February 1984, 23–27.

United States. Department of Labor. Bureau of International Labor Affairs. *Foreign Labor Trends: Panama.* Prepared by United States Embassy in Panama. No. 87–18, 1986.

United States. Department of State. Bureau of Public Affairs. *Aid and U.S. Interests in Latin America and the Caribbean.* Current Policy No. 666. Washington: March 5, 1985.

_____. *Atlas of the Caribbean Basin.* Washington: July 1984.

_____. *The U.S. and Central America: Implementing the National Bipartisan Commission Report.* Special Report No. 148. Washington: August 1986.

United States. Department of State. Embassy in Panama. *1986 Economic Summary: Panama.* Washington: February 12, 1987, mimeo.

United States. General Accounting Office. *U.S. Economic Assistance to Central America.* GAO/NSIAD-84-71. Washington: March 8, 1984.

_____. *Revenue Estimate: Panama Canal Commission Estimated Revenue for Fiscal Year 1988.* GAO/AFMD-87-25. Washington: May 1987.

Washington Institute Task Force. *Central America in Crisis.* Washington: Washington Institute for Values in Public Policy: 1984.

Weeks, John. *The Economies of Central America.* New York: Holmes and Meier, 1985.

_____. "Panama: The Roots of Current Political Instability," *Third World Quarterly,* 9, No. 3, July 1987, 763-87.

World Bank. *Panama: Structural Change and Growth Prospects.* A World Bank Country Study, Report No. 5236-PAN. Washington: 1985.

_____. *World Development Report, 1981.* New York: Oxford University Press, 1981.

_____. *World Development Report, 1984.* New York: Oxford University Press, 1984.

_____. *World Development Report, 1986.* New York: Oxford University Press, 1986.

_____. *World Development Report, 1987.* New York: Oxford University Press, 1987.

(Various issues of the following publications also were used in the preparation of this chapter: Foreign Broadcast Information Service, *Daily Report, Latin America,* January 1982-July 1987; *Latin America Commodities Report,* January 1984-July 1987; *Latin America Regional Reports: Mexico and Central America Report* [London], January 1986-July 1987; *Latin American Weekly Report* [London], January 1986-July 1987; *New York Times,* January 1981- June 1987; *Newsweek,* January 1982-July 1987; *Time,* January 1982-July 1987; *U.S. News and World Report,* January 1982-July 1987; *Wall Street Journal,* January 1982-June 1987; and *Washington Post,* January 1982-July 1987.)

Chapter 4

"Acto Reformatorio de la Constitución Política de la República de Panamá," *Gaceta Oficial* [Panama City], November 16, 1978, 13-24.

Arias Calderón, Ricardo. "Panama: Disaster or Democracy?" *Foreign Affairs,* 66, No. 2, Winter 1987-88, 328-47.

Arias de Para, Raúl. *Así Fue el Fraude: Las Elecciones Presidenciales de Panamá, 1984.* Panama City: Edlito, 1984.

Bagley, Bruce, Roberto Alvarez, and Katherine Hadedorn (eds.). *Contadora and the Central American Peace Process: Selected Documents.* Boulder: Westview Press, 1985.

Baloyra, Enrique. *El Salvador in Transition.* Chapel Hill: University of North Carolina Press, 1982.

Blachman, Morris J., William M. Leogrande, and Kenneth E. Sharpe (eds.). *Confronting Revolution: Security Through Diplomacy in Central America.* New York: Pantheon Books, 1986.

Brown, Esmeralda, et al. "Panama: For Whom the Canal Tolls," *NACLA,* 13, No. 5, September–October 1979, 3–37.

Burns, E. Bradford. "Panama: New Treaties or New Conflicts?," *Current History,* 74, No. 438, February 1978, 74–76.

Código Electoral de la República de Panamá y Normas Complementarias. Panama City: Tribunal Electoral, 1983.

Constitución Política de la República de Panamá de 1972: Reformada por los Actos Reformatorios de 1978 y por el Acto Constitucional de 1983. Panama City: La Imprenta Comercial de la Editora Renovación, 1983.

Constitution of Panama 1972. Washington: General Secretariat, Organization of American States, 1974.

"Exchange of Instruments of Ratification of Panama Canal Treaties," *Department of State Bulletin,* 78, No. 2016, July 1978, 52–57.

Falk, Richard A. "Panama Treaty Trap," *Foreign Policy,* No. 30, Spring 1978, 68–82.

Frost and Sullivan. *Political Risk Report: Panama.* New York: 1987.

Furlong, William L., and Margaret E. Scranton. *The Dynamics of Foreign Policymaking: the President, the Congress, and the Panama Canal Treaties.* Boulder: Westview Press, 1984.

Goldrich, Daniel. *Sons of the Establishment: Elite Youth in Panama and Costa Rica.* Chicago: Rand McNally, 1966.

Jorden, William J. *Panama Odyssey.* Austin: University of Texas Press, 1984.

Kitchel, Denison. *The Truth about the Panama Canal.* New Rochelle, New York: Arlington House, 1978.

LaFeber, Walter. *The Panama Canal: The Crisis in Historical Perspective.* New York: Oxford University Press, 1979.

Liss, Sheldon B. *The Canal: Aspects of United States-Panamanian Relations.* Notre Dame: University of Notre Dame Press, 1967.

Mason, Henry L. *Mass Demonstrations Against Foreign Regimes: A Study of Five Crises.* (Tulane Studies in Political Science.) New Orleans: Tulane University, 1966.

Millan, Victor. "Controlling Conflict in the Caribbean Basin: National Approaches." Pages 41–69 in Michael A. Morris and Victor Millan (eds.), *Controlling Latin American Conflicts: Ten Approaches.* Boulder: Westview Press, 1983.

Minor, Kent Jay. "United States-Panamanian Relations: 1958–1973." (Unpublished Ph.D. dissertation, Department of Modern History, Case Western University, No. 74–16, 508.) Cleveland: 1974.

Moss, Ambler. "The U.S.-Panamanian Relationship: An American Perspective." Pages 7-17 in *Report on Panama: Findings of the Study Group on United States-Panamanian Relations.* Washington: Johns Hopkins University School of Advanced International Studies, April 1987.

Needler, Martin C. "Omar Torrijos, the Panamanian Enigma," *Intellect,* 105, No. 2381, February 1977, 242-43.

Panama Canal Commission. *Annual Report.* Balboa, Panama: 1987.

Pastor, Robert. *Condemned to Repetition: The United States and Nicaragua.* Princeton: Princeton University Press, 1987.

Pearson, Neale J. "Panama." Pages 589-606 in Jack W. Hopkins (ed.), *Latin America and Caribbean Contemporary Record: Volume IV, 1984-85.* New York: Holmes and Meier, 1986.

Report on Panama: Findings of the Study Group on United States-Panamanian Relations. (Central American and Caribbean Program, Occasional Paper No. 13.) Washington: Johns Hopkins University School of Advanced International Studies, April 1987.

Ropp, Steve C. "Cuba and Panama, Signaling Left and Going Right?" *Caribbean Review,* 9, No. 1, Winter 1980, 15-20.

_____. "General Noriega's Panama," *Current History,* 85, No. 512, December 1986, 421-24.

_____. "Military Reformism in Panama: New Directions or Old Inclinations," *Caribbean Studies* [Río Piedras, Puerto Rico], 12, No. 3, October 1972, 45-63.

_____. *Panamanian Politics: From Guarded Nation to National Guard.* New York: Praeger, 1982.

_____. "Panama's Domestic Power Structure and the Canal: History and Future." Pages 482-92 in Howard J. Wiarda and Harvey F. Kline (eds.), *Latin American Politics and Development.* Boston: Houghton Mifflin, 1979.

_____. "Panama's Recent Foreign Policy Toward Central America and the Caribbean: Constraints, Capabilities, and Motivations." (Paper presented to the Latin American Studies Association annual meeting, 1980.)

_____. "Panama's Struggle for Democracy," *Current History,* 86, No. 524, December 1987, 421-24.

_____. "Panama: The Decline of Military Rule." Pages B401-B422 in Jack W. Hopkins (ed.), *Latin America and Caribbean Contemporary Record: Volume V, 1985-86.* New York: Holmes and Meier, 1988.

_____. "Ratification of the Panama Canal Treaties: The Muted Debate," *World Affairs,* 141, No. 4, Spring 1979, 283-92.

Ryan, Paul B. *The Panama Canal Controversy, U.S. Diplomacy and Defense Interests.* Stanford: Hoover Institution Press, 1977.

Sánchez Borbón, Guillermo. "Panama Fallen Among Thieves: Of General Noriega and a Country Convulsed," *Harper's Magazine,* 275, December 1987, 57–67.

Sullivan, Mark P. *Panama's Political Crisis: Prospects and U.S. Policy Concerns.* Washington: Library of Congress Congressional Research Service, November 1987.

Torrijos Herrera, Omar. *La Batalla de Panamá.* Buenos Aires: Editorial Universitaria de Buenos Aires, 1973.

_____. *Nuestra Revolución.* Panama City: Republic of Panama, 1974.

United States. Congress. 95th, 1st Session. Senate. Committee on Foreign Relations. *Background Documents Relating to the Panama Canal.* Washington: GPO, November 1977.

United States. Congress. 95th, 2d Session. House of Representatives. Committee on International Relations. *Congress and Foreign Policy 1977.* Washington: GPO, 1978.

United States. Congress. 95th, 2d Session. Senate. Committee on Foreign Relations. *Panama Canal Treaties.* (Executive Report No. 95–12.) Washington: GPO, 1978.

United States. Congress. 96th, 1st Session. House of Representatives. Committee on Foreign Affairs. *Congress and Foreign Policy 1978.* Washington: GPO, 1979.

United States. Congress. 96th, 1st Session. Senate. Committee on Armed Services. *Panama Canal Treaty Implementing Legislation.* (Hearings, June 26–27, 1979.) Washington: GPO, 1979.

United States. Congress. 96th, 1st Session. Senate. Committee on Foreign Relations. *Senate Debate on the Panama Canal Treaties: A Compendium of Major Statements, Documents, Record Votes, and Relevant Events.* Washington: Library of Congress Congressional Research Service, 1979.

United States. Congress. 99th, 2d Session. House of Representatives. Committee on Foreign Affairs. Subcommittee on Human Rights and International Organizations and on Western Hemisphere Affairs. *Human Rights and Political Developments in Panama.* (Hearings, April 29 and July 23, 1986.) Washington: GPO, 1986.

United States. Congress. 99th, 2d Session. Senate. Committee on Foreign Relations. Subcommittee on Western Hemisphere Affairs. *The Situation in Panama.* (Hearings, March 10 and April 21, 1986.) Washington: GPO, 1986.

United States. Department of State. Bureau of Public Affairs. *Documents Associated with the Panama Canal Treaties.* (Selected Documents, Inter-American Series, No. 6B.) Washington: September 1977.

_____. *The Meaning of the New Panama Canal Treaties.* (Selected Documents, No. 6C.) Washington: January 1978.

_____. *Texts of Treaties Relating to the Panama Canal.* (Selected Documents, Inter-American Series, No. 6A.) Washington: September 1977.

United States. Department of State. Embassy in Panama. *Economic Trends Report for Panama.* Washington: October 1987.

_____. *Fact Sheet on Panamanian Political Parties.* Washington: September 3, 1986.

United States. General Accounting Office. *Panama Canal: Establishment of Commission to Study Sea-Level Canal and Alternatives.* Washington: 1986.

United States. *Panama Canal Act of 1979.* (Public Law 96-70.) Washington: GPO, 1979.

United States Southern Command. *Fact Sheet: An Overview of the United States Southern Command.* Panama: 1987.

Viola, Oscar Luis. *Malvinas: Derrota Diplomática y Militar.* Buenos Aires: Tinta Nueva, 1983.

Wesson, Robert (ed.). *The Latin American Military Institution.* New York: Praeger, 1986.

Wheaton, Philip, and Mario R. Villalobos. *Treaty for Us. Treaty for Them: Two Analyses of the Panama Canal Treaties.* Washington: EPICA Task Force, November 1977.

(Various issues of the following publications were also used in the preparation of this chapter: *Central American Report* [Guatemala City], November 1985–June 1987; *Christian Science Monitor,* January–December 1987; *Crítica* [Panama City], June–December 1987; *Financial Times* [London], June–December 1987; Foreign Broadcast Information Service, *Daily Report, Latin America,* March 1985–December 1987; *La Nación Internacional* [San José, Costa Rica], April–May 1983; *La Prensa Digest* [Panama City], December 1987; *La República* [Panama City], December 1987; *Latin America Regional Reports: Mexico and Central America Report* [London], September 1983–December 1987; *Latin American Weekly Report* [London], April 1984–December 1987; *New York Times,* January 1986–December 1987; *Panama Star and Herald* [Panama City], June 1987; *San Diego Union,* February 1986; *St. Louis Post and Dispatch,* July–September 1987; *Tico Times* [San José, Costa Rica], December 1987; and *Washington Post,* June–December 1987.)

Chapter 5

Anguizola, Gustave. *The Panama Canal: Isthmian Political Stability from 1821 to 1977.* Washington: University Press of America, 1977.

Barber, Willard F., and C. Neale Ronning. *Internal Security and Military Power.* Columbus: Ohio State University Press, 1966.

Busey, James L. *Political Aspects of the Panama Canal.* (Comparative Government Series.) Tucson: University of Arizona Press, 1974.

Ealy, Lawrence O. *Yanqui Politics and the Isthmian Canal.* University Park: Pennsylvania State University Press, 1971.

International Institute for Strategic Studies. *The Military Balance 1986-1987.* London: Garden City Press, 1986.

Kennan, George F. *The Cloud of Danger.* Boston: Little, Brown, 1977.

LaFeber, Walter. *The Panama Canal: The Crisis in Historical Perspective.* New York: Oxford University Press, 1979.

Liss, Sheldon B. *The Canal: Aspects of United States-Panamanian Relations.* Notre Dame: University of Notre Dame Press, 1967.

McAlister, Lyle N., et al. *The Military in Latin American Sociopolitical Evolution.* Washington: Center for Research in Social Systems, 1970.

McDonald, Vincent P. "The Panama Canal for Panamanians," *Military Review,* 55, No. 12, December 1975, 7-16.

McGee, Gale. "After Panama: Some Lessons and Opportunities in the Aftermath of the Canal Treaties Debate," *South Atlantic Quarterly,* 78, No. 1, Winter 1979, 1-16.

Mellander, G.A. *The United States in Panamanian Politics: The Intriguing Formative Years.* Danville, Illinois: Interstate, 1971.

Miller, Robert Howard, Jr. *Military Government and Approaches to National Development: A Comparative Analysis of the Peruvian and Panamanian Experiences.* (Ph.D. dissertation.) University of Miami, Coral Gables, Florida, 1975.

Norman, Albert. *The Panama Canal Treaties of 1977: A Political Evaluation.* Northfield, Vermont: Norman, 1978.

Pereira, Renato. *Panamá: fuerzas armadas y política.* Panama City: Nueva Universidad, 1979.

Peters, Joan. "Panama's Genial Despot," *Harper's Magazine,* No. 256, April 1978, 61-68, 70.

Pippin, Larry LaRae. *The Remón Era: An Analysis of a Decade of Events in Panama (1947-1957).* Stanford: Institute of Hispanic American and Luso-Brazilian Studies, 1964.

Ropp, Steve C. "General Noriega's Panama," *Current History,* 85, No. 512, December 1986, 421-24.

_____. "Military Reformism in Panama: New Directions or Old Inclinations," *Caribbean Studies* [Río Piedras, Puerto Rico], 12, No. 3, October 1972, 45-63.

_____. "Panama: The Decline of Military Rule." Pages B401–B422 in Jack W. Hopkins (ed.), *Latin America and Caribbean Contemporary Record: Volume V, 1985–86*. New York: Holmes and Meier, 1988.

_____. *Panamanian Politics: From Guarded Nation to National Guard*. New York: Praeger, 1982.

Ruhnke, Volko F. (ed.). *Defense and Foreign Affairs Handbook*. Washington: Perth Corporation, 1986.

Ryan, Paul B. *The Panama Canal Controversy, U.S. Diplomacy and Defense Interests*. Stanford: Hoover Institution Press, 1977.

St. John, Jeffrey. *The Panama Canal and Soviet Imperialism*. Washington: Heritage Foundation, 1978.

Sossa, José Antonio. *Imperialismos, fuerzas armadas, y partidos políticos en Panamá*. Panama City: Ediciones Documentos, 1977.

Stockholm International Peace Research Institute. *World Armaments and Disarmament*. New York: Oxford University Press, 1986.

Storrs, K. Larry, and Rosemary P. Jackson. "Panama Canal Treaties: Consideration by the Congress," (Library of Congress Congressional Research Service, Major Issues System, IB78026.) Washington: January 2, 1979 (mimeo.).

United States. Congress. 94th, 2d Session. House of Representatives. Committee on International Relations. *A New Panama Canal Treaty: A Latin America Imperative Report of a Study Mission to Panama*. Washington: GPO, February 24, 1976.

United States. Congress. 95th, 1st Session. Senate. Committee on Foreign Relations. *A Chronology of Events Relating to the Panama Canal*. (Library of Congress Congressional Research Service.) Washington: GPO, December 1977.

United States. Congress. 95th, 2d Session. Senate. Committee on Foreign Relations. *Report on Panama Canal Treaties with Supplemental and Minority Views*. Washington: GPO, February 3, 1978.

United States. Congress. 96th, 1st Session. Senate. Committee on Armed Services. *Panama Canal Treaty Implementing Legislation*. (Hearings, June 26–27, 1979.) Washington: GPO, 1979.

United States. Congress. 99th, 2d Session. Senate. Committee on Foreign Relations. Subcommittee on Western Hemisphere Affairs. *The Situation in Panama*. (Hearings, March 10–April 21, 1986.) Washington: GPO, 1986.

United States. Department of Defense. Security Assistance Agency. *Foreign Military Sales, Foreign Military Construction Sales, and Military Assistance Facts*. Washington: 1986.

United States. Department of State. Bureau of Public Affairs. *Documents Associated With the Panama Canal Treaties*. (Selected Documents, Inter-American Series, No. 6B.) Washington: September 1977.

————. *Texts of Treaties Relating to the Panama Canal.* (Selected Documents, Inter-American Series, No. 6A.) Washington: September 1977.

United States. *Panama Canal Act of 1979.* (Public Law 96–70.) Washington: GPO, 1979.

Wesson, Robert (ed.). *The Latin American Military Institution.* New York: Praeger, 1986.

(Various issues of the following publications were also used in the preparation of this chapter: *Defensa* [Panama City], December 1979–December 1986; *Central American Report* [Guatemala City], September–November, 1986; *Miami Herald,* October 1985; and *New York Times,* May–July 1987.)

Glossary

ADO—Alianza Democrática de Oposición (Democratic Opposition Alliance). Opposition alliance of three major parties and several smaller parties formed to contest the 1984 elections. Remained officially in place in late 1987.

balboa (B)—Panama's monetary unit, in practice consisting only of coins. Official value is B1 equals US$1. United States currency used for paper money.

CCN—Crusada Civilista Nacional (National Civic Crusade). Business-led coalition that organized popular civic opposition to government and FDP (q.v.) in 1987 demonstrations and unrest.

Central America—Region between Mexico and Panama including present-day Belize, Guatemala, Honduras, El Salvador, Nicaragua, and Costa Rica.

CFZ—Colón Free Zone. Free-trade zone in Panama. Goods from foreign countries are landed and stored or repackaged there and shipped onward without being subject to Panama's customs duties.

Contadora peace process—A diplomatic initiative launched by a January 1983 meeting on Contadora Island off the Pacific coast of Panama, by which the "Core Four" mediator countries of Mexico, Venezuela, Colombia, and Panama sought to prevent through negotiations a regional conflagration among the Central American states of Guatemala, El Salvador, Honduras, Nicaragua, and Costa Rica. In September 1984 the negotiating process produced a draft treaty, the Contadora *Acta,* which was judged acceptable by the government of Nicaragua but rejected by the other four Central American states concerned. The governments of Peru, Uruguay, Argentina, and Brazil formed a Contadora Support Group in 1985 in an effort to revitalize the faltering talks. The process was suspended unofficially in June 1986 when the Central American governments refused to sign a revised *Acta.* The Contadora process was effectively superseded by direct negotiations among the Central American states.

DENI—Departamento Nacional de Investigaciones (National Department of Investigations). Undercover secret police.

Eurocurrency—A country's currency on deposit outside the country. Most Eurocurrency claims are Eurodollars, which are dollar claims on banks located outside the United States. The Eurocurrency market is a wholesale market.

313

FDP—Fuerzas de Defensa de Panamá (Panama Defense Forces). Panama's military forces. Includes former National Guard as well as all military and police forces. FDP commander was de facto head of government in late 1987.

fiscal year (FY)—Calendar year.

FRAMPO—Frente Amplio Popular (Broad Popular Front). Small left-of-center party that was part of pro-government coalition, UNADE (*q.v.*), in 1984 elections, but lost legal status by failing to win 3 percent of total vote.

GDP—gross domestic product. A measure of the total value of goods and services produced by the domestic economy during a given period, usually one year. Obtained by adding the value contributed by each sector of the economy in the form of profits, compensation to employees, and depreciation (consumption of capital). The income arising from investments and possessions owned abroad is not included, only domestic production. Hence, the use of the word ''domestic'' to distinguish GDP from GNP (*q.v.*).

GNP—gross national product. Total market value of all final goods and services produced by an economy during a year. Obtained by adding GDP (*q.v.*) and the income received from abroad by residents less payments remitted abroad to nonresidents.

IMF—International Monetary Fund. Established along with the World Bank (*q.v.*) in 1945, the IMF is a specialized agency affiliated with the United Nations that takes responsibility for stabilizing international exchange rates and payments. The main business of the IMF is the provision of loans to its members when they experience balance-of-payment difficulties. These loans often carry conditions that require substantial internal economic adjustments by the recipients.

mola—Literally, clothing, dress, or blouse in Cuna dialect, but has come to mean simply the single panel of a Cuna woman's appliqued blouse. The panels feature colorful, intricately stitched abstract or geometric designs; scenes of everyday Cuna life, lore, myths, legends, flora, and fauna; or ideas or images from the outside world.

MOLIRENA—Movimiento Liberal Republicano Nacional (National Liberal Republican Movement). Pro-business coalition of several center-right political movements. Part of opposition coalition ADO (*q.v.*).

offshore banking—Term applied to banking transactions conducted between participants located outside the country. Such transactions increased rapidly worldwide after the mid-1960s because of the growth and liquidity of Eurocurrency (*q.v.*) markets.

PALA—Partido Laborista Agrario (Labor and Agrarian Party, often referred to simply as the Labor Party). Despite title, generally right-of-center, pro-business. Part of pro-government coalition, UNADE (*q.v.*).

Panama Canal net ton—Measure used to assess tolls for the Panama Canal based on 100 cubic feet of a vessel's net earning capacity, usually meaning its cargo space.

PAPO—Partido de Acción Popular (Popular Action Party). Minor independent party that contested 1984 elections, but lost legal status by failing to garner 3 percent of total vote.

PDC—Partido Demócrato Cristiano (Christian Democratic Party). Centrist opposition party. Part of opposition coalition, ADO (*q.v.*).

PdP—Partido del Pueblo (People's Party). Far left, orthodox communist, pro-Moscow party. Ran candidates in 1984 elections, but lost legal status by failing to win 3 percent of total vote.

PLN—Partido Liberal Nacional (National Liberal Party). Generally right-of-center. Part of pro-government coalition, UNADE (*q.v.*).

PNP—Partido Nacionalista Popular (Popular Nationalist Party). Minor party that contested 1984 elections, but lost legal status by failing to receive 3 percent of total vote.

PP—Partido Panameñista (Panameñista Party). Small break-away faction of Panameñistas. Part of pro-government coalition, UNADE (*q.v.*), in 1984 elections, but lost legal status by failing to win 3 percent of total vote.

PPA—Partido Panameñista Auténtico (Authentic Panameñista Party). Nation's leading opposition party. Strongly nationalist and populist. Part of opposition coalition, ADO (*q.v.*). Led by veteran politician Arnulfo Arias Madrid.

PPP—Partido Panameño del Pueblo (Panamanian People's Party). Far left communist party.

PR—Partido Republicano (Republican Party). Right-of-center party. Part of pro-government coalition, UNADE (*q.v.*).

PRD—Partido Revolucionario Democrático (Democratic Revolutionary Party). Official government party founded by Torrijos. Part of pro-government coalition, UNADE (*q.v.*).

Roosevelt Corollary—Policy enunciated by President Theodore Roosevelt in 1904 specifying that if a country in the Western Hemisphere failed to maintain internal order or to pay its international debts, the United States could intervene with military force to rectify the situation. Policy was bitterly resented by Latin American nations.

terms of trade—Number of units that must be given up for one unit of goods received by each party (e.g., nation) to a transaction. The terms of trade are said to move in favor of the party that gives up fewer units of goods than it did previously for one unit of goods received, and against the party that gives up more units of goods for one unit of goods received. In international economics, the concept of ''terms of trade'' plays an important role in evaluating exchange relationships between nations.

UNADE—Unión Nacional Democrática (National Democratic Union). Pro-government coalition of six parties formed to contest 1984 elections; remained officially in place in late 1987.

World Bank—Informal name used to designate a group of three affiliated international institutions: the International Bank for Reconstruction and Development (IBRD), the International Development Association (IDA), and the International Finance Corporation (IFC). The IBRD, established in 1945, has the primary purpose of providing loans to developing countries for productive projects. The IDA, a legally separate loan fund administered by the staff of the IBRD, was set up in 1960 to furnish credits to the poorest developing countries on much easier terms than those of conventional IBRD loans. The IFC, founded in 1956, supplements the activities of the IBRD through loans and assistance designed specifically to encourage the growth of productive private enterprises in less developed countries. The president and certain senior officers of the IBRD hold the same positions in the IFC. The three institutions are owned by the governments of the countries that subscribe their capital. To participate in the World Bank group, member states must first belong to the IMF (*q.v.*).

Yankee—Generally pejorative term used in Latin America to refer to United States citizens.

Index

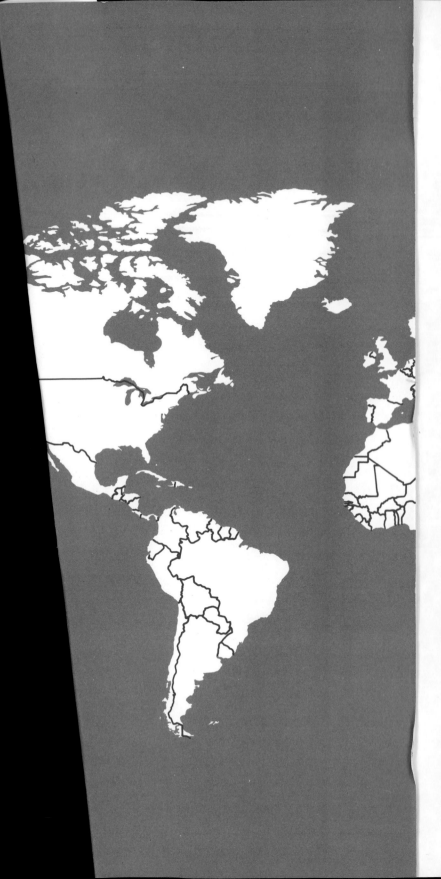

Published Country Studies

(Area Handbook Series)

550-65	Afghanistan	550-174	Guinea
550-98	Albania	550-82	Guyana
550-44	Algeria	550-151	Honduras
550-59	Angola	550-165	Hungary
550-73	Argentina	550-21	India
550-169	Australia	550-154	Indian Ocean
550-176	Austria	550-39	Indonesia
550-175	Bangladesh	550-68	Iran
550-170	Belgium	550-31	Iraq
550-66	Bolivia	550-25	Israel
550-20	Brazil	550-182	Italy
550-168	Bulgaria	550-69	Ivory Coast
550-61	Burma	550-30	Japan
550-50	Cambodia	550-34	Jordan
550-166	Cameroon	550-56	Kenya
550-159	Chad	550-81	Korea, North
550-77	Chile	550-41	Korea, South
550-60	China	550-58	Laos
550-26	Colombia	550-24	Lebanon
550-33	Commonwealth Caribbean, Islands of the	550-38	Liberia
550-91	Congo	550-85	Libya
550-90	Costa Rica	550-172	Malawi
550-152	Cuba	550-45	Malaysia
550-22	Cyprus	550-161	Mauritania
550-158	Czechoslovakia	550-79	Mexico
550-52	Ecuador	550-49	Morocco
550-43	Egypt	550-64	Mozambique
550-150	El Salvador	550-88	Nicaragua
550-28	Ethiopia	550-157	Nigeria
550-167	Finland	550-94	Oceania
550-155	Germany, East	550-48	Pakistan
550-173	Germany, Fed. Rep. of	550-46	Panama
550-153	Ghana	550-156	Paraguay
550-87	Greece	550-185	Persian Gulf States
550-78	Guatemala	550-42	Peru
550-72	Philippines	550-62	Tanzania
550-162	Poland	550-53	Thailand
550-181	Portugal	550-89	Tunisia
550-160	Romania	550-80	Turkey
550-51	Saudi Arabia	550-74	Uganda
550-70	Senegal	550-97	Uruguay
550-180	Sierra Leone	550-71	Venezuela
550-184	Singapore	550-32	Vietnam
550-86	Somalia	550-183	Yemens, The
550-93	South Africa	550-99	Yugoslavia
550-95	Soviet Union	550-67	Zaire
550-179	Spain	550-75	Zambia
550-96	Sri Lanka	550-171	Zimbabwe
550-27	Sudan		
550-47	Syria